EVENT HISTORY
ANALYSIS
WITH STATA

Event History Analysis With Stata

Edited by

Hans-Peter Blossfeld
Otto-Friedrich Universitat Bamberg

Katrin Golsch
University of Cologne

Götz Rohwer
Ruhr–Universitat Bochum

LAWRENCE ERLBAUM ASSOCIATES, PUBLISHERS
2007   Mahwah, New Jersey   London

Senior Acquisitions Editor: Debra Riegert
Editorial Assistant: Rebecca Larsen
Cover Design: Kathryn Houghtaling-Lacey

Lawrence Erlbaum Associates, Inc., Publishers
10 Industrial Avenue
Mahwah, New Jersey 07430
www.erlbaum.com

CIP information for this volume can be obtained
from the Library of Congress

ISBN   978–0–8058–6046–7 — 0–8058–6046–0   (case)
ISBN   978–0–8058–6047–4 — 0–8058–6047–9   (paper)
ISBN   978–1–4106–1429–2 — 1–4106–1429–8   (e book)

Books published by Lawrence Erlbaum Associates are printed
on acid-free paper, and their bindings are chosen for strength
and durability.

Printed in the United States of America

10 9 8 7 6 5 4 3 2 1

Contents

Preface

This book provides an updated introductory account of event history modeling techniques using the statistical package Stata (version 9). The specific emphasis is on the usefulness of event history models for causal analysis in the social sciences. The literature distinguishes between discrete-time and continuous-time models. This volume is intended to introduce the reader to the application of continuous-time models. It is both a student textbook and a reference book for research scientists in sociology, economics, political sciences, and demography. It may be used in undergraduate and graduate courses.

There are three main goals in writing this book. First, was to demonstrate that event history models are an extremely useful approach to uncover causal relationships or to map out a system of causal relations. Event history models are linked very naturally to a causal understanding of social processes because they allow for modeling a theoretically supposed change in future outcomes of a process to (time-constant or changing) conditions in related other processes in the past.

Second, to demonstrate the application of the statistical package Stata in the analysis of event histories and to give the reader the opportunity to compare these models with the TDA examples used in the book by Blossfeld and Rohwer (2002).[1] In economics and the social sciences, Stata is a widely used software package that provides tools for data analysis, data management, and graphics. We refer the reader to the Stata homepage.[2] A file with the data used in the examples throughout the book and a series of files containing the Stata setups for the examples in the book can be downloaded.[3] Thus the reader is offered the unique opportunity to easily run and modify all the application examples of the book on the computer. In fact, we advise the event history analysis beginner to go through the application examples of the book on his or her own computer step by step. Based on our teaching experience from many workshops and introductory classes, this seems to be the most efficient and straightforward way to get familiar with these complex analysis techniques.

We emphasize the strengths and limitations of event history modeling techniques in each example. In particular, we complement each practical application with a short exposition of the underlying statistical concepts. The examples start with an introduction of the substantive background for the specific model. Then we demonstrate how to organize the input data

---

[1] Details about the book can be downloaded at www.erlbaum.com.

[2] http://www.stata.com/products/overview.html

[3] http://web.uni-bamberg.de/sowi/soziologie-i/eha/stata/

and use the statistical package Stata. Finally, a substantive interpretation of the obtained results is given.

Our third goal is to supplement the textbooks *Event History Analysis* by Blossfeld, Hamerle, and Mayer (1989) and *Techniques of Event History Modeling* by Blossfeld and Rohwer (2002). This new book extends the practical application of event history analysis. It heavily builds on the Blossfeld, Hamerle, and Mayer volume with regard to statistical theory, which will not be repeated to the same extent here. It also takes up most of the examples given in the Blossfeld and Rohwer volume for the computer program *Transition Data Analysis* (TDA). Therefore, based on the complementary character of the three volumes, we recommend a combination of those books for courses in applied event history analysis.

Acknowledgments

We received support for our work from several sources and various places. In particular, we received support from the GLOBALIFE (*Life Courses in the Globalization Process*) project at the Otto Friedrich University of Bamberg, Germany (and financed by the Volkswagen Foundation, Hannover), the Department of Social Sciences at the University of Bochum, and the Department of Empirical Social and Economic Research at the University of Cologne, Germany.

To produce the camera-ready copy for this book, we used Donald Knuth's typesetting program TEX in connection with Leslie Lamport's LATEX and Tomas Rokicki's DVIPS PostScript driver.

The data used in our examples were taken from the German Life History Study (GLHS) and were anonymized for data protection purposes. The GLHS study was conducted by Karl Ulrich Mayer, as principal investigator at the Max Planck Institute for Human Development and Education in Berlin, now at Yale University, USA. The original data collection was funded by the Deutsche Forschungsgemeinschaft (DFG) within its Sonderforschungsbereich 3 "Mikroanalytische Grundlagen der Gesellschaftspolitik." We would like to thank Professor Mayer for his kind permission to use a sample of 600 job episodes in the GLHS as a basis for our practical examples. We also thank Ulrich Pötter for valuable comments concerning model parameterizations.

Hans-Peter Blossfeld, Otto Friedrich University of Bamberg

Katrin Golsch, University of Cologne

Götz Rohwer, Ruhr University of Bochum

EVENT HISTORY
ANALYSIS
WITH STATA

Chapter 1
Introduction

Over the last two decades, social scientists have been collecting and analyzing event history data with increasing frequency. This is not an accidental trend, nor does it reflect a prevailing fashion in survey research or statistical analysis. Instead, it indicates a growing recognition among social scientists that event history data are often the most appropriate empirical information one can get on the substantive process under study.

James Coleman (1981: 6) characterized this kind of substantive process in the following general way: (1) there is a collection of units (which may be individuals, organizations, societies, or whatever), each moving among a finite (usually small) number of states; (2) these changes (or events) may occur at any point in time (i.e., they are not restricted to predetermined points in time); and (3) there are time-constant and/or time-dependent factors influencing the events.

Illustrative examples of this type of substantive process can be given for a wide variety of social research fields: in *labor market studies*, workers move between unemployment and employment,[1] full-time and part-time work,[2] or among various kinds of jobs;[3] in *social inequality studies*, people become a home-owner over the life course;[4] in *demographic analyses*, men and women enter into consensual unions, marriages, or into father-/motherhood, or are getting a divorce;[5] in *sociological mobility studies*, em-

---

[1] See, e.g., Heckman and Borjas 1980; Andreß 1989; Galler and Pötter 1990; Huinink et al. 1995; Bernardi, Layte, Schizzerotto and Jacobs 2000; McGinnity 2004; Blossfeld et al. 2005; Blossfeld, Mills and Bernardi 2006; Blossfeld and Hofmeister 2006; Blossfeld, Buchholz and Hofäcker 2006; Golsch 2005.

[2] See, e.g., Bernasco 1994; Blossfeld and Hakim 1997; Blossfeld, Drobnič and Rohwer 1998; Courgeau and Guérin-Pace 1998; Bernardi 1999a, 1999b; Cramm, Blossfeld and Drobnič 1998; Smeenk 1998; Blossfeld and Drobnič 2001.

[3] See, e.g., Sørensen and Tuma 1981; Blossfeld 1986; Carroll and Mayer 1986; Carroll and Mosakowski 1987; Mayer and Carroll 1987; DiPrete and Whitman 1988; Blossfeld and Mayer 1988; Hachen 1988; Diekmann and Preisendörfer 1988; Andreß 1989; Becker 1993; DiPrete 1993; Brüderl, Preisendörfer and Ziegler 1993; Esping-Andersen, Leth-Sørensen and Rohwer 1994, Mach, Mayer and Pohoski 1994; Blau 1994; Allmendinger 1994; Huinink et al. 1995; Jacobs 1995; Halpin and Chan 1998; Blau and Riphahn 1999; Drobnič and Blossfeld 2004.

[4] See, e.g., Mulder and Smits 1999; Kurz 2000; Kurz and Blossfeld 2004.

[5] See, e.g., Hoem 1983, 1986, 1991; Rindfuss and John 1983; Rindfuss and Hirschman 1984; Michael and Tuma 1985; Hoem and Rennermalm 1985; Papastefanou 1987; Huinink 1987, 1993, 1995; Mayer and Schwarz 1989; Leridon 1989; Hannan and Tuma 1990; Wu

1

ployees shift through different occupations, social classes, or industries;[6] in *studies of organizational ecology*, firms, unions, or organizations are founded or closed down;[7] in *political science research*, governments break down, voluntary organizations are founded, or countries go through a transition from one political regime to another;[8] in *migration studies*, people move between different regions or countries;[9] in *marketing applications*, consumers switch from one brand to another or purchase the same brand again; in *criminology studies*, prisoners are released and commit another criminal act after some time; in *communication analysis*, interaction processes such as interpersonal and small group processes are studied;[10] in *educational studies*, students drop out of school before completing their degrees, enter into a specific educational track, or later in the life course, start a program of further education;[11] in *analyses of ethnic conflict*, incidences of racial and ethnic confrontation, protest, riot, and attack are studied;[12] in *socialpsychological studies*, aggressive responses are analyzed;[13] in *psychological studies*,

---

1990; Mayer, Allmendinger and Huinink 1991; Liefbroer 1991; Grundmann 1992; Klijzing 1992; Sørensen and Sørensen 1985; Diekmann 1989; Diekmann and Weick 1993; Blossfeld, De Rose, Hoem, and Rohwer 1995; Teachman 1983; Lillard 1993; Lillard and Waite 1993; Wu and Martinson 1993; Lauterbach 1994; Manting 1994; Bernasco 1994; Blossfeld 1995; Lillard, Brien and Waite 1995; Yamaguchi and Ferguson 1995; Huinink et al. 1995; Courgeau 1995; Manting 1996; Blossfeld and Timm 1997; Li and Choe 1997; Defo 1998; Ostermeier and Blossfeld 1998; Timm, Blossfeld and Müller 1998; Brian, Lillard and Waite 1999; Blossfeld et al. 1999; Diekmann and Engelhardt 1999; Mills 2000b; Blossfeld and Timm 2003; Blossfeld and Müller 2002/2003; Nazio and Blossfeld 2003.

[6]See, e.g., Sørensen and Blossfeld 1989; Mayer, Featherman, Selbee, and Colbjørnsen 1989; Featherman, Selbee, and Mayer 1989; Blossfeld 1986; Carroll and Mayer 1986; Carroll and Mosakowski 1987; Mayer and Carroll 1987; DiPrete and Whitman 1988; Blossfeld and Mayer 1988; Allmendinger 1989a, 1989b; Esping-Andersen 1990, 1993; Blossfeld and Hakim 1997; Drobnič, Blossfeld and Rohwer 1998; Blossfeld, Drobnič and Rohwer 1998; Cramm, Blossfeld and Drobnič 1998; Blossfeld and Drobnič 2001.

[7]See, e.g., Carroll and Delacroix 1982; Hannan and Freeman 1989; Freeman, Carroll, and Hannan 1983; Preisendörfer and Burgess 1988; Brüderl, Diekmann, and Preisendörfer 1991; Brüderl 1991a; Hedström 1994; Greve 1995; Lomi 1995; Brüderl and Diekmann 1995; Popielarz and McPherson 1996; Hannan et al. 1998a, 1998b; Carroll and Hannan 2000.

[8]See, e.g., Strang 1991; Strang and Meyer 1993; Popielarz and McPherson 1996; Chaves 1996; Soule and Zylan 1997; Ramirez, Soysal, and Shanahan 1997; Box-Steffensmeier and Bradford 1997, 2004.

[9]See, e.g., Bilsborrow and Akin 1982; Pickles and Davies 1986; Wagner 1989a, 1989b, 1990; Courgeau 1990; Baccaïni and Courgeau 1996; Courgeau, Leliévre and Wolber 1998.

[10]See, e.g., Eder 1981; Krempel 1987; Snyder 1991.

[11]See, e.g., Blossfeld 1989, 1990; Willett and Singer 1991; Singer and Willett 1991; Becker 1993; Meulemann 1990; Schömann and Becker 1995.

[12]See, e.g., Olzak 1992; Olzak and West 1991; Olzak, Shanahan and West 1994; Olzak and Shanahan 1996, 1999; Rasler 1996; Olzak, Shanahan and McEneaney 1996; Krain 1997; Myers 1997; Minkoff 1997, 1999; Olzak and Olivier 1998a, 1998b; Soule and Van Dyke 1999.

[13]See, e.g., Hser et al. 1995; Yamaguchi 1991; Diekmann et al. 1996.

human development processes are studied;[14] in *psychiatric analysis*, people may show signs of psychoses or neuroses at a specific age;[15] in *social policy studies*, entry to and exit from poverty, transitions into retirement, or the changes in living conditions in old age are analyzed;[16] in *medical and epidemiological applications*, patients switch between the states "healthy" and "diseased" or go through various phases of an addiction career;[17] and so on.

Technically speaking, in all of these diverse examples, units of analysis occupy a discrete state in a theoretically meaningful state space, and transitions between these states can virtually occur at any time.[18] Given an event history data set, the typical problem of the social scientist is to use appropriate statistical methods for describing this process of change, to discover the causal relationships among events, and to assess their importance.

This book was written to help the applied social scientist to achieve these goals. In this introductory chapter we first discuss different observation plans and their consequences for causal modeling. We also summarize the fundamental concepts of event history analysis and show that the change in the transition rate is a natural way to represent the causal effect in a statistical model. The remaining chapters are organized as follows:

- Chapter 2 describes event history data sets and their organization. It also shows how to use such data sets with Stata.

- Chapter 3 discusses basic nonparametric methods to describe event history data, mainly the life table and the Kaplan-Meier (product-limit) estimation methods.

- Chapter 4 deals with the basic exponential transition rate model. Although this very simple model is almost never appropriate in practical applications, it serves as an important starting point for all other transition rate models.

- Chapter 5 describes a simple generalization of the basic exponential model, called the *piecewise constant exponential model*. In our view, this is one of the most useful models for empirical research, and we devote a full chapter to discussing it.

- Chapter 6 discusses time-dependent covariates. The examples are restricted to exponential and piecewise exponential models, but the topic—and part of the discussion—is far more general. In particular, we introduce the problem of how to model parallel and interdependent processes.

---

[14]See, e.g., Yamaguchi and Jin 1999; Mills 2000a.

[15]See, e.g., Eerola 1994.

[16]See, e.g., Allmendinger 1994; Leisering and Walker 1998; Leisering and Leibfried 1998; Zwick 1998; Mayer and Baltes 1996.

[17]See, e.g., Andersen et al. 1993.

[18]See, e.g., Cox and Oakes 1984; Tuma and Hannan 1984; Hutchison 1988a, 1988b; Kiefer 1988.

- Chapter 7 introduces a variety of models with a parametrically specified duration-dependent transition rate, in particular Gompertz-Makeham, Weibull, log-logistic, and log-normal models.

- Chapter 8 discusses the question of goodness-of-fit checks for parametric transition rate models. In particular, the chapter describes simple graphical checks based on transformed survivor functions and generalized residuals.

- Chapter 9 introduces semiparametric transition rate models based on an estimation approach proposed by D. R. Cox (1972).

- Chapter 10 discusses problems of model specification and, in particular, transition rate models with unobserved heterogeneity. The discussion is mainly critical, and the examples are restricted to using a gamma mixing distribution.

1.1   Causal Modeling and Observation Plans

In event history modeling, design issues regarding the type of substantive process are of crucial importance. It is assumed that the methods of data analysis (e.g., estimation and testing techniques) cannot only depend on the particular type of data (e.g., cross-sectional data, panel data, etc.) as has been the case in applying more traditional statistical methodologies. Rather, the characteristics of the specific kind of social process itself must "guide" both the *design of data collection* and *the way that data are analyzed and interpreted* (Coleman 1973, 1981, 1990).

To collect data generated by a continuous-time, discrete-state substantive process, different observation plans have been used (Coleman 1981; Tuma and Hannan 1984). With regard to the extent of detail about the process of change, one can distinguish between cross-sectional data, panel data, event count data, event sequence data, and event history data.

In this book, we do not treat *event count data* (see, e.g., Andersen et al. 1993; Barron 1993; Hannan and Freeman 1989; Olzak 1992; Olzak and Shanahan 1996; Minkoff 1997; Olzak and Olivier 1998a/b), which simply record the number of different types of events for each unit (e.g., the number of upward, downward, or lateral moves in the employment career in a period of 10 years), and *event sequence data* (see, e.g., Rajulton 1992; Abbott 1995; Rohwer and Trappe 1997; Halpin and Chan 1998), which document sequences of states occupied by each unit. We concentrate our discussion on cross-sectional and panel data as the main standard sociological data types (Tuma and Hannan 1984) and compare them with event history data. We use the example shown in Figure 1.1.1. In this figure, an individual's family career is observed in a cross-sectional survey, a panel survey, and an event-oriented survey.

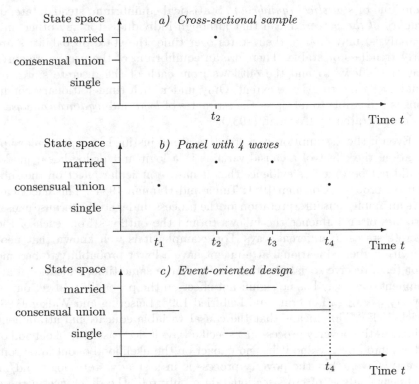

Figure 1.1.1 Observation of an individual's family career on the basis of a cross-sectional survey, a panel study, and an event-history-oriented design.

1.1.1   Cross-Sectional Data

Let us first discuss the *cross-sectional observation*. In the social sciences, this is the most common form of data used to assess sociological hypotheses. The family history of the individual in Figure 1.1.1 is represented in a cross-sectional study by one single point in time: his or her marital state at the time of interview. Thus a cross-sectional sample is only a "snapshot" of the substantive process being studied. The point in time when researchers take that "picture" is normally not determined by hypotheses about the dynamics of the substantive process itself, but by external considerations such as getting research funds, finding an appropriate institute to conduct the survey, and so on.

Coleman (1981) has demonstrated that one must be cautious in drawing inferences about the effects of explanatory variables in logit models on the basis of cross-sectional data because, implicitly or explicitly, social researchers have to assume that the substantive process under study is in some kind of *statistical equilibrium*. Statistical equilibrium, steady-state, or *stability of the process* mean that although individuals (or any other unit of analysis) may change their states over time, the state probabilities are fairly trendless or stable. Therefore an equilibrium of the process requires that the inflows to and the outflows from each of the discrete states be equal over time to a large extent. Only under such time-stationary conditions is it possible to interpret the estimates of *logit* and *log-linear analyses*, as demonstrated by Coleman (1981).

Even if the assumption of a steady state is justified in a particular application, the effect of a causal variable in a logit and/or log-linear model should not be taken as evidence that it has a particular effect on the substantive process (Coleman 1981; Tuma and Hannan 1984). This effect can have an ambiguous interpretation for the process under study because causal variables often influence the inflows to and the outflows from each of the discrete states in different ways. For example, it is well known that people with higher educational attainment have a lower probability to become poor (e.g., receive social assistance); but at the same time, educational attainment obviously has no significant effect on the probability to get out of poverty (see, e.g., Leisering and Leibfried 1998; Leisering and Walker 1998; Zwick 1998). This means that the causal variable educational attainment influences the poverty process in a specific way: it decreases the likelihood of inflows into poverty and it has no impact on the likelihood of outflows from poverty. Given that the poverty process is in a steady state, logit and/or log-linear analysis of cross-sectional data only tells the difference in these two directional effects on the poverty process (Coleman 1981). In other words, cross-sectional logit and/or log-linear models can only show the net effect of the causal variables on the steady state distribution and that can be misleading as the following example demonstrates.

Consider that we are studying a process with two states ("being unemployed" and "being employed"), which is in equilibrium (i.e., the unemployment rate is trendless over time), and let us further assume that the covariate "educational attainment" increases the probability of movement from unemployment to employment (UE → E) and increases the probability of movement from employment to unemployment (E → UE) for each individual. In a cross-sectional logistic regression analysis using the probability of being employed as the dependent variable, the estimated coefficient for "educational attainment" only tells the net effect of both directional effects. Therefore, if the positive effect of educational attainment on UE → E offsets the positive effect on E → UE, the net effect of "educational attainment" in the logistic regression on the steady-state probability will be about zero and not significant. That is, a zero effect of a covariate in a cross-sectional logistic regression analysis could mean two very different things: that there is no effect at all of the respective covariate on UE → E and on E → UE, or that the directional effects on UE → E and on E → UE offset each other. Thus, an insignificant effect in the cross-sectional logit model should not be taken as evidence that a variable is irrelevant to the process, only that it has no net effect on the equilibrium distribution (Tuma and Hannan 1984).

Similarly, if the net effect of "educational attainment" in a cross-sectional logistic regression on the probability of becoming employed is positive, then the following four different interpretations are in principle possible: (1) that the positive effect on UE → E is greater than the positive effect on E → UE, (2) that the negative effect on UE → E is smaller than the negative effect on E → UE, (3) that there is only a positive effect on UE → E and no effect on E → UE, and (4) that there is no effect on UE → E and only a negative effect on E → UE. Conversely, for negative effects in the cross-sectional logistic regression, the four interpretations have to be reversed.

If there is no equilibrium in the process, however, cross-sectional coefficients may not only be ambiguous but also present a completely misleading picture. In a study on unemployment incidence, Rosenthal (1991), for example, demonstrated how confusing cross-sectional estimates can be if the proportion of people being unemployed increases or decreases in a specific region and if the process of change is, therefore, not in equilibrium.

In the social sciences one can expect that stability is very rare. For example, life history studies (Mayer 1990; Blossfeld 1989, 1995; Blossfeld and Hakim 1997; Blossfeld and Drobnič 2001; Blossfeld and Timm 2003; Blossfeld and Müller 2002) show that change across age, cohort, and historical period is an enduring and important feature in all domains of modern individuals' lives (Mayer and Tuma 1990); organizational studies demonstrate that most social organizations seem to follow a program of growth and not of stability (Carroll and Hannan 2000); and most modern societies reveal an accelerating rate of change in almost all of their subsystems (cf. the rapid changes in family systems, job structures, educational systems, etc.; see Heinz 1991a, 1991b, 1992; Mayer 1990; Huinink et al. 1995; Blossfeld and Hakim 1997; Leisering and Leibfried 1998; Blossfeld and Drobnič 2001; Blossfeld and Timm 2003; Blossfeld and Müller 2002). But even in areas considered to be fairly stable, one must ask the crucial methodological question: To what extent is the process under study close to an equilibrium (Tuma and Hannan 1984)? This question can only be answered if longitudinal data are applied, because longitudinal data are the only type of data that indicate whether a steady state actually exists, or how long it will take until a system returns to a new equilibrium after some external upheaval.

Beyond the crucial assumption of process stability, cross-sectional data have several other inferential limitations with regard to causal modeling. We want to address at least some of the more important problems here.[19]

---

[19]These problems are, however, not mutually exclusive.

Direction of Causality. There are only a few situations in which the direction of causality can be established based on cross-sectional data (Davies 1987). For example, consider the strong positive association between parental socioeconomic characteristics and educational attainment of sons and daughters, controlling for other important influences (Shavit and Blossfeld 1993; Erikson and Jonsson 1996). A convincing interpretation of this effect might be that being born into a middle class family increases the likelihood of attaining a university degree because one is unable to think of any other plausible explanation for the statistical association. However, such recursive relationships, in which all the causal linkages run "one way" and have no "feedback" effects, are rare in social science research. For example, there is very often an association between the age of the youngest child and female labor force participation in modern industrialized societies (Blossfeld and Hakim 1997; Blossfeld, Drobnič and Rohwer 1998; Blossfeld and Drobnič 2001). The common interpretation is that there is a one-way causality with young children tending to keep mothers at home. However, it is quite possible that the lack of jobs encourages women to enter into marriage and motherhood, suggesting a reversed relationship (Davies 1987).

The ambiguity of causation seems to be particularly important for the modeling of the *relationship between attitudes and behavior*. There are two interesting aspects of this relationship: There is a direct effect in which behavior affects attitudes, and there is a "feedback" process where attitudes change behavior (Davies 1987).[20] The well-known disputes among sociologists, as to whether value change engenders change in social behavior, or whether structural change in behavior leads to changing values of individuals, often originate from the fact that cross-sectional surveys are used that can only assess the net association of these two processes.

Various Strengths of Reciprocal Effects. Connected with the inability of establishing the direction of causality in cross-sectional surveys is the drawback that these data cannot be used to discover the different strengths of reciprocal effects. For example, many demographic studies have shown that first marriage and first motherhood are closely interrelated (Blossfeld and Huinink 1991; Blossfeld et al. 1999; Blossfeld and Mills 2001). To understand what has been happening with regard to family formation in modern societies, it might be of interest to know not only the effect of marriage on birth rates, but also the effect of pregnancy or first birth on getting married (Blossfeld and Huinink 1991; Blossfeld 1995; Blossfeld et al. 1999; Mills and Trovato 2001; Blossfeld and Mills 2001), and, perhaps, how these effects have changed over historical time (Manting 1994, 1996).

---

[20]The relationship between attitudes and behavior suggests that there is some kind of inertia (or positive feedback), which means that the probability of a specific behavior increases as a monotonic function of attitudes, and attitudes depend on previous behavior (Davies and Crouchley 1985).

Observational Data. Most sociological research is based on nonexperimental observations of social processes, and these processes are highly selective. For example, Lieberson (1985), in a study examining the influence of type of school (private vs. public) on test performance among students, distinguished at least three types of nonrandom processes: (1) *self-selectivity*, in which the units of analysis sort themselves out by choice (e.g., specific students choose specific types of schools); (2) *selective assignment by the independent variable* itself, which determines, say, what members of a population are exposed to specific levels of the independent variable (e.g., schools select their students based on their past achievement); and (3) *selectivity due to forces exogenous to variables under consideration* (socioeconomic background, ethnicity, gender, previous school career, changes of intelligence over age, etc.); and many of these sources are not only *not observed* but also effectively *unmeasurable*. Of course, no longitudinal study will be able to overcome all the problems of identification of these various effects; however, cross-sectional data offer the worst of all opportunities to disentangle the effects of the causal factors of interest on the outcome from other forces operating at the same time because these data are least informative about the process of change. Cross-sectional analysis therefore requires a particularly careful justification, and the substantive interpretation of results must always be appropriately qualified (Davies 1987; Pickles and Davies 1989).

Previous History. There is one aspect of observational data that deserves special attention in the social sciences. Life courses of individuals (and other units of analysis such as organizations, etc.) involve complex and cumulative time-related layers of selectivity (Mayer 1991; Mayer and Müller 1986; Mayer and Schöpflin 1989; Mayer and Tuma 1990; Huinink et al. 1995; Mayer and Baltes 1996). Therefore, there is a strong likelihood that specific individuals have been entering a specific origin state (see, e.g., the discussion in Blossfeld et al. 1999 with regard to consensual unions). In particular, life-course research has shown that the past is an indispensible factor in understanding the present (Buchmann 1989; Heinz 1991a, 1991b, 1992; Mayer 1990; Allmendinger 1994; Huinink et al. 1995; Weymann 1995; Weymann and Heinz 1996). Cross-sectional analysis may be performed with some proxy-variables and with assumptions of the causal order as well as interdependencies between the various explanatory variables. However, it is often not possible to appropriately trace back the time-related selective processes operating in the previous history, because these data are simply not available. Thus the normal control approaches in cross-sectional statistical techniques will rarely be successful in isolating the influence of some specific causal force (Lieberson 1985).

Age and Cohort Effects. Cross-sectional data cannot be used to distinguish age and cohort effects (Tuma and Hannan 1984; Davies 1987).

However, in many social science applications it is of substantive importance to know whether the behavior of people (e.g., their tendency to vote for a specific party) is different because they belong to different age groups or because they are members of different birth cohorts (Blossfeld 1986, 1989; Mayer and Huinink 1990).

Historical Settings. Cross-sectional data are also not able to take into account the fact that processes emerge in particular historical settings. For example, in addition to individual resources (age, education, labor force experience, etc.), there are at least two ways in which a changing labor market structure affects career opportunities. The first is that people start their careers in different structural contexts. It has often been assumed that these specific historic conditions at the point of entry into the labor market have a substantial impact on people's subsequent careers. This kind of influence is generally called a cohort effect (Glenn 1977). The second way that changing labor market structure influences career opportunities is that it improves or worsens the career prospects of all people within the labor market at a given time (Blossfeld 1986). For example, in a favorable economic situation with low unemployment, there will be a relatively wide range of opportunities. This kind of influence is generally called a period effect (Mason and Fienberg 1985). With longitudinal data, Blossfeld (1986) has shown that life-course, cohort, and period effects can be identified based on substantively developed measures of these concepts (see, e.g., Rodgers 1982) and that these effects represent central mechanisms of career mobility that must be distinguished.

Multiple Clocks, Historical Eras, and Point-in-Time Events. From a theoretical or conceptual point of view, multiple clocks, historical eras, and point-in-time events very often influence the substantive process being studied (Mayer and Tuma 1990). For example, in demographic studies of divorce, types of clocks, such as age of respondent, time of cohabitation, duration of marriage, ages of children, as well as different phases in the state of the business cycle, or changes in national (divorce) laws are of importance (Blossfeld, De Rose, Hoem, and Rohwer 1995; Blossfeld and Müller 2002/2003). With respect to cross-sectional data, such relationships can hardly be studied without making strong untestable assumptions.

Contextual Processes at Multiple Levels. Social scientists are very often interested in the influences of contextual processes at multiple aggregation levels (Huinink 1989). Contextual process effects refer to situations where changes in the group contexts themselves influence the dependent variable. For example, career mobility of an individual may be conceptualized as being dependent on changes in resources at the *individual level* (e.g., social background, educational attainment, experience, etc.), the success of the firm in which he or she is employed (e.g., expansion or contraction of the organization) at the *intermediate level*, and changes in the business cycle at the *macro level* (Blossfeld 1986; DiPrete 1993). Cross-sectional data do not provide an adequate opportunity for the study of such influences at different levels (Mayer and Tuma 1990).

Duration Dependence. Another problem of cross-sectional data is that they are *inherently ambiguous with respect to their interpretation at the level of the unit of observation*. Suppose we know that in West Germany 30.6 % of employed women were working part-time in 1970 (Blossfeld and Rohwer 1997a). At the one extreme, this might be interpreted to imply that *each* employed woman had a 30.6 % chance of being employed part-time in this year, but on the other, one could infer that 30.6 % of the employed women always worked part-time and 69.4 % were full-timers only. In other words, cross-sectional data do not convey information about the *time women spent in these different employment forms*. They are therefore open to quite different substantive interpretations (Heckman and Willis 1977; Flinn and Heckman 1982; Blossfeld and Hakim 1997; Blossfeld and Drobnič 2001). In the first case, each woman would be expected to move back and forth between part-time and full-time employment. In the second, there is no mobility between part-time and full-time work, and the estimated percentages describe the proportions of two completely different groups of employed women. From an analytical point of view, it is therefore important to have data about durations in a state. Also, repeated cross-sectional analysis using comparable samples of the same population (e.g., a series of microcensuses or cross-sectional surveys) can only show net change, not the flow of individuals.

Variability in State Dependencies. In many situations, cross-sectional data are problematic because the rate of change is strongly state dependent and *entries into and exits from these states are highly variable over time* (e.g., over the life course and historical period or across cohorts). For example, it is well known that the roles of wives and mothers (the latter in particular) have been central in women's lives. Therefore the *family cycle concept* has frequently been used in sociology to describe significant changes in the circumstances that affect the availability of women for paid work outside the home. The basic idea is that there is a set of ordered stages primarily defined by variations in family composition and size that could be described with cross-sectional data. However, this view often leads to the tendency to assume that what happens to different women in various phases in the family cycle at one point in time is similar to the pattern that women experience when they make these transitions in different historical times (which has been called the *life course fallacy*). Moreover, there is the well-known problem that individuals and families often fail to conform to the assumption of a single progression through a given number of stages in a predetermined order (see, e.g., Blossfeld and Hakim 1997; Blossfeld and

Drobnič 2001). At least three reasons for this may exist (Murphy 1991): (1) the chronology of timing of events may not conform to the ideal model, for example, childbearing may start before marriage; (2) many stages are not reached, for example, by never-married persons; and (3) the full set of stages may be truncated by events such as death or marital breakdown. Such complex constellations between the family cycle and women's labor-force participation could hardly be meaningfully described or studied on the basis of cross-sectional data.

Changes in Outcomes. Cross-sectional models very often have a *tendency to overpredict change* and consistently *overestimate the importance of explanatory variables* (Davies 1987). The reason for this phenomenon is that these data analyses cannot be based on how *changes* in explanatory variables engender *changes* in outcomes. They are only concerned with how *levels* of explanatory variables "explain" an *outcome* at a specific point in time. However, if an outcome at time t (e.g., choice of mode of travel to work in June) is dependent on a previous outcome (e.g., established choice of mode of travel to work), and if both outcomes are positively influenced in the same way by an explanatory variable (e.g., merits of public transport), then the effect of the explanatory variable will reflect both the true positive influence of the explanatory variable on the outcome at time t and a positive spurious element due to that variable acting as a proxy for the omitted earlier outcome (established mode of travel to work). Thus a cross-sectional analysis of the travel to work choice (e.g., public vs. private transport) would have a tendency to overpredict the effect of policy changes (e.g., fare increases or faster buses) because there is a strong behavioral inertia (Davies 1987).

In sum, all these examples show that cross-sectional data have many severe inferential limitations for social scientists. Therefore it is not surprising that causal conclusions based on cross-sectional data have often been radically altered after the processes were studied with longitudinal data (Lieberson 1985).

Longitudinal studies also have a much greater power than cross-sectional ones, both in the estimation of bias from missing data and in the means for correcting it. This is because in longitudinal studies one often has data from previous points in time, thus enabling the characteristics of non-responders or lost units to be assessed with some precision. It is noteworthy that almost all the substantive knowledge concerning the biases associated with missing data, which all studies must seek to minimize, is derived from longitudinal studies (Medical Research Council 1992).

Although longitudinal data are no panacea, they are obviously more effective in causal analysis and have less inferential limitations (Magnusson, Bergmann, and Törestad 1991; Arminger, Clogg and Sobel 1995; Clogg and Arminger 1993; Blossfeld 1995; Mayer 1990; Mayer and Tuma 1990;

Blossfeld and Hakim 1997; Blossfeld and Drobnič 2001; Carroll and Hannan 2000). They are indispensable for the study of processes over the life course (of all types of units) and their relation to historical change. Therefore research designs aimed at a causal understanding of social processes should be based on longitudinal data at the level of the units of analysis.

1.1.2   Panel Data

The temporal data most often available to sociologists are *panel data*. In panel studies the same persons or units are re-interviewed or observed at a series of discrete points in time (Chamberlain 1984; Hsiao 1986; Arminger and Müller 1990; Engel and Reinecke 1994). Figure 1.1.1 shows a four-wave panel in which the family career of the respondent was observed at four different points in time. This means that there is only information on states of the units at pre-determined survey points, but the course of the events between the survey points remains unknown.

Panel data normally contain more information than cross-sectional data, but involve well-known distortions created by the method itself (see, e.g., Magnusson and Bergmann 1990; Hunt 1985).

Panel Bias. Respondents often answer the same questions differently in the second and later waves than they did the first time because they are less inhibited, or they mulled over or discussed the issues between questioning dates.

Modification of Processes. Panel studies tend to influence the very phenomena they seek to observe—this sometimes changes the natural history of the processes being observed.

Attrition of the Sample. In panel studies the composition of the sample normally diminishes selectively over time. These processes normally are particularly strong during the first panel waves and then gradually diminish. Therefore, what researchers observe in a long-term panel may not provide a good picture of what has actually happened to the process under study.

Non-Responses and Missing Data. In a cross-sectional analysis, one can afford to throw out a small number of cases with non-responses and missing data, but in a long-term panel study, throwing out incomplete cases at each round of observation can eventually leave a severely pruned sample having very different characteristics from the original one.

Fallacy of Cohort Centrism. Very often panel studies are focused on members of a specific cohort (cf., e.g., the British National Child Study). In other words, these panels study respondents that were born in, grew up in, and have lived in a particular historical period. There is therefore a danger that researchers might assume that what happens to a particular group of people over time reveals general principles of the life course (fallacy of cohort centrism). Many events may simply be specific for that generation.

Fallacy of Period Centrism. Many panel studies include just a few waves and cover only a short period of historical time (cf. the British Household and Panel Study, which now covers only a few years). At the time of these observations, special conditions may exist (e.g., high unemployment) and this can result in an individual's responding differently than he or she would under different historical conditions (fallacy of historical period).

Confounded Age, Period, and Cohort Effects. In any long-term panel study in sociology, three causal factors—individual's age, cohort, and historical period effect—are confounded (cf. the Panel Study of Income Dynamics). Methodological techniques are needed to unconfound these three factors and reveal the role of each. As discussed in more detail later, panel data do have some specific problems unconfounding the three major factors. However, for gaining scientific insights into the interplay of processes governing life courses from birth to death, they appear to be a better approach than applying cross-sections. But a mechanical and atheoretical cohort analysis is a useless exercise, and statistical innovations alone will not solve the age-period-cohort problem (Blossfeld 1986; Mayer and Huinink 1990).

Most of the previously mentioned difficulties concerning panel studies can be dealt with by better data collection methods, more sophisticated statistical procedures, or more panel waves. However, panel data also lead to a series of deficiencies with respect to the estimation of transition rates (Tuma and Hannan 1984): First, there is the problem of "embeddability," which means that there may be difficulties in embedding a matrix of observed transition probabilities within a continuous-time Markov process (Singer and Spilerman 1976a); second, there is the problem that there may be no unique matrix of transition rates describing the data (Singer and Spilerman 1976b); and third, there is the drawback that the matrix of transition probabilities may be very sensitive to sampling and measurement error (Tuma and Hannan 1984). Multiple waves with irregular spacing or shorter intervals between waves can reduce these problems. However, as Hannan and Tuma (1979) have noted, this only means that the more panel and event history data resemble each other, the less problematic modeling becomes.

Lazarsfeld (1948, 1972) was among the first sociologists to propose panel analysis of discrete variables. In particular, he wanted to find a solution to the problem of ambiguity in causation. He suggested that if one wants to know whether a variable X induces change in another variable Y, or whether Y induces change in X, observations of X and Y at two points in time would be necessary. Lazarsfeld applied this method to dichotomous variables whose time-related structure he analyzed in a resulting sixteenfold table. Later on, Goodman (1973) applied log-linear analysis to such tables. For many years, such a cross-lagged panel analysis for qualitative and quantitative variables (Campbell and Stanley 1963; Shingles 1976) was considered to be a powerful quasi-experimental method of making causal inferences. It was also extended to multiwave-multivariable panels to study more complex path models with structural-equation models (Jöreskog and Sörbom 1993). However, it appears that the strength of the panel design for causal inference was hugely exaggerated (Davis 1978). Causal inferences in panel approaches are much more complicated than has been generally realized. There are several reasons for this.

Time Until the Effect Starts to Occur. It is important to realize that the role of time in causal explanations does not only lie in specifying a *temporal order* in which the effect follows the cause in time. In addition, it implies that there is a *temporal interval* between the cause and its impact (Kelly and McGrath 1988). In other words, if the cause has to precede the effect in time, it takes some finite amount of time for the cause to produce the effect. The time interval may be very short or very long but can never be zero or infinity (Kelly and McGrath 1988). Some effects take place almost instantaneously. For example, if the effect occurs at microsecond intervals, then the process must be observed in these small time units to uncover causal relations. However, some effects may occur in a time interval too small to be measured by any given methods, so that cause and effect *seem to occur* at the same point in time. Apparent simultaneity is often the case in those social science applications where basic observation intervals are relatively crude (e.g., days, months, or even years), such as, for example, yearly data about first marriage and first childbirth (Blossfeld, Manting, and Rohwer 1993). For these parallel processes, the events "first marriage" and "first childbirth" may be interdependent, but whether these two events are observed simultaneously or successively depends on the degree of temporal refinement of the scale used in making the observations. Other effects need a long time until they start to occur. Thus, there is a *delay* or *lag* between cause and effect that must be specified in an appropriate causal analysis. However, in most of the current sociological theories and interpretations of research findings, this interval is left unspecified. In most cases, at least implicitly, researchers assume that the effect takes place almost immediately and is then constant (Figure 1.1.2b). Of course, if this is the case, then there seems to be no need for theoretical statements about the time course of the causal effect. A single measurement of the effect at some point in time after a cause has been imposed might be sufficient for catching it (see Figure 1.1.2a). However, if there is a reason to assume that there is a lag between cause and effect, then a single measurement of the outcome is inadequate for describing the process (see Figure 1.1.2b), and the interpretation based on a single measurement of the outcome will then be a function of the point in time chosen to measure the effect (the substantial conclusion based on

p_3 or p_4 would be obviously different).

Thus a *restrictive assumption of panel designs* is that either cause and effect occur almost simultaneously, or the interval between observations is of approximately the same length as the true causal lag. The greater the discrepancy, the greater the likelihood that the panel analysis will fail to discover the true causal process. Thus, as expressed by Davis (1978), if one does not know the causal lag exactly, panel analysis is not of much use to establish causal direction or time sequencing of causal effects. Unfortunately, we rarely have enough theoretically grounded arguments about the structure of a social process to specify the lags precisely.

Temporal Shapes of the Unfolding Effect. In addition to the question of how long the delay between the timing of the cause and the beginning of the unfolding of the effect is, there might be *different shapes of how the effect develops in time*. Although the problem of time lags is widely recognized in social science literature, considerations with respect to the temporal shape of the effect are quite rare (Kelly and McGrath 1988). In fact, social scientists seem to be quite ignorant with respect to the fact that causal effects could be highly time-dependent.

Figure 1.1.2 illustrates several possible shapes these effects may trace over time. In Figure 1.1.2a, there is an almost simultaneous change in the effect that is then maintained; in Figure 1.1.2b, the effect occurs with some lengthy time lag and is then time-invariant; in Figure 1.1.2c, the effect starts almost immediately and then gradually increases; in Figure 1.1.2d, there is an almost simultaneous increase, which reaches a maximum after some time and then decreases; finally, in Figure 1.1.2e, a cyclical effect pattern over time is described.

If the effect increases or decreases monotonically or linearly, oscillates in cycles, or shows any other complicated time-related pattern, then the strength of the observed effect in a panel study is dependent on the timing of the panel waves. A panel design might be particularly problematic if there are non-monotonic cycles of the effect because totally opposite conclusions about the effects of the explanatory variable can be arrived at, depending on whether the panel places measurement points at a peak or at an ebb in the curve (see Figures 1.1.2d and 1.1.2e).

Reciprocal Effects with Different Time Paths. In cases of reciprocal causality, additional problems will arise in panel studies if the time structure of the effects of X_1 on X_2 and of X_2 on X_1 are different with respect to lags and shapes. In these situations, a panel design might turn out to be completely useless for those wishing to detect such time-related recursive relationships.

Observational Data and Timing of Measurement of Explanatory Variables. Most sociological research is based on observational data, mean-

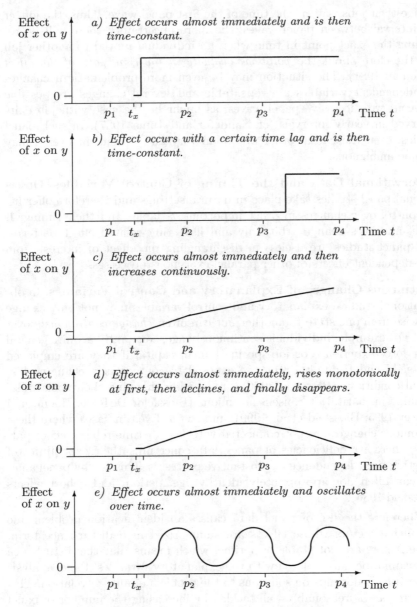

Figure 1.1.2 Different temporal lags and shapes of how a change in a variable x, occurring at point in time t_x, effects a change in a variable y.

ing that manipulation of the timing of the independent variables is generally not possible. For example, if the researcher is going to study the effects of job mobility on marriage behavior, it is impossible to force respondents to change their jobs, say, at the time of the first panel wave. Thus, the longer the interval between panel waves, the more uncertainty there will be regarding the exact point in time when an individual moved to another job and therefore about the *point we evaluate in the time path of the effect* (Coleman 1981). The situation may be even more problematic if changes in independent variables are repeatable and several changes are possible between two successive panel waves, as might be the case with job exits observed in yearly intervals (cf. Sandefur and Tuma 1987). In such panel studies, even the causal order of explanatory and dependent events may become ambiguous.

Observational Data and the Timing of Control Variables. Observational panel studies take place in natural settings and therefore offer little control over changes in other important variables and their timing. If these influences change arbitrarily and have time-related effect patterns, then panel studies are useless in disentangling the effect of interest from time-dependent effects of other parallel exogenous processes.

Continuous Changes of Explanatory and Control Variables. In observational studies, explanatory and control variables may not only change stepwise from one state to another but can often *change continuously* over time. For example, individuals continuously age, constantly acquire general labor force experience or job-specific human capital if they are employed (Blossfeld and Huinink 1991), are exposed to continuously changing historical conditions (Blossfeld 1986), are steadily changing their social relationships in marital or consensual unions (Blossfeld, De Rose, Hoem, and Rohwer 1995; Blossfeld et al. 1999), and so on. Even in cases where these continuous changes are not connected with lags or time-related effect patterns, there are deficiencies of panel data concerning their capabilities of detecting time dependence in substantive processes. This is why panel analysis can often not appropriately identify age, period, and cohort effects (Blossfeld 1986).

Therefore the use of panel data causes an identification problem due to omitted factors whose effects are summarized in a disturbance term. These factors are not stable over time, which means that the disturbance term cannot be uncorrelated with the explanatory variables. Panel analysis thus critically depends on solutions to the problem of autocorrelation. This problem can be reasonably well tackled by increasing the number of panel waves and modifying their spacing. Panel analysis is particularly sensitive to the *length of the time intervals between waves relative to the speed of the process* (Coleman 1981). They can be too short, so that too few events will be observed, or too long, so that it is difficult to establish a time-order between events (Sandefur and Tuma 1987). A major advantage of the continuous-time observation design in event history analysis is that it makes the timing between waves irrelevant (Coleman 1968).

1.1.3   Event History Data

For many processes in the social sciences, a continuous measurement of qualitative variables seems to be the only adequate method of assessing empirical change. This is achieved by utilizing an *event oriented observation design*, which records all the changes in qualitative variables and their timing. As shown in Figure 1.1.1, the major advantage of event history data is that they provide the *most complete data possible on changes in qualitative variables that may occur at any point in time*. The observation of events therefore provides an attractive alternative to the observation of states for social scientists.

Event history data, mostly *collected retrospectively* via *life history studies*, cover the whole life course of individuals. An example for such a study is the German Life History Study (GLHS; Mayer and Brückner 1989). Retrospective studies have the advantage of normally being *cheaper* than the collection of data with a long-term panel study. They are also systematically *coded to one framework of codes and meanings* (Dex 1991). But retrospective (in contrast to prospective) studies suffer from several limitations that have been increasingly acknowledged (Medical Research Council 1992).

Nonfactual Data. It is well known that retrospective questions concerning motivational, attitudinal, cognitive, or affective states are particularly problematic because the respondents can hardly recall the timing of changes in these states accurately (Hannan and Tuma 1979). This type of data is not verifiable even in principle because these states exist only in the minds of the respondents and are only directly accessible, if at all, to the respondent concerned (Sudman and Bradburn 1986). For these nonfactual data, panel studies have the advantage of being able to repeatedly record current states of the same individual over time. Thus, for studies aiming to model the relationship between attitudes and behavior over time, panel observations of attitudinal states, combined with retrospective information on behavioral events since the last sweep, appear to be an appropriate design.

Recall Problems with Regard to Behavior or Facts. Behavioral or factual questions ask the respondents about characteristics, things they have done, or things that have happened to them, which in principle are verifiable by an external observer. Most surveys (cross-sectional, panel, or event oriented) elicit retrospective information on behavior or facts (e.g., by asking people about their education, social origin, etc.), so that the disadvantages of retrospection are only a matter of degree. However, event history studies are particularly ambitious (see Mayer and Brückner 1989). They try to collect continuous records of qualitative variables that have a high potential for bias because of their strong reliance on (autobiographic) memory. However, research on the accuracy of retrospective data shows that individuals' marital and fertility histories, family characteristics and education, health service usage, and employment history can be collected to a reasonable degree of accuracy. A very good overview concerning the kinds of data that can be retrospectively collected, the factors affecting recall accuracy, and the methods improving recall has been presented by Dex (1991).

Unknown Factors. Retrospective designs cannot be used to study factors involving variables that are not known to the respondent (e.g., emotional and behavioral problems when the respondent was a child). In such cases, panel studies are indispensable (Medical Research Council 1992).

Limited Capacity. There is a limit to respondents' tolerance for the amount of data that can be collected on one occasion (Medical Research Council 1992). A carefully corsetted panel design can therefore provide a broader coverage of variables (if these are not unduly influenced by variations at the time of assessment).

Only Survivors. Due to their nature, retrospective studies must be based on survivors. Thus, those subjects who have died or migrated from the geographical area under study will necessarily be omitted. If either is related to the process (as often may be the case), biases will arise. This problem is particularly important for retrospective studies involving a broad range of birth cohorts, such as the German Life History Study (GLHS) or international migration studies (Blossfeld 1987b).

Misrepresentation of Specific Populations. Retrospective studies also may result in a misrepresentation of specific populations. For example, Duncan (1966) has shown that if men are asked about their fathers, men from earlier generations who had no sons, or whose sons died or emigrated are not represented in a retrospective father-son mobility table. So, part of the population at risk might not be considered in an analysis (see Blossfeld and Timm 2003, who discuss that problem with regard to studies of educational homogamy which often exclude singles at the time of the interview).

To avoid these problems concerning retrospective event history data, a mixed design employing a follow-up (or "catch-up") and a follow-back strategy appears to combine the strengths of traditional panel designs with the virtues of retrospective event history studies. Therefore, in modern panel studies, event histories are collected retrospectively for the period before the panel started and between the successive panel waves. Sometimes complete administrative records also contain time-related information about events in the past. All of these procedures (retrospective, combined follow-up and back-up, or available registers) offer a comparatively superior opportunity for modeling social processes, regardless of which method is selected.

One aim of our book is to show that event history models are a useful approach to uncovering causal relationships or mapping out a system of causal relations. As becomes apparent later on in the book, event history models are linked very naturally to a causal understanding of social processes because they relate change in future outcomes to conditions in the past and try to predict future changes on the basis of past observations (Aalen 1987).

1.2   Event History Analysis and Causal Modeling

The investigation of causal relationships is an important but difficult scientific endeavor. As shown earlier, opportunities for assessing causal inferences vary strongly with the type of observation available to the social scientist. That is because they determine the extent to which the researcher is forced to make untested assumptions. The overall goal of research design therefore should not merely be to produce data, but to produce the most appropriate data about the intended aspects of the social world. In this section, we discuss the role of time in causal inferences. In particular, we show how the idea of causal relations can be represented in the statistical models of event history analysis.

Correlation and Causation

To begin with, statements about causation should be distinguished from statements about association. In making correlational inferences, one can be satisfied to observe how the values of one variable are associated with the values of other variables over the population under study and, perhaps, over time. In this context, time is only important insofar as it determines the population under analysis or specifies the operational meaning of a particular variable (Holland 1986). Although one always looks at data through the medium of some implicit or explicit theory (Fox 1992), statements about associations are quite different from causal statements because the latter are designed to say something about how events are produced or conditioned by other events. We are often interested in causal mechanisms that we think lie behind the correlation in the data (see Popper Shaffer 1992).

Sometimes social scientists argue that because the units of sociological analysis continuously learn and change and involve actors with goals and beliefs, sociology can at best only provide systematic descriptions of phenomena at various points in history. This position is based on the view that causal statements about events are only possible if they are regulated by "eternal," timeless laws (Kelly and McGrath 1988). Of course, the assumption that such laws can be established with regard to social processes can reasonably be disputed (see, e.g., Giere 1999). In particular, we are not forced to accept a simple contrast: either describing contingent events or assuming "eternal" laws. Many social phenomena show *systematic temporal variations* and *patterned regularities* under specific conditions that themselves are a legitimate focus of our efforts to understand social change (Kelly and McGrath 1988; Goldthorpe 2000). Thus, sociology can do more than just describe the social world. This book therefore emphasizes the usefulness of techniques of event history modeling as "new" approaches to the investigation of causal explanations.[21]

Role of Causal Models and Empirical Research

There is a long-standing philosophical debate on the question whether causality is a property of the real world, so that in causal models crucial variables can be identified and the functional form of their relationships can be discovered (this position might be called the realist perspective), or whether it is only a humanly created concept, so that the variables and relationships are only constructions embedded in a theoretical framework (this position might be called the social constructivist perspective). Recently, this kind of debate was enriched by an intriguing proposal of Giere (1999) who suggested that one could think about the representation in scientific models in analogy to road maps. A map may, for example, be more or less accurate, more or less detailed, of smaller or larger scale. Maps (as well as causal models) require a large background of human convention for their production and use (Giere 1999: 24). Insuring that a map correctly represents the intended space requires much deliberate care. Mistakes can easily be made. Moreover, one can deliberately construct mistaken maps, or even maps of completely fictional places. Mapmaking and mapusing takes advantage of similarities in spatial structures. But one cannot understand map-making solely in terms of abstract, geometrical relationships. Interpretative relationships are also necessary. One must be able to understand that a particular area on a map is intended to represent something specific. These two features of representation using maps, similarity of structure and of interpretation, carry over to an understanding of how social researchers use causal models to represent aspects of the social world. That is, thinking about causal models in terms of maps combines what is valuable in both constructivism and realism, but it requires abandoning the universal applicability of either view (Giere 1999). One can agree that scientific representations are socially constructed, but then one must also agree that some socially constructed representations can

---

[21]We speak of a "new" approach just to emphasize the contrast to traditional "causal analysis" based on structural equation models, which are basically time-less models. See the discussion in Bollen (1989); Campbell, Mutran, and Nash Parker (1987); or Faulbaum and Bentler (1994). Structural equation models normally fit a deterministic structure across the observed points in time and do not distinguish between a completed past, the present, and a conditionally open future.

be discovered to provide a good picture of aspects of the world, while others are mere constructions with little genuine connection to the world (Giere 1999).

This epistemological perspective suggests that causal models only provide partial access to social reality (Giere 1999). Some ways of constructing models of the social world do provide resources for capturing some aspects of the social world more or less well. Other ways may provide resources for capturing other aspects more or less well. Both ways, however, may capture some aspects of social reality and thus be candidates for a realistic understanding of the social world. That is, there is no such thing as a perfect causal model, complete in all details. The fit of causal models is always partial and imperfect. However, that does not prevent causal models from providing us with deep und useful insights into the workings of the social world. In this view, the empirical question is not whether causal models about the social world, as ontologically well-defined entities, are empirically true or not, but how well causal models fit the intended aspects of the social world. In other words, there may exist several valid theoretical models and statistical analyses, and one causal model may fit the social world more or less well in something like the way maps fit the world more or less well (Giere 1999; see also Pötter and Blossfeld 2001). In such a framework, it is sufficient that empirical evidence can sometimes help us decide that one type of model fits better than another type in some important respect. This means sometimes a fortunate combination of data and research design will make us justifiably confident that a particular model is wellfitting, that is, that this model is judged to exhibit a structure similar to the social world itself. However, often the situation in nonexperimental social science research is less ideal (Popper Shaffer 1922), and a scientific consensus may then rest more on shared values than on empirical data. We will come back to these ambiguities of empirical social research in the final chapter.

Causal Mechanisms and Substantive Theory

The identification of causal mechanisms has been one of the classic concerns in sociology (Weber 1972). Causal statements are made to explain the occurrence of events, to understand why particular events happen, and to make predictions when the situation changes (Marini and Singer 1988). Although sociologists sometimes seem to be opposed to using the word *cause*, they are far less reluctant to apply very similar words such as *force*, *agency*, or *control* when trying to understand social phenomena.

As discussed earlier, there seems to be a consensus that causal inferences cannot simply and directly be made from empirical data, regardless of whether they are collected through ingenious research designs or summarized by particularly advanced statistical models. Thus using event history observation plans and event history models per se will not allow us to prove causality, as is the case for all other statistical techniques. However, as already shown in section 1.1, event-oriented observation designs offer richer information and, as we try to demonstrate in this book, event history models provide more appropriate techniques for exploring causal relations.

If we treat causality as being a property of theoretical statements rather than the empirical world itself (Goldthorpe 1996, 2000), then causal statements are based primarily on substantive hypotheses that the researcher develops about the social world. In this sense, causal inference is theoretically driven (Freedman 1991), and it will always reflect the changing state of sociological knowledge in a field.[22] Of course, descriptive statements are also dependent on theoretical views guiding the selection processes and providing the categories underlying every description. The crucial point in regard to causal statements is, however, that they need a *theoretical argument* specifying the *particular mechanism of how a cause produces an effect* or, more generally, *in which way interdependent forces affect each other in a given setting over time*.

Therefore, the important task of event history modeling is not to demonstrate causal processes directly, but to establish relevant empirical evidence that can serve as a link in a chain of reasoning about causal mechanisms (Goldthorpe 1996, 2000). In this respect, event history models might be particularly helpful instruments because they allow a time-related empirical representation of the structure of causal arguments.

Attributes, Causes, and Time-Constant Variables

Holland (1986) tried to establish some links between causal inference and statistical modeling. In particular, he emphasized that for a conception of causality it is essential that each unit of a population must be exposable to any of the various levels of a cause, at least hypothetically. He argued, for example, that the schooling a student receives can be a cause of the student's performance on a test, whereas the student's race or sex cannot. In the former case it seems possible to contemplate measuring the causal effect, whereas in the latter cases, where we have the enduring attributes of a student, all that can be discussed is association (Yamaguchi 1991).

---

[22]Causal relations are always identified against the background of some field, and what is to be taken as background and field will always be relative to the conceptual framework under consideration (Marini and Singer 1988). Thus, observed relations between stochastic processes generally depend on the number of processes that are considered. If further processes are taken into account, the causal relationships between them may change. Because the theoretical background in the social sciences will rarely be specific enough to determine exactly what processes have to be considered, there may exist several valid causal analyses based on different sets of stochastic processes (see Pötter and Blossfeld 2001).

We agree with Holland that causal mechanisms imply a counterfactual reasoning: *if* the cause *had been* different, there *would have been* another outcome, at least with a certain probability. In this sense, counterfactual statements reflect imagined situations. It is not always clear, however, which characteristics of a situation can sensibly be assumed to be variable (i.e. can be used in counterfactual reasoning) and which characteristics should be regarded as fixed. At least to some degree, the distinction depends on the field of investigation. For example, from a sociological point of view, what is important with regard to sex is not the biological attributes per se, but the social meaning attached to these attributes. The social meaning of gender can change regardless of whether their biological basis changes or not. For example, societal rules might change to create more equality between the races or sexes. We therefore think that, in sociological applications, counterfactuals can also be meaningfully applied to such attributes. They can be represented as *time-constant* "variables" in statistical models to investigate their possible impact on some outcome to be explained. It is, however, important to be quite explicit about the sociological meaning of causal statements that involve references to biological or ethnic attributes. There is, for example, no eternal law connecting gender and/or race with wage differentials. But probably there are *social* mechanisms that connect gender and ethnic differences with different opportunities in the labor market.

Causes and Time-Dependent Variables

The meaning of the counterfactual reasoning of causal statements is that causes are states that could be different from what they actually are. However, the consequences of conditions that could be different from their actual state are obviously not observable.[23] To find an empirical approach to causal statements, the researcher must look at conditions that actually do change in time. These changes are events. More formally, an event is a change in a variable, and this change must happen at a specific point in time. This implies that the most obvious empirical representation of causes is in terms of variables that can change their states over time. In chapter 6, we see that this statement is linked very naturally with the concept of *time-dependent covariates*. The role of a time-dependent covariate in event history models is to indicate that a (qualitative or metric) causal factor has changed its state at a specific time and that the unit under study is exposed to another causal condition. For example, in the case of gender the causal events might be the steps in the acquisition of gender roles over the life course or the exposure to sex-specific opportunities in the labor market at a spe-

---

[23]Holland (1986) called this "the fundamental problem of causal inference." This means that it is simply impossible to observe the effect that *would have* happened on the same unit of analysis, *if* it were exposed to another condition at the same time.

cific historical time. Thus, a time-constant variable "gender" should ideally be replaced in an empirical analysis by time-changing events assumed to produce sex-specific differences in the life history of men and women. Of course, in empirical research that is not always possible, so one often has to rely on time-constant "variables" as well. However, it is important to recognize that for these variables the implied *longitudinal causal relation* is not examined. For example, if we observe an association among people with different levels of educational attainment and their job opportunities, then we can normally draw the conclusion that changes in job opportunities are a result of changes in educational attainment level. The implied idea is the following: If we started having people with the lowest educational attainment level and followed them over the life course, they would presumably differ in their rates to attaining higher levels of educational attainment and this would produce changes in job opportunities. Whether this would be the case for *each* individual is not very clear from a study that is based on people with *different* levels of educational attainment. In particular, one would expect that the causal relationship between education and job opportunities would radically be altered if all people acquired a higher (or the highest) level of educational attainment.[24] Thus, the two statements—the first about associations across different members of a population and the second about dependencies in the life course for each individual member of the population—are quite different; one type of statement can be empirically true while the other one can be empirically false. Therefore statements of the first type cannot be regarded as substitutes for statements of the second type. However, because all causal propositions have consequences for longitudinal change (see Lieberson 1985), only time-changing variables provide the most convincing empirical evidence of causal relations.[25]

---

[24]However, a longitudinal approach would provide the opportunity to study these kinds of changes in the causal relationships over time.

[25]There is also another aspect that is important here (see Lieberson 1985): Causal relations can be symmetric or asymmetric. In examining the causal influence of a change in a variable X on a change in a dependent variable Y, one has to consider whether shifts to a given value of X from either direction have the same consequences for Y. For example, rarely do researchers consider whether an upward shift on the prestige scale, say from 20 to 40, will lead to a different outcome of Y (say family decisions) than would a downward shift of X from 60 to 40. In other words, most researchers assume symmetry. However, even if a change is reversible, the causal *process* may not be. The question is, if a change in a variable X causes a change in another one, Y, what happens to Y if X returns to its earlier level? "Assuming everything else is constant, a process is *reversible*, if the level of Y also returns to its initial condition; a process is irreversible if Y does not return to its earlier level. Observe that it is the *process*—not the *event*—that is being described as reversible or irreversible" (Lieberson 1985: 66).

Time Order and Causal Effects

We can summarize our view of causal statements in the following way:

$$\Delta X_t \longrightarrow \Delta Y_{t'}$$

meaning that a *change* in variable X_t at time t is a cause of a *change* in variable $Y_{t'}$ at a later point in time, t'. It is not implied, of course, that X_t is the only cause that might affect $Y_{t'}$. So we sometimes speak of *causal conditions* to stress that there might be, and normally is, a quite complex set of causes.[26]

Thus, if causal statements are studied empirically, they must intrinsically be related to time. There are three important aspects. First, to speak of a change in variables necessarily implies *reference to a time axis*. We need at least two points in time to observe that a variable has changed its value. Of course, at least approximately, we can say that a variable has changed its value *at a specific point in time*.[27] Therefore we use the symbols ΔX_t and ΔY_t to refer to changes in the values of the time-dependent variable X_t and the state variable Y_t at time t. This leads to the important point that causal statements relate *changes* in two (or more) variables.

Second, there is a *time ordering between causes and effects*. The cause must *precede* the effect in time: $t < t'$, in the formal representation given earlier. This seems to be generally accepted.[28] As an implication, there must be a *temporal interval* between the change in a variable representing a cause and a change in the variable representing a corresponding effect. This time interval may be *very short* or *very long*, but can never be *zero* or *infinity* (Kelly and McGrath 1988). Thus *the cause and its effect logically cannot occur at the same point in time*. Any appropriate empirical representation of causal effects in a statistical model must therefore take into account that there may be various *delays* or *lags* between the events assumed to be causes and the unfolding of their effects (see *a* and *b* in Figure 1.1.2).

This immediately leads to a third point. There may be a variety of different *temporal shapes (functional forms) in which the causal effect Y_t unfolds*

---

[26]It is important to note here that the effect of a variable X is always measured relative to other causes. A conjunctive plurality of causes occurs if various factors must be jointly present to produce an effect. Disjunctive plurality of causes, alternatively, occurs if the effect is produced by each of several factors alone, and the joint occurrence of two or more factors does not alter the effect (see the extensive discussion in Marini and Singer 1988; and the discussion in regard to stochastic processes in Pötter and Blossfeld 2001).

[27]Statements like this implicitly refer to some specification of "point in time." The meaning normally depends on the kind of events that are to be described, for instance, a marriage, the birth of a child, or becoming unemployed. In this book, we always assume a continuous time axis for purposes of mathematical modeling. This should, however, be understood as an idealized way of representing social time. We are using mathematical concepts to speak about social reality, so we disregard the dispute about whether time is "continuous" (in the mathematical sense of this word) or not.

[28]See, for instance, the discussion in Eells (1991, ch. 5).

over time. Some of these possibilities have been depicted in Figure 1.1.2.
Thus an appropriate understanding of causal relations between variables
should take into account that the *causal relationship itself may change over
time*. This seems particularly important in sociological applications of causal
reasoning. In these applications we generally cannot rely on the assumption
of eternal, timeless laws, but have to recognize that the causal mechanisms
may change during the development of social processes.

Actors and Probabilistic Causal Relations

It seems agreed that social phenomena are always directly or indirectly
based on actions of individuals. This clearly separates the social from the
natural sciences. Sociology therefore does not deal with associations among
variables per se, but with variables that are associated via acting people. There are at least three consequences for causal relations. First, in
methodological terms, this means that if individuals relate causes and effects through their actions, then research on social processes should at best
be based *on individual longitudinal data* (Coleman and Hao 1989; Coleman
1990; Blossfeld and Prein 1998; Goldthorpe 2000). This is why life history
data on individuals, and not aggregated longitudinal data, provide the most
appropriate information for the analyses of social processes. Only with these
data can one trace the courses of action at the level of each individual over
time. Second, in theoretical terms, it means that the explaining or understanding of social processes requires a time-related specification of (1) the
past and present conditions under which people act,[29] (2) the many and possibly conflicting goals that they pursue at the present time, (3) the beliefs
and expectations guiding the behavior, and (4) the actions that probably
will follow in the future.[30] Third, if it is people who are doing the acting,
then causal inference must also take into account the free will of individuals
(Blossfeld and Prein 1998). This introduces an essential element of inde-
terminacy into causal inferences. This means that in sociology we can only
reasonably account for and model the *generality* but not the determinacy of

---

[29]These conditions are, of course, heavily molded by social structural regularities in the
past and the present. Sociology must always be a historical discipline (Goldthorpe 1991,
2000).

[30]Sometimes it is argued that, because human actors act intentionally and behavior is
goaloriented, the intentions or motives of actors to bring about some effect in the future
causes the actor to behave in a specific way in the present (e.g., Marini and Singer 1988).
This does not, however, contradict a causal view. One simply has to distinguish intentions, motives, or plans as they occur in the present from their impact on the behavior
that follows their formation temporally, and from the final result, as an outcome of the
behavior. An expectation about a future state of affairs should clearly be distinguished
from what eventually happens in the future. Therefore the fact that social agents can
behave intentionally, based on expectations, does not reverse the time order underlying
our causal statements.

behavior. The aim of substantive and statistical models must therefore be to capture common elements in the behavior of people, or patterns of action that recur in many cases (Goldthorpe 1996, 2000). This means that in sociological applications randomness has to enter as a defining characteristic of causal models. We can only hope to make sensible causal statements about how a given (or hypothesized) change in variable X_t in the past affects the *probability of a change* in variable $Y_{t'}$ in the future. Correspondingly, the basic causal relation becomes

$$\Delta X_t \longrightarrow \Delta \Pr(\Delta Y_{t'}) \quad t < t' \tag{1.1}$$

This means that a change in the time-dependent covariate X_t will *change the probability* that the dependent variable $Y_{t'}$ will change in the future $(t' > t)$. In sociology, this interpretation seems more appropriate than the traditional deterministic approach. The essential difference is not that our knowledge about causes is insufficient because it only allows probabilistic statements, but instead that *the causal effect to be explained is a probability*. Thus probability in this context is not just a technical term anymore, but is considered as a theoretical one: it is the propensity of social agents to change their behavior.

Causal Statements and Limited Empirical Observations

A quite different type of randomness related to making inferences occurs if causal statements are applied to real-world situations in the social sciences. There are at least four additional reasons to expect further randomness in empirical studies. These are basically the same ones that occur in deterministic approaches and are well known from traditional regression modeling (Lieberson 1991). The first one is *measurement error*, a serious problem in empirical social research, which means that the observed data deviate somewhat from the predicted pattern without invalidating the causal proposition. The second reason is particularly important in the case of nonexperimental data. It is often the case that *complex multivariate causal relations* operate in the social world. Thus a given outcome can occur because of the presence of more than one influencing factor. Moreover, it may also not occur at times because the impact of one independent variable is outweighed by other influences working in the opposite direction. In these situations, the observed influence of the cause is only approximate unless one can control for the other important factors. The third motive is that sociologists often do *not know* or are *not able to measure* all of the important factors. Thus social scientists have to relinquish the idea of a complete measurement of causal effects, even if they would like to make a deterministic proposition. Finally, sometimes *chance* affects observed outcomes in the social world. It is not important here to decide whether chance exists per se or whether it is

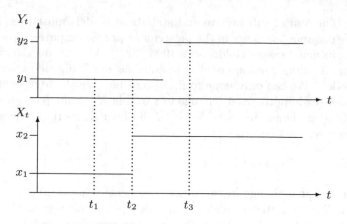

Figure 1.2.1 Observation of a simple causal effect.

only a surrogate for the poor state of our knowledge of additional influences and/or inadequate measurement.

In summary, these problems imply that social scientists can only hope to make empirical statements with a probabilistic character. This situation can lead to problems, as is discussed in chapter 10. Without strong assumptions about missing information and errors in the available data, it is generally not possible to find definite statements about causal relations (see, e.g., Arminger 1990).

A Simplistic Conception of Causal Relations

At this point it is important to stress that the concept of causal relation is a rather special abstraction implying a time-related structure that does not immediately follow from our sensory impressions. Consider the following example in Figure 1.2.1 where we characterize the necessary time-related observations of a unit being affected by a causal effect. This figure shows that an empirical representation of the most simple causal effect (i.e., (1) where the condition X_t changes—from one state $X_{t_1} = x_1$ to another one $X_{t_2} = x_2$—and (2) is then constant afterward, (3) the change in Y_t—from $Y_{t_2} = y_1$ to $Y_{t_3} = y_2$—takes place almost instantaneously and (4) is then also time-constant afterward) needs at least three points in time where the researcher must note the states of the independent and dependent variables, respectively.[31] This is because, if we assume that a change in the independent variable X_t has taken place at t_2, then to be able to fix the particular change in the condition in the past, we need to know the state of the independent variable X_t at an earlier time, t_1 (see Figure 1.2.1). For the

---

[31] This example is instructive because Lazarsfeld (1948, 1972) and many others after him have argued that for causal inferences two observations of the units would be sufficient.

dependent variable Y_t we need an observation before the effect has started to occur. Assuming everything else is constant, this observation can be made, at the latest point t_2, because the effect has to *follow* the cause in time. To evaluate whether the hypothesized effect has indeed taken place at a later time, t_3, we must again note the state of the dependent variable Y_t. Thus, a *simplistic representation of a causal effect* exists when we compare the change in the observations for the independent variable in the past and the present with the change in the observations for the dependent variable in the present and in the future and link both changes with a substantive argument.[32]

However, as already demonstrated in section 1.1, this is only a simple and fairly unrealistic example of a causal effect. In the case of observational data in the social sciences, where there are many (qualitative and metric) causal variables that might change their values at any point in time, when their causal effects might have various delays and different shapes in time (see Figure 1.1.2), then the quantity of the observed causal effect as shown in Figure 1.2.1 will strongly depend on when the measurements at the three points in time are taken.

Thus, what can we say about the causal effect(s) at any given point in time if the situation is more complex? A paradox occurs: The concept of causal effect depends intrinsically on comparisons between changes in both the independent and dependent variables in at least three points in time. Yet the concept of causal effect should itself reflect a state of a unit of observation at any point in time as being an appropriate one in real empirical situations. Thus, what is still needed in our discussion is a concept that represents the quantity of the causal effect at any point in time.

Causal Effects and Changes in Transition Rates

If the dependent variable is discrete and can change its state at any time, then the transition rate framework offers a time-point-related representation for the causal effect. We briefly want to develop this idea.

Let us first start with the dependent variable, Y_t, and its changes in the future (as a consequence of a change in a causal factor). In particular, we are interested in changes of states occupied by the units of analysis. The state space is assumed to be discrete, and so the possible changes are discrete. We assume that a unit enters at time t_0 into the (origin) state j, that is, $Y_{t_0} = j$. The basic form of change to be explained in the transition rate framework is the probability of a change in Y_t from an origin state j to a destination state k (while $t > t_0$).

Now we need a concept that allows describing the development of the

---

[32]Indeed, such a simplistic idea of the causal effect is the basis of all panel designs, as shown in section 1.1.

process at every point in time, while the process is evolving, and that, for its definition, only relies on information about the past development of the process. The crucial concept that can be used for this purpose is the *transition rate*. To define this concept, let us first introduce a random variable T to represent the duration, beginning at t_0, until a change in the dependent variable, that is, a transition from (origin) state j to (destination) state k, occurs. To simplify the notation we will assume that $t_0 = 0$. Then, the following probability can be defined:

$$\Pr(t \leq T < t' \mid T \geq t) \quad t < t' \tag{1.2}$$

This is the probability that an event occurs in the time interval from t to t', given that no event (transition) has occurred before, that is, in the interval from 0 to t. This probability is well defined and obviously well suited to describe the temporal evolution of the process. The definition refers to each point in time while the process is evolving and thereby can express the idea of change during its development. Also, the definition only relies on information about the past of the process, what has happened up to the present point in time, t. Therefore the concept defined in (1.2) can sensibly be used to describe the process before it has finished for all individuals in the population. Assume that we know the probabilities defined in (1.2) for all points in time up to a certain point t^*. Then we have a description of the process up to this point, and this description is possible without knowing how the process will develop in the future (i.e., for $t > t^*$).

Because our mathematical model is based on a continuous-time axis, one can in the expression (1.2) let $t' - t$ approach zero. However, as the length of the time interval approaches zero, the concept of change in the dependent variable would simply disappear because the probability that a change takes place in an interval of zero length is zero:

$$\lim_{t' \to t} \Pr(t \leq T < t' \mid T \geq t) = 0$$

To avoid this, we regard the *ratio* of the transition probability to the length of the time interval to represent the probability of future changes in the dependent variable per unit of time (Coleman 1968); that is, we consider

$$\Pr(t \leq T < t' \mid T \geq t) \, / \, (t' - t)$$

This allows us to define the limit

$$r(t) = \lim_{t' \to t} \frac{\Pr(t \leq T < t' \mid T \geq t)}{t' - t} \tag{1.3}$$

and we arrive at the central concept of the *transition rate*. Because of the various origins of transition rate framework in the different disciplines, the transition rate is also called the *hazard rate, intensity rate, failure rate, transition intensity, risk function*, or *mortality rate*.

The transition rate concept obviously provides the possibility of giving a local, time-related description of how the process (defined by a single episode) evolves over time. We can interpret $r(t)$ as the *propensity* to change the state, from origin j to destination k, at t. But one should note that this propensity is defined in relation to a risk set, the risk set at t (i.e., the set of individuals who can experience the event because they have not already had the event before t).

The transition rate is also an appropriate tool to model the *time arrow* (Conveney and Highfield 1990) of social processes and to distinguish conceptually at each point in time the *presentness* from a *closed past* and an *open future*. The transition rate allows one to connect the events of the closed past with the intensity of *possible future changes* at each point in time. Thus the transition rate is particularly suited for causal analysis because stochastic processes require an approximation of the *underlying distribution* from which future realizations of events are "drawn" (March, Sproull and Tamuz 1991). The appropriate focus of causal analysis based on stochastic processes is the *distribution of possible future events* (or their potentiality), *not their concrete "realizations."*

Having introduced the basic concept of a transition rate, we can finally formulate our basic modeling approach. The preliminary description in (1.1) can now be restated in a somewhat more precise form as

$$r(t) = g(t, x) \tag{1.4}$$

This is the basic form of a transition rate model. The central idea is to make the transition rate, which describes a process evolving in time, dependent on time and on a set of covariates, x. Obviously, we also need the "variable" time (t) on the right-hand side of the model equation. However, it must be stressed that a sensible causal relation can only be assumed for the dependency of the transition rate on the covariates. The causal reasoning underlying the modeling approach (1.4) is

$$\Delta X_t \longrightarrow \Delta r(t') \quad t < t'$$

As a causal effect, the changes in some covariates in the past may lead to changes in the transition rate in the future, which in turn describe the propensity that the units under study will change in some presupposed state space. As discussed earlier, this causal interpretation requires that we take the temporal order in which the process evolves very seriously. At any given point in time, t, the transition rate $r(t)$ can be made dependent on conditions that happened to occur in the past (i.e., before t), but not on what is the case at t or in the future after t.

There are many possibilities to specify the functional relationship $g(.)$ in (1.4). Some of these possibilities are discussed extensively in subsequent chapters. We particularly discuss how the formal dependence of the transition rate on time, t, can be interpreted from a causal point of view in chapters 6 and 7.

It is sometimes argued that sociologists should give up the causal analytical point of view in favor of a systems view because the operation of causal forces is mutually interdependent, and variables change each other more or less simultaneously in many systems (Marini and Singer 1988). However, even in systems of interdependent processes time does not run backward, and change in one of the interdependent variables will take (at least a small amount of) time to produce a change in another one. Thus, in systems of variables there cannot be any simultaneity of causes and their effects. This allows us to demonstrate in chapter 6 that a causal approach to interdependent systems is possible with the help of the transition rate concept. In other words, the systems view is not a substitute for a proper causal approach in our field (Kelly and McGrath 1988).

Additional Statistical Concepts

Because the transition rate is indeed an abstraction, it is necessary to relate it back to quantities that are directly observable, that is, to frequencies of state occupancies at particular points in time. To support such inferences, some additional statistical concepts are useful.

We begin with the basic concept to describe the probability distribution of T, that is, the distribution function

$$F(t) = \Pr(T \leq t)$$

It is the probability that the episode's duration is less than or equal to t, or put otherwise, the probability that an event happens in the time interval from 0 to t. Equivalently, we can describe the probability distribution of T by a *survivor function*, defined by

$$G(t) = 1 - F(t) = \Pr(T > t)$$

This is the probability that the episode's duration is at least t, and that the event by which the current episode comes to an end occurs later than t.

Both concepts, the distribution function and the survivor function, are mathematically equivalent. However, in describing event histories one generally prefers the survivor function because it allows for a more intuitive description. We can imagine a population of individuals (or other units of analysis) all beginning a certain episode with origin state j at the same point in time $t = 0$. Then, as time goes on, events occur (i.e., individuals

leave the given origin state). Exactly this process is described by the survivor function. If N is the size of the population at $t = 0$, then $N \cdot G(t)$
is the number of individuals who have not yet left the origin state up to t.
Sometimes this is called the "risk set" (i.e., the set of individuals who remain exposed to the "risk" of experiencing the event that ends the current
episode).

Finally, because T is a continuous random variable, its distribution can
also be described by a density function, $f(t)$, which is related to the distribution function by

$$F(t) = \int_0^t f(\tau) \, d\tau$$

The meaning of the density function is similar to (1.3). In fact, we can write
its definition in the following way:

$$f(t) = \lim_{t' \to t} \frac{F(t') - F(t)}{t' - t} = \lim_{t' \to t} \frac{\Pr(t \leq T < t')}{t' - t}$$

On the right-hand side, before going to the limit, we have the probability
that the event occurs in the time interval from t to t'. $f(t)$ is approximately
proportional to this probability, if the time interval becomes very short.

Distribution function, survivor function, and density function are quite
familiar concepts to describe the probability distribution of a random variable. However, these functions do not make explicit that our random variable
T has a quite specific meaning: the duration of an episode. Our mathematical concepts are intended to describe a *process evolving in time*. In defining
such a process, we refer to a population of individuals (or other units of
analysis) who are seen as "bearing" the process. These individuals evolve
over time, and their behavior generates the process. With respect to these
individuals, and while the process is evolving, there is always a distinction
in past, present, and future. This is particularly important for a causal view
of the process. The past conditions the present, and what happens in the
present shapes the future. The question is how these temporal aspects of
the process can be made explicit in our concepts to describe the process.
As we have seen, the development of an episode can be represented by a
random variable T, and statistics offers familiar concepts to describe the
distribution of the variable. However, these concepts have hidden the temporal nature of the process. This becomes clear if we ask the question, *when*
does a description of the distribution of T become available? At the earliest,
this is when the current episode has ended for all individuals of the population. Therefore, although a description of the distribution of T provides
a description of the process *as it had evolved*, to make a causal assessment
of how the process evolves we need a quite different description. We need
a concept that allows describing the development of the process at every

point in time, while the process is going on, and that, for its definition, only relies on information about the past development of the process.

Now we can investigate the relationship with the transition rate again. By definition, we have

$$\Pr(t \leq T < t' \mid T \geq t) = \frac{\Pr(t \leq T < t')}{\Pr(T \geq t)}$$

Therefore, definition (1.3) can also be written as

$$r(t) = \lim_{t' \to t} \frac{\Pr(t \leq T < t')}{t' - t} \frac{1}{\Pr(T \geq t)} = \frac{f(t)}{G(t)} \tag{1.5}$$

This shows that the transition rate is a conditional density function, that is, the density function $f(t)$ divided through the survivor function $G(t)$.

The transition rate allows for a local description of the development of a process. To calculate $r(t)$ one needs information about the local probability density for events at t, given by $f(t)$, and about the development of the process up to t, given by $G(t)$. Of course, if we know the transition rate for a time interval, say t to t', we have a description of how the process evolves during this time interval. And if we know the transition rate for all (possible) points in time, we eventually have a description of the whole process, which is mathematically equivalent to having a complete description of the distribution of T.

There is a simple relationship between the transition rate and the survivor function. First, given the survivor function $G(t)$, we can easily derive the transition rate as (minus) its logarithmic derivative:[33]

$$\frac{\mathrm{d}\log(G(t))}{\mathrm{d}t} = \frac{1}{G(t)} \frac{\mathrm{d}G(t)}{\mathrm{d}t} = \frac{1}{G(t)} \frac{\mathrm{d}}{\mathrm{d}t}(1 - F(t)) = -\frac{f(t)}{G(t)} = -r(t)$$

Using this relation, the other direction is provided by integration. We have

$$-\int_0^t r(\tau)\,\mathrm{d}\tau = \log(G(t)) - \log(G(0)) = \log(G(t))$$

since $G(0) = 1$. It follows the basic relation, often used in subsequent chapters, that

$$G(t) = \exp\left(-\int_0^t r(\tau)\,\mathrm{d}\tau\right) \tag{1.6}$$

The expression in brackets,

$$\int_0^t r(\tau)\,\mathrm{d}\tau$$

---

[33]Throughout this book, we use log(.) to denote the natural logarithm.

is often called the *cumulative hazard rate*.

Finally, one should note that $r(t)$ is a transition *rate*, not a transition probability. As shown in (1.5), $r(t)$ is similar to a density function. To derive proper probability statements, one has to integrate over some time interval, as follows:

$$\Pr(t \leq T < t' \mid T \geq t) \;=\; \frac{G(t) - G(t')}{G(t)} = 1 - \frac{G(t')}{G(t)}$$

$$= \; 1 - \exp\left(-\int_{t}^{t'} r(\tau)\, d\,\tau\right)$$

One easily verifies, however, that $1 - \exp(-x) \approx x$ for small values of x. Therefore, the probability that an event happens in a *small* time interval (t, t') is approximately equal to $r(t)$:

$$\Pr(t \leq T < t' \mid T \geq t) \approx (t' - t)\, r(t)$$

It follows that there is a close relationship between concepts based on a discrete and a continuous time axis. It is most obvious when one considers unit time intervals.

Chapter 2

Event History Data Structures

This chapter discusses event history data structures. We first introduce the basic terminology used for event history data and then give an example of an event history data file. Finally, we show how to use it with Stata.

2.1 Basic Terminology

Event history analysis studies *transitions* across a set of discrete states, including the length of *time intervals* between entry to and exit from specific states. The basic analytical framework is a state space and a time axis. The choice of the *time axis* or *clock* (e.g., age, experience, marriage duration, etc.) used in the analysis must be based on theoretical considerations and affects the statistical model. In this book, we discuss only methods and models using a *continuous* time axis. An *episode, spell, waiting time,* or *duration*—terms that are used interchangeably—is the time span a unit of analysis (e.g., an individual) spends in a specific state. The *states* are *discrete* and usually small in number. The definition of a set of possible states, called the *state space* $\mathcal{Y}$, is also dependent on substantive considerations. Thus a careful, theoretically driven choice of the time axis and design of state space are important because they are often serious sources of misspecification. In particular, misspecification of the model may occur because some of the important states are not observed. For example, in a study analyzing the determinants of women's labor market participation in West Germany, Blossfeld and Rohwer (1997a) have shown that one arrives at much more appropriate substantive conclusions if one differentiates the state "employed" into "full-time work" and "part-time work." One should also note here that a small change in the focus of the substantive issue in question, leading to a new definition of the state space, often requires a fundamental reorganization of the event history data file.

The most restricted event history model is based on a process with only a *single episode* and *two states* (one *origin* and one *destination* state). An example may be the duration of *first* marriage until the end of the marriage, for whatever reason. In this case each individual who entered into first marriage (origin state) started an episode, which could be terminated by a transition to the destination state "not married anymore." In the *single episode* case, each unit of analysis that entered into the origin state is represented by one episode. If more than one destination state exists, we

refer to these models as *multistate models*. Models for the special case, with
a single origin state but two or more destination states, are also called *models with competing events* or *risks*. For example, a housewife might become
"unemployed" (meaning entering into the state "looking for work") or start
being "full-time" or "part-time employed." If more than one event is possible
(i.e., if there are repeated events or transitions over the observation
period), we use the term *multiepisode models*. For example, an employment
career normally consists of a series of job exits. Figure 1.1.1c (p. 5) describes
a *multistate-multiepisode* process. The individual moves repeatedly between
several different states. As shown in Blossfeld, Hamerle, and Mayer (1989),
most of the basic concepts for the one-episode and one-event case can simply
be extended and applied to more complex situations with *repeated episodes*
and/or *competing events*. In this book, we mainly stick to the more complex
notation for the multistate-multiepisode case. Thus if one has a sample of
$i = 1, \ldots, N$ multistate-multiepisode data, a complete description of the
data[1] is given by

$$(u_i, m_i, o_i, d_i, s_i, t_i, x_i) \qquad i = 1, \ldots, N$$

where u_i is the identification number of the individual or any other unit of
analysis the ith episode belongs to; m_i is the serial number of the episode;
o_i is the origin state, the state held during the episode until the ending time;
d_i is the destination state defined as the state reached at the ending time of
the episode; and s_i and t_i are the starting and ending times, respectively.
In addition, there is a covariate vector x_i associated with the episode. We
always assume that the starting and ending times are coded such that the
difference $t_i - s_i$ is the duration of the episode and is positive and greater
than zero. There is also an ordering of the episodes for each individual, given
by the set of serial numbers of the episodes. Although it is not necessary
that these serial numbers be contiguous, it is required that the starting time
of an episode be not less than the ending time of a previous episode.

   Observations of event histories are very often *censored*. Censoring occurs
when the information about the duration in the origin state is incompletely
recorded. Figure 2.1.1 gives examples of different types of censoring created
by an observation window (see also Yamaguchi 1991; Guo 1993). The hori-
zontal axis indicates historical time, and the observation period is usually of
finite length, with the beginning and end denoted by τ_a and τ_b, respectively.

1. *Episode A* is fully censored on the left, which means that the starting
   and ending times of this spell are located before the beginning of the
   observation window. Left censoring is normally a difficult problem, because it is not possible to take the effects of the unknown episodes in

---

[1] A complete history of state occupancies and times of changes is often called a "sample
path" (see Tuma and Hannan 1984).

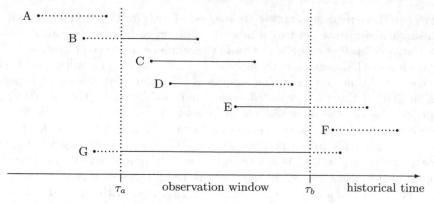

Figure 2.1.1 Types of censoring in an observation window.

the past into account. It is only easy to cope with if the assumption of a Markov process is justified (i.e., if the transition rates do not depend on the duration in the origin state).

2. *Episode B* is partially censored on the left, so that the length of time a subject has already spent in the origin state is unkown. In this case, we have the same problems as for A-type episodes. However, sometimes (e.g., in a first panel wave) we have additional retrospective information about the time of entry into the origin state of Episode B. In this case, usually called a *left truncated* observation (see Guo 1993), we can reconstruct the full duration of Episode B, but do not have information about episodes of type A. This creates a sample selection bias for the period before the observation window. The earlier the starting time of the episode and the shorter the durations, the less likely it is that these episodes will appear in the observation window. One solution to this problem is that one starts to analyze the process at the beginning of the observation window and evaluates only the part of the duration that reaches into the observation window, beginning with time τ_a and ending with t_i. This means that the analysis is conditional on the fact that the individual has survived up to τ_a (see Guo 1993).

3. *Episode C* is complete. There is no censoring on the left or right.

4. *Episode D* is a special case. This episode is censored on the right within the observation window. If the censoring is a result of a random process, then event history analysis methods can take these episodes into account without any problems, as is shown later (Kalbfleisch and Prentice 1980: type II censoring). Technically speaking, it can be treated in the same way as Episode E. However, this type of censoring might occur because of attrition or missing data in a panel study. Such dropouts or missing data are normally not random, and the characteristics of the lost individuals

are very often related to the process under study. Such selectivity bias creates problems and cannot easily be corrected in an event history analysis (see chapter 10).

5. *Episode E* is right censored because the observation is terminated at the right-hand side of the observation window. This type of censoring typically occurs in life course studies at the time of the retrospective interview, or in panel studies at the time of the last panel wave. Because the end of the observation window, τ_b, is normally determined independently from the substantive process under study, this type of right censoring is unproblematic. It can be handled with event history methods (Kalbfleisch and Prentice 1980: type I censoring).

6. *Episode F* is completely censored on the right. Entry into and exit from the duration occurs after the observation period. This type of censoring normally happens in retrospective life history studies in which individuals of various birth cohorts are observed over different spans of life. To avoid sample selection bias, such models have to take into account variables controlling for the selection, for example, by including birth cohort dummy variables and/or age as a time-dependent covariate.

7. *Episode G* represents a duration that is left and right censored.[2] Such observations happen, for example, in panel studies in which job mobility is recorded. In such cases one knows that a person is in a specific job at the first sweep and in the same job up to the second one, but one has no information about the actual beginning and ending times.

In the examples in this book, which are based on the German Life History Study (GLHS), we do not have left censored data because all the life histories of the birth cohorts 1929–31, 1939–41, and 1949–51 were collected retrospectively from the time of birth up to the date of the interview (1981–1983, see Mayer and Brückner 1989; Mayer 1987, 1988, 1991). Thus we do not have data of the type A, B, and G. Type D censoring can only occur due to missing data, not due to attrition, because the GLHS is a retrospective study. Because we are studying different birth cohorts in our analyses (data of types E and F), we have to control for the fact that members of these birth cohorts could only be observed over various age spans (1929–31: up to the age of 50; 1939–41: up to the age of 40; and 1949–51: up to the age of 30).

---

[2] A special case of such data type are "current-status" data. These data comprise information on whether an event has or has not been reached at the time of a survey, and information on age at the time of the survey. If the event has occurred, one has incomplete information on when it occurred. Conversely, we do not know when it will happen (if ever) for those respondents who have not experienced the event at the time of the survey (see Diamond and McDonald 1992).

2.2   Event History Data Organization

Event history data are more complex than cross-sectional ones because, for each episode, information about an *origin state* and a *destination state*, as well as the *starting* and *ending times*, are given. In most studies, there are also *repeated episodes* from *various parallel processes* (e.g., job, marital, or residential histories, etc.) at *different levels* (e.g., job history of an individual, histories of the firm where the individual worked at the mesolevel, and/or structural changes in the labor market at the macrolevel) for each unit of analysis. Therefore, large event history data sets have often been stored in data bank systems. In this book, we do not discuss the advantages and disadvantages of different data bank systems for event histories in terms of efficiency, convenience, data handling, and retrieval. We do, however, stress that event history data have to be organized as a *rectangular data file* in order to analyze the data with standard programs such as SPSS, SAS, or GLIM (e.g., see Blossfeld, Hamerle, and Mayer 1989), or the program that is used throughout this book, Stata.

In an event-oriented data set *each record of the file is related to a duration in a state or episode* (see Carroll 1983). As shown previously, type and number of states for each unit of analysis are dependent on the substantive question under consideration. Changes in the state space usually lead to a new definition of episodes and very often entail a fundamental reorganization of the data file. If, for each unit of analysis, only one episode is considered (e.g., entry into first marriage), then the number of records in the data file corresponds to the number of units. In an analysis concerned with repeated events (e.g., consecutive jobs in an individual's career), whose number may vary among individuals, the sum of these person-specific episodes represents the number of records in the data set.

In the examples throughout this book, we use event history data from the GLHS. The GLHS provides detailed retrospective information about the life histories of men and women from the birth cohorts 1929–31, 1939–41, and 1949–51, collected in the years 1981–1983 (Mayer and Brückner 1989). For our didactical task in this book, we only use an event history data file of 600 job episodes from 201 respondents (arbitrarily selected and anonymized). Each record in this file represents an employment episode, and the consecutive jobs of a respondent's career are stored successively in the file. For some individuals there is only a single job episode, whereas for others there is a sequence of two or more jobs.

The data file, `rrdat1.dta`, is a Stata system file, which contains 12 variables that are described briefly in Box 2.2.1.

id   identifies the individuals in the data set. Because the data file contains information about 201 individuals, there are 201 different ID numbers. The numbers are arbitrarily chosen and are not contiguous.

Box 2.2.1 Variables in data file `rrdat1.dta`

```
Contains data from rrdat1.dta
  obs:           600
  vars:           12
  size:        13,800 (98.7% of memory free)
-----------------------------------------------------------------
              storage  display
variable name   type    format    variable label
-----------------------------------------------------------------
id              int     %8.0g     ID of individual
noj             byte    %8.0g     Serial number of the job
tstart          int     %8.0g     Starting time of the job
tfin            int     %8.0g     Ending time of the job
sex             byte    %8.0g     Sex (1 men, 2 women)
ti              int     %8.0g     Date of interview
tb              int     %8.0g     Date of birth
te              int     %8.0g     Date of entry into the labor market
tmar            int     %8.0g     Date of marriage (0 if no marriage)
pres            byte    %8.0g     Prestige score of job i
presn           byte    %8.0g     Prestige score of job i+1
edu             byte    %8.0g     Highest educational attainment
-----------------------------------------------------------------
Sorted by:  id  noj
```

Box 2.2.2 First records of data file `rrdat1.dta`

	id	noj	tstart	tfin	sex	ti	tb	te	tmar	pres	presn	edu
1.	1	1	555	982	1	982	351	555	679	34	-1	17
2.	2	1	593	638	2	982	357	593	762	22	46	10
3.	2	2	639	672	2	982	357	593	762	46	46	10
4.	2	3	673	892	2	982	357	593	762	46	-1	10
5.	3	1	688	699	2	982	473	688	870	41	41	11
6.	3	2	700	729	2	982	473	688	870	41	44	11
7.	3	3	730	741	2	982	473	688	870	44	44	11
8.	3	4	742	816	2	982	473	688	870	44	44	11
9.	3	5	817	828	2	982	473	688	870	44	-1	11

noj   gives the serial number of the job episode, always beginning with job number 1. For instance, if an individual in our data set has had three jobs, the data file contains three records for this individual entitled job numbers 1, 2, and 3. Note that only job episodes are included in this data file. If an individual has experienced an interruption between two consecutive jobs, the difference between the ending time of a job and the starting time of the next job may be greater than 1 (see Figure 2.2.1b).

tstart   is the starting time of the job episode, in century months. (A century month is the number of months from the beginning of the century; 1 =

January 1900.) The date given in this variable records the first month in a new job.

tfin   is the ending time of the job episode, in century months. The date given in this variable records the last month in the job.

sex   records the sex of the individual, coded 1 for men and 2 for women.

ti   is the date of the interview, in century months. Using this information, one can decide in the GLHS data set whether an episode is right censored or not. If the ending time of an episode (tfin) is less than the interview date, the episode ended with an event (see Figure 2.2.1c), otherwise the episode is right censored (see Figures 2.2.1a and 2.2.1b).

tb   records the birth date of the individual, in century months. Therefore, tstart minus tb is the age, in months, at the beginning of a job episode.

te   records the date of first entry into the labor market, in century months.

tmar   records whether/when an individual has married. If the value of this variable is positive, it gives the date of marriage (in century months). For still unmarried individuals at the time of the interview, the value is 0.

pres   records the prestige score of the current job episode.

presn   records the prestige score of the consecutive job episode, if there is a next job, otherwise a missing value (-1) is coded.

edu   records the highest educational attainment before entry into the labor market. In assigning school years to school degrees, the following values have been assumed (Blossfeld 1985, 1992): Lower secondary school qualification (*Hauptschule*) without vocational training is equivalent to 9 years, middle school qualification (*Mittlere Reife*) is equivalent to 10 years, lower secondary school qualification with vocational training is equivalent to 11 years, middle school qualification with vocational training is equivalent to 12 years. *Abitur* is equivalent to 13 years, a professional college qualification is equivalent to 17 years, and a university degree is equivalent to 19 years.

Box 2.2.2 shows the first nine records of data file rrdat1.dta. Note that all dates are coded in *century months*. Thus 1 means January 1900, 2 means February 1900, 13 means January 1901, and so on. In general:

$$\text{YEAR} \;=\; (\text{DATE} - 1) \;/\; 12 + 1900$$
$$\text{MONTH} \;=\; (\text{DATE} - 1) \;\% \; 12 + 1$$

where DATE is given in century months, and MONTH and YEAR refer to calendar time. "/" means *integer division* and "%" is the *modulus operator*.[3] For instance, the first individual (ID = 1) has a single job episode. His starting

---

[3]In Stata you specify mod(x,y) to ask for the modulus of x with respect to y. Given two integer numbers, x and y, mod(x,y) is the remainder after dividing x by y. For instance: display mod(13,12) = 1.

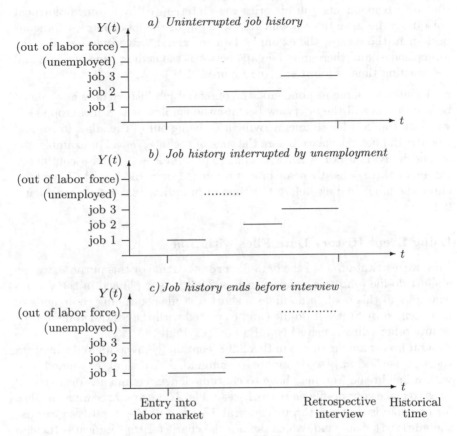

Figure 2.2.1 Examples of job histories included in the GLHS data set.

time is given in terms of century month 555, corresponding to March 1946, and the ending time is 982 ≡ October 1981. Because this is equal to the interview month, the episode is right censored.

The panels in Figure 2.2.1 demonstrate the three basic types of job careers included in the example data file:

a) For some respondents, the file `rrdat1.dta` contains an uninterrupted job history from the time of entry into the labor market until the time of the retrospective interview. If there is more than one job for respondents, the ending time of job n (`tfin`) and the starting time of job $n+1$ (`tstart`) are contiguous. For example, the first individual in the data set (`id = 1`, see Box 2.2.2), who is a man (`sex = 1`), has had only one job from first entry into the labor market (`tstart = 555`) up to the time of the interview (`tfin = 982` equals `ti = 982`). So this episode is right censored.

b) Some respondents' job histories were interrupted by an unemployment episode, or because the respondents were out of the labor market for some period. In these cases the example data set `rrdat1.dta` only contains the job episodes, and there may be gaps between the ending time of job n and the starting time of job $n + 1$ (see Figure 2.2.1b).

c) Finally, for some respondents, the observed job history may have ended before the time of the interview because the employment career stopped or was interrupted (due to unemployment or being out of the labor force) and re-entry did not take place before the time of the interview. For example, the second individual (`id = 2`), who is a woman (`sex = 2`), had a continuous career of three jobs, then an interruption (`tfin = 892`), and did not re-enter the labor market before the time of interview (`ti = 982`; see Figure 2.2.1c).

Using Event History Data Files with Stata

Here we use Stata to read the data file `rrdat1.dta`. For this purpose, we use a short do-file (`ehb1.do`), shown in Box 2.2.3.[4] As explained in the various examples in this book, a do-file is a short text file containing commands to be executed by Stata. A do-file can be created with the Stata Do-file Editor or any other editor, such as NotePad or TextPad.

Our first example, shown in Box 2.2.3, contains eight commands. In Stata there are several ways to terminate a command. As a default, commands end with a line break. You may have to continue longer commands over several lines to make your do-file more easily readable. There are three ways to allow for commands that run through several lines of a do-file. First, you can use the `#delimit` command, which defines the character that indicates the end of a command (carriage return or semicolon). If you change the delimiter to a semicolon, each piece of text, up to a terminating semicolon, will be interpreted by Stata as a single command. Second, three slashes at the end of a line (///) can be used to continue commands across lines. Alternatively, you may also type /* at the end of a line and restart the following line with */. To include a line of comments, you put an asterisk (*) at the beginning of a line. Also, anything following two slashes (//) will be ignored by Stata.

Every do-file in this textbook begins with a series of commands. Stata is continually being improved, and hence do-files written for earlier versions of Stata might produce an error message. To ensure that future versions of Stata will continue to execute your commands, you specify the version of Stata for which the do-file was written at the top of your do-

---

[4]The naming convention to identify do-files is: `ehxn.do`, where the single letter x is one of the series `a,b,c,...` referring to the successive chapters, and n numbers the do-files in each chapter. As far as possible, the do-files correspond to the TDA command files that were used in Blossfeld and Rohwer (2002).

Box 2.2.3 Do-file ehb1.do

```
version 9
capture log close
set more off
log using ehb1.log, replace

use rrdat1, clear

describe

list id noj tstart tfin sex ti tb te tmar pres presn edu in 1/9, sepby(id)

log close
```

file. Once you submit a command, the results will appear in the Stata Results Window. Stata pauses after the Results Window is filled up. With `set more off`, you ask Stata to run a do-file without interruption. Note that these results are only temporarily stored. In every Stata session you should therefore ensure that the commands and results of your do-file are saved in a so-called log file. In Stata the command `log using` allows you to make a full record of your Stata session. The command `log close` will close log files. If no log file is open, this command will produce an error message, and Stata will stop running the do-file. We therefore place `capture` before this command and instruct Stata to pay no attention to any error message from this command. You can open a Stata-format data set with the command `use`. Once you have set your working directory to the correct directory, you can load the file `rrdat1.dta` by simply typing `use rrdat1`.[5] For other data formats, you have to use other commands. Stat/Transfer (`http://www.stattransfer.com`) is a very useful program to convert system files from another statistical package such as SAS or SPSS or ASCII data to Stata and vice versa. There are also various Stata commands for reading external data: `infile` (free-format files), `infix` (ASCII data), `insheet` (spreadsheets), `fdause` and `fdasave` (SAS Xport). Once you load the data file, you can look at its contents by typing `describe`. Using the command `list`, you can look at all the contents and every single observation of the data file. The `in` qualifier in do-file `ehb1.do` tells Stata to list only the first nine observations; with `sepby(id)` you draw a separator line whenever the `id` changes to make the output more easily readable (see Box 2.2.2). In Stata it is possible to use abbreviations for commands as well as

---

[5]We do without path statements and assume that you have copied our example data set and all do-files into your working directory. To change the working directory to the correct drive and directory, use the command `cd drive:directory_name`. The path of your current working directory is displayed in the bottom of your Stata window and will also be shown in the Results Window if you type `cd`.

variable names as long as the abbreviations are not ambiguous. For example, to create or change the contents of a variable you can use the command `generate`. A simple `g` would do. Note, however, that many abbreviations in a do-file may also result in a lack of clarity. In this book, we will use abbreviations for several commands shown in do-files, but the full names of all commands will be given in the text. One should also note that Stata is casesensitive and that we use lowercase for variable names. In Stata you can ask for onscreen help. To display the online help system, you type `help` at the command line. If you want to learn more about a specific command, you type `help command` in the command line and press the Return key.

Executing Stata with a Do-File

Having prepared a do-file, one can get Stata to execute the commands. There are different ways to do this. First, to run the do-file, you type

    do filename

at the command line where `filename` is the name of a do-file and press the Return key. If you have saved your file in your current working directory you can omit any path statement. Another command to cause Stata to execute the commands of your do-file is `run`. In contrast to the command `do`, `run` will not display the commands and results in the Stata Results Window. Alternatively, you may also use the pull-down menu, Files > Do. If you are using the Stata Do-File Editor, you can select Tools > Do and Tools > Run from the top menu bar. Stata tries to find the do-file, reads the commands given in the file, and tries to execute the commands, possibly producing error messages. Any output will be written to the Results Window, though these results are only temporarily stored. To make a full record of all commands and results produced in your Stata session you need to open a Stata log file. When executing do-file `ehb1.do`, Stata will open the data set `rrdat1.dta` consisting of 600 cases and 12 variables, describe the data, and list values of all variables for the first nine records of the data set (see Boxes 2.2.1 and 2.2.2). If the user wants any further actions, these must be specified by additional commands. For instance, one can request a table of summary statistics of the variables by using the command `table`. As an example, add the command

    table noj

to the do-file to obtain a frequency distribution of variable `noj` (i.e., the distribution of the number of job episodes in the data file). If one intends to use the data as a set of event history data, Stata must be explicitly informed about how to interpret the data matrix as a set of episodes. In fact, there are two different ways of interpreting the data matrix as a set of episodes: single episode data and multiepisode data.

Single Episode Data

When working with single episode data, the implicit assumption is that all individual episodes are statistically independent.[6] Before defining episode data, two basic dimensions must be specified: the state space and the time axis. The state space is the set of possible origin and destination states. Values can be arbitrarily assigned. For instance, if we are only interested in job duration, the origin state of each job episode may be coded 0, and the destination state may be coded 1. This implies that we do not distinguish between different ways to leave a job. There is just a single transition: from 0 (being in a job) to 1 (having left that job). Of course, some episodes may be right censored. In these cases, individuals are still in the origin state at the observed ending time of the episode. Note, however, that Stata does not explicitly use the concept of a state space. All calculations are based on just one origin and one destination state. Censored and uncensored episodes are distinguished using a censoring indicator.

In addition to a state space, one needs a time axis. For instance, in our example data file, the jobs are coded in historical time defined in century months. The implied origin of this time axis is the beginning of January 1900. The easiest way to define the process time axis, for example, is to define the time of entry into the episode as zero and the ending time as the episode duration.[7] Do-file `ehb2.do`, shown in Box 2.2.4, illustrates the definition of single episode data with our example data set. The state space is $\mathcal{Y} = \{0, 1\}$: $0 \equiv$ being in a job episode, $1 \equiv$ having left the job. This is achieved by defining a new variable, `des`, serving as the censoring indicator: `des` is assigned zero or one, depending on whether the episode is right censored or not. An episode is right censored in the GLHS data set if its ending time (`tfin`) is equal to the interview date (`ti`). Therefore, if `tfin` is equal to `ti`, variable `des` becomes zero, otherwise one. Because we are only interested in job duration in this example, starting and ending times are given on a process time axis, that is, the starting time is always zero and the ending time equals the (observed) duration of the episode. This is achieved in Stata by defining a variable `tf` for the ending time. The variable `tf` is calculated as the difference between historical ending time (`tfin`) and historical starting time (`tstart`). To avoid zero durations, we have added one month to the job duration. For example, it might happen that an individual enters a job on the first day of a month and then leaves it during that same month. Because starting and ending times refer to the month where an individual occupies the current job, starting and ending times would be

---

[6]This may not be true if some individuals contribute more than a single episode and if the dependencies are not sufficiently controlled for by covariates (see section 4.3).

[7]It should be noted here that the time of entry into the origin state is sometimes hard to determine. For example, consider the case when people start a consensual union, begin a friendship, or are looking for a marriage partner.

Box 2.2.4 Do-file ehb2.do

```
version 9
capture log close
set more off
log using ehb2.log, replace

use rrdat1, clear

gen org = 0                    /*origin state*/
gen des = tfin==ti             /*destination state*/
gen tf  = tfin - tstart + 1    /*ending time*/

stset tf, f(des)    /*define single episode data*/

stdes    /*describe survival-time data*/
stsum    /*summarize survival-time data*/

stci, by(org des) emean /*calculate the mean survival time*/

log close
```

equal, and the duration would be zero. Thus we assume in our examples that any employment duration in the last month can be treated as a full month. The Stata command to create a new variable is **generate**. In Stata you can use the following operators:

Arithmetic		Logical		Relational	
+	addition	∼	not	>	greater than
−	subtraction	!	not	<	less than
⋆	multiplication	|	or	>=	greater or equal
/	division	&	and	<=	less or equal
∧	power			==	equal
				∼=	not equal
				!=	not equal

For example, to create the variable **tf** you type: **gen tf = tfin - tstart + 1** (see Box 2.2.4). Note that a double equal sign (==) is used for equality testing. Next, we use the **stset** command to declare the data set **rrdat1.dta** to be single-record event-history data: **stset timevar, failure(failvar)**. The variable **timevar** measures the duration before either a particular event ("failure") occurs or the observation is terminated at the right-hand side of the observation window due to censoring. The variable **failvar** records whether an episode ends with an event or censoring. By specifying **failure(des)**, all episodes for which the variable **des** is equal to 0 or missing will be considered as censored. You can also specify a list of codes that resemble events: **failure(des==1)**. All other values of the variable **des** will

be considered as indicators for censoring. For our example, type: stset tf,
f(des). There are several options for use with the Stata command stset,
although not all of them are relevant for this simple example. We assume
that all individual episodes are statistically independent, so it is not necessary to note individual case identification numbers. We will discuss repeated
events in the next section on multiple record data. The option origin is
used to identify when a subject becomes at risk. By default, Stata assumes
that our variable ts, the onset of risk, is 0, and this is exactly what our
data set looks like. When you declare your data to be event history data
by using the stset command, Stata checks the consistency of your data.[8]
At the same time, the command stset automatically creates the following
new variables:

_t0   analysis time when record begins

_t   analysis time when record ends

_d   1 if failure, 0 if censored

_st   1 if the record is to be used, 0 if ignored

The first two variables inform you about the process time. In our example,
_t0 is equal to zero for all job episodes; _t is equal to our variable tf.
The dummy _d contains the same type of information as our variable des.
The variable _st is not relevant here, but we will get back to this issue
in the next section on multiple-record data. It is important to note that
most of Stata's event history analysis commands require that the data have
previously been declared as single episode or multiepisode data by specifying
the stset command. This command need only be run once. If you want to
save the data to preserve this information, type save, replace and you
will overwrite the existing data set. To see how your current data set is
set, simply type st. Once you have declared your data set to be single
episode data, you can produce a summary of this data set by using the
Stata commands stdes, stsum, and stci. Executing the do-file ehb2.do
with Stata can be achieved in the following way: do ehb2. The output of
the Results Window is shown in Box 2.2.5. First, Stata shows how the data
set has been declared. You can see that 458 out of all 600 job episodes end
with an event. The total analysis time at risk is 40782 months, and the
last exit is observed after a duration of 428 months. The second part of the
output in the Results Window yields a brief description of how our survival-
time data are structured, though some of this information has already been

---

[8]Once you have declared your data to be event history data, Stata may warn you about
inconsistent records. For example, Stata will recognize if the event time or entry time is
missing, it will mark records if the observed entry is on or after the observed exit, and it
will warn you about any overlapping records. Exclusions of observations may result (the
automatically created variable _st will be equal to zero for these observations).

Box 2.2.5   Result of using do-file `ehb2.do` (Box 2.2.4)

```
    stset tf, f(des=1)   /*define single episode data*/

    failure event:  des == 1
    obs. time interval:  (0, tf]
    exit on or before:  failure

    ------------------------------------------------------------------------
      600  total obs.
        0  exclusions
    ------------------------------------------------------------------------
      600  obs. remaining, representing
      458  failures in single record/single failure data
    40782  total analysis time at risk, at risk from t =           0
                                 earliest observed entry t =       0
                                    last observed exit t =       428

    . stdes   /*describe survival-time data*/

            failure _d:  des == 1
       analysis time _t:  tf

                               |-------------- per subject --------------|
    Category             total       mean        min     median       max
    ------------------------------------------------------------------------
    no. of subjects        600
    no. of records         600          1          1          1          1

    (first) entry time                  0          0          0          0
    (final) exit time               67.97          2         37        428

    subjects with gap        0
    time on gap if gap       0
    time at risk         40782       67.97          2         37        428

    failures               458   .7633333          0          1          1
    ------------------------------------------------------------------------

    . stsum   /*summarize survival-time data*/

            failure _d:  des == 1
       analysis time _t:  tf

                   |              incidence     no. of   |------ Survival time -----|
                   | time at risk    rate      subjects    25%        50%        75%
    ---------------+--------------------------------------------------------------------
        total |        40782    .0112304         600       20         44        121

    . stci, by(org des) emean /*calculate the mean survival time*/

            failure _d:  des == 1
       analysis time _t:  tf

    org        |   no. of    extended
    des        |  subjects      mean
    -----------+----------------------
        0 0 |       142           .
        0 1 |       458     49.30349(*)
    -----------+----------------------
        total |       600     116.1306

    (*) no extension needed
```

produced by the `stset` command. In this simple example we have only one record per subject, so the number of subjects is equal to the number of records, and the minimum and maximum of records per subject is 1. The starting time (first entry time) is zero for all job episodes, and the first exit occurs after two, the last after 428 months (final exit time). By specifying `stsum`, Stata presents summary statistics (third part of the output in Box 2.2.5). The hazard rate, called incidence rate here, is $458/40782 = 0.011$. The percentiles of survival times are derived from a Kaplan-Meier survivor function (see chapter 3). This function estimates about a 25% chance of ending a job episode within 20 months, and 50% within 44 months. Finally, as can be seen on the bottom output in Box 2.2.5, the command `stci` can be used to calculate the mean survival time by exponentially extending the survival time to zero. The option `by(des)` requests separate summaries for each group of `des`, along with an overall total. The mean value of `tf` - `ts` is 49.3, but this is, of course, no proper estimate if some episodes are right censored.

Multiepisode Data

For multiepisode data, one needs two additional pieces of information. First, one must know which episodes belong to which individual; second, one must have knowledge about the serial (sequence) number of the episodes. The first piece of information is normally provided by an ID variable that identifies episodes belonging to the same individual.

To illustrate, we use the GLHS data set. Because in this data set not all people who have left a job also enter another one (i.e., they might become unemployed or stay out of work; see Figure 2.2.1c), it is useful to construct the state space in the following way:

1 Entry into 1st job: origin state
2 Exit from 1st job: destination state
3 Entry into 2nd job: origin state
4 Exit from 2nd job: destination state
   and so on.

As in the case of single episode data, right-censored episodes are identified by the fact that their destination state equals their origin state.

To define a time axis, one has at least two options. One can reset the clock at the beginning of each new episode (e.g., we use job-specific labor force experience as process time), or one can use a common process time axis where the first episode for each individual begins at time zero (e.g., we use general labor force experience over the life time as time axis). In the latter case, consecutive episodes are evaluated according to their starting

Box 2.2.6 Do-file ehb3.do for multiepisode data

```
version 9
capture log close
set more off
log using ehb3.log, replace
use rrdat1, clear

gen org       = 1+2*(noj-1)                          /*origin state*/
gen des       = org                                  /*destination state*/
replace des = org+1 if tfin<ti
gen tfc       = tstart if noj==1      /*general labor force experience*/
replace tfc = tfc[_n-1] if id==id[_n-1]
gen tsp       = tstart - tfc                         /*starting time*/
gen tfp       = tfin - tfc + 1                       /*ending time*/

list id noj tstart tfin org des tfc tsp tfp in 1/9, sepby(id)

stset tfp, f(des) id(id) exit(time .)    /*define multiepisode data*/


stdes                    /*describe survival-time data*/
stsum                    /*summarize survival-time data*/
stci, by(org,des) /* calculate median survival times*/
log close
```

Box 2.2.7 Example of multiepisode data for three individuals

```
    +---------------------------------------------------------+
    | id   noj   tstart   tfin   org   des   tfc   tsp   tfp |
    |---------------------------------------------------------|
 1. | 1     1     555     982    1     1     555    0    428 |
    |---------------------------------------------------------|
 2. | 2     1     593     638    1     2     593    0     46 |
 3. | 2     2     639     672    3     4     593   46     80 |
 4. | 2     3     673     892    5     6     593   80    300 |
    |---------------------------------------------------------|
 5. | 3     1     688     699    1     2     688    0     12 |
 6. | 3     2     700     729    3     4     688   12     42 |
 7. | 3     3     730     741    5     6     688   42     54 |
 8. | 3     4     742     816    7     8     688   54    129 |
 9. | 3     5     817     828    9    10     688  129    141 |
    +---------------------------------------------------------+
```

and ending time on this common process time axis, for example, in time-
dependent parametric models (see chapter 7). We use this latter option to
illustrate the setup of multiepisode data with our example data set. The
example do-file ehb3.do is shown in Box 2.2.6.

The serial number of episodes is given by the variable noj. To define the
common process time axis "general labor force experience," we have first

Box 2.2.8 Result of using do-file `ehb3.do` (Box 2.2.6)

```
. stset tfp, f(des) id(id) exit(time .)   /*define multiepisode data*/

              id:  id
   failure event:  des != 0 & des < .
obs. time interval:  (tfp[_n-1], tfp]
 exit on or before:  time .

     600  total obs.
       0  exclusions
-----------------------------------------------------------------------
     600  obs. remaining, representing
     201  subjects
     600  failures in multiple failure-per-subject data
   45441  total analysis time at risk, at risk from t =         0
                             earliest observed entry t =         0
                                last observed exit t =         465

. stdes   /*describe survival-time data*/

        failure _d:  des
   analysis time _t:  tfp
 exit on or before:  time .
              id:  id

                            |--------- per subject ------------|
Category                  total       mean     min    median       max
-----------------------------------------------------------------------
no. of subjects             201
no. of records              600   2.985075       1         3         9

(first) entry time                     0       0         0         0
(final) exit time              226.0746       7       192       465

subjects with gap             0
time on gap if gap            0         .       .         .         .
time at risk              45441   226.0746       7       192       465

failures                    600   2.985075       1         3         9
-----------------------------------------------------------------------

. stsum   /*summarize survival-time data*/

        failure _d:  des
   analysis time _t:  tfp
 exit on or before:  time .
              id:  id

         |              incidence  no. of  |------ Survival time ----|
         | time at risk     rate  subjects     25%       50%       75%
---------+-------------------------------------------------------------
   total |      45441  .0132039       201       18        37        85
```

Box 2.2.8 (cont.) Result of using do-file `ehb3.do` (Box 2.2.6)

```
. stci, by(org des) /*calculate median survival times*/

        failure _d:  des
   analysis time _t:  tfp
  exit on or before:  time .
               id:  id

org        |   no. of
des        |  subjects    50%    Std. Err.    [95% Conf. Interval]
-----------+----------------------------------------------------------
      1  1 |        16    188    6.242794         103         388
      1  2 |       185     32    2.405658          26          37
      3  3 |        36    175    6.580907         147         271
      3  4 |       126     41    4.625901           9          52
      5  5 |        38    163    .9890538          49         285
      5  6 |        69     10          .           .           .
      7  7 |        24    165    .9504057         127         197
      7  8 |        38     18          .           .           .
      9  9 |         9    163    2.829488         144         266
      9 10 |        23     60    1.06111           46          85
     11 11 |         8    181          .          181         283
     11 12 |        12    150    .9536436          99         169
     13 13 |         7    181    1.033404         157         331
     13 14 |         4    129          .           .           .
     15 15 |         3    139          .           .           .
     15 16 |         1      .          .           .           .
     17 17 |         1      .          .           .           .
-----------+----------------------------------------------------------
     total |       201     37    3.599101          29          43
```

defined a new variable

```
gen tfc = tstart if noj==1
replace tfc = tfc[_n-1] if id==id[_n-1]
```

meaning that for all sets of episodes that belong to the same ID, `tfc` equals
the starting time of the episode with serial number 1.[9] This variable is then
subtracted from the original starting and ending times to get their values on
the process time axis. Again, we have added one month to the ending times
to get positive durations. Box 2.2.7 shows, for the first three individuals in
our example data set, how the common process time axis is created from
the calendar time axis.

---

[9]Explicitly formulated, the definition is: if `noj` is equal to 1, `tfc` should be equal to
`tstart`; otherwise `tfc` should be equal to its predecessor. Of course, this definition relies
on the fact that in our example data file the episodes are ordered with respect to their
serial numbers. One should note here that `_n` is a Stata system variable that indicates
the position of an observation in the data set. Therefore, the `if` qualifier restricts the
command to successive records where the value of variable `id` is equal.

In the single-record-per-subject data set each observation represents a different subject. For multiepisode data, in which the same individual might contribute more than one record to the data, you have to modify your `stset` command and include the option `id(idvar)`, where `idvar` records the subject-id variable. Yet, typing `stset tfp, f(des) id(id)` will not yield the expected result. It is important to understand that Stata expects a specific data structure. The starting time of the first record per subject should always be zero, and there should not be gaps between subsequent episodes. The destination state should be zero for all but possibly the last episode per person in which we might observe an event. Our example data `rrdat1` contain multiple events (see Box 2.2.7). If you do not take this into account, Stata will remove the subject from the risk pool after the first event occurs. We therefore specify `exit(time .)` to keep all records for a subject until their final exit. In our example, the variable `tfp` indicates elapsed time before failure or censoring; `des` indicates whether an event (1) or censoring (0) occurred at this time. The variable `id` identifies the individuals in the data set. To set the data for event history analysis, type:

```
stset tfp, f(des) id(id) exit(time .)
```

Stata's output from the execution of do-file `ehb3.do` is shown in Box 2.2.8. The tables are similar to the tables shown in Box 2.2.5; the main difference is that in the case of multiepisode data one has to distinguish episodes with respect to their serial (sequence) number and their changing starting times. The first part of the table shows the Stata standard output after `stset`. The second table describes the multiepisode data. We can see that there are up to nine records per individual and that the first episode for each individual begins at time zero. Because each record in our example data represents an employment episode, the minimum and maximum number of failures is equal to the number of records. The incidence rate appears to be 0.013 (see the third part of the table). The last part of the table in Box 2.2.8 shows which types of episodes (transitions) are found in the data set.

Chapter 3
Nonparametric Descriptive Methods

In this chapter we discuss nonparametric estimation methods that can be used to describe the characteristics of the process under study. Because these methods do not make any assumptions about the distribution of the process, they are particularly suited for first exploratory data analyses. Stata contains procedures to calculate life tables and Kaplan-Meier (or product limit) estimates. Both of these methods are helpful for graphical presentations of the survivor function (and their transformations) as well as the transition rate. The life table method is the more traditional procedure and has been used in the case of large data sets because it needs less computing time and space. However, compared to the Kaplan-Meier estimator, the life table method has the disadvantage that the researcher has to define discrete time intervals, as is shown later. Given the capabilities of modern computers, there seems to be no reason anymore to prefer the life table method on the basis of computer time or storage space. We therefore give only a few examples for the life table method and discuss the Kaplan-Meier estimator in more detail.

3.1 Life Table Method

The life table method enables the calculation of nonparametric estimates of the survivor function, the density function, and the transition rate for durations given in a set of episodes.[1] There are two drawbacks to this method. First, it is necessary to group the durations into fixed intervals. The results therefore depend more or less on these arbitrarily defined time intervals. Second, it is only sensible to use this method if there is a relatively large number of episodes, so that estimates conditional for each interval are reliable. However, if this second requirement is fulfilled, the method gives good approximations that can be easily calculated.

Time intervals are defined by split points on the time axis

$$0 \leq \tau_1 < \tau_2 < \tau_3 < \ldots < \tau_L$$

with the convention that $\tau_{L+1} = \infty$, there are L time intervals, each includ-

---

[1] An extensive discussion of the life table method has been given by Namboodiri and Suchindran (1987).

ing the left limit, but not the right one.

$$I_l = \{t \mid \tau_l \le t < \tau_{l+1}\} \qquad l = 1, \ldots, L$$

Given these time intervals, the calculation of life tables by Stata is always done using episode durations. In the following description we therefore assume that all episodes have starting time zero. In addition, we assume that the time intervals start at zero (i.e., $\tau_1 = 0$).

The calculation depends somewhat on the type of input data. The following possibilities are recognized by Stata.[2] (1) If the input data are split into groups, a separate life table is calculated for each of the groups. (2) If there is more than one origin state, the life table calculation is done separately for each subset of episodes having the same origin state. Consequently, the life table calculation is always conditional on a given origin state. (3) If, for a given origin state, there is only a single destination state, an ordinary life table is calculated. If there are two or more destination states, a so-called multiple-decrement life table is produced.

To explain the formulas used for the life table calculation, we proceed in two steps. We first consider the case of a single transition (i.e., only a single origin and a single destination state), then we take into account the possibility of competing risks (i.e., two or more destination states). In both cases, to simplify notation, we assume a sample of N episodes all having the same origin state.

Single Transitions

All formulas used in the calculation of single transition life tables are based on the following quantities, defined for each interval I_l, $l = 1, \ldots, L$.

$$E_l \;=\; \text{the number of episodes with events in } I_l$$

$$Z_l \;=\; \text{the number of censored episodes ending in } I_l$$

The next important point is the definition of a *risk set*, $\mathcal{R}_l$, for each of the time intervals, that is, the set of units (episodes) that are at risk of having an event during the lth interval.[3] Two steps are required to take into account episodes that are censored during the interval. First the number of episodes, N_l, that enter the lth interval, is defined recursively by

$$N_1 = N, \quad N_l = N_{l-1} - E_{l-1} - Z_{l-1}$$

---

[2] In Stata, there are four kinds of weights: frequency weights (`fweights`), analytic weights (`aweights`), sampling weights (`pweights`), and importance weights (`iweights`). To learn more about these weighting types, enter the command `help weights` at the command line. The Stata command for life tables allows for `fweights`. For a discussion of using weights in longitudinal data analyses, see Hoem (1985, 1989).

[3] We generally denote the risk set by the symbol $\mathcal{R}$, and the number of units contained in the risk set by the symbol R.

Second, one has to decide how many of the episodes that are censored during an interval should be contained in the risk set for that interval. A standard assumption is that one half of their number should be contained, but, clearly, this is a somewhat arbitrary assumption.[4] To provide the possibility of changing this assumption, we assume a constant ω $(0 \le \omega \le 1)$ for the definition of the fraction of censored episodes that should be contained in the risk set. The number of elements in the risk set is defined, then, by

$$R_l = N_l - \omega Z_l$$

Using these basic quantities, it is easy to define all other concepts used in the life table setup. First, the conditional probabilities for having an event in the lth interval, q_l, and for surviving the interval, p_l, are

$$q_l = \frac{E_l}{R_l} \quad \text{and} \quad p_l = 1 - q_l$$

As an implication, one gets the following estimator for the survivor function:

$$G_1 = 1, \quad G_l = p_{l-1} G_{l-1}$$

Note, however, that in the output of Stata's life table procedure values of the survivor function are given for end points of time intervals.

Having estimates of the survivor function, the density function is evaluated approximately at the midpoints of the intervals as the first derivative

$$f_l = \frac{G_l - G_{l+1}}{\tau_{l+1} - \tau_l} \quad l = 1, \ldots, q-1$$

Of course, if the last interval is open on the right side, it is not possible to calculate the survivor function for this interval. Also, estimates of the transition rate, r_l, are calculated at the midpoints of the intervals. They are defined by

$$r_l = \frac{f_l}{\bar{G}_l} \quad \text{where} \quad \bar{G}_l = \frac{G_l + G_{l+1}}{2}$$

and this can also be written as

$$r_l = \frac{1}{\tau_{l+1} - \tau_l} \frac{q_l}{1 - q_l/2} = \frac{1}{\tau_{l+1} - \tau_l} \frac{E_l}{R_l - E_l/2}$$

Finally, it is possible to calculate approximate standard errors for the estimates of the survivor and density function, and for the transition rates, by

---

[4]See the discussion given by Namboodiri and Suchindran (1987: 58ff).

Box 3.1.1 Do-file `ehc1.do` (life table estimation)

```
version 9
capture log close
set more off
log using ehc1.log, replace

use rrdat1, clear

gen des = tfin ~= ti          /*destination state*/
gen tf  = tfin - tstart + 1   /*ending time*/

ltable tf des, intervals(30) su h f   /*command for life table estimation*/

log close
```

the formulas

$$\text{SE}(G_l) = G_l \left[\sum_{i=1}^{l-1} \frac{q_i}{p_i R_i} \right]^{1/2}$$

$$\text{SE}(f_l) = \frac{q_l G_l}{\tau_{l+1} - \tau_l} \left[\frac{p_l}{q_l R_l} + \sum_{i=1}^{l-1} \frac{q_i}{p_i R_i} \right]^{1/2}$$

$$\text{SE}(r_l) = \frac{r_l}{\sqrt{q_l R_l}} \left[1 - \left[\frac{r_l(\tau_{l+1} - \tau_l)}{2} \right]^2 \right]^{1/2}$$

Given large samples, it may be assumed that the values of the survivor, density, and rate functions, divided by their standard errors, are approximately standard normally distributed. In these cases it is then possible to calculate confidence intervals.

As an example of life table estimation with Stata, we examine the length of durations until job exit. This means that there is only one type of event: "job exit" from the origin state "being in a job" to the destination state "having left the job." For didactical purposes, we start with a simple example and assume in this application that all job episodes in the data file `rrdat1` (see Boxes 2.2.1 and 2.2.2) can be considered as independent from each other (single episode case) and that there is no important heterogeneity among the individuals.[5] Thus we are going to estimate "average" survivor and transition rate functions across all the job spells and individuals.

In Box 3.1.1 the do-file (`ehc1.do`) for the life table estimation with Stata is shown. The upper part of this file is identical to do-file `ehb2.do`, shown in Box 2.2.4, which was used to define single episode data. In order to

---

[5]Of course, this is an unrealistic assumption because the individuals are represented in the data file (`rrdat1`) with varying numbers of job spells. Thus there are dependencies between the episodes of each individual.

Box 3.1.2 Result of using do-file `ehc1.do` (Box 3.1.1)

Interval		Beg. Total	Deaths	Lost	Survival	Std. Error	[95% Conf. Int.]	
0	30	600	223	28	0.6195	0.0201	0.5788	0.6574
30	60	349	113	23	0.4121	0.0208	0.3712	0.4524
60	90	213	51	15	0.3098	0.0199	0.2711	0.3492
90	120	147	25	16	0.2541	0.0192	0.2172	0.2924
120	150	106	24	15	0.1922	0.0182	0.1578	0.2291
150	180	67	9	5	0.1654	0.0177	0.1323	0.2016
180	210	53	4	9	0.1517	0.0175	0.1193	0.1878
210	240	40	3	5	0.1396	0.0175	0.1075	0.1758
240	270	32	0	5	0.1396	0.0175	0.1075	0.1758
270	300	27	2	7	0.1277	0.0179	0.0952	0.1651
300	330	18	2	5	0.1112	0.0190	0.0775	0.1517
330	360	11	2	1	0.0900	0.0205	0.0552	0.1352
360	390	8	0	3	0.0900	0.0205	0.0552	0.1352
390	420	5	0	4	0.0900	0.0205	0.0552	0.1352
420	450	1	0	1	0.0900	0.0205	0.0552	0.1352

Interval		Beg. Total	Deaths	Lost	Cum. Failure	Std. Error	[95% Conf. Int.]	
0	30	600	223	28	0.3805	0.0201	0.3426	0.4212
30	60	349	113	23	0.5879	0.0208	0.5476	0.6288
60	90	213	51	15	0.6902	0.0199	0.6508	0.7289
90	120	147	25	16	0.7459	0.0192	0.7076	0.7828
120	150	106	24	15	0.8078	0.0182	0.7709	0.8422
150	180	67	9	5	0.8346	0.0177	0.7984	0.8677
180	210	53	4	9	0.8483	0.0175	0.8122	0.8807
210	240	40	3	5	0.8604	0.0175	0.8242	0.8925
240	270	32	0	5	0.8604	0.0175	0.8242	0.8925
270	300	27	2	7	0.8723	0.0179	0.8349	0.9048
300	330	18	2	5	0.8888	0.0190	0.8483	0.9225
330	360	11	2	1	0.9100	0.0205	0.8648	0.9448
360	390	8	0	3	0.9100	0.0205	0.8648	0.9448
390	420	5	0	4	0.9100	0.0205	0.8648	0.9448
420	450	1	0	1	0.9100	0.0205	0.8648	0.9448

Interval		Beg. Total	Cum. Failure	Std. Error	Hazard	Std. Error	[95% Conf. Int.]	
0	30	600	0.3805	0.0201	0.0157	0.0010	0.0137	0.0177
30	60	349	0.5879	0.0208	0.0134	0.0012	0.0110	0.0158
60	90	213	0.6902	0.0199	0.0094	0.0013	0.0069	0.0120
90	120	147	0.7459	0.0192	0.0066	0.0013	0.0040	0.0092
120	150	106	0.8078	0.0182	0.0092	0.0019	0.0056	0.0129
150	180	67	0.8346	0.0177	0.0050	0.0017	0.0017	0.0083
180	210	53	0.8483	0.0175	0.0029	0.0014	0.0001	0.0057
210	240	40	0.8604	0.0175	0.0028	0.0016	0.0000	0.0059
240	270	32	0.8604	0.0175	0.0000	.	.	.
270	300	27	0.8723	0.0179	0.0030	0.0021	0.0000	0.0071
300	330	18	0.8888	0.0190	0.0046	0.0032	0.0000	0.0110
330	360	11	0.9100	0.0205	0.0070	0.0049	0.0000	0.0167
360	390	8	0.9100	0.0205	0.0000	.	.	.
390	420	5	0.9100	0.0205	0.0000	.	.	.
420	450	1	0.9100	0.0205	0.0000	.	.	.

request life table estimation we added the `ltable` command. One needs a specification of time intervals. This is done with the option `intervals`:

```
ltable tf des,intervals(30)
```

This defines time intervals, each having a duration of 30 months, and beginning at time zero: $0 \leq t < 30$, $30 \leq t < 60$, and so on. With the `intervals` option you can also define cutoff points by specifying more than one number as the argument.

As a default, `ltable` displays the estimates of the survivor function. Specifying the option `failure` one gets the cumulative failure table (1 - survival). To obtain estimates of the transition rate, we type `hazard`.

Executing do-file `ehc1.do` with Stata you will get the survival and failure table as well as the estimates of the transition rate aggregated in 30-month intervals. The results of do-file `ehc1.do` are shown in Box 3.1.2.

We want to give a short example of how the numbers in the life table of our example are related to the formulas developed earlier. In the third column of the life table in Box 3.1.2, the number of episodes entering into the successive intervals is given. In the first interval, all 600 episodes entered: $N_1 = N = 600$. The numbers of the following intervals $l = 2, 3, \ldots$ are calculated as

$$N_l = N_{l-1} - E_{l-1} - Z_{l-1}$$

where E_l, the number of events in the lth interval, is printed in column 4, and Z_l, the number of censored episodes in the lth interval, is printed in column 5. In our example:

$$N_1 = 600$$
$$N_2 = 600 - 223 - 28 = 349$$
$$N_3 = 349 - 113 - 23 = 213$$

Under the assumption that censored episodes are equally distributed within each interval ($w = 0.5$), one is able to estimate the number of episodes at risk in each interval. For the lth interval:

$$\hat{R}_l = N_l - 0.5 Z_l$$

In our example:

$$\hat{R}_1 = 600 - 0.5 \cdot 28 = 586.0$$
$$\hat{R}_2 = 349 - 0.5 \cdot 23 = 337.5$$

The conditional probability of having an event in the lth interval is given as

$$\hat{q}_l = \frac{E_l}{\hat{R}_l}$$

In our example:

$$\hat{q}_1 = \frac{223}{586.0} = 0.38055$$

$$\hat{q}_2 = \frac{113}{337.5} = 0.33481$$

The conditional probability of experiencing no event in the lth interval is then

$$\hat{p}_l = 1 - \hat{q}_l$$

In our example:

$$\hat{p}_1 = 1 - 0.38055 = 0.61945$$
$$\hat{p}_2 = 1 - 0.33481 = 0.66519$$

Based on these estimates, one can compute estimates of the survivor function (column 6 of the upper panel of the life table):

$$\hat{G}_1 = 1$$
$$\hat{G}_l = \hat{p}_{l-1} \cdot \hat{p}_{l-2} \cdots \hat{p}_1$$

In our example:

$$\hat{G}_1 = 1$$
$$\hat{G}_2 = 0.61945 \cdot 1 = 0.61945$$
$$\hat{G}_3 = 0.66519 \cdot 0.61945 \cdot 1 = 0.41205$$

Finally, we also have to consider the length of the intervals, $\tau_{l+1} - \tau_l$ (for the lth interval). The duration density function is given as

$$\hat{f}_l = \frac{\hat{G}_l - \hat{G}_{l-1}}{\tau_{l+1} - \tau_l}$$

In our example:

$$\hat{f}_1 = \frac{1.00000 - 0.61945}{30 - 0} = 0.01268$$

$$\hat{f}_2 = \frac{0.61945 - 0.41205}{60 - 30} = 0.00691$$

The "average" transition rate, evaluated at the midpoint of each interval, is printed in column 6 of the bottom panel in the life table:

$$\hat{r}_l = \frac{1}{\tau_{l+1} - \tau_l} \frac{E_l}{\hat{R}_l - 0.5\,E_l}$$

Box 3.1.3 Do-file `ehc2.do` to plot a survivor function

```
version 9
set scheme sj
capture log close
set more off
log using ehc2.log, replace

use rrdat1, clear

gen des = tfin ~= ti         /*destination state*/
gen tf  = tfin - tstart + 1  /*ending time*/

ltable tf des, intervals(30) gr title("Life Table Survivor Function")  ///
ysc(r(1)) ylabel(0(0.2)1) xtitle("analysis time") ///
saving("Figure 3_1_1",replace)

log close
```

In our example:

$$\hat{r}_1 = \frac{1}{30-0}\frac{223}{586.0-0.5\cdot223} = 0.01567$$

$$\hat{r}_2 = \frac{1}{60-30}\frac{113}{337.5-0.5\cdot113} = 0.01340$$

The standard errors for the survivor function, cumulative failure table, and the rate function are printed in column 7 of each table, and the 95% confidence interval is printed in columns 8 and 9.

Life tables, as shown in Box 3.1.2, are very complex and are not easily interpreted. It is therefore better to plot the interval-related information of the survival or failure function. An example of a Stata do-file, `ehc2.do`, which can be used to generate a plot of the survivor function, is shown in Box 3.1.3.[6] To draw a graph of the survivor function you simply add the `graph` option to the `ltable` command.[7] The resulting plot is shown in Figure 3.1.1. A similar do-file can be used to generate plots for the failure function.

The plot of the survivor function shows estimates of the proportions of respondents who have not yet changed their jobs up to a specific duration. For example, after 10 years (or 120 months) about 25% of respondents are still in their jobs, while about 75% have already left.

---

[6]Because there may be a considerable number of intervals during which no events take place, and hence the hazard estimate is zero, a graph of the rate function is best created by using a kernel smooth. To plot the results of the hazard table, you employ the command `sts graph`. However, this command is not illustrated here.

[7]The appearance of a Stata graph in the Stata Graph Window is specified by a graph scheme. To ensure that you obtain the same results as in this textbook, type `set scheme sj` and change to the Stata Journal scheme. We use various options to specify the title, scale, and labels of the graph. To learn more about the options possible with `ltable`, type `help ltable` and `help twoway options`.

Box 3.1.4 Do-file `ehc3.do` (life table estimation)

```
version 9
set scheme sj
capture log close
set more off
log using ehc3.log, replace

use rrdat1, clear

gen des = tfin ~= ti          /*destination state*/
gen tf  = tfin - tstart + 1   /*ending time*/

label define sex 1 "Men" 2 "Women"
label value sex sex

ltable tf des, intervals(30) su h f by(sex) /*command for life table estimation*/

ltable tf des, intervals(30) by(sex) gr overlay ///
ysc(r(1)) ylabel(0(0.2)1) xlabel(0(100)500) xtitle("analysis time") ///
saving("Figure 3_1_2",replace)

log close
```

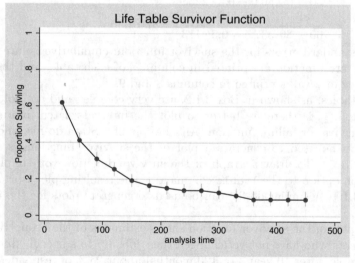

Figure 3.1.1 Plot of the survivor function generated with do-file `ehc2.do`.

Life Table Estimation for Different Groups

Life tables are particularly useful for comparisons of the behavior of subgroups. We therefore extend the example in Box 3.1.1 and demonstrate how separate life tables for men and women can be estimated with Stata. This can be achieved by adding the `by(varname)` option. Box 3.1.4 shows the do-file `ehc3.do`, which is just a modification of do-file `ehc2.do`. The vari-

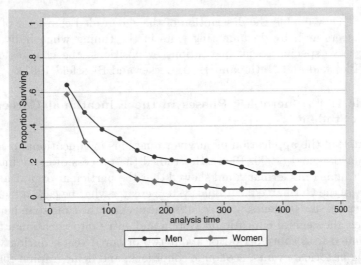

Figure 3.1.2 Plot of survivor functions for men and women, generated with do-file `ehc3.do`.

able `sex` is the indicator variable for men and women.[8] The command to request life table estimation is basically the same. We only added the option `by(sex)` in order to separate life tables for both groups.[9]

As a result of using do-file `ehc3.do`, separate tables for men and women are presented. To save space, these tables are not shown here. Instead, Figure 3.1.2 shows a plot of the survivor functions. It is easy to see that at the beginning the process for men and women is quite similar. But after a duration of about three years the survivor function of women decreases more steeply than the survivor function for men. Thus women tend to leave their jobs sooner than men do. After 20 years, about 20 % of men, but only about 5 % of women are still in their jobs. The median job durations are about 57 months for men and about 40 months for women.

Examples of the Application of Survivor Functions in Social Research

In modern social research, survivor functions have been increasingly used to study social change. They are particularly suited to the analysis of how changing historical conditions affect life course transitions of successive birth

---

[8]In Stata, linking value labels and variables is a two-step process. First, one has to define a value label by using the command `label define`, then one specifies `label value` to attach its contents to a variable.

[9]By default, Stata draws a separate graph within the same image for each group defined with the `by()` option. Sometimes it is useful to overlay these plots on the same graph. To do so, we specify the option `overlay`.

cohorts.[10] They enable the description of the age-graded character of roles and behaviors and, by documenting exits in the timing when individuals enter or leave specific social institutions or positions, the changes of life phases (Blossfeld and Nuthmann 1990; Becker and Blossfeld 1991).

Example 1: "Vulnerable" Phases in the Educational Careers of German Students

An example of the application of survivor functions in educational research is given in Blossfeld (1990, 1992). He studied the process of entry into vocational training in Germany and showed that the particular organizational structure of the German educational system creates what he calls a "vulnerable" life phase for students. *Vulnerability* means that the time span between having left the general educational system and entry into vocational training is limited to a short period of about two or three years, during which prevailing historical events, economic conditions, and demographic constellations strongly determine the opportunities of each generation to acquire vocational training.

The survivor functions in Figure 3.1.3 demonstrate this "vulnerable" phase for three different birth cohorts, and for men and women. They show the proportions of school leavers who did not yet enter the German vocational training system for every point in time after leaving the general educational system. The curves are very different for the three birth cohorts and for men and women. In particular, the economic and political breakdown in the immediate postwar period (1945–50) had a strong negative effect on enrollment in vocational training for the 1929–31 cohort. Confronted with the existing historical conditions, school leavers of this birth cohort did not rank entering vocational training highly because they had more urgent problems to deal with (e.g., making a living), and it would have been very difficult to find trainee positions at all (Mayer 1987, 1988, 1991). Compared to this immediate postwar period, the later social and economic development until the mid-1970s led to a constant rise in the standard of living, a decrease in unemployment, and a substantial growth in the number of trainee positions offered in the private sector.

The upper part of Figure 3.1.3 shows that about 50% of men in the 1929–31 birth cohort started vocational training immediately after leaving the general educational system. An additional 27% of these men undertook vocational training within three years of leaving the general educational system. But about 23% never entered vocational training. In comparison, about 71% and 79% of the men in the 1939–41 and 1949–51 birth cohorts, respectively, began vocational training immediately, and an additional 14%

---

[10]See Mayer and Schwarz 1989; Hogan 1978, 1981; Marini 1978, 1984, 1985; Elder 1975, 1978, 1987.

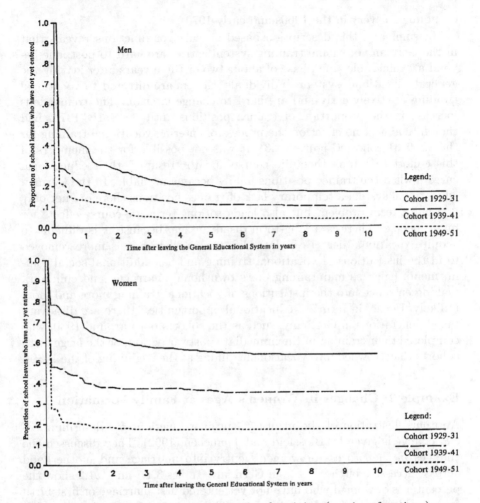

Figure 3.1.3 Process of entering vocational training (survivor functions).

of the men in both cohorts started within three years. Thus only about 15 %
of the men in the 1939–41 cohort and about 7 % of the men in the 1949–51
cohort never entered vocational training.

For women (lower part of Figure 3.1.3), these differences were even more
pronounced. Within three years of leaving the general educational system,
only 40 % of the women in the 1929–31 cohort, but 60 % of the women in the
1939–41 cohort, and 80 % of the women in the 1949–51 cohort undertook
vocational training. In other words, with regard to educational opportunities, women in particular carried the burden of the immediate postwar social
and economic crises, but they also profited more than men from the rapid

economic recovery in the 1960s and early 1970s.

In summary, this description based on survivor functions reveals that in the German vocational training system entries are hard to postpone beyond a "vulnerable" life phase of about two or three years after leaving the general educational system. Individuals' careers are directed to vocational training relatively early and are hard to change later on. The tremendous increase in the proportion of trainee positions until the early 1970s had therefore almost no effect on the process of entering vocational training for the 1929–31 cohort (Figure 3.1.3). It was not possible for the members of this cohort to "stop" their life course and to "resume" their educational careers when the trainee positions finally became available. In the German educational system a temporary lack of trainee positions therefore not only is a short-term problem but also leads to long-term life-course effects for many people. There is a long-term disadvantage, because it is difficult to acquire vocational degrees in later life stages when one is more removed from the institutions of vocational training and has additional social commitments (such as maintaining one's own home, marriage, and children), making entrance into the institutions of vocational training more and more unlikely. Hence, in terms of educational opportunities, there are disadvantaged generations in Germany, such as the cohorts born around 1930, who completed their training in the immediate postwar period, or the large birth cohorts that crowded into vocational training at the beginning of the 1980s.

Example 2: Changes in Women's Ages at Family Formation

Another illustration of the utility of survivor functions for describing social change is given by Blossfeld and Jaenichen (1992). They discussed the changes in the process of women's entry into marriage and motherhood across successive birth cohorts in Germany. Tables 3.1.1 and 3.1.2 show the percentages of women who have not yet entered first marriage or first birth for each birth cohort and specific ages. These percentages are based on life table estimates of survivor functions for each cohort for the events of entry into marriage and first birth.

As shown in Table 3.1.1, age at first marriage fell sharply from the 1919–23 cohort to the 1944–48 cohort, and has since been rising again until the youngest birth cohort. The greatest movements occurred among women aged 20–24, where the unmarried proportion dropped from 46 % to 15 % and subsequently increased again to 40 %. The result is that as far as the youngest cohorts, 1964–68 and 1959–63, can be followed, they have more or less the same age pattern at entry into marriage as we find for the oldest cohorts, 1924–28 and 1919–23.

Looking at ages at first birth in Table 3.1.2, we observe a similar trend. Again, it is the 1944–48 cohort that entered motherhood at the youngest

Table 3.1.1 Changes in the timing of entry into marriage, as measured by proportions unmarried at specific ages (percentages).

Birth cohort	Proportion of unmarried women at age							
	20	24	28	32	36	40	44	48
1964–68	89	–	–	–	–	–	–	–
1959–63	78	40	–	–	–	–	–	–
1954–58	73	32	19	–	–	–	–	–
1949–53	65	24	11	7	–	–	–	–
1944–48	65	15	7	4	3	–	–	–
1939–43	80	21	8	5	3	3	–	–
1934–38	76	23	9	6	5	5	4	–
1929–33	86	32	13	7	6	5	5	4
1924–28	90	40	16	11	8	6	5	5
1919–23	90	46	20	13	10	9	7	7

Table 3.1.2 Changes in the timing of entry into motherhood, as measured by proportions childless at specific ages (percentages).

Birth cohort	Proportion of childless women at age							
	20	24	28	32	36	40	44	48
1964–68	92	–	–	–	–	–	–	–
1959–63	90	57	–	–	–	–	–	–
1954–58	84	55	30	–	–	–	–	–
1949–53	78	47	21	15	–	–	–	–
1944–48	77	32	16	11	9	–	–	–
1939–43	87	41	18	13	10	10	–	–
1934–38	83	45	18	13	11	11	11	–
1929–33	92	54	28	19	16	16	16	16
1924–28	87	56	26	19	15	14	14	14
1919–23	91	57	30	19	15	15	15	15

ages. For this cohort, not only marriages but entries into motherhood were highly concentrated. And again, we find more or less the same time pattern of entry into motherhood for the youngest cohorts, 1964–68 and 1959–63, and the oldest cohorts, 1924–28 and 1919–23, at least as far as the youngest cohorts can be followed.

Both tables show that in Germany the delay of entry into marriage and motherhood seems to be less dramatic than has been shown for other countries, such as the Scandinavian ones, especially Sweden (see Blossfeld 1995; Hoem 1986, 1991; Hoem and Rennermalm 1985). In Germany, more or less the same entrance pattern of ages into marriage and motherhood is observed as was established 50 years ago. However, it is also clear that in

Germany the earlier movement toward younger and universal marriage and
motherhood had come to a halt at the end of the 1960s and the beginning of
the 1970s. But this reversal of the timing of marriage and motherhood is not
in line with the monotonic trend in women's educational attainment across
cohorts (Blossfeld and Shavit 1993). It is therefore questionable whether
changes in marriage and motherhood can be attributed mainly to women's
growing economic independence (see Blossfeld 1995), as argued for example
by Becker (1981).

3.2   Product-Limit Estimation

Another method for the nonparametric estimation of the survivor function
and its derivatives is the product-limit, also called the Kaplan-Meier (1958),
method. One of the advantages of this approach, compared with the life
table method, is that it is not necessary to group the episode durations
according to arbitrarily defined time intervals. Instead, the product-limit
method is based on the calculation of a risk set at every point in time where
at least one event occurred. In this way, the information contained in a set
of episodes is optimally used. The only drawback of this method results
from the fact that all episodes must be sorted according to their ending
(and starting) times, but with efficient sorting algorithms the method can
be employed with fairly large sets of episodes.

This section describes the product-limit estimation method and its implementation in Stata.[11] The options, depending on the type of input data,
are essentially the same as with the life table method: (1) If the input data
are split into groups, separate product-limit estimates are calculated for
each of the groups. (2) If there is more than a single origin state, one or
more product-limit estimates are calculated for each subset of episodes having the same origin state. (3) If there is more than a single destination state,
separate product-limit estimates are calculated for each transition found in
the input data.

The following description proceeds in two steps. First, we consider the
case of a single transition, then the case of two or more destination states.

Single Transitions

We assume a sample of N episodes, all having the same origin state and
either having the same destination state or being right censored. If groups
are defined, it is assumed that all episodes belong to the same group. For
the moment we also assume that all episodes have the starting time zero.

---

[11] You must declare your data to be event history data before you can use the Stata command for product-limit estimation. If you work with weighted data, fweights, iweights,
and pweights may be specified at this point.

The first step is to consider the points in time where at least one of the episodes ends with an event. There are, say, q such points in time.

$$\tau_1 < \tau_2 < \tau_3 < \ldots < \tau_q$$

The second step is to define three basic quantities, all defined for $l = 1, \ldots, q$, with the convention that $\tau_0 = 0$.

E_l = the number of episodes with events at τ_l

Z_l = the number of censored episodes ending in $[\tau_{l-1}, \tau_l)$

R_l = the number of episodes in the risk set at τ_l, denoted $\mathcal{R}_l$, that is, the number of episodes with starting time less than τ_l and ending time $\geq \tau_l$

Note that the implied definition of the risk set allows the handling of episodes with starting times greater than zero. Also note that the risk set at τ_l includes episodes that are censored at this point in time. It is assumed that a censored episode contains the information that there was no event up to *and including* the observed ending time of the episode. As sometimes stated, censoring takes place an infinitesimal amount to the right of the observed ending time.

Given these quantities, the product-limit estimator of the survivor function is defined as

$$\hat{G}(t) = \prod_{l:\tau_l < t} \left(1 - \frac{E_l}{R_l} \right)$$

This is a step function with steps at the points in time, τ_l. The commonly used formula to calculate estimates of standard errors for the survivor function is

$$\mathrm{SE}(\hat{G}(t)) = \hat{G}(t) \left[\sum_{l:\tau_l < t} \frac{E_l}{R_l \, (R_l - E_l)} \right]^{1/2}$$

In addition to survivor function estimates, the product-limit method gives a simple estimate of the cumulated transition rate.

$$\hat{H}(t) = -\log\left(\hat{G}(t) \right)$$

This is again a step function. It is especially useful for simple graphical checks of distributional assumptions about the underlying durations (see chapter 8).

Unfortunately, unlike the life table estimation, the product-limit method does not provide direct estimates of transition rates. Of course, it is possible

Box 3.2.1 Do-file ehc5.do (Kaplan-Meier estimation)

```
version 9
capture log close
set more off
log using ehc5.log, replace

use rrdat1, clear

gen des = tfin ~= ti          /*destination state*/
gen tf  = tfin - tstart + 1   /*ending time*/

stset tf, f(des)    /*define single episode data*/

sts list /*list survivor function*/

log close
```

Box 3.2.2 Result of do-file ehc5.do (Box 3.2.1)

```
        failure _d:  des
  analysis time _t:  tf
        Beg.          Net    Survivor      Std.
  Time  Total  Fail  Lost   Function     Error   [95% Conf. Int.]
  -----------------------------------------------------------------
     2   600     2     1     0.9967      0.0024  0.9867    0.9992
     3   597     5     2     0.9883      0.0044  0.9757    0.9944
     4   590     9     0     0.9732      0.0066  0.9567    0.9835
     5   581     3     1     0.9682      0.0072  0.9506    0.9796
     6   577    10     0     0.9514      0.0088  0.9309    0.9660
     7   567     9     1     0.9363      0.0100  0.9136    0.9533
     8   557     6     3     0.9262      0.0107  0.9022    0.9446
     9   548     7     1     0.9144      0.0115  0.8889    0.9343
    10   540     8     4     0.9009      0.0123  0.8739    0.9223
                     output omitted
    42   273     1     0     0.5040      0.0209  0.4623    0.5442
    43   272     2     1     0.5003      0.0209  0.4586    0.5405
    44   269     5     1     0.4910      0.0210  0.4493    0.5313
    45   263     1     0     0.4891      0.0210  0.4474    0.5295
                     output omitted
   275    26     1     0     0.1345      0.0175  0.1025    0.1709
                     output omitted
   293    20     1     0     0.1278      0.0179  0.0953    0.1652
                     output omitted
   312    16     1     1     0.1198      0.0185  0.0866    0.1588
   326    14     1     0     0.1112      0.0190  0.0775    0.1518
                     output omitted
   332    11     1     0     0.1011      0.0198  0.0666    0.1440
                     output omitted
   350     9     1     0     0.0899      0.0205  0.0550    0.1353
                     output omitted
   428     1     0     1     0.0899      0.0205  0.0550    0.1353
```

to get estimates by numerical differentiation of $\hat{H}(t)$, but this requires that one first applies a smoothing procedure to the cumulative rate.

In illustrating the application of the product-limit estimator with Stata in Box 3.2.1, we again apply the job-exit example in which we assumed that there are only single episodes and two states ("being in a job" and "having

Box 3.2.3   Do-file `ehc6.do` to plot a survivor function

```
version 9
set scheme sj
capture log close
set more off
log using ehc6.log, replace

use rrdat1, clear

gen des = tfin ~= ti          /*destination state*/
gen tf  = tfin - tstart + 1   /*ending time*/

stset tf, f(des)    /*define single episode data*/
sts graph, title("Product-Limit Survivor Function") saving("Figure 3_2_1", replace)

log close
```

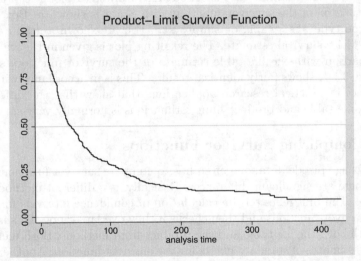

Figure 3.2.1 Plot of survivor function (product-limit estimation)
generated with do-file `ehc6.do`.

left the job"). To estimate the Kaplan-Meier survivor function, type `sts`
`list`. The default is to list the function at all the unique time values in the
data. To reduce output, you can also choose the points in time at which
the estimated survivor function is to be listed. This is achieved by using the
option `at()`. In our example, the following command will produce the output
shown in Box 3.2.2: `sts list, at(0 2/10 42/45 275 293 312 326 332`
`350 428)`.[12]

The column labeled `Time` shows the points in time where at least one
event takes place. The risk set is given in the second column. For example,

---

[12]If you are not yet familiar with number lists in Stata, type `help numlist`.

at the job duration of two months, 600 episodes are still at risk. The number
of events is given in column 3. For example, at a job duration of 6 months
we observe 10 job moves, and at a job duration of 42 months we observe
1 event. The last four columns show estimates of the survivor function,
its standard errors, and the 95 % confidence intervals. For example, after
about 4 years (or 45 months) a proportion of 0.4891 of workers are still in
the same job. The survivor function of the product-limit estimator is only
defined up to the highest event time. The highest event time in Box 3.2.2
is 350 months. Eight additional censored cases with longer job durations
follow. Under these circumstances, the estimated survivor function can no
longer approach zero and can only be interpreted up until 350 months.

Again, the survivor function in Box 3.2.2 is not very comprehensible. The
shape of the function can be evaluated more easily, if it is plotted against
job duration. An example do-file, `ehc6.do`, in order to plot the product-
limit estimator of the survivor function with Stata is shown in Box 3.2.3.
When you type `sts graph`, or simply `sts`, you are shown a graph of the
Kaplan-Meier survival estimate. The resulting plot is given in Figure 3.2.1.
A comparison with the life table estimate of the survivor function, shown
in Figure 3.1.1, shows fairly identical results. This is in accordance with our
experience in practical research applications that show that the difference
between life table and product-limit estimations is normally very small.

3.3   Comparing Survivor Functions

In analyzing episode data, one often has to compare survivor functions and
test if there are significant differences. Basically, two different methods are
available. The first relies on the calculation of confidence intervals for each
of the survivor functions and then checks if they overlap or not. This is possible with both the life table and the product-limit methods. Both methods
provide estimates of standard errors for the survivor function. Another possibility is to calculate specific test statistics to compare two or more survivor
functions. This section describes both possibilities.

Defining Groups of Episodes

To make any comparisons, there must be two or more groups of episodes.
This is easily done using indicator variables that define membership in a
group. In Stata, the syntax is

```
sts list, by(varlist)
```

In our example we specify a single `by()` variable, `by(sex)`, but it is also
possible to select up to five variables. The set of episodes given in the current
data matrix is then split into groups, and separate calculations are pursued
for each group identified by equal values of the variables in `varlist`.

Box 3.3.1 Do-file `ehc7.do` (comparing survivor functions)

```
version 9
set scheme sj
capture log close
set more off
log using ehc7.log, replace

use rrdat1, clear

gen des = tfin ~= ti          /*destination state*/
gen tf  = tfin - tstart + 1   /*ending time*/

label define sex 1 "Men" 2 "Women"
label value sex sex

stset tf, f(des)     /*define single episode data*/

sts list, by(sex)

sts graph, by(sex) gwood saving("Figure 3_3_1", replace)

sts test sex              /*Log-rank test for equality of survivor functions*/
sts test sex, wilcoxon    /*Wilcoxon (Breslow)*/
sts test sex, tware       /*Wilcoxon (Taron-Ware)*/
sts test sex, peto        /*Wilcoxon (Prentice)*/

log close
```

To illustrate grouping in the case of product-limit estimation, we extend the example in Box 3.2.1. The new do-file, `ehc7.do`, is a small modification of do-file `ehc5.do` already shown in Box 3.2.1. The additional commands are shown in Box 3.3.1.

Using this modified do-file, a product-limit estimation is done separately for men and women. The results window contains two tables, one with estimates for men, another one for women. Figure 3.3.1 shows a plot of these two survivor functions. In Stata, you can obtain this plot with the following command: `sts graph, by(sex)`. The option `gwood` is used to show the pointwise Greenwood confidence bands around the survivor function.[13] After about 3 years, the confidence bands of the survivor functions of men and women no longer intersect. Thus there are statistically significant differences in the job-exit behavior of men and women for greater durations.

Construction of Test Statistics

Many different test statistics have been proposed to compare two or more survivor functions. We describe four that can be calculated with Stata. All of them are based on product-limit estimates of survivor functions.

It is assumed that m groups have been defined that do not intersect.

---

[13]If you specify `gwood` to draw pointwise confidence bands, the curves are automatically placed on separate graphs.

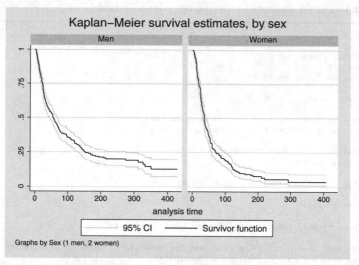

Figure 3.3.1 Plots of survivor functions (product-limit estimation) for men and women with 95 % confidence intervals (grey-scaled). The plot has been generated with do-file `ehc7.do`.

The whole sample is implicitly defined as the set of all episodes that are contained in one of these groups. Then, in exactly the same way as explained in connection with the product-limit method, all calculations are done for each transition in the whole sample separately. Therefore we only consider a sample of episodes that have the same origin state and are censored or have the same destination state.

In general, a sample defined this way consists of m groups, and the following table can be calculated.

$$
\begin{array}{ccccccc}
\tau_1 & R_{11} & E_{11} & R_{12} & E_{12} & \ldots & R_{1m} & E_{1m} \\
\tau_2 & R_{21} & E_{21} & R_{22} & E_{22} & \ldots & R_{2m} & E_{2m} \\
& & & & \vdots & & & \\
\tau_q & R_{n1} & E_{q1} & R_{q2} & E_{q2} & \ldots & R_{qm} & E_{qm}
\end{array}
$$

These are the basic quantities for the product-limit estimation, for the whole sample, and for each group separately. $\tau_1 < \tau_2 < \ldots < \tau_q$ are the points in time where at least one episode contained in the sample has an event. E_{lg} is the number of episodes contained in group g and having an event at τ_l; R_{lg} is defined as the number of elements in the risk set at τ_l for the episodes contained in group g (i.e., all episodes belonging to group g that have starting times less than τ_l and ending times equal to or greater than τ_l). All together, these quantities are sufficient for a product-limit estimation in each of the m groups.

Given this, the four test statistics can be defined, and they are denoted S_ν ($\nu = 1, \ldots, 4$). Because the calculations only differ in different weights, we give their definitions first. The weights are denoted $W_l^{(\nu)}$, and they are defined for $l = 1, \ldots, q$ by

$$
\begin{aligned}
W_l^{(1)} &= 1 \\
W_l^{(2)} &= R_l \\
W_l^{(3)} &= \sqrt{R_l} \\
W_l^{(4)} &= \prod_{i=1}^{l} \frac{R_i - E_i + 1}{R_i + 1}
\end{aligned}
\tag{3.1}
$$

The next step is to construct for each of the four test statistics one (m)-vector $U^{(\nu)}$ and one (m, m)-matrix $V^{(\nu)}$. The definitions are[14]

$$
U_g^{(\nu)} = \sum_{l=1}^{q} W_l^{(\nu)} \left(E_{lg} - R_{lg} \frac{E_{l0}}{R_{l0}} \right)
$$

$$
V_{g_1 g_2}^{(\nu)} = \sum_{i=1}^{n} W_l^{(\nu)2} \frac{E_{l0}(R_{l0} - E_{l0})}{R_{l0} - 1} \frac{R_{lg_1}}{R_{l0}} \left(\delta_{g_1 g_2} - \frac{R_{lg_2}}{R_{l0}} \right)
$$

Finally, the test statistics are defined by

$$
S_\nu = U^{(\nu)'} V^{(\nu)-1} U^{(\nu)}
\tag{3.2}
$$

All of them follow a χ^2-distribution with $m - 1$ degrees of freedom given the null hypothesis that there are no significant differences. Note that, accordingly, the rank of $V^{(\nu)}$ is only $m - 1$. Therefore in the calculation of (3.2), one can use a generalized inverse or omit the last dimension without loss of generality. Stata follows the latter of these two possibilities.

Unfortunately, there is no uniform convention to name the different test statistics, so we state the names used by Stata and give some remarks about other naming conventions. In the order given by (3.1), we have

1. *Log-Rank.* Other names are *Generalized Savage Test* (Andreß 1985, p. 158; 1992). The same name is used by BMDP, with *Mantel-Cox* added. SAS calculates this test statistic under the name *Logrank*.

2. *Wilcoxon-Breslow-Gehan.* BMDP gives the name *Generalized Wilcoxon (Breslow)*. SAS uses only the label *Wilcoxon*.

3. *Tarone-Ware.* This test statistic was proposed by Tarone and Ware (1977) and is named accordingly. It is also calculated by BMDP, using the label *Tarone-Ware*.

---

[14]δ_{ij} is the Kronecker symbol, which is one if $i = j$ and zero otherwise.

Box 3.3.2 Results of do-file `ehc7.do` (Box 3.3.1)

```
. sts test sex
        failure _d:  des
   analysis time _t:  tf

Log-rank test for equality of survivor functions
         |   Events          Events
sex      |  observed        expected
---------+------------------------------
Men      |      245           290.89
Women    |      213           167.11
---------+------------------------------
Total    |      458           458.00

                                 chi2(1) =     20.60
                                 Pr>chi2 =    0.0000


. sts test sex, wilcoxon
        failure _d:  des
   analysis time _t:  tf

Wilcoxon (Breslow) test for equality of survivor functions
         |   Events          Events        Sum of
sex      |  observed        expected        ranks
---------+----------------------------------------------
Men      |      245           290.89        -11883
Women    |      213           167.11         11883
---------+----------------------------------------------
Total    |      458           458.00             0

                                     chi2(1) =      9.36
                                     Pr>chi2 =     0.0022


. sts test sex, tware
        failure _d:  des
   analysis time _t:  tf

Tarone-Ware test for equality of survivor functions
         |   Events          Events        Sum of
sex      |  observed        expected        ranks
---------+----------------------------------------------
Men      |      245           290.89       -717.3311
Women    |      213           167.11        717.3311
---------+----------------------------------------------
Total    |      458           458.00             0

                                     chi2(1) =     14.33
                                     Pr>chi2 =    0.0002


. sts test sex, peto
        failure _d:  des
   analysis time _t:  tf

Peto-Peto test for equality of survivor functions
         |   Events          Events        Sum of
sex      |  observed        expected        ranks
---------+----------------------------------------------
Men      |      245           290.89       -21.622585
Women    |      213           167.11        21.622585
---------+----------------------------------------------
Total    |      458           458.00             0

                                     chi2(1) =     10.70
                                     Pr>chi2 =    0.0011
```

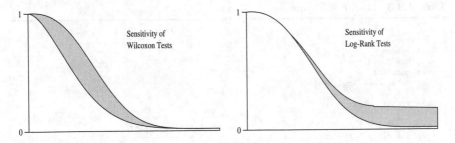

Figure 3.3.2 Regions of sensitivity for Wilcoxon and Log-Rank tests.

4. *Peto-Peto-Prentice.* Finally, there is a test statistic explained by Lawless (1982, p. 423) with reference to R. L. Prentice.

The Stata command to request calculation of test statistics to compare survivor functions is `sts test` as shown in Box 3.3.1. The `sts test` command, by default, performs the log-rank test. To compute the other test statistics you have to select one of the following options: `wilcoxon` to specify the Wilxocon-Breslow-Gehan test, `tware` to conduct the Taron-Ware test, or `peto` to run the Peto-Peto-Prentice test.[15] The results of the do-file `ehc7.do` is shown in Box 3.3.2. All test statistics are based on the null hypothesis that the survivor functions of men and women do not differ. They are χ^2-distributed with $m - 1$ degrees of freedom (in the example we have two groups, men and women: $m = 2$). In our example, all four test statistics are significant. In other words, the null hypothesis that survivor functions of men and women do not differ must be rejected. However, it is easy to see that there is a great difference between the Log-Rank (or Savage) test statistic and the other test statistics. The reason for this is that the Wilcoxon tests stress differences of the survivor functions at the beginning of the duration, whereas the Log-Rank (or Savage) test statistic stresses increasing differences at the end of the process time (see Figure 3.3.2).

Multiple Destination States

We now turn to the case of multiple transitions. Here we have a situation of competing risks conditional on a given origin state. There are different concepts to describe such a situation. The simplest generalization of the single transition case leads to product-limit estimates for pseudosurvivor functions.[16]

---

[15]You may also obtain the test statistic for the Cox test and the Fleming-Harrington test, which are not discussed here. For more details you are referred to the Stata manual.

[16]This generalization is commonly used with the product-limit method. See, for instance, the discussion in Lawless (1982, p. 486f) and Tuma and Hannan (1984, p. 69f).

Box 3.3.3 Do-file `ehc9.do`

```
version 9
set scheme sj
capture log close
set more off
log using ehc9.log, replace

use rrdat1, clear

gen     des = 2                          /*destination state*/
replace des = 1 if (presn/pres -1)>0.2
replace des = 3 if (presn/pres -1)<0.0
replace des = 0 if presn==-1

gen tf = tfin - tstart + 1               /*ending time*/

stset tf, f(des=1) /* upward moves */
sts list if pres <= 65, at(0 2 4 6/8 160 170 326 428)
sts gen surv1 = s

stset tf, f(des=2) /* lateral moves */
sts list, at(0 3 4/7 184 194 209 350 428)
sts gen surv2 = s

stset tf, f(des=3) /* downward moves */
sts list, at(0 2/6 275 293 312 332 428)
sts gen surv3 = s

for any surv1 surv2 surv3 \ any "upward" "lateral" "downward": label var X "Y"

graph twoway line surv1 surv2 surv3 _t, sort ///
ysc(r(0 1)) ylabel(0(0.2)1) xtitle("analysis time")legend(row(1))

log close
```

The method is analogous to the single transition case. One starts with N episodes having the same origin state. Then, for each possible destination state k, one looks at the points in time, $\tau_{k,l}$, where at least one transition to destination state k takes place. There are, say, $l = 1, \ldots, q_k$ such points in time.

Let $E_{k,l}$ denote the number of events at $\tau_{k,l}$, and let $\mathcal{R}_l$ denote the risk set at the same point in time. Note that the risk set does not depend on the destination state, but is defined as in the single transition case as the set of all episodes with a starting time less than $\tau_{k,l}$, and with an ending time equal to or greater than $\tau_{k,l}$. The product-limit estimate of the pseudosurvivor functions may then be formally defined by

$$\tilde{G}_k(t) = \prod_{l:\tau_{k,l}<t} \left(1 - \frac{E_{k,l}}{R_l}\right)$$

Obviously, a calculation of this estimate can use the same algorithm as in the single transition case. In the calculation for a specific destination state,

Box 3.3.4a   Part 1 (upward moves)

```
        failure _d:  des == 1
 analysis time _t:   tf
               Beg.              Survivor    Std.
   Time       Total     Fail     Function    Error      [95% Conf. Int.]
 -----------------------------------------------------------------------
      0          0        0       1.0000        .          .         .
      2        591        1       0.9983      0.0017     0.9880    0.9998
      4        582        2       0.9949      0.0030     0.9842    0.9983
      6        569        3       0.9896      0.0042     0.9771    0.9953
      7        559        1       0.9879      0.0046     0.9747    0.9942
      8        549        1       0.9861      0.0049     0.9723    0.9930
    160         61       74       0.7301      0.0316     0.6625    0.7864
    170         58        1       0.7175      0.0334     0.6459    0.7772
    326         14        1       0.6663      0.0583     0.5382    0.7664
    428          1        0       0.6663      0.0583     0.5382    0.7664
 -----------------------------------------------------------------------
 Note:  Survivor function is calculated over full data and evaluated at
 indicated times; it is not calculated from aggregates shown at left.
```

Box 3.3.4b   Part 2 (lateral moves)

```
        failure _d:  des == 2
 analysis time _t:   tf

               Beg.              Survivor    Std.
   Time       Total     Fail     Function    Error      [95% Conf. Int.]
 -----------------------------------------------------------------------
      0          0        0       1.0000        .          .         .
      3        597        2       0.9966      0.0024     0.9867    0.9992
      4        590        4       0.9899      0.0041     0.9776    0.9954
      5        581        2       0.9865      0.0047     0.9732    0.9932
      6        577        4       0.9796      0.0058     0.9644    0.9884
      7        567        3       0.9745      0.0065     0.9580    0.9845
    184         53      201       0.4181      0.0316     0.3557    0.4791
    194         50        1       0.4097      0.0321     0.3466    0.4717
    209         41        1       0.3997      0.0328     0.3353    0.4632
    350          9        1       0.3553      0.0510     0.2571    0.4546
    428          1        0       0.3553      0.0510     0.2571    0.4546
 -----------------------------------------------------------------------
 Note:  Survivor function is calculated over full data and evaluated at
 indicated times; it is not calculated from aggregates shown at left.
```

one only has to treat *all* episodes that do not end in this destination as if they were censored.

As an illustration, we use (in do-file `ehc9.do` in Box 3.3.3) our example data set, `rrdat1`, and construct a new variable, `des`, to distinguish three different destination states.[17] Variable `des` takes the values 1, 2, and 3 for

---

[17]We defined upward shifts as job mobility leading to an increase in the prestige score of 20 % or more, downward shifts as job mobility connected with a decrease in the prestige score, and lateral shifts as having no effect or experiencing an increase in the prestige score of up to 20 %. It is important to note here that the prestige score in our example data varies between 18 and 78. Those already in good positions with a prestige score greater than 65 are no more at risk to experience an upward career move. These records

Box 3.3.4c Part 3 (downward moves)

```
          failure _d:  des == 3
    analysis time _t:  tf

            Beg.              Survivor     Std.
  Time     Total     Fail    Function     Error      [95% Conf. Int.]
----------------------------------------------------------------------
     0         0        0     1.0000        .              .        .
     2       600        1     0.9983      0.0017       0.9882   0.9998
     3       597        3     0.9933      0.0033       0.9823   0.9975
     4       590        3     0.9883      0.0044       0.9755   0.9944
     5       581        0     0.9883      0.0044       0.9755   0.9944
     6       577        3     0.9831      0.0053       0.9689   0.9909
   275        26       84     0.6468      0.0445       0.5522   0.7263
   293        20        1     0.6144      0.0528       0.5025   0.7084
   312        16        1     0.5760      0.0619       0.4458   0.6862
   332        11        0     0.5760      0.0619       0.4458   0.6862
   428         1        0     0.5760      0.0619       0.4458   0.6862
----------------------------------------------------------------------
 Note:  Survivor function is calculated over full data and evaluated at
 indicated times; it is not calculated from aggregates shown at left.
```

upward, lateral, and downward moves, respectively, or the value 0 for right censored episodes.

Moreover, we change the content of this new variable des to zero for subjects who have left their last job before the interview date because these subjects are no more at risk. In our example, we simply add the line replace des = 0 if presn==-1 because the prestige score of the consecutive job episode, presn, is -1 for both censored observations and all records with ending times before the date of the interview. Executing the do-file ehc9.do, shown in Box 3.3.3, with Stata generates three tables with product-limit estimates for the three destination states at specified times. We can also plot the results. First, you need to generate a new variable containing the estimated survivor function. The syntax is: sts generate newvar = s. Next we use the graph command as shown in Box 3.3.3.

Figure 3.3.3 shows the survivor functions for these three directional moves. One observes that workers move down faster than they move up. After a duration of approximately 120 months (or 10 years) in a job, only about 22 % have experienced an upward move, while about 24 % moved down.[18]

---

are therefore excluded from the analysis.

[18] These results differ from the results in Blossfeld and Rohwer (2002) because we have taken into account here the ceiling effect for upward moves (only people who can experience a 20 % or more increase in the prestige score from job n to job $n + 1$ are at risk to move upward), the bottom effect (only people who are not already at the bottom of the prestige score are at risk to move downward), and we have corrected for all job exits without a job destination (in this case presn is coded -1).

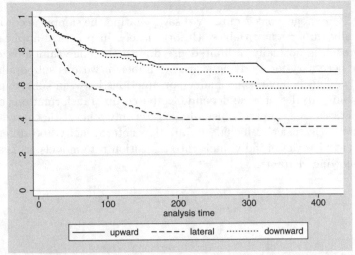

Figure 3.3.3 Plot of survivor functions (product-limit estimation) for upward, lateral, and downward moves. The plot was generated with do-file ehc9.do.

Multiepisode Data (or Repeating Events)

The presentation of the life table method and the product-limit estimation in this book has been limited to the special case of single episodes (with competing risks). For didactical reasons we assumed in our practical examples that the episodes in the data set rrdat1 are statistically independent from each other and that the population is homogeneous. Of course, this is not the case because, in the GLHS, complete job histories of men and women up to the time of the interview are recorded. Thus individuals with a higher number of jobs are represented in the file rrdat1 more often than individuals with a lower number. One solution to this problem is that one only looks at episodes of a certain job number. For example, one could study job behavior in only the first job, second job, and so on. Another solution would be that one compares survivor functions for several—say the first four—jobs (using the variable "serial number of job" as a group variable) and tests whether the survivor functions are equal. If they do not significantly differ, one could pool them and continue as in the single episode case.

Generally, great differences in the number of episodes between observation units suggests that the sample is quite heterogeneous. However, even in the case of single episodes, homogeneous populations are assumed. Neglected (or unobserved) heterogeneity between observation units can lead to apparent time-dependence (see chapter 10) and wrong substantive conclusions. One should therefore be careful and only estimate survivor functions for actually homogeneous groups by disaggregating the sample according to theoretically important variables. Unfortunately, in practical applications, this approach is normally of limited use due to the huge sample size that would be necessary for studying a great number of various subpopulations separately. Thus comparisons of survivor functions between subgroups and the possibility to detect time-dependence based on transformations of survivor functions (see chapter 8) usually possess only a heuristic character. In many cases it is easier to include population heterogeneity and differences in the event histories of individuals into transition rate models, as is shown in the following chapters.

Chapter 4

Exponential Transition Rate Models

In practical research, the analysis of event history data with nonparametric estimation methods is associated with several disadvantages. First, as discussed in the previous chapter, with an increasing number of subgroups normally a point is rapidly reached, at which it is no longer sensible to estimate and compare survivor functions due to the small number of cases left in the various subgroups. Second, even in the case where it is feasible to estimate a rising number of survivor functions for important subgroups, comparisons of these functions quickly become complex and interpretation difficult. Third, in the case of quantitative characteristics (e.g., income, age, etc.), variables must be grouped (e.g., "high income group" vs. "low income group," etc.), with a loss of information, to be able to estimate and compare survivor functions. Finally, multiepisode processes can hardly be analyzed with nonparametric methods. Over the last 20 years, transition rate models have therefore increasingly been used in practical research for the analysis of event history data instead of nonparametric methods.

Transition rate models are a general statistical technique through which one can analyze how the transition rate is dependent on a set of covariates. As discussed in section 1.2, viewing the transition rate as a function of change in covariates is naturally linked with a causal approach to the study of social processes. In general, this modeling approach requires that covariates be measured on an interval or ratio scale, but nominal and ordinal covariates can be incorporated into the models through the use of "dummies" (i.e., by substituting the original variables by a set of 0-1 variables). If permitted by measurement, there is also the interesting possibility of controlling for various factors by introducing their metric versions as proxies in the analysis.[1] Well-known examples are the inclusion of social inequality via metric prestige scores (Treiman 1977; Handl, Mayer, and Müller 1977; Wegener 1985; Shavit and Blossfeld 1993) or the approximation of qualification levels by the average number of school years necessary to obtain a specific level of educational attainment (Blossfeld 1985; Shavit and Blossfeld 1993). The previous history of the process can also be easily taken into account in transition rate models. For example, in the job duration example, the history of the process might be incorporated through a variable "general la-

---

[1] In this case it is assumed that qualitative states reflect points (or intervals) on an underlying metric scale. If the states are ordered, one might argue that the sequence of states corresponds to segments of an underlying continuous variable.

bor force experience" (measured in number of months worked) or a variable
"number of previously held jobs." The application of these metric versions
of important factors makes it possible to study or control for a great number of effects without significantly increasing the number of parameters to
be estimated in the models. Finally, and most importantly, transition rate
models also permit the analysis of the impact of duration dependence and
the influence of one or more parallel processes by the use of (qualitative
and/or quantitative) time-dependent covariates.

In this chapter, we discuss the application of the basic exponential model.
We start by describing the characteristics of the exponential transition rate
model and its estimation using the maximum likelihood method. Then we
estimate exponential models without covariates and with time-constant covariates and give detailed interpretations. We also demonstrate how to deal
with multiple destination states and multiple episodes as well as the application of equality constraints. Extensions of the basic exponential model are
discussed in the next two chapters.

4.1   The Basic Exponential Model

The exponential model is the most simple transition rate model. It assumes
that the duration variable T can be described by an exponential distribution
with density, survivor, and transition rate function given, respectively, by

$$
\begin{aligned}
f(t) &= a \exp(-at) \qquad a > 0 \\
G(t) &= \exp(-at) \\
r(t) &= a
\end{aligned}
$$

A general definition of the model, for transitions to destination state k,
always assuming a given origin state, can be written as

$$
r_k(t) \equiv r_k = \exp\left(\alpha_{k_0} + A_{k_1}\,\alpha_{k_1} + \ldots\right) = \exp\left(A_k\,\alpha_k\right)
$$

r_k is the time-constant transition rate to destination state k. The exit rate
(i.e., the rate of leaving the origin state for any one of the possible destination states) is

$$
r = \sum_{k \in \mathcal{D}} r_k
$$

with $\mathcal{D}$ denoting the set of all possible destination states. The survivor
function for the duration in the origin state can easily be formulated with
the help of this exit rate:

$$
G(t) = \exp\left(-\int_0^t r\,\mathrm{d}\tau\right) = \exp\left(-rt\right)
$$

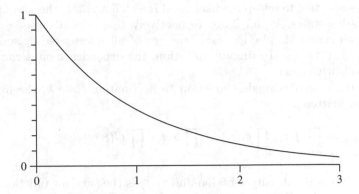

Figure 4.1.1 Survivor function of the standard ($r = 1$) exponential distribution.

The exponential model assumes that the transition rate $r_k(t)$ to destination state k can vary with different constellations of covariates but is time-constant: $r_k(t) = r_k$. In other words, it is assumed that the process is not time-dependent. The relationship between the transition rate and the (row) vector of covariates A_k is specified as log-linear to make sure that estimates of the transition rate cannot become negative.[2] The (column) vector of unknown parameters α_k and the vector of observed covariates A_k are specific for each destination state k. The vector of parameters also includes a constant term, α_{k_0}, which can be estimated even if no covariates are included in the model. The covariates in the vector A_k are assumed to be measured at the beginning of each episode and to be time-constant.

Figure 4.1.1 shows the density and survivor function of a standard exponential distribution where the transition rate is $r = 1$. In this case, both functions are identical. In general, the density function is the survivor function multiplied by the transition rate (see section 1.2). By definition, the distribution is only defined on a nonnegative time axis.

4.1.1 Maximum Likelihood Estimation

The exponential model, like all parametric transition rate models,[3] is estimated using the maximum likelihood method. To explain the general setup of the likelihood for parametric transition rate models, we proceed in two steps: first we consider the case of a single transition, then situations with two or more destination states.

---

[2]We generally adopt the convention of writing covariates as row vectors and the associated coefficients as column vectors.

[3]See chapters 5, 6, and 7.

The notation to set up the likelihood is as follows. $\mathcal{D}$ is the set of possible destination states. $\mathcal{N}$ and $\mathcal{Z}$ are, respectively, the set of all episodes and the set of all censored episodes. $\mathcal{E}_k$ is the set of all uncensored episodes with destination state k. To simplify notation, the dependence on parameters is not explicitly shown.

In the case of a single transition to destination state k, the likelihood may be written as

$$\mathcal{L}_k = \prod_{i \in \mathcal{E}_k} f(t_i) \prod_{i \in \mathcal{Z}} G(t_i) = \prod_{i \in \mathcal{E}_k} r(t_i) \prod_{i \in \mathcal{N}} G(t_i)$$

where $f(t)$ is the density function and $G(t)$ is the survivor function for the single transition. The contribution to the likelihood of an episode with an event at t_i is given by the density function, evaluated at the ending time t_i and with appropriate covariate values. The contribution of a censored episode is given by the survivor function evaluated at the censored ending time t_i, but possibly depends on covariates changing their values during the episode. Remember that, at the moment, we assume that all episodes have the starting time zero. The likelihood can be expressed, then, by using only the transition rate and the survivor function.

The next step is to look at the case with two or more destination states; the destination state space is $\mathcal{D}$. The likelihood may then be written as

$$\mathcal{L} = \prod_{k \in \mathcal{D}} \prod_{i \in \mathcal{E}_k} \tilde{f}_k(t_i) \prod_{i \in \mathcal{Z}} G(t_i)$$

The contribution of an episode with an event at t_i is again given by the density function but is now transition-specific, according to the underlying model. It is, in fact, a subdensity function, $\tilde{f}_k(t)$, with the interpretation that $\tilde{f}_k(t)\,dt$ is the probability of leaving the origin state for the destination state k in a small time interval at t. The contribution to the likelihood of a right-censored episode is the value of the survivor function at t_i, denoted by $G(t_i)$, that is, the probability that the episode has no event until t_i.

It is now possible to factor the likelihood in a product of transition-specific terms. First, the likelihood may be rewritten as

$$\mathcal{L} = \prod_{k \in \mathcal{D}} \prod_{i \in \mathcal{E}_k} r_k(t_i) \prod_{i \in \mathcal{N}} G(t_i)$$

This can be rewritten by using so-called pseudosurvivor functions, defined by

$$\tilde{G}_k(t) = \exp\left(-\int_0^t r_k(\tau)\,d\tau\right)$$

Using this definition, the survivor function $G(t)$ can be written as a product of pseudosurvivor functions:

$$G(t) = \prod_{k \in \mathcal{D}} \tilde{G}_k(t)$$

Inserting this, the likelihood becomes

$$\mathcal{L} = \prod_{k \in \mathcal{D}} \prod_{i \in \mathcal{E}_k} r_k(t_i) \prod_{k \in \mathcal{D}} \prod_{i \in \mathcal{N}} \tilde{G}_k(t_i)$$

or, with terms rearranged:

$$\mathcal{L} = \prod_{k \in \mathcal{D}} \left\{ \prod_{i \in \mathcal{E}_k} r_k(t_i) \prod_{i \in \mathcal{N}} \tilde{G}_k(t_i) \right\}$$

All models described in this book are estimated using the logarithm of this likelihood, that is

$$\ell = \sum_{k \in \mathcal{D}} \sum_{i \in \mathcal{E}_k} \log \{ r_k(t_i) \} + \sum_{i \in \mathcal{N}} \log \left\{ \tilde{G}_k(t_i) \right\} \tag{4.1}$$

The fact that the total likelihood can be expressed as a product of transition-specific factors implies that, in the case of several transitions, a model for each transition can be estimated separately. The estimation for a transition to destination state k is done using all episodes starting in the given origin state; the episodes ending in destination state k are regarded as having an event, and *all other* episodes are included as censored.

Moreover, the possibility of factoring the total likelihood offers an easy way to estimate models with different specifications of transition rates for different transitions. A different model can be assumed for each transition, and then each of these models can be estimated separately.

All parametric transition rate models offered by Stata are estimated by maximizing the log likelihood (4.1) separately for destination states $k \in \mathcal{D}$, which must be specified by the user. Note, however, that log likelihoods are defined only up to an arbitrary additive constant; values may therefore differ between different computer programs.[4]

4.1.2 Models without Covariates

We begin with a simple exponential model and then gradually introduce complexity. To illustrate the interpretation of the basic exponential model, we first estimate a model without any covariates (i.e., we only analyze the

---

[4]The log-likelihood value reported by Stata is the unmodified value ℓ plus $\Sigma_{i \in \mathcal{E}_k} \log(t_i)$.

Box 4.1.1 Do-file `ehd1.do` (exponential model without covariates)

```
version 9
capture log close
set more off
log using ehd1.log, replace

use rrdat1, clear

gen des = tfin ~= ti        /*destination state*/
gen tf  = tfin - tstart + 1 /*ending time*/

stset tf, failure(des)      /*define single episode data*/

streg, dist(e) nohr         /*fit parametric survival model*/

log close
```

average job change behavior of individuals). For didactic purposes we further
assume that the episodes in the data file **rrdat1** are independent of each
other and that there is only one origin state ("being in a job") and one
destination state ("having left the job"). Thus the exponential model to be
estimated is

$$r(t) \equiv r = \exp(\alpha_0)$$

Box 4.1.1 shows how to estimate this exponential model with Stata. Most
of the do-file **ehd1.do** is again identical to previously used do-files and deals
with loading the data file (**rrdat1.dta**) and defining variables as well as
episode data. In addition, we use the command

```
streg, distribution(exponential) nohr
```

to request the estimation of an exponential transition rate model. The option
`distribution(exponential)` specifies the exponential model to be fitted.
By default, hazard ratios are reported but one may also ask Stata to display
coefficients by typing **nohr**.

The result of **ehd1.do** is shown in Box 4.1.2. The value of the log likelihood function is -937.9681,[5] and the estimated coefficient is -4.4891. The
estimated average rate of job exit is therefore

$$r = \exp(-4.4891) = 0.0112.$$

You can calculate this rate directly within Stata using the **display** com-

---

[5] In this example, $\Sigma_{i \in \mathcal{E}_k} \log(t_i) = 1576.0520$, the unmodified log likelihood, is therefore
$-937.9681 - 1576.0520 = -2514.0201$.

Box 4.1.2 Results of using do-file ehd1.do (Box 4.1.1)

```
            failure _d:  des
     analysis time _t:  tf

Iteration 0:   log likelihood =  -937.9681
Iteration 1:   log likelihood =  -937.9681

Exponential regression -- log relative-hazard form

No. of subjects =           600   Number of obs    =        600
No. of failures =           458
Time at risk    =         40782
                                  LR chi2(0)       =       0.00
Log likelihood  =     -937.9681   Prob > chi2      =          .

------------------------------------------------------------------
   _t |     Coef.   Std. Err.      z    P>|z|    [95% Conf. Interval]
------+-----------------------------------------------------------
_cons |  -4.489127   .0467269  -96.07   0.000    -4.58071   -4.397544
------------------------------------------------------------------
```

mand. Type: `display exp(_b[_cons])`.[6] Alternatively, you may also want
to use the postestimation command `predict`: `predict hazard, hazard`.
To derive the estimated survivor function, type `predict surv, surv`.

Because for exponentially distributed durations the number of events N
within a specified time interval is characterized by a Poisson distribution
with an expected value of

$$E(N) = rt = 0.0112 \cdot t$$

we expect an annual average number of job exits of $0.0112 \cdot 12 \approx 0.13$.

An estimate of the average duration in a job may be obtained in the
exponential model via the relationship (see Blossfeld, Hamerle, and Mayer
1989)

$$E(T) = \frac{1}{r} = \frac{1}{0.0112} \approx 89 \text{ months}$$

This means that on the average about 7.5 years pass before individuals
exit their jobs. If you use `predict` after `streg` and specify the option `mean
time`, the predicted mean survival time is calculated within Stata. For our
example, type: `predict meantime, mean time`.

---

[6]After `streg` all coefficients are stored in a matrix called `e(b)`. You can access the
values contained in this matrix for further calculations. With `_b[varname]` you refer to
the coefficient for a specific variable; with `_b[_cons]` you turn to the constant of the
model.

Based on the survivor function

$$G(t) = \exp(-rt)$$

one can get an estimate of the median duration M, defined by $G(M) = 0.5$. Inserting the estimated rate

$$G(\hat{M}) = \exp(-0.0112\,\hat{M}) = 0.5$$

our estimate is $\hat{M} \approx 62$ months. Again you can use Stata to calculate the median survival time: `predict mediantime, median time`. Because the exponential distribution is skewed to the right (see Figure 4.1.1), the median is smaller than the mean of the job duration. In general, for the exponential model, the median (M) is about 69.3 % of the mean $(\mathrm{E}(T))$:

$$0.5 = \exp\left(-\frac{1}{\mathrm{E}(T)}\,M\right)$$

The probability that an individual is still employed in the same job after ten years is $G(120) = \exp(-0.0112 \cdot 120) = 0.26$, or 26 %, and the probability that he or she has left the job by this time is $1 - G(120) = 1 - 0.26 = 0.74$, or 74 %. If you have used `predict` after `streg` to obtain each observation's predicted survivor probability, you can simply type `tab surv if _t==120` to get $G(120)$.

4.1.3   Time-Constant Covariates

The simple model without covariates treats the data as a sample of homogeneous individual job episodes, meaning that, in estimating such a model, we abstract from all sources of heterogeneity among individuals and their job episodes. Of course, social scientists are normally more interested in finding differences (i.e., in investigating how the transition rate describing the process under study depends on observable characteristics of the individuals and their environment).

To do so, one has to include covariates into the model. The most simple way is to include time-constant covariates. This means that the values of these covariates are fixed *at the beginning* of the episodes under study, that is, they do not change their values over the process time. As noted by Yamaguchi (1991), basically two groups of time-constant covariates can be distinguished: *Ascribed statuses* that are (normally) constant throughout individuals' lives, such as race, gender, or social origin, and *statuses attained prior to* (or at the time of) entry into the process time and that remain constant thereafter.[7] Examples are the highest educational attainment at

---

[7]In the case of multiepisode processes, the status must be attained prior to the *first* entry into the process.

time of marriage or age at marriage in the analysis of divorce from first marriage. It should be noted that very often selection bias exists with regard to such states at entry, and this must be carefully considered in event history models.

A special case of time-constant covariates is *information about the history of the process itself*, evaluated at the beginning of the episodes under study. For instance, in the job duration example, the dependence between successive job episodes might be controlled for by including information about the number of previous jobs (and unemployment episodes) and their durations.[8] To include such information is important from a substantive point of view because life course research has shown that, in the case of repeated events, the past course of the process is a crucial factor in understanding the present. But it is also important from a statistical point of view because model estimation is based on the assumption of conditionally independent episodes (i.e., conditional on the covariates that are accounted for in the model specification).[9]

To estimate a model with time-constant covariates, we use the do-file `ehd2.do`, a small modification of `ehd1.do`. The modifications are shown in Box 4.1.3. We define the additional covariates required and then include these covariates into the model specification.

First, to include an individual's highest educational attainment at the beginning of each job, we use `edu` as a metric proxy variable. This variable is already contained in our data file `rrdat1` and measures the average number of school years necessary to obtain a certain educational attainment level in Germany. Second, to distinguish between the three birth cohorts, two dummy variables, `coho2` and `coho3`, are defined in the following way (using `coho1` as the reference group):

	coho2	coho3
Cohort 1929-31	0	0
Cohort 1939-41	1	0
Cohort 1949-51	0	1

Third, a variable `lfx` is constructed to measure, approximately, "general labor force experience" at the beginning of each job episode. This variable

---

[8]Heckman and Borjas (1980) called the effect of the number of previous occupancy of labor force states (e.g., jobs) "occurrence dependence" and the effect of the durations in previous states (e.g., general labor force experience) "lagged duration dependence."

[9]Maximum likelihood estimation assumes independent episodes. The better the dependencies between the episodes are controlled for in the case of repeated events, the less biased are the estimated parameters. However, in practical research it is very difficult to achieve this goal completely. Therefore it is always a source of possible misspecification; see chapter 10.

Box 4.1.3 Do-file `ehd2.do` (exponential model with covariates)

```
version 9
capture log close
set more off
log using ehd2.log, replace

use rrdat1, clear

gen des = tfin ~= ti              /*destination state*/
gen tf  = tfin - tstart + 1       /*ending time*/

gen coho2 = tb >= 468 & tb <= 504 /*cohort 2*/
gen coho3 = tb > =588 & tb <= 624 /*cohort 3*/
gen lfx   = tstart - te           /*labor force experience*/
gen pnoj  = noj - 1               /*previous number of jobs*/

stset tf, failure(des)            /*define single episode data*/

streg edu coho2 coho3 lfx pnoj pres, dist(e) nohr
                                  /*fit parametric survival model*/

display 2*(e(ll)-e(ll_0))    /*likelihood ratio test*/

* percentage change in the rate, given that only one covariate
* changes its value

display (exp(_b[edu])-1)*100      /*education*/
display (exp(_b[coho2])-1)*100    /*cohort 2*/
display (exp(_b[coho3])-1)*100    /*cohort 3*/
display (exp(_b[lfx])-1)*100      /*labor force experience*/
display (exp(_b[pres])^10-1)*100 /*prestige scale (increase by 10 units)*/

* simultaneous change in covariates: change in prestige score and lfx
display (exp(_b[pres])^10*exp(_b[lfx])^12-1)*100

* selected subgroups (edu==13,coho2==0,coho3==0,lfx==0,pnoj==0,pres==60)
display exp(_b[_cons]+_b[edu]*13+_b[pres]*60)    /*rate*/
display 1/exp(_b[_cons]+_b[edu]*13+_b[pres]*60) /*average job duration*/

log close
```

is computed as the difference, in months, between the beginning of the respective job episode (`tstart`) and the time of first entry into the labor force (`te`).[10] Fourth, we define a variable `pnoj` to capture information about

---

[10]Of course, this variable is only a very rough proxy, because it assumes that individuals have been continuously employed. In a "real" job-exit analysis, one would construct the variable "general labor force experience" for each individual on the basis of the number of months he or she had actually worked.

Box 4.1.4 Results of using do-file `ehd2.do` (Box 4.1.3)

```
             failure _d:  des
       analysis time _t:  tf

Iteration 0:   log likelihood = -937.9681
Iteration 1:   log likelihood = -892.94482
Iteration 2:   log likelihood = -889.94245
Iteration 3:   log likelihood = -889.93527
Iteration 4:   log likelihood = -889.93527


Exponential regression -- log relative-hazard form

No. of subjects =          600      Number of obs    =         600
No. of failures =          458
Time at risk    =        40782
                                    LR chi2(6)       =       96.07
Log likelihood  =   -889.93527      Prob > chi2      =      0.0000

-----------------------------------------------------------------------
     _t |      Coef.   Std. Err.       z    P>|z|    [95% Conf. Interval]
--------+--------------------------------------------------------------
    edu |   .0773013   .0247033     3.13   0.002     .0288837    .125719
  coho2 |   .6080358   .1135509     5.35   0.000     .3854802   .8305914
  coho3 |   .6107997    .118542     5.15   0.000     .3784617   .8431377
    lfx |  -.0031793   .0009378    -3.39   0.001    -.0050174  -.0013412
   pnoj |   .0596384   .0441525     1.35   0.177    -.026899   .1461758
   pres |  -.0280065   .0055303    -5.06   0.000    -.0388457  -.0171672
  _cons |  -4.489445   .2795003   -16.06   0.000    -5.037255  -3.941634
-----------------------------------------------------------------------
```

the number of previously held jobs. The value of this covariate is simply the serial number of the current job minus one. Finally, we use a variable `pres` to capture the prestige score of the current job. This information is already contained in our data file.

Model specification is done again with the `streg` command. In order to include covariates, we simply add the variable names to the command line:

```
streg edu coho2 coho3 lfx pnoj pres, dist(e) nohr
```

Using a log-linear link function between the transition rate and the vector of explaining time-constant covariates, the model that will be estimated is

$$r(t) \equiv r = \exp(A\alpha)$$

where A is the row vector of covariates and α is a corresponding column vector of coefficients.

Estimation results for this model are shown in Box 4.1.4. First of all, we get a value of the log likelihood function: -889.93527. Thus one can compare this model with the exponential model without covariates (in Box 4.1.2) using a likelihood ratio test. Under the null hypothesis that the additionally included covariates do not significantly improve the model fit, the likelihood ratio test statistic (LR) follows approximately a χ^2-distribution with m degrees of freedom where m is the number of additionally included covariates. These test statistics can be calculated as two times the difference of the log likelihoods:

$$LR = 2 \; (\text{LogLik(present model)} - \text{LogLik(reference model)})$$

For our example, the test statistic is

$$LR = 2 \, ((-889.9353) - (-937.9681)) = 2 \cdot 48.0328 = 96.07.$$

with six degrees of freedom (the six additionally included covariates). In Stata, the `display` command can be used to show the test statistic. The command `streg` saves the value of the log likelihood function of the present model and the constant-only model in a matrix called `e(b)`.[11] You can now access the values contained in this matrix. The computation of the test statistic would then look like this:

```
display 2*(e(ll)-e(ll_0))
```

Alternatively, you may also use the command `lrtest`, a postestimation tool for `streg`. Before you can issue this command, both the present model and the reference model must be estimated and the results stored using the command `estimates store`. For our example you simply type:

```
streg, dist(e) nohr
estimates store ll_0
streg edu coho2 coho3 lfx pnoj pres, dist(e) nohr
lrtest ll_0
```

Given a significance level of 0.05, we conclude that the null hypothesis should be rejected. At least one of the included covariates significantly improves the model fit.

In addition, the maximum likelihood estimation provides standard errors for the estimated coefficients. These standard errors are useful to assess the precision of the estimates of the model parameters. In particular, one can check whether the estimated coefficients are significantly different from zero. Dividing the estimated coefficients (column `Coef.` in Box 4.1.4) by the estimated standard error (column `Std. Err.`) produces a test statistic

---

[11] Stata saves various other results in this matrix. If you type `ereturn list` you will get the names and contents of all saved results.

(column z) approximately normally distributed if the model is correct and the sample is large. Assuming this, one can apply a formal test (see Blossfeld, Hamerle, and Mayer 1989). If one uses, for instance, a 0.05 significance level and a two-sided test, then a covariate A_j has a significant (nonzero) effect, if the following relationship is satisfied:[12]

$$\left| \frac{\hat{\alpha}_j}{\hat{\sigma}(\hat{\alpha}_j)} \right| > 1.96$$

$\hat{\alpha}_j$ is the estimated coefficient for covariate A_j, and $\hat{\sigma}_j$ is the associated standard error. In Box 4.1.4 all covariates, with the exception of pnoj ("previous number of jobs"), have a significant effect.

The effect of a covariate on the transition rate reflects both its impact on the speed of the dependent process and its impact on the proportion of people who have experienced an event after a certain time (see Bernardi 2001). The effect of a covariate can easily be interpreted when one examines the percentage change in the rate, given that only one covariate changes its value. The formula (see Blossfeld, Hamerle, and Mayer 1989) is

$$\Delta \hat{r} = (\exp(\hat{\alpha}_j)^{\Delta A_j} - 1) \cdot 100\,\%$$

ΔA_j is the change in variable A_j. $\Delta \hat{r}$ is the resulting percentage change in the estimated rate. $\exp(\alpha_j)$, the antilogarithm of the coefficient α_j, is referred to in the literature as the "alpha effect" (see Tuma and Hannan 1984). It takes the value 1 when the covariate has no effect ($\alpha_j = 0$); it is smaller than 1 if $\alpha_j < 0$ and greater than 1 if $\alpha_j > 0$. If the value of the covariate is increased by just one unit, then the rate changes by

$$\Delta \hat{r} = (\exp(\hat{\alpha}_j) - 1) \cdot 100\,\%$$

In Box 4.1.4, the coefficient of the covariate edu ("educational attainment level") has a positive sign. Therefore each additional school year increases

---

[12]It is important to distinguish statistical from substantive significance in empirical analysis. Given a fixed significance level, statistical significance is dependent on the ratio of effect size (column Coef.) and estimated standard error (column Std. Err.) and the standard error is inversely related to the number of events. Thus if the number of events is increasing in a sample, then the standard error is declining and the test statistic (column z) is increasing, with the consequence that these tests have an increasing likelihood to produce a statistically significant finding (given a fixed significance level). In other words, statistical significance is strongly dependent on the number of events, while substantive significance (an evaluation based on a substantive theory) is not. Therefore often some variables may be substantively significant, but given a small sample size, the results of the test might not be statistically significant; and in many cases some variables may be without any substantive significance (meaning), but given a big sample size, the test produces a statistically significant finding. Taken together, these arguments point against a mechanical use of statistical tests, stress the importance of substantive theory in the interpretation of test results, and underline that interpretations are often quite ambiguous.

the job-exit rate by about $\exp(0.0773) - 1) \cdot 100\% = 8\%$. This means that better educated workers are more mobile than less educated ones. As shown in do-file `ehd2.do` in Box 4.1.3, you can calculate this amount directly within Stata using the `display` command. However, this estimate is hard to interpret in substantive terms because theory suggests that educational attainment should have a positive effect on upward moves and a negative effect on downward moves, while the effects of educational attainment on lateral moves are theoretically still quite open (Blossfeld and Mayer 1988; Blossfeld 1989). Thus a reasonable substantive interpretation of the effect of variable `edu` can only be achieved if we estimate models with directional moves (see next section).

Each younger birth cohort is more mobile. Compared to the reference group (individuals born 1929-31), the job-exit rate of people born 1939-41 (`coho2`) is about 83.7% higher: $(\exp(0.6080) - 1) \cdot 100\%$, and of the people born in 1949-51 (`coho3`), about 84.2% higher: $(\exp(0.6108) - 1) \cdot 100\%$.[13]

The effect of labor force experience (`lfx`) is negative. Thus in our example, each additional year of labor force experience decreases the job-exit rate by 3.2%. This is in accordance with the human capital theory, which predicts that with increasing general labor force experience, additional investments into human capital decline, and as a consequence, job-exits decrease.[14]

Also, the number of previously held jobs (`pnoj`) has a positive effect, but this variable is not statistically significant. Therefore in our example, this part of the job history has no effect on the job-exit rate.

Finally, the prestige score of the current job (`pres`) influences the job-exit rate negatively. An increase by 10 units on the magnitude prestige scale (Wegener 1985) decreases the job-exit rate by about 24%.[15]

It is important to note that the effects of the covariates are not independent of each other. They are related *multiplicatively*. For example, a simultaneous change in prestige by 10 units and in labor force experience by one year decreases the job-exit rate by 27.3%:

$$\left(\exp(-0.0280)^{10} \cdot \exp(-0.0032)^{12} - 1 \right) \cdot 100\% \approx -27.3\%$$

For selected subgroups one can also predict the average job duration, the

---

[13] At that point in our analysis, it is unclear whether younger birth cohorts have indeed a higher mobility rate, e.g., because of modernization processes, or whether this is only a methodological artefact (younger birth cohorts are still in a life phase with higher mobility rates compared to the cohort 1929-31).

[14] Also, in this case, the effect on directional moves can be better interpreted in substantive terms (see next section).

[15] Again, in substantive terms this result is more easily interpreted for directional moves. For example, vacancy competition theory (Sørensen 1977, 1979) argues that upward moves are increasingly less likely the higher the job is located in the pyramid of inequality (see next section).

median of the duration, the average number of exits in a given duration interval, and the probability of remaining in the same job up to a given point in time. For example, for an individual with Abitur (edu = 13) of the birth cohort 1929-31 (coho2 = 0 and coho3 = 0), just entering the labor market (lfx = 0 and pnoj = 0) into a job with prestige level pres = 60 on the Wegener scale, we can calculate the following rate:

$$r = \exp(-4.4894 + 0.0773 \cdot 13 - 0.028 \cdot 60) \approx 0.0057$$

Consequently, we expect an average job duration of about 175 months, or 15 years ($1/0.0057 \approx 175$), for individuals with these characteristics. Analogously, the median job duration for this group of individuals can be calculated as about 69.3 % of the mean duration, which is about 10 years ($175 \cdot 0.693 \approx 121$). Finally, the probability that individuals with the assumed characteristics are still employed in the same job after 8 years is about 58 %. This is calculated by using the survivor function $G(96) = \exp(-0.0057 \cdot 96) \approx 0.58$. Similar predictions can be made for other subgroups too, so that one obtains a quite differentiated picture of job-exit behavior in the sample.

4.2 Models with Multiple Destinations

So far we have only considered job-exits. More important are situations where, from a given origin state, individuals can move to any one of a set of destination states ("competing risks"). Defining an appropriate state space is a matter of substantive consideration. For example, as shown in the previous section, it is very hard to interpret the effect of educational attainment on the rate of job-exit because theory predicts contradictory effects of educational attainment on upward and downward moves. Furthermore, the effect of educational attainment on lateral moves is theoretically still quite open. Thus in the causal analysis of transitions, the specification of the state space might turn out to be a serious source of misspecification (see chapter 10). Origin and destination states must be carefully selected, and the effects of covariates must be related to the specific transitions in a theoretically meaningful way.

In this section, we extend the exponential model with time-constant covariates to study transitions from the origin state "being in a job" to a better job (upward exit), a worse job (downward exit), and to a job of about the same reward level (lateral exit). In other words, we are estimating a model with one origin state and three destination states or competing risks. Part of the do-file (ehd3.do) is shown in Box 4.2.1. The first part, specifying the data file rrdat1 and providing definitions of the basic variables, is identical with the do-file in Box 4.1.1. In addition, we specify, first, that we now have three destination states. They are 1 ("better job"), 2 ("same job level"),

Box 4.2.1 Do-file ehd3.do

```
version 9
capture log close
set more off
log using ehd3.log, replace

use rrdat1, clear

gen     des = 2                           /*lateral moves*/
replace des = 1 if (presn/pres -1)>0.2    /*upward moves*/
replace des = 3 if (presn/pres -1)<0.0    /*downward moves*/
replace des = 0 if presn==-1

gen tf    = tfin - tstart + 1   /*ending time*/

gen coho2 = tb >= 468 & tb <= 504   /*cohort 2*/
gen coho3 = tb >= 588 & tb <= 624   /*cohort 3*/
gen lfx   = tstart - te             /*labor force experience*/
gen pnoj  = noj - 1                 /*previous number of jobs*/

*define single episode data and fit parametric survival model

stset tf, fail(des==1)   /*upward*/
streg edu coho2 coho3 lfx pnoj pres if pres <= 65, dist(e) nohr

stset tf, fail(des==2)   /*lateral*/
streg edu coho2 coho3 lfx pnoj pres, dist(e) nohr

stset tf, fail(des==3)   /*downward*/
streg edu coho2 coho3 lfx pnoj pres, dist(e) nohr

log close
```

and 3 ("worse job").[16] Second, as in Box 4.1.3, we define a set of covariates to be used in the model specification. Finally, an exponential model is selected with the **streg, dist(e)** command, and the covariates to be included in the model are specified. One should note that we estimate a separate model for each of the possible transitions. In our example, we have three possible transitions: (0-1), (0-2), and (0-3), so we use the **stset** and **streg** commands three times to declare our data to be event history data and estimate an exponential model.[17]

---

[16]This is in accordance with section 3.3 (see Box 3.3.3), where we defined upward exits as job mobility leading to an increase in the prestige score of 20 % or more, downward exits as job mobility connected with a decrease in the prestige score, and lateral exits as having no change in the prestige score or experiencing an increase in the prestige score of up to 20 %.

[17]In this example, the same list of covariates is linked to each of the three transitions. In general, it would be possible to use different sets of covariates for each transition.

Using do-file `ehd3.do`, Stata's output is shown in Box 4.2.2.[18] The tables report estimates for the rates of upward (`des = 1`), lateral (`des = 2`), and downward moves (`des = 3`). The results for lateral moves are presented but not interpreted.

The *positive effect of education* (`edu`) *on upward moves* is in accordance with status attainment theory (e.g., Blau and Duncan 1967; Sewell and Hauser 1975; Goldthorpe 1987; Erikson and Goldthorpe 1991), human capital theory (Becker 1975), and vacancy competition theory (Sørensen 1979). However, the three theories offer different explanations.[19] Status attainment theory claims that increases in educational attainment always lead to better job opportunities and will have a positive effect on upward moves. Under the condition of an imperfect labor market, human capital theory predicts that upward exits are more likely if employees are underrewarded; and the likelihood of being underrewarded increases with increasing personal resources (Tuma 1985). Education will therefore have a positive effect on upward moves. Finally, vacancy competition theory explains this positive effect of education in terms of the ability of higher educated persons to get better places in the labor queue and to therefore be in a better position to take advantage of opportunities.

The *positive effects of the cohort dummy variables* for the birth cohorts 1939-49 (`coho2`) and 1949-51 (`coho3`) on all directional moves show that each younger cohort is more mobile, independently of whether we focus on upward, downward, or lateral job-exits. However, one must be careful in interpreting this result in substantive terms. A methodological reason for the cohort effects may be that the younger cohorts with shorter job histories simply remember job shifts better than the older ones with longer job histories. Finally, we also know that job mobility decreases with age. Thus people with longer histories should have a higher average job duration. We therefore only consider the cohort variables as technical control variables for the different lengths of job histories in the GLHS.

The *negative effect of prestige on upward moves* can also be interpreted in light of two different theories. For Sørensen, opportunities for even better jobs decline as the level of attainment (measured here in terms of prestige scores) already achieved increases. In this theoretical model, employees have

---

[18]These results differ from the results in Blossfeld and Rohwer (2002) because we have taken into account here the ceiling effect for upward moves (only people who can experience a 20 % or more increase in the prestige score from job n to job $n + 1$ are at risk to move upward), the bottom effect (only people who are not already at the bottom of the prestige score are at risk to move downward), and we have corrected for all job-exits without a job destination (in this case `presn` is coded -1).

[19]This is a good example of the well-known situation in the social sciences where the causal effect can be explained by different theories. Comparing the relative merits of these competing theories is very difficult, simply because it is difficult to find a "crucial test" (see Lieberson 1985).

Box 4.2.2 Results of using do-file `ehd3.do` (Box 4.2.1)

```
          failure _d:  des == 1
     analysis time _t:  tf

Exponential regression -- log relative-hazard form
No. of subjects =        591          Number of obs  =    591
No. of failures =         84
Time at risk    =      40161
                                      LR chi2(6)     = 131.39
Log likelihood  =   -253.68509        Prob > chi2    = 0.0000


------------------------------------------------------------------------
    _t |     Coef.    Std. Err.      z    P>|z|     [95% Conf. Interval]
-------+----------------------------------------------------------------
   edu |   .3020663    .0429622     7.03   0.000     .2178619    .3862708
 coho2 |   .6366232    .2713856     2.35   0.019     .1047172    1.168529
 coho3 |   .7340517    .2766077     2.65   0.008     .1919105    1.276193
   lfx |  -.0022632    .0020781    -1.09   0.276    -.0063363    .0018098
  pnoj |   .1734636    .1003787     1.73   0.084    -.0232751    .3702022
  pres |   -.143771    .0142008   -10.12   0.000     -.171604    -.115938
 _cons |  -5.116249    .6197422    -8.26   0.000    -6.330922   -3.901577

          failure _d:  des == 2
     analysis time _t:  tf

Exponential regression -- log relative-hazard form
No. of subjects =        600          Number of obs  =    600
No. of failures =        219
Time at risk    =      40782
                                      LR chi2(6)     =  39.89
Log likelihood  =    -595.272         Prob > chi2    = 0.0000


------------------------------------------------------------------------
    _t |     Coef.    Std. Err.      z    P>|z|     [95% Conf. Interval]
-------+----------------------------------------------------------------
   edu |   .0033448     .037983     0.09   0.930    -.0711004     .07779
 coho2 |   .6722249    .1642522     4.09   0.000     .3502966    .9941533
 coho3 |   .6843349    .1732453     3.95   0.000     .3447803    1.023889
   lfx |   -.003085    .0013664    -2.26   0.024     -.005763    -.000407
  pnoj |   .0322934    .0644585     0.50   0.616     -.094043    .1586298
  pres |   .0081357      .00806     1.01   0.313    -.0076616    .0239329
 _cons |  -5.804317    .4054322   -14.32   0.000    -6.598949   -5.009684

          failure _d:  des == 3
     analysis time _t:  tf

Exponential regression -- log relative-hazard form
No. of subjects =        600          Number of obs  =    600
No. of failures =         96
Time at risk    =      40782
                                      LR chi2(6)     =  17.34
Log likelihood  =   -345.80692        Prob > chi2    = 0.0081


------------------------------------------------------------------------
    _t |     Coef.    Std. Err.      z    P>|z|     [95% Conf. Interval]
-------+----------------------------------------------------------------
   edu |  -.0542781    .0640498    -0.85   0.397    -.1798134    .0712572
 coho2 |   .5946145    .2431647     2.45   0.014     .1180204    1.071209
 coho3 |   .5510851    .2620141     2.10   0.035      .037547    1.064623
   lfx |  -.0040521    .0021377    -1.90   0.058    -.0082419    .0001377
  pnoj |   .0388227    .0990888     0.39   0.695    -.1553878    .2330332
  pres |   .0034328    .0123049     0.28   0.780    -.0206844     .02755
 _cons |  -5.699672    .6715966    -8.49   0.000    -7.015977   -4.383367
```

control over the decision to leave their job. This control over the decision to leave the job is derived from job-specific skills, collective action, and so on. Thus employees will only leave jobs when a better job is available, but the higher the attainment level already achieved, the harder it will be to find an even better job in a given structure of inequality. It should be noted that within the framework of vacancy competition theory, the size of the coefficient of prestige is also a measure of the opportunity structure of a given society: The larger the absolute magnitude of this coefficient, the fewer the opportunities for gains that are available in a society (Sørensen and Blossfeld 1989). A competing explanation is given by human capital theory, which assumes that there are costs of job searches and that there is imperfect information. In this case, upward moves are more likely if employees are underrewarded, and the likelihood of being underrewarded decreases with increasing job rewards. In other words, the higher the prestige score of the origin job, the less upward moves are to be expected (Tuma 1985).

Also in accordance with this modified form of human capital theory (Tuma 1985) is the *negative effect of education on downward moves* (although not significant in our didactical example because of the small number of events). Downward moves should be more likely if employees are overrewarded; and the likelihood of being overrewarded rises with decreasing personal resources, for example, educational attainment. Another reason can be seen in the specific type of labor market organization found in Germany. For example, Blossfeld and Mayer (1988) have shown that labor market segmentation in Germany is much more the result of qualification barriers, and that educational certificates tend to protect workers against downward exits to the secondary labor market (see also Blossfeld, Giannelli, and Mayer 1993).

Even if human capital and vacancy competition theories are able to explain some of the estimated coefficients in Box 4.2.2, there are also results that contradict these theories. Most important, vacancy competition theory regards downward moves as an exception. However, this is not the case. The number of downward moves ($n_{\text{down}} = 96$) is greater than the number of upward moves ($n_{\text{up}} = 84$).[20] Further, according to the vacancy competition model, the effect of time spent in the labor force (or labor force experience) on upward moves should not be significant once education and prestige are controlled for. Otherwise, this variable is no adequate proxy of the discrepancy between resources and current job rewards.[21] An explanation for the

---

[20]These numbers are also a function of the technical definition of upward, downward, and lateral moves. In our example, the number of upward moves stays, however, more or less the same if we lower the threshold from a 20 % increase to a 10 % or even 5 % increase in the prestige score. However, there are good theoretical reasons to classify job moves only as upward moves, if they are connected with a significant step upward (Blossfeld 1986).

[21]Similar problems exist with regard to the effect of labor market experience on downward exits.

negative effect of the covariate "general labor force experience" on upward moves is, however, given by Mincer (1974). He argued that people invest in their resources as long as their expected returns exceed their expected costs. Therefore training is concentrated mainly in the earlier phases of employment, where more time is left to recover training costs. In this way, the job mobility process is time-dependent because time spent in the labor force (or general labor force experience) reduces the likelihood of new training and consequent gains in attainment.

It should also be noted that human capital theory is interesting for sociological mobility research only insofar as an imperfect labor market is assumed. As shown by Tuma (1985), human capital theory only leads to specific hypotheses about mobility if imperfect information and search costs are assumed. Otherwise the labor market would be in equilibrium, and in equilibrium job-exits only occur randomly, because no one can improve his or her present situation.

Comparison of Covariate Effects Across Destinations

In comparing the statistical significance of covariate effects across various destinations in competing risks models, one must be careful, because statistical significance tests of parameters (see section 4.1.3) are normally affected by a varying number of competing events. For example, in Box 4.2.2 these tests are based on 84 upward moves, 219 lateral moves, and 96 downward moves.[22] Given a fixed size of an effect for all directional moves, the results of the significance tests are therefore dependent on the number of events. Thus it is more likely that the statistical test provides a significant result for lateral moves than for downward moves, and it is more likely there than for upward moves.

To demonstrate the impact of the various number of events, we standardize the number of events across the three directional moves. Because the number of upward moves is smallest, we use this number as the baseline and standardize the number of events by drawing probability samples from the input data for lateral and downward job moves (Box 4.2.3).

First, we specify the initial value of the random-number seed to ensure that we obtain at all times the same results: set seed 33948773. Next the command gen r = uniform() generates uniformly distributed pseudorandom numbers on the interval [0,1]. In Box 4.2.3, an episode is randomly selected if a random number is less than or equal to the value 84/219, the number of upward moves divided by the number of lateral moves. Box 4.2.4 shows that this do-file selects 224 episodes with 84 events. In the next step,

---

[22]These results differ from the results in Blossfeld and Rohwer (2002), because we have taken into account here the ceiling and bottom effects, and we have corrected for all job-exits without a job destination.

Box 4.2.3 Do-file ehd4.do

```
version 9
capture log close
set more off
log using ehd4.log, replace

use rrdat1, clear

gen     des = 2                          /*lateral moves*/

replace des = 1 if (presn/pres -1)>0.2  /*upward moves*/
replace des = 3 if (presn/pres -1)<0.0  /*downward moves*/
replace des = 0 if presn==-1

gen tf     = tfin - tstart + 1    /*ending time*/

gen coho2 = tb >= 468 & tb <= 504  /*cohort 2*/
gen coho3 = tb >= 588 & tb <= 624  /*cohort 3*/
gen lfx     = tstart - te          /*labor force experience*/
gen pnoj   = noj - 1               /*previous number of jobs*/

set seed 339487731 /* specify initial value of the random-number seed */

gen r = uniform()  /* uniformly distributed pseudorandom numbers */
                   /* on the interval [0,1) */

stset tf, fail(des==2)   /*define single episode data*/

streg edu coho2 coho3 lfx pnoj pres if r <=84/219, ///
dist(e) nohr          /*fit parametric survival model: lateral*/

stset tf, fail(des==3)   /*define single episode data*/

streg edu coho2 coho3 lfx pnoj pres if r <=84/96, ///
dist(e) nohr          /*fit parametric survival model: downward*/

log close
```

the estimation of the exponential model is restricted to those observations where the random number is less than or equal to the value 84/96, the number of upward moves divided by the number of downward moves. Box 4.2.5 shows that this procedure selects 533 episodes with 85 events.

The unstandardized and standardized estimation results for upward, lateral, and downward moves are again summarized in Box 4.2.6 to make comparison easier. In each cell of the three tables, Stata reports the coefficient, followed by its standard error. In the case of lateral moves, the effect of the covariate lfx is no longer significant in the standardized estimation. Thus there is a chance that one could come to quite different substantive conclusions if the number of events in the comparisons of effects across various

Box 4.2.4 Results of using do-file `ehd4.do` (lateral moves; Box 4.2.3)

```
 failure _d:  des == 2
  analysis time _t:  tf

Exponential regression -- log relative-hazard form

No. of subjects =          224        Number of obs   =        224
No. of failures =           84
Time at risk    =        16331
                                       LR chi2(6)      =      25.09
Log likelihood  =    -225.3563         Prob > chi2     =     0.0003


------------------------------------------------------------------------
   _t |     Coef.   Std. Err.      z    P>|z|    [95% Conf. Interval]
------+-----------------------------------------------------------------
  edu |   .0659433   .0629674    1.05   0.295   -.0574706    .1893572
coho2 |   1.054293   .2664299    3.96   0.000    .5321003   1.576486
coho3 |   .7635633   .2935898    2.60   0.009    .1881378   1.338989
  lfx |  -.0023364   .0024646   -0.95   0.343   -.0071668    .002494
 pnoj |  -.0498902   .1118115   -0.45   0.655   -.2690367   .1692563
 pres |   .0041175   .0139569    0.30   0.768   -.0232376   .0314726
_cons |  -6.465483   .6487527   -9.97   0.000   -7.737015  -5.193951
------------------------------------------------------------------------
```

transitions is taken into account. As a rule, if one wants to compare the statistical significance of effects of covariates across competing transitions, one should always be aware that different event numbers might have an effect on statistical tests.

Continuous Time, Continuous State Space Models

Our job-exit example with directional moves has the disadvantage that a continuous state space of inequality (measured in terms of prestige levels of jobs) has to be collapsed into a set of ordered destination states ("better job," "job of same level," and "worse job"). Thus for job moves, the exact size of the increases in prestige scores could not be evaluated. To solve this problem, Petersen (1988a) suggested a method for analyzing what he calls continuous time, continuous state space failure time processes. In these processes, the dependent variable is continuous but stays constant for finite periods of time in contrast to diffusion processes. He shows that the likelihood for this type of process can be written as the product of the transition rate of a change in the state variable $Y(t)$ and the density for the new value of $Y(t)$, given that a change in $Y(t)$ has occurred. For the first term, transition rate models for the analysis of duration data apply, as shown previously. For the second term, transition rate models for the outcomes of continuous dependent variables can be used. It is simple to introduce covariates into

Box 4.2.5 Results of using do-file ehd4.do (downward moves), (Box 4.2.3)

```
        failure _d:  des == 3
  analysis time _t:  tf

Exponential regression -- log relative-hazard form

No. of subjects =          533         Number of obs   =        533
No. of failures =           85
Time at risk    =        35892
                                        LR chi2(6)      =      16.90
Log likelihood  =   -301.81197          Prob > chi2     =     0.0097


----------------------------------------------------------------------
   _t |     Coef.   Std. Err.     z    P>|z|    [95% Conf. Interval]
------+---------------------------------------------------------------
  edu | -.0085059   .0654301   -0.13   0.897   -.1367465    .1197346
 coho2|  .6229421   .2598822    2.40   0.017    .1135824   1.132302
 coho3|  .4685549   .2795808    1.68   0.094   -.0794134   1.016523
  lfx | -.0046318   .0023692   -1.95   0.051   -.0092755    .0000118
 pnoj |  .0336741   .1078372    0.31   0.755   -.1776828    .2450311
 pres | -.0005333   .0127877   -0.04   0.967   -.0255967    .0245301
_cons | -5.99383    .6702314   -8.94   0.000   -7.307459    -4.6802
----------------------------------------------------------------------
```

both model equations. Petersen (1988a) illustrated this method, analyzing
first the rate of upward exits in socioeconomic status and then the new value
of socioeconomic status, given that an upward exit has occurred.

Another methodological solution for the analysis of continuous time,
continuous outcome processes has been suggested by Hannan, Schömann,
and Blossfeld (1990). They analyzed wage trajectories across job histories
of men and women and estimated (1) the wage rate at time of first entry
into the labor market, (2) wage changes when workers changed jobs, and (3)
wage growth within jobs. Especially for estimating the wage growth within
jobs, a stochastic differential equation model was applied.

4.3   Models with Multiple Episodes

As demonstrated in this chapter, transitions to a destination job are modeled
as a function of the time since entry into an origin job in most studies
of social mobility research (e.g., Sørensen and Tuma 1981; Sørensen 1984;
Carroll and Mayer 1986; Tuma 1985; Sørensen and Blossfeld 1989). The
career trajectory of an individual is therefore divided into a series of job
spells (single episodes), each starting with time equal to 0. The process
time is job-specific labor force experience. The effects of causal variables
are mostly regarded as independent of the different job episodes and are

Box 4.2.6 Comparison of standardized and unstandardized estimates

Variable	unstandardized_upward	standardized_upward
edu	.30206634	.30206634
	.04296223	.04296223
coho2	.6366232	.6366232
	.27138561	.27138561
coho3	.73405171	.73405171
	.27660773	.27660773
lfx	-.00226324	-.00226324
	.00207813	.00207813
pnoj	.17346355	.17346355
	.10037868	.10037868
pres	-.14377097	-.14377097
	.01420076	.01420076
_cons	-5.1162495	-5.1162495
	.61974219	.61974219

Variable	unstandardized_lateral	standardized_lateral
edu	.00334481	.06594331
	.03798296	.06296742
coho2	.67222494	1.0542932
	.16425219	.26642988
coho3	.68433485	.76356331
	.17324528	.29358982
lfx	-.00308502	-.00233641
	.00136635	.00246456
pnoj	.03229343	-.0498902
	.06445853	.11181148
pres	.00813567	.0041175
	.00805998	.01395692
_cons	-5.8043167	-6.465483
	.40543215	.6487527

Variable	unstandardized_downward	standardized_downward
edu	-.05427811	-.00850594
	.0640498	.06543006
coho2	.59461447	.62294208
	.24316469	.25988218
coho3	.55108507	.46855489
	.26201405	.27958079
lfx	-.00405212	-.00463183
	.00213768	.00236925
pnoj	.03882273	.03367415
	.09908881	.10783718
pres	.00343279	-.00053329
	.01230494	.01278769
_cons	-5.6996718	-5.9938297
	.67159658	.67023141

legend: b/se

therefore estimated as constant across episodes.[23] Blossfeld and Hamerle (1989b; Hamerle 1989, 1991) called this type of job-exit model *uni-episode analysis with episode-constant coefficients*.[24]

Another way to model job mobility is to regard job transitions as being dependent on the time a person spent in the labor force since entry into the labor market. Process time in this case is the amount of *general labor force experience*.[25] Starting and ending times of the job spells in a person's career are then given as the time since entry into the labor market.[26] The coefficients of covariates may be estimated as constant or as changing across episodes. One can term this type of job-exit analysis *multiepisode models with episode-constant or episode-changing coefficients* (Blossfeld and Hamerle 1989b).

In the case of an exponential model, for which we assume that general labor force experience does not affect job-exit rates, an interesting application of a multiepisode model could be to study how covariate effects change across episodes. Such a model is estimated with do-file ehd7.do, shown in Box 4.3.1.

However, before we begin to describe this do-file, we should make some more general comments. It is important to note here that, compared to American workers, German workers have considerably fewer jobs and change jobs less frequently. The average time in a given job for a man in Germany is about 6 years (Carroll and Mayer 1986), while in the United States it is only 2.2 years (Tuma 1985). The stable nature of job trajectories in Germany implies that a job change is more likely to be substantively meaningful than is a job-exit in the United States. But, conversely, it also means that the distribution of job episodes is clustered more to the left of the mean, with extreme values to the right (see Box 2.2.8). This has consequences for the analysis of career mobility as a multiepisode process: The smaller the number of job transitions for a given serial job number, the more likely it is to produce statistically insignificant results; hence, a comparison of episode-specific parameters across spell numbers based on significance tests

---

[23]In the case of exponential models, for example, interaction terms between the serial number of the job (or a set of dummy variables for it) and the other time-constant covariates could be used to study changes of such covariate effects across spells.

[24]In the literature, these models normally also include job duration dependence (see chapters 5, 6, and 7). But in this case, time-dependence means that the event of a job-exit primarily depends on the time spent in each of these jobs (or job-specific labor force experience), regardless of the specific location of the job in an individual's job career (which is general labor force experience).

[25]Again, definitions of different clocks or process times are particularly important in the case of models with time-dependence (chapter 7) and semiparametric (Cox) models (chapter 9).

[26]In time-dependent models, the event of a job-exit depends on the specific location of the spell in a person's life course. Consequently, the job spells of a person's career are not treated as autonomous entities.

Box 4.3.1 Do-file `ehd7.do` (multiepisode exponential model)

```
version 9
capture log close
set more off
log using ehd7.log, replace

use rrdat1, clear

keep if noj <= 4    /*keep only episodes with serial number <= 4*/

gen des = tfin ~= ti            /*destination state*/
gen tf  = tfin - tstart + 1     /*ending time*/

gen coho2 = tb >= 468 & tb <= 504  /*cohort 2*/
gen coho3 = tb >= 588 & tb <= 624  /*cohort 3*/
gen lfx   = tstart - te            /*labor force experience*/
gen pnoj  = noj - 1                /*previous number of jobs*/

stset tf, failure(des)             /*define single episode data*/

stci, by(noj des) emean
/*descriptive statistics for the individuals' first four jobs*/

by noj, sort: streg edu coho2 coho3 lfx pres, dist(e) nohr
/*fit parametric survival models*/

log close
```

may be misleading; and the number of serial job episodes that can be used to study career mobility as a multiepisode process is limited. In such a model, it is not wise to include episodes of serial numbers with a very small number of job transitions. Therefore based on the distribution of job transitions, as displayed in Box 2.2.8, only the first four job episodes are used for our estimation of the multiepisode model. This ensures that the number of job spells and transitions in each episode is great enough to compare the estimates across episodes in a meaningful way. In addition, it guarantees that only a few job spells are lost in the analysis. On the basis of this decision, about 89 % (532/600) of all job spells and 91 % (418/458) of all job moves (or events) are included in this multiepisode model.

The do-file `ehd7.do`, estimating this multiepisode model, is shown in Box 4.3.1. First, we select episodes with the `keep` command. Using `keep if noj <= 4` tells Stata to keep only job episodes with a serial number (`noj`) less than or equal to 4. The episodes (jobs) belonging to each individual are distinguished by their serial number given by the `noj` variable. As discussed in chapter 2, the serial numbers must be positive integers and should be contiguous. We sort the data by `noj` and `des` and display descriptive statis-

Box 4.3.2a Result (first part) of using do-file `ehd7.do` (Box 4.3.1)

```
          failure _d:  des
    analysis time _t:  tf

noj        |   no. of    extended
des        |  subjects      mean
-----------+----------------------
    1 0 |      16        .
    1 1 |     185     52.72973(*)
    2 0 |      36        .
    2 1 |     126     52.30159(*)
    3 0 |      38        .
    3 1 |      69     50.36232(*)
    4 0 |      24        .
    4 1 |      38     37.71053(*)
-----------+----------------------
   total |     532     112.7138
```

tics for the individuals' first four jobs by using the command `by noj des:
summarize tf`.

We sort the data by `noj` and use the `by` prefix to repeat the `streg`
command for the first four job episodes. Note that the covariate `lfx`, general
labor force experience measured at the beginning of each new job episode,
cannot be included as a covariate for the *first* job episode because this
variable is zero for all first episodes (or workers). With the exception of this
variable, all other covariates are time-constant because they do not change
their value after the beginning of the process time, which is the *time of
entry into the first job*. Variable `lfx` ("general labor force experience at
the beginning of each new job") is a special form of a (process-related)
time-dependent covariate because it changes its value at the beginning of
each job. Using this covariate in a multiepisode exponential model whose
process time is defined by the clock "general labor force experience" would
be meaningless. If, on the one hand, the assumption of the exponential model
is correct, then this covariate cannot have a significant effect, because the
process does not depend on history, and the rate of job change is constant
across the process time (i.e., general labor force experience). If, on the other
hand, the covariate "general labor force experience" had a significant effect,
then the assumption of an exponential distribution would be wrong, and one
should use a model with a time-dependent transition rate. The transition
rate would then become a function of time so that events become either
less likely (negative duration dependence) or more likely (positive duration
dependence) as the clock, general labor force experience, progresses. Thus
this multiepisode model can serve as a test for the assumption that the job
history process is *time stationary* or *time homogeneous* (i.e., transitions do
not depend on time).

Box 4.3.2b Result (second part) of using do-file `ehd7.do` (Box 4.3.1)

```
-> noj = 1

note: lfx dropped due to collinearity
Exponential regression -- log relative-hazard form
No. of subjects =          201        Number of obs   =         201
No. of failures =          185
Time at risk    =        13490
                                      LR chi2(4)      =       21.90
Log likelihood  =   -320.73616        Prob > chi2     =      0.0002

-----------------------------------------------------------------------------
     _t |     Coef.    Std. Err.      z     P>|z|    [95% Conf. Interval]
--------+--------------------------------------------------------------------
    edu |   .0622383   .0326678     1.91   0.057   -.0017894     .126266
  coho2 |   .7220939   .1888079     3.82   0.000    .3520372     1.09215
  coho3 |   .6637726   .1791567     3.70   0.000    .3126319     1.014913
   pres |   -.009535   .0091225    -1.05   0.296   -.0274147     .0083448
  _cons |  -5.017885   .4173747   -12.02   0.000   -5.835924    -4.199846
-----------------------------------------------------------------------------


-> noj = 2

Exponential regression -- log relative-hazard form
No. of subjects =          162        Number of obs   =         162
No. of failures =          126
Time at risk    =        11996
                                      LR chi2(5)      =       42.88
Log likelihood  =   -237.89354        Prob > chi2     =      0.0000

-----------------------------------------------------------------------------
     _t |     Coef.    Std. Err.      z     P>|z|    [95% Conf. Interval]
--------+--------------------------------------------------------------------
    edu |   .1261256   .0516029     2.44   0.015    .0249857     .2272655
  coho2 |   .3422823   .2157199     1.59   0.113   -.0805208     .7650855
  coho3 |   .2703772   .2334466     1.16   0.247   -.1871696     .7279241
    lfx |  -.0061697   .0018403    -3.35   0.001   -.0097767    -.0025627
   pres |  -.0510282   .0110363    -4.62   0.000    -.072659    -.0293974
  _cons |  -3.735184   .5778047    -6.46   0.000   -4.867661    -2.602708
-----------------------------------------------------------------------------


-> noj = 3

Exponential regression -- log relative-hazard form
No. of subjects =          107        Number of obs   =         107
No. of failures =           69
Time at risk    =         8101
                                      LR chi2(5)      =       18.00
Log likelihood  =   -152.73377        Prob > chi2     =      0.0029

-----------------------------------------------------------------------------
     _t |     Coef.    Std. Err.      z     P>|z|    [95% Conf. Interval]
--------+--------------------------------------------------------------------
    edu |   .0522256   .0748627     0.70   0.485   -.0945026     .1989538
  coho2 |   .1975193    .297243     0.66   0.506   -.3850663     .7801048
  coho3 |   .7143032   .3288906     2.17   0.030    .0696895     1.358917
    lfx |  -.0039478   .0019895    -1.98   0.047   -.0078472    -.0000483
   pres |  -.0223009   .0139315    -1.60   0.109   -.0496061     .0050044
  _cons |  -4.262784   .7396699    -5.76   0.000   -5.712511    -2.813058
-----------------------------------------------------------------------------
```

Box 4.3.2b (cont.) Result (second part) of using do-file `ehd7.do` (Box 4.3.1)

```
-> noj = 4

Exponential regression -- log relative-hazard form
No. of subjects =          62      Number of obs   =         62
No. of failures =          38
Time at risk    =        3481
                                   LR chi2(5)      =      21.98
Log likelihood  =  -73.004575      Prob > chi2     =     0.0005


-----------------------------------------------------------------------
    _t |      Coef.   Std. Err.      z    P>|z|     [95% Conf. Interval]
-------+---------------------------------------------------------------
   edu |   .0437997   .1329081    0.33   0.742    -.2166953    .3042947
 coho2 |   1.135352   .3830044    2.96   0.003     .384677     1.886027
 coho3 |   .3163115   .4492212    0.70   0.481    -.5641459    1.196769
   lfx |  -.0051987   .0027173   -1.91   0.056    -.0105246    .0001272
  pres |  -.0654294   .0204556   -3.20   0.001    -.1055215   -.0253372
 _cons |   -2.22315    1.34894   -1.65   0.099    -4.867025    .4207244
```

Estimation results using do-file `ehd7.do` (Box 4.3.1) are shown in Boxes 4.3.2a and 4.3.2b. Box 4.3.2a shows some descriptive statistics for the individuals' first four jobs, and Box 4.3.2b provides the job-number-specific estimates for the covariates. It is easy to see that the covariate "general labor force experience" (`lfx`) has significant effects on the rate of job change for episode numbers 2 and 3, and is almost significant for the fourth job. This means that the job history is not time stationary or time homogeneous, but that the movement rate becomes less likely as general labor force experience increases.

It is interesting to see how the effects of covariates change across the number of episodes. For mobility out of the first job, only the cohort dummy variables are statistically significant. The parameters for `coho2` and `coho3` are quite similar in size. Thus the greatest difference is between the reference group (birth cohort 1929–31) and the two younger birth cohorts (1939–41 and 1949–51). After having left the first job and entered the second one, the educational attainment level has a positive impact, and prestige of the job has a negative impact on job mobility. In the third job, only the birth cohort 1949–51 (`coho3`) behaves differently. Members of this cohort move to a fourth job significantly more often. Finally, in the fourth job, the birth cohort 1939–41 (`coho2`) is more mobile, and the prestige level (`pres`) reduces job mobility. Of course, all of these estimates are based on a small number of events, and the interpretation given here only serves for didactical purposes.

Chapter 5

Piecewise Constant Exponential Models

In most applications of transition rate models, the assumption that the forces of change are constant over time is not theoretically justified. It is therefore important for an appropriate modeling of social processes to be able to include time-dependent covariates in transition rate models. Before discussing this topic more deeply in chapter 6, we survey the *piecewise constant exponential model*. This is a simple generalization of the standard exponential model (chapter 4), but it is extremely useful in many practical research situations. It is particularly helpful when researchers are not in a position to measure and include important time-dependent covariates explicitly or when they do not have a clear idea about the form of the time-dependence of the process. In both of these situations, a small modification of the exponential model leads to a very flexible instrument of analysis. The basic idea is to split the time axis into time periods and to assume that transition rates are constant in each of these intervals but can change between them.

5.1 The Basic Model

If there are L time periods, the piecewise constant transition rate is defined by L parameters. In Stata there are two different options to include covariates, which are demonstrated in this section. The first is to assume that only a baseline rate, given by period-specific constants, can vary across time periods, but the covariates have the same (proportional) effects in each period.[1] The second option allows for period-specific effects of covariates. We begin by demonstrating the first option.

Stata 9 does not have a built-in command for piecewise constant exponential models. But Stata provides a solution: You have to split episodes into two or more episodes and estimate an exponential model using the command `streg`. There is an even smarter solution. You can also install an ado-file that will automatically split the episodes and estimate the piecewise

---

[1]The exponential model and the piecewise constant exponential model, in which the covariates have the same effects across the time periods, are both special cases of the more general proportional transition rate models (see chapter 9).

constant exponential model.[2] Both procedures will lead to exactly the same estimation results. We will discuss both ways in this chapter.

The commands require a definition of time periods. This is based on split points on the time axis

$$0 = \tau_1 < \tau_2 < \tau_3 < \ldots < \tau_L$$

With $\tau_{L+1} = \infty$, one gets L time periods[3]

$$I_l = \{t \mid \tau_l < t \leq \tau_{l+1}\} \qquad l = 1, \ldots, L$$

Given these time periods, the transition rate from a given origin state to destination state k is

$$r_k(t) = \exp\left\{\bar{\alpha}_l^{(k)} + A^{(k)}\alpha^{(k)}\right\} \quad \text{if} \quad t \in I_l \tag{5.1}$$

For each transition to destination state k, $\bar{\alpha}_l^{(k)}$ is a constant coefficient associated with the lth time period. $A^{(k)}$ is a (row) vector of covariates, and $\alpha^{(k)}$ is an associated vector of coefficients assumed not to vary across time periods. Note that with this model the vector of covariates cannot contain an additional constant.

Maximum Likelihood Estimation

The maximum likelihood estimation of this model is done following the outline given in section 4.1.1. To simplify notation we omit indices for transitions and define $l[t]$ to be the index of the time period containing t (so $t \in I_{l[t]}$ always). Also the following notation is helpful:

$$\delta[t, l] = \begin{cases} 1 & \text{if} \quad t \in I_l \\ 0 & \text{otherwise} \end{cases}$$

$$\Delta[s, t, l] = \begin{cases} t - \tau_l & \text{if} \quad s \leq \tau_l, \ \tau_l < t < \tau_{l+1} \\ \tau_{l+1} - \tau_l & \text{if} \quad s \leq \tau_l, \ t \geq \tau_{l+1} \\ \tau_{l+1} - s & \text{if} \quad t \geq \tau_{l+1}, \ \tau_l < s < \tau_{l+1} \\ 0 & \text{otherwise} \end{cases}$$

---

[2]The Statistical Software Components (SSC) archive maintained by Boston College (http://www.repect.org) provides user-written Stata commands. To install the Stata program to estimate piecewise constant exponential models, the ssc install command is used: ssc install stpiece. This command will download the ado-file and implement the new Stata command stpiece.

[3]This definition is used by Stata. Note that TDA uses time intervals that are closed on the left-hand side and open on the right-hand side. Because many ending times in the data set rrdat1 coincide with the split points used in the following examples, estimation results produced by Stata differ from those produced by TDA.

The conditional survivor function may then be written as

$$G(t \mid s) = \exp\left\{ -\sum_{l=1}^{L} \Delta[s, t, l] \exp(\bar{\alpha}_l + A\alpha) \right\}$$

Using this expression, the log likelihood can be written as

$$\ell = \sum_{i \in \mathcal{E}} (\bar{\alpha}_{l[t_i]} + A_i\alpha) - \sum_{i \in \mathcal{N}} \sum_{l=1}^{L} \Delta[s_i, t_i, l] \exp(\bar{\alpha}_l + A_i\alpha)$$

5.2   Models without Covariates

As an illustration of the piecewise constant exponential model, we continue with the example in Box 4.1.1 (section 4.1), but now allow for the possibility that the transition rate varies across time periods.

Generally, time periods can be arbitrarily defined, but there is some trade-off. If one chooses a large number of time periods, one will get a better approximation of the unknown baseline rate, but this implies a large number of coefficients to be estimated. Alternatively, if one chooses a small number of periods, there are fewer estimation problems, but there is probably a poorer approximation of the baseline rate. Therefore, in most cases, some compromise is needed.

Another important requirement is that there should be some episodes with ending event times within the interval for all time periods. Otherwise it is generally not possible to reach sensible estimates.

We already have some information about the length of episodes in our example data set. We know that the mean duration of episodes with an event is about 49 months (see Box 2.2.5). Therefore it seems appropriate to use eight time periods, each having a length of one year, plus an additional open-ended interval.

First, as shown in do-file `ehe1.do` (Box 5.2.1), we generate a new ID variable and declare the data to be event history data.[4] Next, we have to split the records into two or more episodes using the command

```
stsplit time, at(0 (12) 96)
```

Stata will split records at specified times and create 2115 episodes.[5] In the next step, you generate time dummies named `t1` to `t9`: `tab time, ge(t)`. We then fit an exponential model that includes these time dummies as

---

[4]Note that _u is a Stata system variable that indicates the position of an observation in the data set.

[5]Notice that it is necessary to define an ID variable before using the command `stsplit`. We use the option `at(numlist)` to define time periods. Type `help numlist` to learn more about number lists in Stata.

Box 5.2.1 Do-file `ehe1.do` (piecewise constant exponential model)

```
version 9
set scheme sj
capture log close
set more off
log using ehe1.log, replace

use rrdat1, clear

* 1st option: use stsplit

gen des = tfin ~= ti          /*destination state*/
gen tf  = tfin - tstart + 1   /*ending time*/

gen newid = _n
stset tf, failure(des) id(newid) /*define single episode data*/

stsplit time, at(0 (12) 96)   /*split records*/
tab time, ge(t)               /*generate time dummies*/

stset tf, failure(des) id(newid) /*define single episode data*/

streg t1 t2 t3 t4 t5 t6 t7 t8 t9, ///
dist(exp) nohr noconstant     /*fit parametric survival model*/

predict hazard, hazard        /*obtain predictions*/

line hazard _t, sort title("Piecewise Constant Exponential Rate") ///
xtitle("analysis time") saving("Figure 5_2_1",replace)

drop time t1-t9 hazard
stjoin

* 2nd option: use stpiece

ssc install stpiece
/*install wrapper to estimate piecewise-constant hazard rate models*/

stset tf, failure(des) id(newid) /*define single episode data*/

stpiece, tp(0(12)96) nohr /*fit piecewise constant exponential model*/

log close
```

covariates. Alternatively, you may also want to use a wrapper that does all these steps automatically for you (see the second part of do-file `ehe1.do`). Before we explain this procedure we introduce another command that is very helpful after episode splitting. The command `stjoin` joins episodes if this can be achieved without losing information. That is, two records can be joined if they are adjacent and contain the same data. In our example,

Box 5.2.2 Part of estimation results of do-file `ehe1.do` (Box 5.2.1)

```
         failure _d:  des
   analysis time _t:  tf
                 id:  newid

Iteration 0:   log likelihood = -1002.8964
Iteration 1:   log likelihood =  -892.003
Iteration 2:   log likelihood = -888.99801
Iteration 3:   log likelihood = -888.99048
Iteration 4:   log likelihood = -888.99048

Exponential regression -- log relative-hazard form

No. of subjects =          600        Number of obs   =      2715
No. of failures =          458
Time at risk    =        40782
                                       Wald chi2(9)    =   8882.37
Log likelihood  =    -888.99048        Prob > chi2     =    0.0000
```

_t	Coef.	Std. Err.	z	P>|z|	[95% Conf. Interval]	
t1	-4.360092	.1072113	-40.67	0.000	-4.570223	-4.149962
t2	-4.063008	.1031421	-39.39	0.000	-4.265162	-3.860853
t3	-3.920421	.1097643	-35.72	0.000	-4.135555	-3.705287
t4	-4.413101	.1581139	-27.91	0.000	-4.722999	-4.103204
t5	-4.219508	.1561738	-27.02	0.000	-4.525603	-3.913413
t6	-4.558253	.2041241	-22.33	0.000	-4.958329	-4.158177
t7	-4.995652	.2773501	-18.01	0.000	-5.539248	-4.452056
t8	-5.175585	.3162278	-16.37	0.000	-5.79538	-4.55579
t9	-5.223871	.1230915	-42.44	0.000	-5.465126	-4.982616

we first need to remove from the data set all variables created by `stsplit` before typing `stjoin`. This is achieved by using the command `drop`. Then you can issue the new Stata command `stpiece`. The definition of the split points is achieved by specifying the option `tp(0(12)96)`.

The results of both ways are exactly the same so we report only part of the estimation results in Box 5.2.2. The estimated parameters for the baseline transition rate at first increase, from -4.36 to -3.92, and then decrease. In our application example this means that with increasing duration in a specific job the force of job exit (or the job-exit rate) is nonmonotonic. This can be seen more easily when the estimation result in Box 5.2.2 is plotted in Figure 5.2.1. The commands that plot the estimated rates of the piecewise constant exponential model are

```
predict hazard, hazard
line hazard _t, sort
```

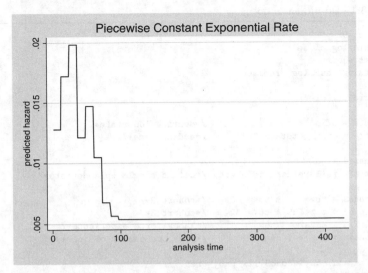

Figure 5.2.1 Piecewise constant transition rate, estimated with do-file `ehe1.do`.

In substantive terms this bell-shaped rate pattern might be interpreted as an interplay of two opposing causal forces (increases in job-specific invest-ments and decreases in the need to resolve mismatches) that cannot easily be measured, so that the duration in a job has to serve as a proxy variable for them. The argument is that when people are matched to jobs under the condition of imperfect information and high search costs, mismatches can occur. Particularly during the first months of each new employment, there will be an intensive adjustment process in which the respective expecta-tions of the employer and the employee are confronted with reality. German labor law, for example, allows for a probationary period of six months dur-ing which it is relatively easy for employers to fire somebody if they are not satisfied. But employees also quit their jobs more at the beginning of each new employment, because their job-specific investments are still low. Consequently, one would expect that the rate of moving out of the job in-creases at the beginning of each new employment. However, as mismatches have been increasingly resolved and investments in job-specific human cap-ital are continuously rising, a point will be reached at which both of these forces will become equally strong. This is where the peak of the transition rate of moving out of the job is reached (Figure 5.2.1). In our example, this point is reached after about 2 years of employment in a new job. After this job duration, further increases in job-specific investments will more and more outweigh the force of resolving mismatches, so that the job-exit rate declines with increasing duration.

Box 5.3.1 Do-file ehe2.do

```
version 9
capture log close
set more off
log using ehe2.log, replace

use rrdat1, clear

gen des = tfin ~= ti            /*destination state*/
gen tf  = tfin - tstart + 1     /*ending time*/

gen newid = _n
stset tf, failure(des) id(newid) /*define single episode data*/

gen coho2 = tb>=468 & tb<= 504  /*cohort 2*/
gen coho3 = tb>=588 & tb<= 624  /*cohort 3*/
gen lfx   = tstart - te         /*labor force experience*/
gen pnoj  = noj - 1             /*previous number of jobs*/

stpiece edu coho2 coho3 lfx pnoj pres, ///
tp(0(12)96) nohr  /*fit piecewise constant exponential model*/

log close
```

5.3   Models with Proportional Covariate Effects

The problem with the analysis without covariates in the previous section is that important heterogeneity between the individuals has not been taken into account. Thus, in the next step, we study whether the nonmonotonic pattern of the job-exit rate will still be there if time-constant covariates are included. This can be done by a simple modification of the do-file ehe1.do (Box 5.2.1). The new do-file, ehe2.do, is shown in Box 5.3.1. The modification simply consists in constructing the covariates and adding the names of covariates to be included into the model to the stpiece command.

The estimation results of using do-file ehe2.do are shown in Box 5.3.2. Based on these parameter estimates, one can draw at least two conclusions: First, the nonmonotonic rate pattern of the piecewise constant exponential model without covariates (Box 5.2.2) has not changed. Thus this pattern of time-dependence cannot be explained by the additionally included time-constant covariates.[6] Second, the parameter estimates for the time-constant covariates resemble the estimates for the basic exponential model in Box 4.1.5. Thus the parameter estimates for the time-constant covariates in the exponential model seem to be quite robust.[7]

---

[6]In chapter 10 we give some examples of how unobserved time-constant heterogeneity can produce time-dependent rates.

[7]We shall see in the next chapters that the parameter estimates for the time-constant

Box 5.3.2 Estimation results of do-file `ehe2.do` (Box 5.3.1)

```
        failure _d:  des
  analysis time _t:  tf
             id:  newid

Iteration 0:   log likelihood = -1002.8964
Iteration 1:   log likelihood = -854.90874
Iteration 2:   log likelihood = -851.88418
Iteration 3:   log likelihood = -851.86828
Iteration 4:   log likelihood = -851.86828

Exponential regression -- log relative-hazard form

No. of subjects =        600    Number of obs   =      2715
No. of failures =        458
Time at risk    =      40782
                               Wald chi2(15)   =   8626.69
Log likelihood  =  -851.86828  Prob > chi2     =    0.0000
```

_t	Coef.	Std. Err.	z	P>|z|	[95% Conf. Interval]	
tp1	-4.25273	.294021	-14.46	0.000	-4.829001	-3.676459
tp2	-3.916678	.2920046	-13.41	0.000	-4.488996	-3.344359
tp3	-3.738957	.2925247	-12.78	0.000	-4.312295	-3.165619
tp4	-4.22092	.3133731	-13.47	0.000	-4.83512	-3.60672
tp5	-4.009912	.3122496	-12.84	0.000	-4.62191	-3.397914
tp6	-4.323992	.3395438	-12.73	0.000	-4.989486	-3.658498
tp7	-4.772435	.3848382	-12.40	0.000	-5.526704	-4.018166
tp8	-4.940688	.4134257	-11.95	0.000	-5.750988	-4.130389
tp9	-4.95165	.2898812	-17.08	0.000	-5.519807	-4.383493
edu	.0635991	.0248868	2.56	0.011	.0148219	.1123763
coho2	.4572261	.1153366	3.96	0.000	.2311704	.6832817
coho3	.3521179	.122506	2.87	0.004	.1120105	.5922254
lfx	-.0037174	.0009285	-4.00	0.000	-.0055373	-.0018976
pnoj	.0595917	.0442055	1.35	0.178	-.0270495	.1462329
pres	-.0252979	.0054807	-4.62	0.000	-.0360398	-.0145559

5.4 Models with Period-Specific Effects

In this section we further generalize the piecewise constant exponential model by also allowing the effects of the time-constant covariates (i.e., their associated parameters) to vary across time periods.[8] This model was first proposed by Tuma (1980).

---

covariates are surprisingly stable across a broad range of different models.

[8]One should note that this is not the same as a standard exponential model with interaction effects between covariates and time periods. Such interaction effects with process time would lead to heavily biased estimation results.

To request estimation of an exponential model with period-specific effects, you can use the `streg` command. Yet it is important to note here that you need to generate period-specific dummies that will then be included in the `streg` command. One way to do this is shown in Box 5.4.1.

Time periods are defined by split points on the time axis in exactly the same way as for the standard exponential model with time periods. Given, then, time periods defined by split points $\tau_1, \tau_2, \ldots, \tau_L$, the transition rate to destination state k is

$$r_k(t) = \exp\left\{\bar{\alpha}_l^{(k)} + A^{(k)}\alpha_l^{(k)}\right\} \quad \text{if} \quad \tau_l < t \leq \tau_{l+1} \tag{5.2}$$

For each transition to destination state k, $\bar{\alpha}_l^{(k)}$ is a constant coefficient associated with the lth time period. The (row) vector of covariates is $A^{(k)}$, and $\alpha_l^{(k)}$ is an associated vector of coefficients, showing the effects of these covariates in the lth time period.

Obviously, the standard exponential model with time periods defined in (5.1) (see section 5.1) is a special case of the model defined in (5.2). In fact, estimating the latter model with constraints that require the $\alpha_l^{(k)}$ parameters to be equal across time periods would give identical results to the standard exponential model with time periods.

Maximum likelihood estimation. The maximum likelihood estimation of this model is similar to the standard piecewise constant exponential model described earlier. Using the same abbreviations, $l[t]$ and $\Delta[s, t, l]$, the conditional survivor function is

$$G(t \mid s) = \exp\left\{-\sum_{l=1}^{L} \Delta[s, t, l]\exp(\bar{\alpha}_l + A\alpha_l)\right\}$$

and using this expression, the log likelihood can be written as

$$\ell = \sum_{i \in \mathcal{E}} (\bar{\alpha}_{l[t_i]} + A_i\alpha_{l[t_i]}) - \sum_{i \in \mathcal{N}} \sum_{l=1}^{L} \Delta[s_i, t_i, l]\exp(\bar{\alpha}_l + A_i\alpha_l)$$

Initial estimates to begin the iterative process of maximizing the log likelihood are calculated in the same way as for the standard piecewise constant exponential model.

An application. In the context of our job-exit example, the piecewise constant exponential model with period-specific effects is particularly interesting because it provides the opportunity to assess hypotheses based on the *filter* or *signaling theory* (Arrow 1973; Spence 1973, 1974). This labor market theory contends that, in the hiring process, easily observable characteristics (such as educational qualifications, number of previously held

Box 5.4.1 Do-file `ehe3.do`

```
version 9
capture log close
set more off
log using ehe3.log, replace

use rrdat1, clear

gen des = tfin ~= ti          /*destination state*/
gen tf  = tfin - tstart + 1   /*ending time*/

gen newid = _n
stset tf, failure(des) id(newid) /*define single episode data*/

gen coho2 = tb>=468 & tb<= 504    /*cohort 2*/
gen coho3 = tb>=588 & tb<= 624    /*cohort 3*/
gen lfx   = tstart - te          /*labor force experience*/
gen pnoj  = noj - 1              /*previous number of jobs*/

stsplit time, at(0,24,60)        /*split records*/
tab time, ge(t)                  /*generate time dummies*/

*generate period-specific dummies
for any edu edu edu      \ any t1 t2 t3: gen eduY  = X*Y
for any coho2 coho2 coho2 \ any t1 t2 t3: gen coho2Y= X*Y
for any coho3 coho3 coho3 \ any t1 t2 t3: gen coho3Y= X*Y
for any lfx lfx lfx      \ any t1 t2 t3: gen lfxY  = X*Y
for any pnoj pnoj pnoj   \ any t1 t2 t3: gen pnojY = X*Y
for any pres pres pres   \ any t1 t2 t3: gen presY = X*Y

stset tf, failure(des) id(newid)  /*define single episode data*/

streg t1 t2 t3 edut* coho2t* coho3t* lfxt* pnojt* prest*, ///
dist(exp) nohr noconstant /*fit piecewise constant exponential model*/

log close
```

jobs, or years of labor force experience) serve as signals for employers. In particular, these characteristics are used by employers to infer differences in productivity among people applying for a given job. Thus they are very important for employment decisions as well as in a starting phase of each new job. With increasing job duration, however, the employer is able to gain more direct information on the employee and is increasingly less forced to rely on such signals to evaluate the competence or productivity of employees. Thus the expectation is that, for job decisions, the importance of such signals declines with increasing duration in a job. On the other hand, one can also assume that job decisions of an employee, especially at the beginning of each new job, depend strongly on the image (or prestige) of the job position and that the relevance of these characteristics for his or her job

Box 5.4.2 Estimation results of do-file ehe3.do (Box 5.4.1)

```
        failure _d:  des
  analysis time _t:  tf
               id:  newid

Iteration 0:   log likelihood = -1002.8964
Iteration 1:   log likelihood =  -859.0758
Iteration 2:   log likelihood =  -853.15786
Iteration 3:   log likelihood =  -853.13814
Iteration 4:   log likelihood =  -853.13814


Exponential regression -- log relative-hazard form

No. of subjects =          600        Number of obs   =       1202
No. of failures =          458
Time at risk    =        40782
                                       Wald chi2(21)   =    8642.88
Log likelihood  =   -853.13814         Prob > chi2     =     0.0000
```

_t	Coef.	Std. Err.	z	P>|z|	[95% Conf. Interval]	
t1	-4.35138	.4224051	-10.30	0.000	-5.179279	-3.523481
t2	-3.32689	.4831846	-6.89	0.000	-4.273915	-2.379866
t3	-5.615024	.5755181	-9.76	0.000	-6.743019	-4.487029
edut1	.1097628	.0357066	3.07	0.002	.0397792	.1797464
edut2	.0011625	.0481818	0.02	0.981	-.093272	.0955971
edut3	.0682161	.0492593	1.38	0.166	-.0283304	.1647626
coho2t1	.5809915	.1917358	3.03	0.002	.2051963	.9567867
coho2t2	.4070205	.1892725	2.15	0.032	.0360532	.7779879
coho2t3	.4125671	.2304085	1.79	0.073	-.0390254	.8641595
coho3t1	.5206901	.1931976	2.70	0.007	.1420298	.8993504
coho3t2	.0866651	.2018906	0.43	0.668	-.3090332	.4823634
coho3t3	.7097271	.2600232	2.73	0.006	.2000909	1.219363
lfxt1	-.004681	.0015347	-3.05	0.002	-.007689	-.001673
lfxt2	-.0041873	.001523	-2.75	0.006	-.0071723	-.0012023
lfxt3	-.0011644	.0018192	-0.64	0.522	-.00473	.0024011
pnojt1	.1455211	.0681359	2.14	0.033	.0119773	.279065
pnojt2	.0229359	.0750371	0.31	0.760	-.1241341	.1700059
pnojt3	-.0477606	.0940906	-0.51	0.612	-.2321749	.1366536
prest1	-.0371613	.0082883	-4.48	0.000	-.0534062	-.0209165
prest2	-.0189583	.0094382	-2.01	0.045	-.0374569	-.0004597
prest3	-.0075705	.0116297	-0.65	0.515	-.0303643	.0152232

decisions declines with increasing experience in the job. In summary, both arguments lead to the hypothesis that the effects of those time-constant covariates that serve as signals decline over job duration.

In the following example, we therefore divide the duration in a job into periods and estimate period-specific effects of covariates with a piecewise constant exponential model. We use a new do-file, ehe3.do, as shown in Box 5.4.1. It is basically the same as do-file ehe2.do already used for the standard piecewise constant exponential model. One should note, however, the new specification of time periods. Because our model estimates parameters for all covariates in each time period separately, we have to use a reasonably small number of periods to get sensible estimates with the 600 job episodes in our example data set.[9] Thus we only define three periods (t1, t2, t3) by using three split points, namely, 0, 24, and 60 months. There are several ways to generate period-specific dummies. Here we use the for command, which repeats the generate command for each variable in the forlist where X refers to the first list of variables and Y to the second. To save space we use abbreviations for variable names (*) when specifying streg.

Part of the estimation result is shown in Box 5.4.2. It supports our hypothesis that the effects of the signaling or filter variables, such as educational attainment (edu), general labor force experience at the beginning of each job (lfx), number of previously held jobs (pnoj), or prestige of the job (pres), are strong in the first phase of each job (period up to 2 years), and then decline in importance across later periods. In the third period (job duration greater than 5 years), none of these signaling or filter variables is significant anymore.

---

[9]It is obvious that a model that tries to estimate changing effects of covariates across a number of time periods requires, in general, a large data set, even in the case of moderate numbers of periods and covariates.

Chapter 6

Exponential Models with Time-Dependent Covariates

In our view, the most important step forward in event history analysis, with respect to the empirical study of social change, has been to explicitly measure and include time-dependent covariates in transition rate models. In such cases, covariates can change their values over process time. Time-dependent covariates can be qualitative or quantitative, and may stay constant for finite periods of time or change continuously.

Three basic approaches can be distinguished to include time-dependent covariates in transition rate models. Time-dependent covariates can be included (1) by using a piecewise constant exponential model as shown in the previous chapter, (2) by applying the method of episode splitting in parametric and semiparametric transition rate models, and (3) by specifying the distributional form of the time-dependence and directly estimating its parameters using the maximum likelihood method (see chapter 7). In this chapter we begin with a general discussion of time-dependent covariates in the framework of parallel and interdependent processes, and then focus on the method of episode splitting.[1] Parametric models of time-dependence are presented in chapter 7.

6.1 Parallel and Interdependent Processes

In applying time-dependent covariates, the effects of change over time in one phenomenon on change in another one can be studied (Tuma and Hannan 1984).[2] From a substantive point of view, it is therefore useful to conceptualize time-dependent covariates as observations of the sample path of parallel processes (Blossfeld, Hamerle, and Mayer 1989).[3] These processes can operate at different levels. For example:

---

[1]See, e.g., Petersen 1986a, 1986b; Blossfeld, Hamerle, and Mayer 1989. The method of episode splitting can also be applied in the case of parametric models of time-dependence (see chapter 7) or semiparametric (Cox) models (see chapter 9). Because the logic of including time-dependent covariates for all parametric models is the same, we only demonstrate this method for exponential models.

[2]In this book, we only focus on continuous-time, discrete-state dependent processes.

[3]A complete history of state occupancies and times of changes is referred to as a *sample path* (Tuma and Hannan 1984).

1. There can be *parallel processes at the level of the individual in different domains of life* (e.g., one may ask how upward and downward moves in an individual's job career influence his or her family trajectory); compare Blossfeld and Huinink (1991), Blossfeld et al. (1999), Mills (2000b), Blossfeld and Timm (2003);

2. There may be *parallel processes at the level of some few individuals interacting with each other* (e.g., one might study the effect of the career of the husband on his wife's labor force participation); see Bernasco (1994), Blossfeld and Drobnič (2001);

3. There may be *parallel processes at the intermediate level* (e.g., one can analyze how organizational growth influences career advancement or how changing household structure determines women's labor force participation); see Blossfeld and Hakim (1997), Blossfeld and Drobnič (2001);

4. There may be *parallel processes at the macrolevel* (e.g., one may be interested in the effect of changes in the business cycle on family formation or career advancement); see Blossfeld (1987a) and Huinink (1989, 1992, 1993);

5. There may be *any combination of such processes of type* (1) *to* (4). For example, in the study of life-course, cohort, and period effects, time-dependent covariates at different levels must be included simultaneously (Blossfeld 1986; Mayer and Huinink 1990). Such an analysis combines processes at the individual level (life-course change) with two kinds of processes at the macrolevel: variations in structural conditions across successive (birth, marriage, entry, etc.) cohorts, and changes in historical conditions affecting all cohorts in the same way.

In dealing with such systems of parallel processes, the issue of reverse causation is normally addressed in the methodological literature (see, e.g., Kalbfleisch and Prentice 1980; Tuma and Hannan 1984; Blossfeld, Hamerle, and Mayer 1989; Yamaguchi 1991; Courgeau and Lelièvre 1992). Reverse causation refers to the (direct or indirect) effect of the dependent process on the independent covariate process. Reverse causation is seen as a problem because the effect of a time-dependent covariate on the transition rate is confounded with a feedback effect of the dependent process on the values of the time-dependent covariate.[4] However, in the literature, two types of time-dependent covariates have been described as not being subject to reverse causation (Kalbfleisch and Prentice 1980):

1. *Defined time-dependent covariates*, whose total time path (or functional form of change over time) is *determined in advance in the same way for all*

---

[4] In other words, the value of the time-dependent covariate carries information about the state of the dependent process.

subjects under study. For example, process time, such as age or duration in a state (e.g., job-specific labor force experience), is a defined time-dependent covariate because its values are predetermined for all the subjects. Thus, by definition, the values of these time-dependent covariates cannot be affected by the dependent process under study.

2. *Ancillary time-dependent covariates*, whose time path is the output of a stochastic process that is *external* to the units under study. Again, by definition, the values of these time-dependent covariates are not influenced by the dependent process itself. Examples of time-dependent covariates that are *approximately external* in the analysis of individual life courses are variables that reflect *changes at the macrolevel* of society (unemployment rates, occupational structure, etc.) or the *population level* (composition of the population in terms of age, sex, race, etc.), provided that the contribution of each unit is small and does not really affect the structure in the population (Yamaguchi 1991). For example, consider the changes in the occupational structure. Although a job move by an individual might contribute to the change in the occupational structure, its effect on the job structure is negligibly small.[5]

In contrast to defined or ancillary time-dependent covariates, *internal time-dependent covariates* are referred to as being problematic for causal analysis with event history models (e.g., Kalbfleisch and Prentice 1980; Tuma and Hannan 1984; Blossfeld, Hamerle, and Mayer 1989; Yamaguchi 1991; Courgeau and Lelièvre 1992). An internal time-dependent covariate X_t describes a stochastic process, considered in a causal model as being the cause, that is in turn affected by another stochastic process Y_t, considered in the causal model as being the effect. Thus there are direct effects in which the processes autonomously affect each other (X_t affects Y_t, and Y_t affects X_t), and there are "feedback" effects in which these processes are affected by themselves via the respective other process (Y_t affects Y_t via X_t, and X_t affects X_t via Y_t). In other words, such processes are interdependent and form what has been called a dynamic system (Tuma and Hannan 1984). Interdependence is typical at the individual level for processes in different domains of life and at the level of few individuals interacting with each other (e.g., career trajectories of partners). For example, the empirical literature suggests that the employment trajectory of an individual is influenced by his or her marital history and marital history is dependent on the employment trajectory.

---

[5]As noted by Yamaguchi (1991), selection bias may exist for the effects of ancillary time-dependent covariates. For example, if regional unemployment rates or crime rates reflect the composition of the population in each region, a transition rate model will lead to biased estimates and erroneous conclusions if it fails to include (or control for) these differences.

In dealing with dynamic systems, at least two main approaches have been suggested. We consider both and call them the "system approach" and the "causal approach."

6.2   Interdependent Processes: The System Approach

The system approach in the analysis of interdependent processes, suggested in the literature (see, e.g., Tuma and Hannan 1984; Courgeau and Lelièvre 1992), defines change in the system of interdependent processes as a new "dependent variable." Thus, instead of analyzing one of the interdependent processes with respect to its dependence on the respective others, the focus of modeling is a system of state variables.[6] In other words, interdependence between the various processes is taken into account only implicitly.

We first demonstrate the logic of this approach for a system of *qualitative* time-dependent variables and give some examples, then discuss its limitations, and finally describe the causal approach, which, we believe, is more appropriate for an analysis of coupled processes from an analytical point of view.

Suppose there are J interrelated qualitative time-dependent variables (processes): $Y_t^A, Y_t^B, Y_t^C, \ldots, Y_t^J$. A new time-dependent variable (process) Y_t, representing the system of these J variables, is then defined by associating each discrete state of the ordered J-tuple with a particular discrete state of Y_t. As shown by Tuma and Hannan (1984), as long as change in the whole system only depends on the various states of the J qualitative variables and on exogenous variables, this model is identical to modeling change in a single qualitative variable.[7] Thus the idea of this approach is to simply define a new *joint* state space, based on the various state spaces of the coupled qualitative processes, and then to proceed as in the case of a single dependent process.

For example, suppose we have repeated episodes from two interdependent processes, "employment trajectory" and "marital history," represented by two dichotomous variables Y_t^A and Y_t^B, where Y_t^A takes the values 1 ("not employed") or 2 ("employed") and Y_t^B takes the values 1 ("not mar-

---

[6]There have also been other suggestions for the analysis of dynamic systems based on this approach (e.g., Klijzing 1993).

[7]The basic model for the development of Y_t is a Markov model. It makes two assumptions: First, it assumes that the episodes defined with respect to Y_t are independent of previous history. Thus, when the past of the process makes the episodes dependent, it is crucial to include these dependencies as covariates in transition rate models at the beginning of each new episode of the Y_t process (Courgeau and Lelièvre 1992). Second, the model assumes that transitions to a destination state of the system are not allowed to depend on the episode's duration, but only on the type of states. However, this is not a necessary assumption. The model for the system could also be formulated as a semi-Markov model allowing for duration dependence in the various origin states.

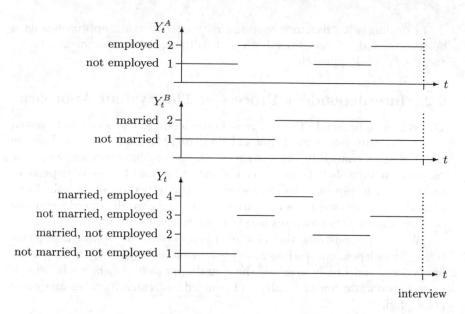

Figure 6.2.1 Hypothetical sample paths of two coupled processes, Y_t^A and Y_t^B, and the sample path of the combined process, Y_t.

ried") or 2 ("married"). Then, as shown in Figure 6.2.1, a new variable Y_t, representing the bivariate system, has $L = 4$ different states:[8]

$1 \equiv (1, 1)$ "not employed and not married"
$2 \equiv (1, 2)$ "not employed and married"
$3 \equiv (2, 1)$ "employed and not married"
$4 \equiv (2, 2)$ "employed and married"

In general, with L different states in the combined process, there are $L(L-1)$ possible transitions. However, if one excludes the possibility of simultaneous changes in two or more of the processes,[9] the number of possible transitions is reduced by the number of simultaneous transitions. Then, in our example of two dichotomous variables, eight transition rates describe the joint process completely, as can be seen in Figure 6.2.2. Each of these origin and

---

[8]The number of distinct values L of the system variable Y_t is given by the product of the distinct values for each of the J variables. When the system is formed by J dichotomous variables, then the number of distinct values is $L = 2^J$. Of course, some of these combinations may not be possible and must then be excluded.

[9]If the modeling approach is based on a continuous time axis, this could then formally be justified by the fact that the probability of simultaneous state changes is zero; see Coleman (1964).

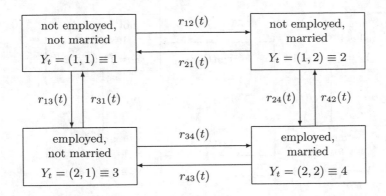

Figure 6.2.2 States and transitions for the system Y_t consisting of employment and marital histories.

destination specific rates can be estimated in a model without covariates or with respect to its dependence on exogenous covariates.

In the case of coupled processes, and if one considers only irreversible events, for example, first marriage and first pregnancy, the diagram of possible transitions can further be simplified to four possible transitions, as shown in Figure 6.2.3. As demonstrated by Courgeau and Lelièvre (1992), one can use equality tests comparing origin and destination specific transition rates to determine whether (see Figure 6.2.3):[10]

1. The two processes are independent: $r_{12} = r_{34}$ and $r_{13} = r_{24}$.
2. One of the two processes is exogenous and the other endogenous:[11]
   a) $r_{12} = r_{34}$ and $r_{13} \neq r_{24}$: pregnancy affects marriage positively: $r_{13} < r_{24}$, pregnancy affects marriage negatively: $r_{13} > r_{24}$, or
   b) $r_{12} \neq r_{34}$ and $r_{13} = r_{24}$: marriage affects pregnancy positively:

---

[10]In this example, a problem might arise when the analysis is only based on observed behavior. For example, it might happen that a couple first decides to marry, then, following this decision, the woman becomes pregnant, and finally the couple marries. In this case, we would observe pregnancy occurring before marriage and assume that pregnancy increases the likelihood of marriage. However, the time order between the processes is the other way around: The couple decides to marry and then the woman gets pregnant. Because the time between decisions and behavior is probably not random and is different for various couples, an analysis that only uses behavioral observations can lead to false conclusions. Courgeau and Lelièvre (1992) have introduced the notion of "fuzzy time" for the time span between decisions and behavior. Note, however, that this issue does not alter the key temporal issues embedded within the causal logic (see section 1.2). There is clearly a time order with regard to decisions and behavior. However, as this example demonstrates, only using the time order of behavioral events without taking into account the timing of decisions could lead to serious misspecification.

[11]Courgeau and Lelièvre (1992) called this specific case "unilateral dependence" or "local dependence."

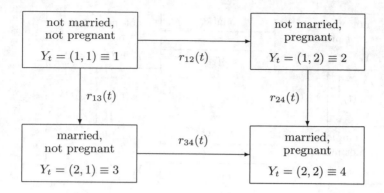

Figure 6.2.3 States and transitions for the system Y_t consisting of first marriage and first pregnancy.

$r_{12} < r_{34}$, marriage affects pregnancy negatively: $r_{12} > r_{34}$.

3. The processes are interdependent (or endogenous) and affect each other: $r_{12} \neq r_{34}$ and $r_{13} \neq r_{24}$.

These equality tests can easily be conducted, as long as there are no covariates involved and only baseline transition rates for specific origin and destination states have to be estimated. However, if the episodes are heterogeneous and a greater number of covariates has to be taken into account to make the episodes in each origin state independent of each other, the number of possible equality tests will quickly rise, presenting practical problems for comparisons (Courgeau and Lelièvre 1992).

Thus, although the system approach provides some insight into the behavior of the dynamic system as a whole, it has several disadvantages: (1) From a causal analytical point of view, *it does not provide direct estimates of effects of coupled processes* on a process under study. In other words, using the system approach, one normally does not know to what extent one or more of the other coupled processes affect the process of interest, controlling for other exogenous variables and the history of the dependent process. It is only possible to compare transition rates for general models without covariates, as shown in the previously mentioned pregnancy-marriage example. (2) In particular, a *mixture of qualitative and quantitative processes*, in which the transition rate of a qualitative process depends on the levels of one or more metric variables, turns out to be a problem in this approach.[12] Tuma and Hannan (1984) suggested in these situations to collapse each quantitative variable into a set of ordered states. But in many situations

---

[12]Tuma and Hannan (1984) called this type of coupling between processes "cross-state dependence."

this is not very useful. (3) This approach is also unable to handle *interdependencies* between coupled processes *occurring only in specific phases of the process* (e.g., processes might be interdependent only in specific phases of the life course) or interdependencies that are dynamic over time (e.g., an interdependence might be reversed in later life phases; see Courgeau and Lelièvre 1992). (4) Finally, the number of origin and destination states of the combined process Y_t, representing the system of J variables, may lead to practical problems. Even when the number of variables and their distinct values is small, the *state space of the system variable is large*. Therefore, event history data sets must contain a great number of events, even if only the most general models of change (i.e., models without covariates) are to be estimated. In summary, the system approach has many limitations for analyzing interdependent processes. We therefore suggest using a different perspective in modeling dynamic systems, which we call the "causal approach."

6.3   Interdependent Processes: The Causal Approach

The underlying idea of the causal approach in analyzing interdependent processes can be outlined as follows (Blossfeld 1994): Based on theoretical reasons, the researcher focuses on one of the interdependent processes and considers it the dependent one. The future changes of this process are linked to the present state and history of the whole dynamic system as well as to other exogenous variables (see Blossfeld 1986; Gardner and Griffin 1986; Blossfeld and Huinink 1991). Thus, in this approach, the variable Y_t, representing the system of joint processes at time t, is not used as a multivariate dependent variable. Instead, the history and the present state of the system are seen as a condition for change in (any) one of its processes.

The question of how to find a more precise formulation for the causal approach remains. Two ideas may be helpful. First, it seems somewhat misleading to regard processes as causes. As argued in section 1.2, only events, or changes in a state variable, can sensibly be viewed as possible causes. Consequently, we would not say that a process Y_t^B is a cause of a process Y_t^A, but that *a change* in Y_t^B could be a cause (or provide a new condition) of a change in Y_t^A. This immediately leads to a second idea: that each event needs some time to become the cause of an effect, because effects follow their causes in time (see section 1.2). This time span may be very short, but it, nonetheless, does not seem sensible to assume an instantaneous reaction, at least not in the social world where most effects are mediated by decision-making agents.[13]

---

[13] In this respect, our approach to the analysis of interdependent systems significantly differs from the approach by Lillard (1993), Lillard and Waite (1993), Lillard, Brien, and Waite (1995); and Brien, Lillard, and Waite (1999) who estimate the hazard rate of a

Of course, we only consider here interdependent processes that are not just an expression of another underlying process, so that it is meaningful to assess the properties of the two processes without regarding the underlying one. This means, for instance, that what happens next to Y_t^A should not be directly related to what happens to Y_t^B at the same point in time, and vice versa. This condition, which we call local autonomy (see Pötter and Blossfeld 2001), can be formulated in terms of the uncorrelatedness of the prediction errors of both processes, Y_t^A and Y_t^B, and excludes stochastic processes that are functionally related.

Combining these ideas, a causal view on parallel and interdependent processes becomes easy, at least in principle. Given two parallel processes, Y_t^A and Y_t^B, a change in Y_t^A at any (specific) point in time t' may depend on the history of both processes *up to, but not including, t'*. Or stated in another way: What happens with Y_t^A at any point in time t' is *conditionally* independent of what happens with Y_t^B at t', conditional on the history of the joint process $Y_t = (Y_t^A, Y_t^B)$ up to, but not including, t'. Of course, the same reasoning can be applied if one focuses on Y_t^B instead of Y_t^A as the "dependent variable." We call this the *principle of conditional independence* for parallel and interdependent processes.[14]

Conditional independence is a regulative idea in the modeling of causal relationships. It is not an empirical concept and therefore cannot be demonstrated from observation alone (see Pötter and Blossfeld 2001). In particular, it is dependent on the number of processes that are considered in a particular analysis. If a process is added or removed from the analysis, the conditional independence may change. Although the theoretical background on which an analysis is grounded will to a certain extent always determine the histories and processes to be excluded and included, it will rarely be specific enough to determine exactly which processes are to be considered (see Pötter and Blossfeld 2001). In this sense, there may exist several valid causal analyses based on different sets of stochastic processes (see Giere 1999).

The same idea can be developed more formally. Beginning with a transition rate model for the joint process, $Y_t = (Y_t^A, Y_t^B)$, and assuming the principle of conditional independence, the likelihood for this model can be factorized into a product of the likelihoods for two separate models: a transition rate model for Y_t^A, which is dependent on Y_t^B as a time-dependent covariate, and a transition rate model for Y_t^B, which is dependent on Y_t^A as a time-dependent covariate.[15]

---

dependent process as a function of the *actual current state* of an independent process as well as on its simultaneous (unobserved) *hazard rate*.

[14] The terminology is adapted from Gardner and Griffin (1986) and Pötter (1993).

[15] The mathematical steps leading to this factorization are, in principle, very easy but unfortunately need a complex terminology. The mathematical apparatus is therefore not

This result has an important implication for the modeling of event histories. From a technical point of view, there is no need to distinguish between defined, ancillary, and internal covariates because all of these time-dependent covariate types can be treated equally in the estimation procedure. A distinction between defined and ancillary covariates on the one hand and internal covariates on the other is, however, sensible from a theoretical perspective because only in the case of internal covariates does it make sense to examine whether parallel processes are independent, whether one of the parallel processes is endogenous and the other ones are exogenous, or whether parallel processes form an interdependent system (i.e., they are all endogenous).[16]

In the next section we show how qualitative time-dependent covariates, whose sample paths follow a step function, can be included in transition rate models on the basis of the episode-splitting method. This procedure leads to direct estimates of how parallel qualitative processes affect the rate of change in another qualitative process and allows the conducting of significance tests of their parameters (see section 4.1.3). Then, in section 6.5, we demonstrate that a generalization of the episode-splitting technique can also be used to include quantitative time-dependent covariates. In particular, this method offers an efficient strategy for approximating (1) the effects of any type of duration dependence in a state, (2) the effects of any sort of parallel quantitative process, as well as (3) complex temporal shapes of effect patterns of covariates over time.

6.4   Episode Splitting with Qualitative Covariates

Estimating the effects of time-dependent processes on the transition rate can easily be achieved by applying the method of episode splitting. The idea of this method can be described as follows: Time-dependent qualitative covariates change their values only at discrete points in time. At all points in time, when (at least) one of the covariates changes its value, the original episode is split into pieces—called *splits* (of an episode) or *subepisodes*. For each subepisode a new record is created containing

---

given here. The mathematics can be found in Gardner and Griffin (1986), Pötter (1993), and Rohwer (1995). An important implication is that because not only the states but also functions of time (e.g., duration) can be included conditionally, the distinction between state and rate dependence proposed by Tuma and Hannan (1984) loses its meaning (see Pötter 1993).

[16]Thus, in a technical sense, there was nothing wrong with the traditional approach, which simply ignored the "feedback" effects and analyzed the impact of processes on the basis of time-dependent covariates as if they were external. However, from a theoretical perspective it was not necessary to "justify" (on theoretical grounds) or to "conclude" (from some preliminary empirical analyses) that a dependent process only has a small effect on the independent one(s) that can be ignored.

1. Information about the origin state of the original episode.

2. The values of all the covariates at the beginning of the subepisode.

3. The starting and ending times of the subepisode (information about the duration would only be sufficient in the case of an exponential model).

4. Information indicating whether the subepisode ends with the destination state of the original episode or is censored. All subepisodes, apart from the last one, are regarded as right censored. Only the last subepisode is given the same destination state as the original episode.

Consider one of the original episodes (j, k, s, t), with single origin and destination states j and k, and with starting and ending times s and t, respectively. It is assumed that the episode is defined on a process time axis so that $s = 0$. Now assume that this episode is split into L subepisodes[17]

$$(j, k, s, t) \equiv \{(j_l, k_l, s_l, t_l) \mid l = 1, \ldots, L\} \qquad (6.1)$$

The likelihood of this episode can be written as the product of a transition rate $r(t)$, and a survivor function $G(t)$. Obviously, only $G(t)$ is influenced by the process of episode splitting. However, $G(t)$ can be written as a product of the conditional survivor functions for each split of the episode:

$$G(t) = \prod_{l=1}^{L} G(t_l \mid s_l)$$

with conditional survivor functions defined by

$$G(t_l \mid s_l) = \frac{G(t_l)}{G(s_l)} = \exp\left\{-\int_{s_l}^{t_l} r(\tau)\, d\tau\right\}$$

On the right-hand side, the transition rate $r(\tau)$ could be specific for each split (j_l, k_l, s_l, t_l) and may depend on covariate values for this split.[18]

It would now be possible to rewrite the general likelihood function for transition rate models given in section 4.1.1 by inserting the product of

---

[17] $j_l = j$ for $l = 1, \ldots, L$; $k_l = j$ for $l = 1, \ldots, L - 1$; and $k_L = k$.

[18] These formulations assume that there is only a single transition, from a given origin state to one possible destination state. It is easy, however, to generalize the result for a situation with many possible destination states. The survivor function then becomes

$$\tilde{G}_k(t) = \prod_{l=1}^{L} \tilde{G}_k(t_l \mid s_l)$$

with conditional pseudosurvivor functions defined by

$$\tilde{G}_k(t_l \mid s_l) = \frac{\tilde{G}_k(t_l)}{\tilde{G}_k(s_l)} = \exp\left\{-\int_{s_l}^{t_l} r_k(\tau)\, d\tau\right\}$$

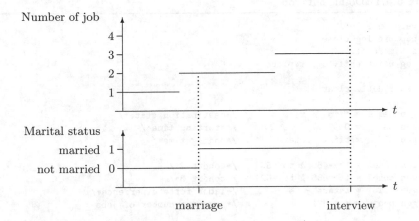

Figure 6.4.1 Modeling the effect of marriage on job mobility as a time-dependent covariate.

conditional pseudosurvivor functions. However, one does not really need to do this. One can write a general likelihood function for transition rate models, assuming a given origin state, as

$$\mathcal{L} = \prod_{k \in \mathcal{D}} \prod_{i \in \mathcal{E}_k} r_k(t_i) \prod_{i \in \mathcal{N}} \tilde{G}_k(t_i \mid s_i) \qquad (6.2)$$

Written this way, the likelihood can also be used with a sample of original (not split) episodes, where all starting times are zero, and with a sample of splits.[19] Of course, it is the responsibility of the user to do any episode splitting in such a way that the splits add up to a sample of meaningful episodes.

The maximum likelihood estimation of transition rate models in Stata is always done using the likelihood (6.2).[20] Therefore the program can easily be used with the episode-splitting method.

Episode Splitting with Stata

Suppose we study job mobility and want to examine whether first marriage has an effect on the job-exit rate. In this case we must first create a time-dependent dummy variable that changes its value from 0 to 1 at the time of first marriage. We must add this information to the original job episodes as a new variable by splitting the original job episodes into two subepisodes

---

[19] Actually, this formula is also used by Stata.

[20] Consequently, using a data set of episode splits will give identical estimation results if the same set of covariates is included in the model.

Box 6.4.1   Do-file `ehf1.do`

```
version 9
capture log close
set more off
log using ehf1.log, replace

use rrdat1, clear

gen des   = tfin ~= ti          /*destination state*/
gen ts    = 0                   /*starting time*/
gen tf    = tfin - tstart + 1   /*ending time*/

gen coho2 = tb>=468 & tb<=504   /*cohort 2*/
gen coho3 = tb>=588 & tb<=624   /*cohort 3*/
gen lfx   = tstart - te         /*labor force experience*/
gen pnoj  = noj - 1             /*previous number of jobs*/

gen marrdate  = tmar - tstart   /*variable for episode splitting*/
gen entrymarr = marrdate>0 & marrdate <tf

gen newid = _n
expand 2 if entrymarr           /*episode splitting*/

by newid, sort: gen postmarr= (_n==2)
by newid, sort: gen t1        = tf        if _n==_N
by newid, sort: replace t1    = marrdate if _n==1 & _N==2
by newid, sort: replace ts    = t1[_n-1] if _n==2
by newid, sort: replace des = 0          if _n==1 & _N==2
gen marr=marrdate <= ts & tmar >0   /*time-dependent dummy variable*/

list newid id des ts tf t1 tmar marrdate marr in 1/20

stset t1, failure(des) id(newid)     /*define single episode data*/

streg marr, dist(exp) nohr           /*fit parametric survival model*/

* percentage change in the rate: entry into marriage
display (exp(_b[marr])-1)*100

log close
```

where the marriage date lies between the starting and ending times of a job spell (see the second job in Figure 6.4.1).

With Stata, we can split the episodes and estimate the coefficients of the time-dependent covariates in one run. First, one has to create a data file containing the split episodes. As an example we use do-file `ehf1.do` shown in Box 6.4.1. Most commands in this file are already familiar from previous do-files. We now add the line

```
gen marrdate = tmar - tstart
```

Box 6.4.2 First records of `rrdat1.dta` with episode splits (generated with `ehf1.do` in Box 6.4.1)

	newid	id	des	ts	tf	t1	tmar	marrdate	marr
1.	1	1	0	0	428	124	679	124	0
2.	1	1	0	124	428	428	679	124	1
3.	2	2	1	0	46	46	762	169	0
4.	3	2	1	0	34	34	762	123	0
5.	4	2	0	0	220	89	762	89	0
6.	4	2	1	89	220	220	762	89	1
7.	5	3	1	0	12	12	870	182	0
8.	6	3	1	0	30	30	870	170	0
9.	7	3	1	0	12	12	870	140	0
10.	8	3	1	0	75	75	870	128	0
11.	9	3	1	0	12	12	870	53	0
12.	10	4	1	0	55	55	872	0	1
13.	11	5	1	0	68	68	701	118	0
14.	12	5	0	0	137	50	701	50	0
15.	12	5	1	50	137	137	701	50	1
16.	13	5	0	0	195	195	701	-87	1
17.	14	6	1	0	26	26	781	90	0
18.	15	6	1	0	26	26	781	53	0
19.	16	6	0	0	76	10	781	10	0
20.	16	6	1	10	76	76	781	10	1

to the do-file in order to define a new variable, `marrdate`, to be used for episode splitting. This variable contains the marriage date (in number of months) relative to the beginning of each job episode. `marrdate` is negative if the individual is not yet married (by the interview date) and if the individual already has been married at the beginning of each job episode, because then `tmar` is smaller than `tstart`. For these individuals our indicator variable `entrymarr` is zero. `marrdate` is positive, but smaller than the duration of the job (`tf`), if the individual marries during that job episode (see Box 6.4.2). For these individuals, `entrymarr` has the value 1, and job episodes are then split by Stata. Finally, `marrdate` is greater than the duration of the job episode (`tf`), when the individual marries after the end of the job. In these cases our indicator variable `entrymarr` is zero. In order to actually perform episode splitting, we create a new ID and use the command

```
expand 2 if entrymarr
```

Given the `if` qualifier, `expand 2` duplicates each episode where `marrdate` contains a value less than the episode's duration and greater than zero

Box 6.4.3 Result of do-file `ehf1.do` (Box 6.4.1)

```
          failure _d:  des
    analysis time _t:  t1
                  id:  newid

Iteration 0:    log likelihood =  -937.9681
Iteration 1:    log likelihood = -922.78222
Iteration 2:    log likelihood =  -922.4817
Iteration 3:    log likelihood = -922.48159
Iteration 4:    log likelihood = -922.48159

Exponential regression -- log relative-hazard form

No. of subjects =           600        Number of obs   =         761
No. of failures =           458
Time at risk    =         40782
                                       LR chi2(1)      =       30.97
Log likelihood  =   -922.48159         Prob > chi2     =      0.0000

------------------------------------------------------------------------------
     _t |      Coef.   Std. Err.      z    P>|z|     [95% Conf. Interval]
--------+---------------------------------------------------------------------
   marr |  -.5211523   .0936828    -5.56   0.000    -.7047673   -.3375374
  _cons |  -4.212944   .0638877   -65.94   0.000    -4.338161   -4.087726
------------------------------------------------------------------------------
```

(`entrymarr=1`). For our data set, Stata creates 161 new episodes. We then generate two new variables, an indicator variable `postmar` for episode splitting, and a new variable `t1` providing the episodes' ending time. We use the `by` prefix to repeat the commands for each group of episodes having the same value of `newid`. The `sort` option specifies that the data are to be sorted first. We use two Stata system variables, `_n` and `_N`, which indicate the position of an observation and the total number of observations in the data set, respectively. The first records of the new data file after episode splitting are shown in Box 6.4.2.

This box shows, for example, that the individual with `id = 1` married after he had been in his first job for 124 months (the total duration in this job is 428 months). Consequently, Stata created two subepisodes out of the original job episode: a first one with `ts = 0`, `t1 = 124`, `des = 0`, and `marrdate = 124`; and a second one with `ts = 124`, `t1 = 428`, `des = 0`, and `marrdate = 124`. Note that the first subepisode is right censored, because it has the same origin and destination states, that is, 0 ("being in a job"). Only the second split is given the same destination state as in the original episode. In this case, the original episode was also censored. This is, for example, not the case for the individual with `id = 2` in Box 6.4.2.

In a second step we create the time-dependent dummy variable `marr` (marriage) by adding the instruction

```
gen marr=marrdate <= ts & tmar >0
```

to create a dummy variable with value 0 until the marriage date and value 1 if the individual has married (compare `ts` in column 4 and `marrdate` in column 8 in Box 6.4.2). Next, we `stset` our data and estimate the effect of `marr` using an exponential model.

Using do-file `ehf1.do`, the estimation results are shown in Box 6.4.3. Obviously, the coefficient for the time-dependent covariate `marr` is statistically significant and has a negative sign. This means that entry into marriage reduces the job-exit rate by about 41 %, calculated as

$$\left(\exp(-0.5212) - 1 \right) \cdot 100 \% = -40.6 \%$$

In other words, marriage makes the individuals less mobile.[21] The question of how this result depends on other covariates now arises. To investigate this question, we use do-file `ehf3.do` in Box 6.4.4.

Part of the output of `ehf3.do` is shown in Box 6.4.5. The effect of the time-dependent covariate is still highly significant and has a negative sign. However, its absolute size is smaller than in Box 6.4.3. Controlling for the time-constant covariables, entry into marriage reduces the job-exit rate by about only 29 %.[22] Thus part of the time-constant heterogeneity between the individuals was captured by the time-dependent covariate "marriage." The estimated effects of the time-constant covariates, however, are very similar compared with the results in Box 4.1.4, where the time-dependent covariate "marriage" was not included.

---

[21] The interpretation of effects of qualitative time-dependent covariates has to be done very carefully. Compared to the effects of time-constant covariates, they seem to be less robust and much more vulnerable with regard to misspecification. For example, in our didactical job-exit example, the time-dependent covariate marriage is likely to pick up various influences of other time-dependent covariates that are correlated with the time-path of the covariate marriage (i.e., the differentiation between the periods before and after marriage) but not controlled for in the analysis. Such variables are (1) birth of a child (which is closely connected with the marriage event and, in traditional societies, should have opposite effects on husbands' and wives' job-exit rates); (2) job duration (job-exit rates normally decline with durations in a job, and longer job durations are much more expected to occur after marriage); (3) general labor force experience (very often people are much more mobile at the beginning of their careers than in later phases; thus they are likely to be more mobile before than after marriage); (4) age (normally, young people are more mobile than older ones; because married people tend to be older, they are likely to be more mobile after marriage; (5) unobserved heterogeneity (see chapter 10) leads to a declining apparent hazard rate over time, thus marriage tends to pick up an apparent high hazard rate before marriage and an apparent low hazard rate after marriage); and so on. These examples make clear that a serious interpretation of the effect of the time-dependent covariate marriage on the job-exit rate would suppose a series of additional controls of time-dependent processes.

[22] $(\exp(-0.3447) - 1) \cdot 100 \% \approx -29.2 \%$.

Box 6.4.4 Do-file `ehf3.do`

```
version 9
capture log close
set more off
log using ehf3.log, replace

use rrdat1, clear

gen des    = tfin ~= ti        /*destination state*/
gen ts     = 0                 /*starting time*/
gen tf     = tfin - tstart + 1 /*ending time*/

gen coho2 = tb>=468 & tb<=504  /*cohort 2*/
gen coho3 = tb>=588 & tb<=624  /*cohort 3*/
gen lfx    = tstart - te       /*labor force experience*/
gen pnoj   = noj - 1           /*previous number of jobs*/

gen marrdate  = tmar - tstart  /*variables for episode splitting*/
gen entrymarr = marrdate>0 & marrdate <tf

gen newid = _n
expand 2 if entrymarr          /*episode splitting*/

by newid, sort: gen postmarr= (_n==2)
by newid, sort: gen t1        = tf        if _n==_N
by newid, sort: replace t1    = marrdate if _n==1 & _N==2
by newid, sort: replace ts    = t1[_n-1] if _n==2
by newid, sort: replace des = 0          if _n==1 & _N==2
gen marr=marrdate <= ts & tmar >0   /*time-dependent dummy variable*/

stset t1, failure(des) id(newid)    /*define single episode data*/

streg edu coho2 coho3 lfx pnoj pres marr, dist(exp) nohr
/*fit parametric survival model*/

* percentage change in the rate: entry into marriage
display (exp(_b[marr])-1)*100

gen marrmen= sex==1 & marrdate <= ts & tmar >0      /*interaction effect*/

streg edu coho2 coho3 lfx pnoj pres marr marrmen, ///
dist(exp) nohr /*fit parametric survival model*/

log close
```

Interaction Effects with Time-Dependent Covariates

Although we get a significant effect for the time-dependent covariate "marriage" in Box 6.4.5, it cannot be easily interpreted in theoretical terms. For example, it is well known from the empirical literature that family events have opposite influences on the job-exit rates for men and women. Marriage,

Box 6.4.5   Result of do-file `ehf3.do` (Box 6.4.4)

```
          failure _d:  des
    analysis time _t:  t1
                  id:  newid

Iteration 0:   log likelihood =  -937.9681
Iteration 1:   log likelihood =   -887.864
Iteration 2:   log likelihood = -884.20472
Iteration 3:   log likelihood = -884.19606
Iteration 4:   log likelihood = -884.19606


Exponential regression -- log relative-hazard form

No. of subjects =          600      Number of obs    =        761
No. of failures =          458
Time at risk    =        40782
                                    LR chi2(7)       =     107.54
Log likelihood  =   -884.19606      Prob > chi2      =     0.0000


------------------------------------------------------------------------
    _t |     Coef.   Std. Err.       z    P>|z|     [95% Conf. Interval]
-------+----------------------------------------------------------------
   edu |   .0770113   .0245584     3.14   0.002     .0288778    .1251448
 coho2 |   .5970898   .1136579     5.25   0.000     .3743244    .8198553
 coho3 |   .6137878   .1188341     5.17   0.000     .3808773    .8466984
   lfx |  -.0022972    .000968    -2.37   0.018    -.0041945      -.0004
  pnoj |   .0645368   .0439811     1.47   0.142    -.0216645    .1507381
  pres |   -.027352    .005522    -4.95   0.000    -.0381748   -.0165291
  marr |  -.3447105   .1022392    -3.37   0.001    -.5450956   -.1443254
 _cons |  -4.387819   .2755794   -15.92   0.000    -4.927944   -3.847693
------------------------------------------------------------------------
```

at least for the older cohorts, increases the rate of moving out of the job for women (because they normally take care of the household and children), while marriage for men decreases the job-exit rate (because they normally carry an additional economic responsibility for the wife and children).

To examine whether these gender-specific relationships between marriage and employment career are true, we create an interaction variable for the joint effect of the time-dependent covariate "marriage" and the time-constant variable "sex." The command is shown in the lower part of Box 6.4.4. The interaction variable **marrmen** has the value 1 as soon as a man marries.

Part of the estimation results of the model with the **marrmen** interaction effect are shown in Box 6.4.6. The estimated parameters are in accordance with our expectations. The effect of marriage on the rate of moving out of a job is *positive* for women. Marriage *increases* the job-exit rate for

Box 6.4.6 Result of do-file ehf3.do (Box 6.4.4)

```
         failure _d:  des
   analysis time _t:  t1
               id:  newid

Iteration 0:    log likelihood =  -937.9681
Iteration 1:    log likelihood = -866.10127
Iteration 2:    log likelihood =  -858.1433
Iteration 3:    log likelihood = -858.12342
Iteration 4:    log likelihood = -858.12342


Exponential regression -- log relative-hazard form

No. of subjects =          600    Number of obs    =         761
No. of failures =          458
Time at risk    =        40782
                                  LR chi2(8)       =      159.69
Log likelihood  =    -858.12342   Prob > chi2      =      0.0000


------------------------------------------------------------------------
     _t |    Coef.    Std. Err.      z     P>|z|    [95% Conf. Interval]
--------+---------------------------------------------------------------
    edu | .0943202    .0234471     4.02    0.000    .0483646    .1402757
   coho2 | .5422956   .1131758     4.79    0.000    .3204752    .764116
   coho3 | .5303917   .1192044     4.45    0.000    .2967555    .764028
    lfx |-.0030792     .000976    -3.16    0.002   -.0049921   -.0011664
   pnoj | .1029071    .0444981     2.31    0.021    .0156924    .1901218
   pres | -.026412    .0053505    -4.94    0.000   -.0368988   -.0159252
   marr | .2734695    .1231325     2.22    0.026    .0321343    .5148047
 marrmen |-1.023141   .1401201    -7.30    0.000   -1.297771   -.7485103
   _cons |-4.584152   .2693982   -17.02    0.000   -5.112163   -4.056141
------------------------------------------------------------------------
```

women by about 31 %.[23] Of course, here the time-dependent covariate marriage also serves as a proxy variable for other time-dependent processes that are connected with the marriage event, such as childbirth, and so on. In a "real" analysis one would therefore also include time-dependent covariates for childbirth and additional possible interaction effects, for example, with the birth cohort.[24]

On the other hand, for men the effect of marriage on the job change rate is *negative*. Marriage *decreases* the rate of moving out of a job by about 53 %.[25] In other words, marriage makes men less mobile.

---

[23] $(\exp(0.2735) - 1) \cdot 100\% \approx 31.5\%$.

[24] New event history analyses show that younger women decreasingly change their employment behavior at the time of marriage, but increasingly at the time when the first baby is born. Thus, the important marker for employment shifted in the first family phase from marriage to the birth of the first child across cohorts (see Blossfeld and Hakim, 1997).

[25] $(\exp(0.2735 - 1.0231) - 1) \cdot 100\% \approx -52.7\%$.

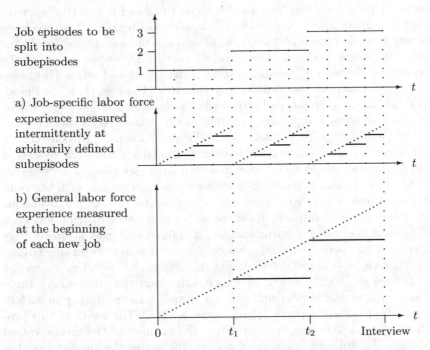

Job episodes to be split into subepisodes

a) Job-specific labor force experience measured intermittently at arbitrarily defined subepisodes

b) General labor force experience measured at the beginning of each new job

Figure 6.5.1 Modeling labor force experience as (a) time-dependent covariate *job-specific labor force experience* and (b) time-constant covariate *general labor force experience*, illustrated with three consecutive job episodes arbitrarily split into subepisodes.

This didactic example again demonstrates how important theory is for modeling event history data. The reason for the negative effect of the time-dependent covariate in Box 6.4.6 is only that the negative effect for men is stronger than the positive effect for women. In general, it is really difficult to evaluate whether an estimated model is appropriate without a strong theory. There are a few technical criteria and approaches that can be applied to assess models (see chapters 8 and 10), but our experience shows that they only give limited help in deciding about competing models. Thus, event history modeling (as is true for all causal modeling) must be guided by theoretical ideas.

6.5 Episode Splitting with Quantitative Covariates

Many of the theoretical models that are of interest to sociologists relate quantitative processes to qualitative outcomes over time. For example, "job-specific labor force experience" can be considered a metric latent (or unobserved) variable. There are good reasons to measure it with the proxy variable "duration in a job." Other examples for metric causal processes are continuously changing "investments into specific marriages" in divorce studies (Blossfeld, De Rose, Hoem, and Rohwer 1993), "career success of the partner" in analyses of parallel careers of husbands and wives (Bernasco 1994), or measures of the continuously changing "business cycle" or "modernization process" in job mobility studies (see Blossfeld 1986). As long as the effects of such quantitative variables can be considered a specific function of process time (e.g., based on a Weibull, Gompertz (-Makeham), a log-logistic, a lognormal, or a sickle model), available parametric models of time-dependence might be selected and estimated (see chapter 7).[26]

However, if these parametric models are not appropriate, or if the sample path of the quantitative covariate is so irregular or complex over time that it is impossible to specify its shape with a parametric distribution, then the method of episode splitting can be generalized and used as an effective instrument to *approximate the sample path of a metric covariate* (Blossfeld, Hamerle, and Mayer 1989). Using this approach, the original episodes are divided arbitrarily into small subepisodes, and the quantitative time-dependent covariate is intermittently measured at the beginning of each of these subepisodes (see panel (a) of Figure 6.5.1).[27] The result of this procedure is a step function approximating the changes of the metric causal variable. The approximation is, of course, the better the smaller the chosen subepisodes are and the more often the metric time-dependent causal variable is intermittently measured.

We use the variable "job-specific labor force experience" as an example. We assume that this (unobserved) variable increases linearly over the time a person spends in a job. In section 4.1.3, labor force experience was only considered in terms of "general labor force experience" measured at the beginning of each new job episode and treated as constant over the whole duration in a job. Panel (b) in Figure 6.5.1 shows that this normally leads to a very bad approximation of what might be called labor force experience, in particular for employees who do not change jobs very often. Now, in addition, we include the variable "job-specific labor force experience," measured intermittently at the beginning of arbitrarily defined subepisodes within each job (see panel (a) in Figure 6.5.1). We start our example by defining subepisodes with a maximal length of 60 months (or 5 years) in the Stata do-file ehf5.do shown in Box 6.5.1. Because the longest duration in a job is 428 months (see Box 2.2.5), we have to define eight intervals

---

[26] In these cases, the values of the causal variables are truly known continuously, that is, at every moment in some interval (Tuma and Hannan 1984).

[27] "Continuous" measurement of quantitative processes usually means that variables are measured intermittently with a very small interval between measurements (see Tuma and Hannan 1984).

Box 6.5.1 Do-file ehf5.do

```
version 9
capture log close
set more off
log using ehf5.log, replace

use rrdat1, clear

gen des   = tfin ~= ti          /*destination state*/
gen ts    = 0                   /*starting time*/
gen tf    = tfin - tstart + 1   /*ending time*/
gen coho2 = tb>=468 & tb<=504   /*cohort 2*/
gen coho3 = tb>=588 & tb<=624   /*cohort 3*/
gen lfx   = tstart - te         /*labor force experience*/
gen pnoj  = noj - 1             /*previous number of jobs*/
gen newid = _n

stset tf, failure(des) id(newid) /*define single episode data*/

stsplit t1, at(60 (60) 420)      /*split time-span records*/

by newid, sort: replace ts = tf[_n-1] if newid == newid[_n-1]

stset tf, failure(des) id(newid) /*define single episode data*/

list newid id des ts tf t1 lfx in 1/20   /*first records of data file*/

gen lfx60=ts
streg edu coho2 coho3 lfx pnoj pres lfx60, dist(exp) nohr

* different episode splits: lfx24
drop t1 ts lfx60  /*drop var with different values across split obs.*/
stjoin            /*combine records*/
gen ts = 0
stsplit t1, at(24 (24) 420)
by newid, sort: replace ts = tf[_n-1] if newid == newid[_n-1]
stset tf, failure(des) id(newid)
list newid id des ts tf t1 lfx in 1/20
gen lfx24=ts
streg edu coho2 coho3 lfx pnoj pres lfx24, dist(exp) nohr

* different episode splits: lfx12
drop t1 ts lfx24
stjoin
gen ts = 0
stsplit t1, at(12 (12) 420)
by newid, sort: replace ts = tf[_n-1] if newid == newid[_n-1]
stset tf, failure(des) id(newid)
list newid id des ts tf t1 lfx in 1/20
gen lfx12=ts
streg edu coho2 coho3 lfx pnoj pres lfx12, dist(exp) nohr

log close
```

Box 6.5.2 First records of data file `rrdat1.dta` with episode splits

	newid	id	des	ts	tf	t1	lfx
1.	1	1	.	0	60	0	0
2.	1	1	.	60	120	60	0
3.	1	1	.	120	180	120	0
4.	1	1	.	180	240	180	0
5.	1	1	.	240	300	240	0
6.	1	1	.	300	360	300	0
7.	1	1	.	360	420	360	0
8.	1	1	0	420	428	420	0
9.	2	2	1	0	46	0	0
10.	3	2	1	0	34	0	46
11.	4	2	.	0	60	0	80
12.	4	2	.	60	120	60	80
13.	4	2	.	120	180	120	80
14.	4	2	1	180	220	180	80
15.	5	3	1	0	12	0	0
16.	6	3	1	0	30	0	12
17.	7	3	1	0	12	0	42
18.	8	3	.	0	60	0	54
19.	8	3	1	60	75	60	54
20.	9	3	1	0	12	0	129

accomplished with the `stsplit` command:

```
stsplit t1, at(60 (60) 420)
```

Once you submit this command, Stata creates 421 new episodes. Box 6.5.2 shows the first records of the data set after episode splitting.

For example, for individual with `id = 1` the original job episode with a duration of 428 months is split into seven subepisodes of 60 months and an eighth subepisode of 8 months. Note again that the first seven subepisodes are right censored, that is, they have the same origin and destination states, that is, 0 ("being in a job"). Only the eighth split is given the same destination state as in the original episode. In this case the original episode was also censored. Now declare your data to be event history data with the command `stset`, and the standard output after `stset` will show you how the total number of observations has changed while the number of individuals and events remain the same.

We use the `streg` command to estimate an exponential model with our standard set of covariates. The estimation results are shown in Box 6.5.3. This box provides estimates of two different forms of labor force experience. The parameter for the variable `lfx` is an estimate for the effect of "*general* labor force experience" and the parameter for variable `lfx60` is an estimate

Box 6.5.3   Result of do-file ehf5.do (Box 6.5.1)

```
           failure _d:  des
     analysis time _t:  tf
                   id:  newid

Iteration 0:   log likelihood =  -937.9681
Iteration 1:   log likelihood = -865.09263
Iteration 2:   log likelihood = -856.34496
Iteration 3:   log likelihood = -856.25564
Iteration 4:   log likelihood = -856.25557


Exponential regression -- log relative-hazard form

No. of subjects =          600    Number of obs   =       1021
No. of failures =          458
Time at risk    =        40782
                                  LR chi2(7)      =     163.43
Log likelihood  =   -856.25557    Prob > chi2     =     0.0000


------------------------------------------------------------------------------
    _t |      Coef.   Std. Err.       z    P>|z|     [95% Conf. Interval]
-------+----------------------------------------------------------------------
   edu |   .0646117   .0248022     2.61   0.009     .0160002    .1132231
 coho2 |   .4073219   .1148612     3.55   0.000     .1821981    .6324456
 coho3 |   .2946223   .1216231     2.42   0.015     .0562455    .5329992
   lfx |  -.0039428   .0009293    -4.24   0.000    -.0057641   -.0021214
  pnoj |   .0647431    .044029     1.47   0.141    -.0215522    .1510384
  pres |  -.0253234    .005449    -4.65   0.000    -.0360032   -.0146435
 lfx60 |  -.0070767   .0009954    -7.11   0.000    -.0090276   -.0051259
 _cons |   -4.01378   .276443   -14.52   0.000    -4.555598   -3.471962
------------------------------------------------------------------------------
```

for the effect of "*job-specific* labor force experience." As expected, both variables have a significantly negative effect. In other words, increases in general and job-specific labor force experience reduce the rate of job mobility. However, as can be seen in the absolute size of the coefficients, job-specific labor force experience reduces job mobility more than does general labor force experience. This is in accordance with the hypotheses suggested in the literature (see chapter 4).

The approximation of job-specific labor force experience in each of the jobs is still relatively rough. We therefore reduce the maximum interval length of subepisodes from 60 months to 24 months and finally to 12 months, and then examine how the estimated coefficients for job-specific labor force experience change. To this end, we first use `stjoin` to reverse episode splitting, adjust the `stsplit` command, create a new variable measuring job-specific labor force experience, and refit the exponential model (see Box 6.5.1) The results of these estimations are shown in Box 6.5.4. In each cell of the table, Stata reports the coefficients first, then their standard errors.

Box 6.5.4 Exponential model with episode splits (60, 24, and 12 months)

Variable	lfx60	lfx24	lfx12
edu	.06461165	.06289739	.06264707
	.02480222	.02479523	.02479745
coho2	.40732186	.40596591	.40490939
	.11486118	.11508234	.11510469
coho3	.29462234	.30063665	.29965295
	.12162307	.12200495	.12203225
lfx	-.00394276	-.00389748	-.00388945
	.00092927	.00092849	.0009282
pnoj	.06474307	.06326584	.0628425
	.04402903	.04405978	.04405985
pres	-.02532336	-.02492895	-.02483508
	.00544898	.00544831	.00544688
lfx60	-.00707673		
	.00099535		
lfx24		-.00631348	
		.00090279	
lfx12			-.00626742
			.00089356
_cons	-4.01378	-3.9498113	-3.9187213
	.27644303	.27888942	.27979706

legend: b/se

One can easily see that the estimates of the three models are quite similar. The estimates of the metric time-dependent covariate change a little when we reduce the maximum length of the subepisodes from 60 to 24 months, but they remain practically unchanged when we reduce the maximum length further from 24 to 12 months. Thus one can conclude that, given a maximum interval length of 24 months, one achieves a relatively good approximation of the linearly changing time-dependent covariate "job-specific labor force experience." Further, one can say that, at least in substantive terms, the coefficients of the time-constant covariates are basically the same as for the exponential model in Box 4.1.4. And finally, all the coefficients (including "job-specific labor force experience") are very similar compared with the equivalent Gompertz model with covariates (see section 7.2).[28]

6.6 Application Examples

To illustrate the utility of the episode-splitting method in empirical research, we refer to four investigations using this method in various ways. We concentrate on the modeling techniques used in these studies and summarize their most important findings.

---

[28] Actually, as is demonstrated in section 7.2, we have only approximated a Gompertz model.

Example 1: A Dynamic Approach to the Study of Life-Course, Cohort, and Period Effects in Career Mobility

Studying intragenerational mobility of German men, Blossfeld (1986) proposed introducing the changing labor market structure into event history models of career mobility in order to treat the time-dependent nature of the attainment process in an adequate manner. There are two main ways in which the changing labor market affects career opportunities. First, people start their careers in different structural labor market contexts (when this influence is more or less stable over people's careers, it is normally called a cohort effect; see also Blossfeld 1986), and second, the labor market structure influences the opportunities of *all* people within the labor market at each moment (this is commonly referred to as a period effect).

Any model using education (in terms of school years), labor market experience (as a life-course measure), year of entry into the labor market (as a cohort measure), and chronological year of measurement (as a period measure) implies an identification problem (Mason and Fienberg 1985) because of a linear dependency of these variables. Blossfeld, starting from a more substantive point of view, tried to find more explicit measures for the theoretically important macro effects. He suggested using 14 time series from official statistics indicating the long-term development of the labor market structure in West Germany.[29] But time series often measure similar features of a process and are highly correlated. Therefore another identification problem invariably arises whenever several time series are included in a model simultaneously. One strategy for solving this problem is to use only one series or to choose only uncorrelated series. The problem then is that the time series chosen may only capture specific features of the labor market structural development. If time series represent aspects of an underlying regularity, it is more appropriate to look for these latent dimensions. A statistical method for doing this is factor analysis. Blossfeld's factor analysis with principal factoring and equimax rotation gave two orthogonal factors explaining 96.4 % of the variance in the 14 time series.

The first factor could be interpreted as representing the changing "level of modernization" and the second one as a measure of the changes in the labor market with regard to the business cycle, so it was called "labor market

---

[29]These included (1) level of productivity, (2) national income per capita (deflated), (3) national income per economically active person (deflated), (4) private consumption (deflated), (5) proportion of expenditure on services in private consumption, (6) proportion of gainfully employed in public sector, (7) proportion of 13-year-old pupils attending German *Gymnasium*, (8) proportion of gainfully employed in service sector, (9) proportion of students in resident population, (10) proportion of civil servants in economically active population, (11) proportion of white-collar employees in economically active population, (12) unemployment rate, (13) proportion of gross national product invested in plant and equipment, and (14) proportion of registered vacancies of all jobs, excluding self-employment.

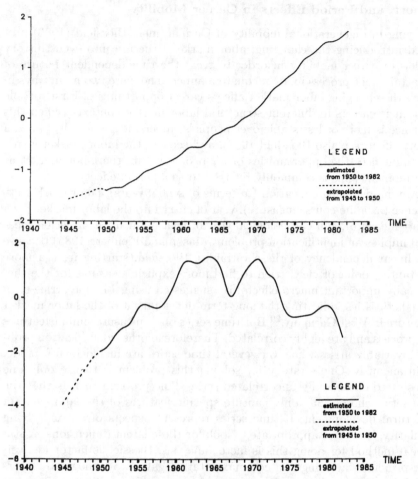

Figure 6.6.1 Development of modernization (upper figure) and labor market conditions (lower figure) in West Germany (plots of factor scores).

conditions." As can be seen from the plots of the scores of the two factors in Figure 6.6.1, the factor "level of modernization" shows a monotonic trend with a slightly increasing slope, while the factor "labor market conditions" shows a cyclical development with downturns around 1967 and 1973. This is in accordance with the historical development of the business cycle in Germany. Because both factors are orthogonally constructed, it is possible to include both measures simultaneously in a model estimation.

To represent the changing conditions under which cohorts enter the labor market, Blossfeld used the factor scores "level of modernization" and "labor market conditions" at the year persons entered the labor force. To introduce period as a time-dependent covariate, he used the method of episode splitting described earlier. In accordance with this method, the original job episodes were split into subepisodes every year so that the factor scores "level of modernization" and "labor market conditions" could be updated in each job episode for all the employees every year. In the terminology of Kalbfleisch and Prentice (1980), the period measures are ancillary time-dependent covariates.

Modeling cohort and period effects this way not only provides more direct and valid measures of the explanatory concepts but also results in the disappearance of the problem of nonestimable parameters. It is therefore not necessary to impose (in substantive terms normally unjustifiable) constraints on the parameters to identify life-course, cohort, and period effects (see, e.g., Mason et al. 1973). The result of the estimation of life-course, cohort, and period effects on upward moves in an exponential model is shown in Table 6.6.1. We focus our attention on Model 5 in this table and do not give substantive interpretations of the effects of the variables "time in the labor force," "education," or "prestige" because these would be basically the same as the ones already given in section 4.1.3.

We mainly concentrate on the interpretation of the effects of changes in the labor market structure. In Model 5, the "level of modernization" at time of entry into the labor market has a negative effect on upward moves. Thus, the higher the level of modernization, the better the first job of beginners and the less likely that there will be further upward moves for them. The same is true for the negative effect of labor market conditions at entry into the labor market. The more favorable the business cycle at entry into the labor market is for a particular cohort, the easier it is for its members to find "good jobs" at the beginning of their careers, and the harder it will be to find even better ones.

Conversely, the period effect of "modernization" is positive on upward moves. Thus the continuous restructuring of the economy in the process of technological and organizational modernization leads to increasing opportunities for all people to move up in the labor market. The same is true for the period effect of the labor market conditions. It is positive for upward mobility and suggests that the better the labor market conditions, the more opportunities the economy will provide.

If we take into account the effect of labor force experience (life-course effect), then this analysis supports the thesis that the career process is strongly affected by cohort, period, and life-course effects. The attainment process is time-dependent in a threefold sense. It depends on the time spent in the labor force, the historical time of entry into the labor market, and the actual historical time. Thus analyses of standard mobility tables (e.g., Erikson and Goldthorpe 1991; Haller 1989; Handl 1988) that distinguish only structural mobility and exchange mobility on a cross-sectional basis

Table 6.6.1 Estimates of models for transition rates to better jobs (upward moves) for German men born 1929–31, 1939–41, and 1949–51.

Estimates for Model	Upward Moves				
	1	2	3	4	5
Log of mean rate	-6.135				
Constant		-4.241*	-4.288*	-4.943*	-5.585*
Time in labor force (life-course effect)		-0.012*	-0.015*	-0.012*	-0.082*
Education			0.187*	0.224*	0.268*
Prestige			-0.042*	-0.041*	-0.042*
Level of modernization at at entry into labor market (cohort effect)				-0.294*	-9.664*
Labor market conditions at entry into labor market (cohort effect)				0.009	-1.394*
Level of modernization (period effect)					9.066*
Labor market conditions (period effect)					1.203*
Number of exits	590	590	590	590	590
Subepisodes	22843	22843	22843	22843	22843
χ^2		842.21	1007.46	1024.02	2165.29
df		1	3	5	7

* statistically significant at 0.001 level. Rates are measured with months as units.

will necessarily provide misleading pictures of the mechanisms of attainment (see also Sørensen 1986). The creation of vacancies and the loss of positions in the course of structural change count as the central mechanisms of career mobility and affect people's mobility changes in different ways.

Example 2: Changes in the Process of Family Formation and the New Role of Women

The second example is based on an investigation by Blossfeld and Huinink (1991). They assessed the hypothesis of the "new home economics" (e.g., Becker 1981) that women's rising educational and career investments will lead to a decline in marriage and motherhood (see also Oppenheimer 1988). Because the accumulation of educational and career resources is a lifetime process, it must be modeled as a dynamic process over the life course. In West Germany in particular it is necessary to differentiate between the accumulation of general and vocational qualifications within the educational

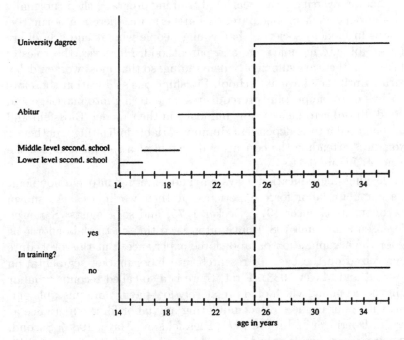

Figure 6.6.2 Educational careers over the life course in West Germany.

system on the one hand, and the accumulation of workplace-related labor force experience on the other.

In order to model the accumulation of general and vocational qualifications in the school system, the vocational training system, and the university system of the Federal Republic of Germany, Blossfeld and Huinink (1991) used the average number of years required to obtain such qualifications (see variable V12 (edu) in Box 2.2.1). However, this variable was not treated as a time-constant variable but as a time-dependent covariate. To model the changes in the accumulation of qualifications over the life course, they updated the level of education at the age when a woman obtained a particular educational rank in the hierarchy. For example, for a woman who attains a lower school qualification at age 14, reaches the intermediate school qualification at age 16, leaves school with an *Abitur* at age 19, and finally finishes university studies at age 25, one would obtain a step function for the highest level of education over the life course as shown in the upper panel of Figure 6.6.2. The hypothesis of the "new home economics" is that such increasing levels of education raise a woman's labor-market attachment, thereby leading to greater delays in marriage and childbirth.

However, from a sociological point of view, one could also expect an effect from the fact that women are enrolled in school. When a woman is attending school, university, or a vocational training program, she is normally economically dependent on her parents. Furthermore, there are normative expectations in modern societies that young people who attend school are "not at risk" of entering marriage and parenthood. Moreover, the roles of students and mothers are sufficiently demanding, so that most women delay childbearing until they have left school. Finishing one's education therefore counts as one of the important prerequisites for entering into marriage and parenthood. In order to include this influence in their model, Blossfeld and Huinink generated a time-dependent dummy variable indicating whether or not a woman is attending the educational system at a specific age (see the lower panel of Figure 6.6.2).

After leaving the educational system and entering into employment, women accumulate labor force experience at their workplaces. As shown earlier, economists (Mincer 1974; Becker 1975) and sociologists (Sørensen 1977; Sørensen and Tuma 1981) have often used time in the labor force as a proxy for the accumulation of labor force experience. But this procedure can be criticized on the basis of research into labor-market segmentation (see Blossfeld and Mayer 1988). First, there is a so-called secondary labor market in the economy, which offers relatively low-paying and unstable employment with poor chances of accumulating any labor force experience at all (see, e.g., Doeringer and Piore 1971; Blossfeld and Mayer 1988). Second, in some positions within so-called internal labor markets, the opportunities to accumulate labor force experience are very unequally distributed (e.g., Doeringer and Piore 1971; Doeringer 1967; Piore 1968; Blossfeld and Mayer 1988). Likewise, differences in the opportunities for acquiring labor force experience may also exist among the self-employed and people working in different kinds of professions. This means that the *speed and levels of the accumulation of labor force experience* must be modeled in dependence of the type of employment. For the dynamic modeling of job-specific investments in human capital over the life course, Blossfeld and Huinink have therefore made the following three conjectures.

Development of Career Resources After Entry Into First Employment. Women who have left the educational system and entered their first jobs accumulate labor force experience with decreasing increments. Because on-the-job training is concentrated mainly in the earlier phases of employment, increases are large at the beginning and level off with increasing time on the job. This means that increments and final levels of labor force experience should be modeled dependent on a measure of how good the job is, for example, the prestige score, P, of jobs. A possible mathematical model of the growth rate $r(P, t)$ of career resources at age t, assuming that the first job was entered at age t_0, is therefore ($t \geq t_0$):

$$r(P, t) = \exp\left(-\alpha(t - t_0)\right)$$

where

$$\alpha = \frac{P_{\max} - P_{\min}}{2} \frac{1}{P} = \frac{83.4}{P}$$

Here P is Wegener's (1985) prestige score, which is used as a proxy measure for the job quality and for the opportunity to accumulate labor force experience within a job. Given this model, the level of career resources $K(P,t)$ within a job episode at age t is then defined as

$$K(P,t) = \exp\left\{\int_{t_0}^{t} r(P,u)\,\mathrm{d}u\right\} - 1$$

Until entry into the first job, the level of career resources $K(P,t)$ is equal to zero. The maximum level of career resources $\max(K(P,t))$, within a job with the lowest prestige score (a helper with a prestige score of 20.0 on the Wegener scale), for example, is reached after 9 months and has the value 0.27. For a job with the highest prestige score on the Wegener scale (a medical doctor), the maximum level of career resources is reached after about 9–10 years and has a value of 8.15.

Change of Jobs. If a woman changes from a job with prestige level P_0 to a job with prestige level $P_h > P_0$ at time t_1, which is an *upward move*, her career resources will increase until the maximum career level of the new job is reached. In this case the career function for $t > t_1$ is[30]

$$K(P_h,t) = \min\left\{K(P_0,t_1) + K(P_h,t-t_1), \max(K(P_h,t))\right\}$$

If a woman changes from a job with prestige level P_0 to a job with a prestige level $P_n < P_0$ at time t_2 (a *downward move*), the career resources of the preceding job decrease linearly over time and the career resources of the successive job are increased over time. However, the maximum career level of the successive job is considered to be the lower limit. Thus, with increasing time, the level of career resources decreases and will approach the maximum career level of the successive job. For $t > t_2$ the level of career resources is obtained as follows:

$$K(P_n,t) = \begin{cases} \min\left\{(1 - (1.5/P_0)\,(t-t_2))\,K(P_0,t_2) + K(P_n,t-t_2),\right. \\ \left.\quad K(P_0,t_2)\right\} \quad \text{if} \quad t - t_2 < P_0/1.5 \\ K(P_n,t-t_2) \quad \text{otherwise} \end{cases}$$

Discontinuity of Work Experience. Besides continuous changes of the level of career resources as a result of upward and downward moves, one

---

[30]In the following formula, $\max(K(P_h,t))$ is the highest value a woman can reach in job h. The formula $K(P_h,t)$ then says that her resources equal a value that increases with time, until the maximum level, $\max(K(Pt,t))$, is reached.

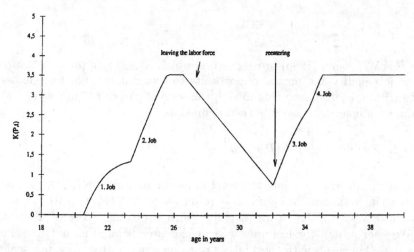

Figure 6.6.3 Career resources over the life course: an occupational career with a phase of nonemployment.

must also recognize that women tend to have several entries into and exits from the labor force after leaving school because of family events (marriage, birth of children, etc.; Mincer and Polachek 1974). Given this discontinuity of work experience, the assumption normally made for the career process of men in labor-market research (Sørensen 1977), that career resources monotonically increase with decreasing increments over the work-life, is no longer valid. If women interrupt their employment careers, then they lose career resources that have to be accumulated again after reentry into the labor force. To model the path of labor force experience of women, Blossfeld and Huinink assumed that career resources decline when women interrupt (I) their employment career at age t_3 as long as women's career resources are still positive. The speed of the decrease is thereby dependent on the prestige level (P_0) of the job held immediately before the interruption of the career. For $t > t_3$ one gets:

$$K(I,t) = \max\left\{0, 1 - \frac{1.5}{P_0}(t - t_3)\,K(P_0, t_3)\right\}$$

Figure 6.6.3 shows an example for a trajectory of career resources including an upward move (from job 1 to job 2), a work interruption, and a reentry into a third job.

The goal of the transition rate analysis in this research was to specify the rates of entry into marriage or motherhood $r(t)$ as a function of time-constant (X_1) and time-dependent covariates ($X_2(t)$) in an exponential model:

$$r(t) = \exp\left(X_1\,\beta_1 + X_2(t)\,\beta_2\right)$$

In this model, observation begins at age 15 and ends with the event of first marriage or the birth of the first child or, for right-censored cases, with the date of the interview or age 45, whichever is earlier.

A combination of two variables was used to control for the well-known nonmonotonic age dependence of the marriage rate and the rate of the first birth (Coale 1971; Bloom 1982). This approach considers women at risk of entering first marriage and having a first child between the ages of 15 and 45 (i is an index for the ith one-month interval):

$$\log\left(D_i\right) = \log\left(\text{current age} - 15\right)$$
$$\log\left(R_i\right) = \log\left(45 - \text{current age}\right)$$

Including these variables in the exponential model as time-dependent covariates,

$$\exp\left(\log(D_i)\,\beta' + \log(R_i)\,\beta''\right) = D_i^{\beta'}\,R_i^{\beta''}$$

the typical bell-shaped curve of the rates of entry into first marriage and first motherhood is modeled. This curve is symmetric around the age of 30 for $\beta' = \beta''$, left-skewed for $\beta' < \beta''$, and right-skewed for $\beta' > \beta''$.

First marriage and first childbirth are interdependent processes and form a dynamic system. Premarital conception increases the readiness of women to enter into marriage, and marriage increases the risk of childbirth. Therefore, Blossfeld and Huinink included time-dependent dummy variables for being pregnant in the marriage model and for being married in the first-birth model.

To control for cohort and period effects of historical and economic developments on family decisions, Blossfeld and Huinink introduced two different types of variables. First, they used two dummy variables for the three birth cohorts (reference group = cohort 1929-31) to measure differences among cohorts. Second, they employed a variable that reflects the continuous development of labor market conditions as a period measure (see Figure 6.6.1 in the previous example).

To include all these various time-dependent covariates in the rate equation, Blossfeld and Huinink (1991) applied the method of episode splitting, as described previously. As time-constant background variables, they incorporated father's social class, residence at age 15 (town vs. country, where country is the reference category), the number of siblings, and the educational level of the partner. We cannot go into the details of this sophisticated dynamic analysis here. We only demonstrate the strength of using

Table 6.6.2 Estimates for models of the rate of entry into marriage (women of cohorts 1929–31, 1939–41, and 1949–51).

Variables	Model						
	1	2	3	4	5	6	7
Intercept	-4.69*	-17.62*	-17.58*	-17.68*	- 16.28*	- 16.28*	-16.04*
Log (current age - 15)		1.76*	1.80*	1.73*	1.46*	1.47*	1.45*
Log (45 - current age)		3.20*	3.27*	3.37*	3.09*	3.09*	2.93*
Number of siblings			-0.00	0.01	0.00	0.00	-0.01
Father's social class 2			-0.13	-0.14	-0.08	-0.08	-0.04
Father's social class 3			-0.31*	-0.31*	-0.14	-0.14	-0.06
Father's social class 4			-0.61*	-0.61*	-0.33*	-0.32*	-0.25
Urban residence at age 15			-0.08	-0.11	-0.05	-0.05	-0.07
Cohort 1939–41				-0.04	-0.04	-0.03	-0.05
Cohort 1949–51				-0.09	-0.01	-0.00	0.00
Economic development				0.19*	0.21*	0.21*	0.18*
In training (dynamic measure)					-0.97*	-0.99*	-0.80*
Level of education (dynamic measure)					-0.01	-0.00	0.00
Level of career resources (dynamic measure)						-0.03	0.04
Is pregnant (dynamic measure)							2.84*
Subepisodes	85404	85404	85404	85404	85404	85404	85404
χ^2		457.80	485.55	525.01	598.39	598.47	1085.47
df		2	7	10	12	13	14

* statistically significant at 0.05 level.

time-dependent covariates by reporting the most important findings of this study.

The first interesting aspect of this analysis is that the effects of the dummy variables for father's social class on entry into marriage and motherhood in Model 3 show that women from lower social classes marry earlier and have their babies sooner than women from higher social classes (see Tables 6.6.2 and 6.6.3). However, when the various time-dependent covariates for women's educational and career investments over the life course are included, this effect disappears completely. Thus, by extending education and improving career opportunities, families of higher social classes *indirectly* delay the rate of getting married and having children. In general, event history analysis provides an opportunity to study the importance of indirect effects that operate by influencing either the timing of entry into or exit from specific states as well as with regard to variations of time-dependence

Table 6.6.3 Estimates for models of the rate of entry into motherhood (women of cohorts 1929–31, 1939–41, and 1949–51).

Variables	Model						
	2	3	4	5	6	7	8
Intercept	-19.33^*	-18.82^*	-18.59^*	-17.64^*	-16.03^*	-16.72^*	-14.21^*
Log (curr. age - 15)	2.17^*	2.19^*	2.08^*	2.11^*	1.68^*	1.76^*	0.08
Log (45 - curr. age)	3.36^*	3.30^*	3.33^*	3.28^*	2.84^*	2.95^*	2.24^*
Number of siblings		0.04^*	0.05^*	0.04^*	0.04^*	0.04^*	0.09^*
Father's social class 2		-0.10	-0.10	-0.03	-0.04	-0.01	0.12
Father's social class 3		-0.34^*	-0.34^*	-0.21	-0.19	-0.18	-0.03
Father's social class 4		-0.45^*	-0.46^*	-0.13	-0.08	-0.05	0.16
Urban residence at age 15		-0.23^*	-0.47^*	-0.18^*	-0.17^*	-0.18^*	-0.23^*
Cohort 1939–41			-0.11	-0.03	-0.07	-0.03	-0.22
Cohort 1949–51			-0.16	-0.02	-0.05	0.03	-0.57^*
Economic development			0.20^*	0.19^*	0.20^*	0.20^*	0.07
In training (dynamic measure)					-1.98^*	-2.24^*	-1.32^*
Level of education (dynamic measure)					0.05	0.08^*	0.08^*
Level of career resources (dynamic measure)						-0.39^*	-0.18^*
Married (dynamic measure)							3.82^*
Subepisodes	99506	99506	99506	99506	99506	99506	99506
χ^2	480.04	518.86	547.14	579.51	674.56	695.86	1744.10
df	2	7	10	11	13	14	15

* statistically significant at 0.05 level.

within states (see also Yamaguchi 1991).

In Model 4 (Tables 6.6.2 and 6.6.3), measures of changes in the historical background, such as cohort membership and economic development, are incorporated. There are no significant cohort effects, but one observes a significant positive effect of the economic conditions. This is to say that women enter into marriage earlier when the economic situation is favorable. In a period of economic expansion, the life-cycle prospects of young people are more predictable, and it is therefore easier for women to make such long-term decisions such as entering into marriage and having a baby.

After having controlled for age dependence (Model 2), social background (Model 3), and changes in the historical setting (Model 4), an answer to the question of how important the improvements in educational and career opportunities have been for women's timing of marriage can be given (Table 6.6.2). We first look at the *dynamic effects of education* in Model 5. This model shows that attending school, vocational training programs, or university does indeed have a strong negative effect on the rate of entry into marriage. What is very interesting, however, is that the effect of the *level of education* is not significant. Women's timing of marriage is therefore independent of the quantity of human capital investments. In assessing the consequences of educational expansion on family formation, one can conclude that marriage is postponed because women postpone their transition from youth to adulthood and not because women acquire greater quantities of human capital, thereby increasing their labor force attachment.

In Model 6 of Table 6.6.2, one can assess the effect of the improvement in women's career opportunities on the timing of their marriage. Again, and of great theoretical interest, this variable proves to be insignificant. Women's entry into marriage seems to be independent of their career opportunities.

Finally, in Model 7 (Table 6.6.2) a time-dependent pregnancy indicator is included. It does not change the substantive findings cited earlier, but its effect is positive and very strong. This indicates that, for women experiencing premarital pregnancy, the marriage rate increases sharply.

Let us now consider the estimates for first motherhood in Table 6.6.3. Again, age dependence, social background, historical period, cohort effects, and partner's educational attainment are controlled for in the first five models. In Model 6, women's continuously changing level of education and an indicator for their participation in school are included to explain the rate of entry into motherhood. Again, as in the marriage model, level of education, which measures women's general human capital investments, has no significant effect on the timing of the first birth. Only attending school negatively affects the women's rate of having a first child. This means that conflicting time commitments with respect to women's roles as students and mothers exist (Rindfuss and John 1983), and that there are normative expectations that young women who attend school are not at risk of entering into motherhood.

If changes in career resources of women over the life course are introduced in Model 7 of Table 6.6.3, the effect of the level of education proves to be significantly positive. This is contrary to the expectations of the economic approach to the family and means that the process of attaining successively higher levels of qualification has an augmenting, rather than a diminishing, effect on the rate of having a first child. The reason for this is that the attainment of increasing levels of education takes time and is connected with an increasing age of women (Figure 6.6.2). Women who remain in school longer and attain high qualifications are subject to pressure not only from the potential increase in medical problems connected with having children late but also from societal age norms ("women should have their first child at least by age 30"; Menken 1985). Thus, not human capital investments, as claimed by the "new home economics," but increasing social pressure might

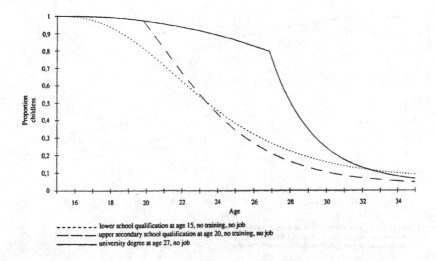

Figure 6.6.4 Estimated cumulative proportion of childless women by education (survivor function).

be at work, if the level of education has an impact on the timing of the first birth.

These relationships are also illustrated in Figure 6.6.4.[31] In this figure, the estimates of the age-specific cumulative proportion of childless women (survivor function) for different levels of education are reported.[32] The longer that women are in school, the more first birth is delayed; therefore there is a high proportion of childless women among the highly educated. After leaving the educational system, those women who have delayed having children "catch up" with their contemporaries who have less education and who got an earlier start. However, they do not only catch up. The positive effect of the educational level pushes the proportion of childless women with upper-secondary school qualifications (at about age 20) and even those with university degrees (at about age 27) below the proportion of childless women with lower school qualifications.

A confirmation of the economic approach to the family may, however, be seen in the negative effect of the *level of career resources* on the rate of

---

[31]Rate function coefficients and their standard errors are helpful in ascertaining how educational and career investments of women influence first motherhood and first birth, in what direction, and at what level of significance. However, the magnitude of the effects and their substantive significance are more easily assessed by examining survivor functions for typical educational and occupational careers that show the probability that a woman remains unmarried or childless until age t.

[32]These estimates were obtained from Model 7 of Table 6.6.3 by holding constant all other variables at the mean and assuming the women were not employed.

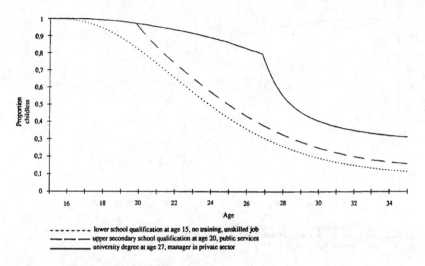

Figure 6.6.5 Estimated cumulative proportion of childless women for ideal-typical career lines (survivor function).

entry into motherhood (Model 7, Table 6.6.3). The accumulation of women's career resources conflicts with societal expectations concerning a woman's role as a mother. Women still take primary responsibility for child care and are still disadvantaged in their careers when they have to interrupt their working life because of the birth of a child. Therefore women who have accumulated a high stock of career resources try to postpone or even avoid the birth of a first child.

Figure 6.6.5 displays examples of age-specific, cumulated proportions of childless women (survivor function) for ideal-typical career lines.[33] This exercise shows that there is a conflict between career and motherhood. An increase in career opportunities augments the proportion of childless women at any age.

Finally, in Model 8 (Table 6.6.3), Blossfeld and Huinink introduced a time-dependent dummy variable that changes its value at marriage and thus shows whether or not a woman was married before the birth of the first child. This variable increases the rate of entry into motherhood remarkably. When this variable is introduced, one can observe that the effects of "in training" and "level of career resources" become weaker. Part of their influence is therefore mediated by the marriage process (see also Blossfeld and De Rose 1992; Blossfeld and Jaenichen 1992; and for an international comparison of these models Blossfeld 1995).

---

[33] Again, these estimates are obtained from Model 7 (Table 6.6.3) by holding constant all other variables at the mean.

In summarizing these results, it is interesting to note that empirical support for the "new home economics" has normally been claimed on the basis of cross-sectional and aggregated time-series data. However, these data do not permit a differentiation between the effect of accumulation of human capital over the life course and the effect of participation in the educational system in keeping women out of the marriage market. Therefore it seems that such empirical support for the "new home economics" is only the result of inappropriate methods and the type of data used.

Example 3: The Effects of Pregnancy on Entry into Marriage for Couples Living in Consensual Unions

We finally report on two investigations by Blossfcld, Manting, and Rohwer (1993) and Blossfeld et al. (1999). These studies are instructive because they demonstrate how sensitive the effects of time-dependent covariates can be with respect to the points in time when they are supposed to change their values.

In substantive terms, the purpose of the first study was to gain insight into the relationship between consensual unions and marriage in West Germany and the Netherlands. The study focused on the effect of pregnancy on the rate of entry into marriage, controlling for other important covariates in a transition rate model.

Historically, marriage has—as a rule—preceded the birth of a child, but in recent decades, the interplay between marriage and childbirth has certainly become more complex. Some cohabiting couples wait until the woman gets pregnant and then marry. For other couples, an accidental pregnancy may lead to a marriage that otherwise might not have taken place. Pregnancy can also lead to a dissolution of the consensual union, if there is strong disagreement over the desirability of having a child. Other couples, wishing to have children in the near future, may decide to marry before the woman gets pregnant. To study these complex relationships, nationally representative longitudinal data were used. In the first analysis by Blossfeld, Manting, and Rohwer (1993), the German Socio-Economic Panel for West Germany and the Netherlands Fertility Survey were applied. Both data sets provide important information about the dynamics of consensual unions in the 1980s. In both countries, attention was limited to members of the cohorts born between 1950 and 1969, who started a consensual union between 1984 and 1989 in West Germany, and between 1980 and 1988 in the Netherlands.[34]

However, we only want to discuss the pregnancy effects here. Pregnancy was included in the transition rate model as a series of time-dependent

---

[34] About 85 % of the entries into consensual unions between 1984 and 1989 were observed for these cohorts.

Table 6.6.4 Piecewise constant exponential model for transitions from consensual unions to marriage and dissolution, for West Germany (FRG) and the Netherlands (NL).

Variable	Entry into Marriage		Dissolution	
	FRG[3]	NL [4]	FRG[3]	NL [4]
Constant	-2.79**	-4.01**	-10.60**	-4.92**
Duration				
less than 2 years	0.08	-0.01	-0.49**	-0.18**
more than 2 years	-0.08	0.01	0.49**	0.18**
Birth cohort				
1950–53[1]	-0.09	0.07	0.37	-0.19
1954–58	0.01	0.16*	0.22	-0.13
1959–63	0.11	0.00	-0.68*	-0.15
1964–69[2]	-0.03	-0.23**	-0.09	0.46**
School enrolment				
at school	-0.16*	-0.36**	-0.40	0.11
not at school	0.16*	0.36**	0.40	-0.11
Educational level				
low	-0.17*	0.14*	0.03	-0.08
medium	-0.09	-0.07	0.29	0.10
high	0.26	-0.07	-0.32	-0.03
Fertility				
not pregnant	-1.19**	-0.43**	5.48**	-0.09
pregnant	1.13**	1.19**	-5.45	0.17
first child birth	1.21**	0.21	-4.75	-0.69
six months after birth	-1.15**	-0.98**	4.72*	0.61*
Sex				
men	-0.08		0.09	
women	0.08		-0.09	
Married before				
no	0.07		-0.01	
yes	-0.07		0.01	

* statistically significant at 0.1 level. ** statistically significant at 0.05 level.
1) For West Germany the birth cohort of 1949 was also included.
2) For West Germany the birth cohort of 1969 was also included.
3) Men and women. 4) Only women.

dummy variables (coded as centered effects)[35] with the following states: "not pregnant," "pregnant," "first childbirth," "6 months after birth." As shown

---

[35] Using effect coding for dummy variables, the differences between the levels of a qualitative variable are expressed as differences from a "virtual mean." The effect of the category chosen as the reference in the estimation can be computed as being the negative sum of the effects of the dummy variables included in the model.

in Table 6.6.4, the effects of the pregnancy dummy variables are significant for both countries, and they basically work in the same direction. As long as women are not pregnant, a comparatively low rate of entry into marriage for people living in a consensual union is observed. But as soon as a woman becomes pregnant (and in West Germany, also around the time when a woman has her child) the rate of entry into marriage increases strongly. Thus there still seems to be a great desire among the young generations in West Germany and the Netherlands to avoid illegitimate births and to legalize the union when a child is born. However, if the couple did not get married within a certain time (around 6 months) after the child was born, the rate of entry into marriage again dropped to a comparatively low level in West Germany. In the Netherlands, this level is even below the "not pregnant" level.

Let us now look at the effects of pregnancy on the dissolution process of consensual unions, which are different in Germany and the Netherlands. In Germany, the dissolution risk is high as long as women are not pregnant. The rate drops strongly for some months when a woman is pregnant and then has her child. But 6 months after childbirth, the dissolution rate rises again. The strong rise 6 months after childbirth can also be observed in the Netherlands. Thus, in Germany and the Netherlands, women living in consensual unions with an illegitimate child have not only a comparatively low rate of entering into marriage but also a comparatively high dissolution risk. In other words, the rise in the number of consensual unions will certainly increase the number of female-headed single-parent families in both countries.

About a year after this comparative study was conducted, Blossfeld et al. (1999) wanted to examine whether these relationships could be reproduced with new data from Germany. They started to conduct some preliminary analyses and used only one dummy variable for the pregnancy process. However, the effect of this variable was insignificant. This was surprising because results of the earlier comparative study were convincing in theoretical terms. After checking the input data and command files, the authors noticed that the programmer had accidentally switched the time-dependent dummy variable at the time of the birth of the child and not at the time when it was clear that there was a conception (i.e., about 8 to 6 months before birth). Thus, a shift in the switch of a time-dependent covariate by 6 months made the effect of pregnancy disappear. This "finding" created a lot of confusion in the research group. What happened to the pregnancy effect? After much discussion, one explanation seemed to unite theory and the seemingly contradictory results of the estimated models: The effect of pregnancy on entry into marriage must be strongly time-dependent. It must start to rise at some time shortly after conception, increase during pregnancy to a maximum, and then decrease again. Thus, when the time-dependent covariate

Table 6.6.5 Exponential model for transitions from consensual unions to marriage, with a series of dummy variables, defined as lags/leads with regard to the month of childbirth.

Variable	Coefficient	p-value
Intercept	-4.4852	0.0000
Dummy: -9 months	1.4094	0.0161
Dummy: -8 months	1.9515	0.0000
Dummy: -7 months	1.7443	0.0006
Dummy: -6 months	1.4567	0.0129
Dummy: -5 months	1.0039	0.1507
Dummy: -4 months	1.3071	0.0257
Dummy: -3 months	0.2657	0.7015
Dummy: -2 months	1.8605	0.0000
Dummy: -1 months	-8.4526	0.0145
Dummy: 0 months	0.2657	0.7015
Dummy: 1 months	-8.4526	0.9114
Dummy: 2 months	0.8743	0.2208
Dummy: 3 months	-0.3593	0.0881

was switched at the time of conception, the effect was strongly positive because it compared the situation before discovery of conception (cumulating a period with a low marriage rate) to the situation after discovery of conception (cumulating a high marriage rate for some months). But when the time-dependent covariate was switched at the time of childbirth, a period with a low marriage rate up to the time of discovery of conception and a period with a high marriage rate during pregnancy were mixed (see Table 6.6.4). Thus the average tendency to marry before the child is born more or less equals the average tendency to marry after the child is born, and the estimated coefficient for the time-dependent covariate "childbirth" is not significantly different from zero. There is, of course, a simple way to test this hypothesis. Blossfeld et al. (1999) used a series of time-dependent dummy variables each indicating a month since the occurrence of conception. And in fact, as shown in Table 6.6.5, the effects of the time-dependent dummy variables at first increase, reach a maximum at about 8 months before birth of a child, and then decrease. Thus, starting with conception, there is an increasing normative pressure to avoid an illegitimate birth that increases the marriage rate, particularly for people who are already "ready for marriage." But with an increasing number of marriages, the composition of the group of still unmarried couples shifts toward couples being "less ready for marriage" or being "not ready for marriage," which, of course, decreases the pregnancy effect again.

Not only is this an important result in substantive terms, but also the methodological lesson is very revealing. One should be very careful in modeling qualitative parallel processes with only one dummy variable, particularly in situations in which it is theoretically quite open, at which point in time the value of the dummy variable must be switched (see also Blossfeld and Mills 2001, as well as Mills and Trovato 2001).

Example 4: An Analysis of Diffusion of Cohabitation Among Young Women in Europe with Individual-Level Event History Models

In a recent paper, Nazio and Blossfeld (2003) used methods of event history analysis with episode splitting to study the diffusion of cohabitation across successive generations of young women in Italy, the capitalist West Germany, and the socialist East Germany. In particular, they were interested in the normative shifts regarding consensual unions from a rare and deviant form of partnership to a common and socially accepted union over the last 30 years. In their analysis, diffusion was considered as an individual-level process by which the practice of cohabitation is communicated through certain channels and adopted or rejected over time among the members of a society (Rogers 1983). The focus of the analysis was on cohabitation before women enter (if ever) into first marriage in order to get a better understanding of the dynamic shifts during the phase of family formation in historical time. In the 1960s, cohabitation clearly was a social innovation. It was perceived as relatively new, at least in the phase of family formation, by most people in Europe. This form of union then gradually became integrated into the process of family formation in varying degrees in most of the Northern European countries. Nazio and Blossfeld wanted to answer the question of what drives the diffusion of consensual unions among young women in Italy, West Germany, and East Germany, and if there is convergence or divergence in this process across countries, which forces are responsible for it.

Using longitudinal data from the Fertility and Family Surveys (see Klijzing and Corijn 2001), Nazio and Blossfeld adopted an individual-level diffusion model (see Strang and Tuma 1993). In these models the individual woman's rate of adoption of cohabitation can be estimated, among other factors, as a function of prior adoptions by other individuals in the social system. In methodological terms, these models are particularly attractive because they allow (1) to estimate a flexible individual-level analogue of the relatively limited standard population-level models of diffusion; (2) to incorporate the influence of time-constant and time-varying individual heterogeneity affecting the intrinsic propensity of women to adopt the cohabitation practice in different stages of their life course; (3) to take into account ideas about structures of communication, knowledge awareness, and structural equivalence; and, (4) to estimate more complex models of temporal variation in the process of diffusion.

The diffusion of cohabitation among young women is a highly complex

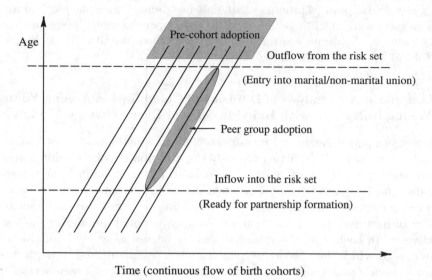

Figure 6.6.6 Time-related dimensions of the diffusion process of pre-marital cohabitation.

time-related process (see Figure 6.6.6). A characteristic of cohabitation before entry (if ever) into marriage is that the time-span of potential adoption for each generation is highly concentrated on the period of transition from youth to adulthood. There is then a continuous succession of birth cohorts over time moving through this life-course window (see Figure 6.6.6). Past research has shown that in modern societies the readiness of young women to form marital or nonmarital unions over the life course is governed to a large extent by organizational rules and institutional structures in the educational and employment systems (Blossfeld 1995). At specific ages, women typically move from one institutional domain to another (e.g., from secondary school to vocational training, or from school to the labor market) and these transitions often serve as markers for the beginning of a life stage where women form partnerships (Blossfeld and Nuthmann 1990; Huinink 1995; Klijzing and Corijn 2001; Blossfeld et al. 2005). It is well-known, that finishing women's education counts as one of the most important transitions in the process of getting ready for entry into marriage (see example 1; Blossfeld and Huinink 1991; Blossfeld 1995).

Figure 6.6.6 presents a stylized picture of the complex dynamics involved in the diffusion of premarital cohabitation among young women. There is a continuous inflow of birth cohorts who are entering into the life stage "ready for partnership formation" and thus are becoming members of the risk set of potential adopters; and, at the same time, there is a continuous outflow of women from this risk set, not only because some young women adopt cohabitation but also because others marry and therefore also leave the risk set. In Figure 6.6.6, dotted lines describe the inflow to and outflow from the risk set given the variable ages at which these entries and exits take place. In other words, in the case of premarital cohabitation, potential adoption is typically confined to a specific window in the life course, and the population of potential adopters is highly dynamic over time. These peculiarities of the adoption process have significant consequences for the mechanisms that drive the diffusion process of premartial cohabitation among young women over time.

Each new cohort of women who enters into the phase of being ready for partnership formation will encounter an increasingly greater proportion of prior adopters from previous cohorts. Each new cohort of women will therefore gradually experience premarital cohabitation as a less deviant (or stigmatized) and more socially acceptable living arrangement right from the beginning. Newspapers, magazines, radio, and television will increasingly disseminate knowledge awareness on the growing popularity of cohabitation among older birth cohorts and enhance social acceptability of nonmarital cohabitation. Nazio and Blossfeld (2003) expected, therefore, that the cumulative proportion of cohabitation adopters from previous cohorts has a positive effect on the conveyance of cohabitation for the following generations of women. This mechanism is represented in the trapezoidal area (Pre-cohort adoption) in Figure 6.6.6.

However, young women often need to confirm their beliefs about cohabitation through more direct experience. They have to be persuaded by further evaluative information about the actual benefits and possible disadvantages of cohabitation through more concrete examples. These examples are most convincing if they come from other individuals like themselves who have previously adopted the innovation, and whose experiences can constitute a sort of vicarious trial for the newcomers (Strang 1991; Kohler 2001). Thus it is not only conversation and personal contact to near peers that counts but also the perception of the practice proper for an individual of their position within the social structure (structural equivalence; see Burt 1987). Cohabitation of peers should therefore constitute a particularly valuable trial example of the new living arrangement. This suggests that at the heart of the diffusion process there is direct social modeling by potential adopters of their peers who have adopted previously. This mechanism is represented in the oval area (Peer group adoption) in Figure 6.6.6.

Blossfeld and Nazio's description of the diffusion process showed that in East and West Germany each successive birth cohort experienced not only an impressive rise in the proportions of cumulative pre-cohort adoption (see Figure 6.6.7) but also a steep increase in the cumulative proportions of peer group adoption (see Figure 6.6.8) at each age. This suggests that there has been an increasing social acceptance of cohabitation for each younger

Figure 6.6.7 Cumulative pre-cohort adoption in West Germany, East Germany and Italy

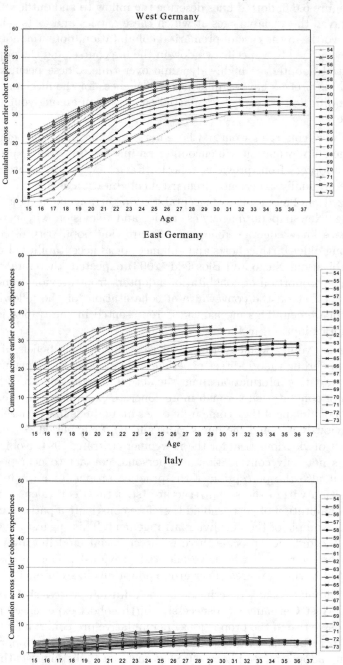

Figure 6.6.8 Cumulative peer group adoption in West Germany, East Germany and Italy

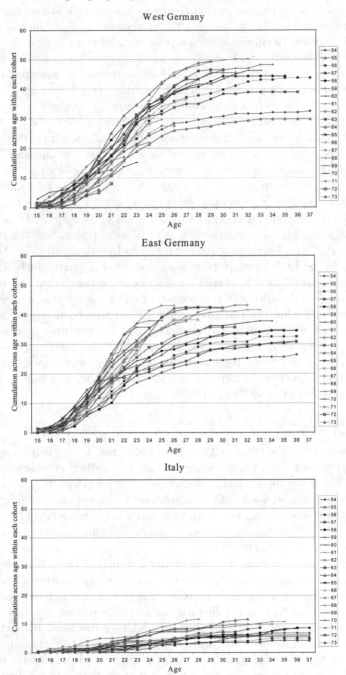

birth cohort in Germany to the extent that cohabitation has become a normal form of partnership in the process of family formation. Among the youngest birth cohorts, about 50 % of women in West Germany and about 40 % in East Germany have adopted cohabitation before they eventually start a first marriage. In contrast, in Italy, even among the youngest birth cohorts not more than about 10 % of women have adopted cohabitation before eventually entering into first marriage (see Figures 6.6.7 and 6.6.8).

In the past, diffusion processes have been generally formulated in terms of population-level epidemic models (Diekmann 1989, 1992). This type of analysis assumes that all members of the population have the same chance of influencing and being influenced by each other (Strang and Tuma 1993). However, the assumption of homogeneous mixing does often not hold in empirical applications (Strang 1991). Nazio and Blossfeld (2003) therefore did not estimate a population-level model but turned to an individual-level model of diffusion as suggested by Strang and Tuma (1993). In these event history models, the individual's rate of adoption of cohabitation can be estimated as a function of prior adoptions by other actors in the social system. In methodological terms, these models are particularly attractive for studying the diffusion of cohabitation because they allow the researcher to incorporate the effects of time-constant and time-varying individual hetero-geneity affecting the intrinsic propensity of women to adopt cohabitation. They can also be used to test ideas about structures of communication and structural equivalence (see Strang and Tuma 1993), or more precisely, the effects of knowledge awareness and direct social modeling. A simple individual-level based diffusion model might be formulated in the following way (see Strang and Tuma 1993):

$$r_n(t) = \exp\left(\alpha + \Sigma_{s \in S(t)} \beta\right)$$

where $r_n(t)$ is the propensity that an individual moves from nonadoption to adoption at time t, α represents the effect of individual characteristics, $S(t)$ consists of the theoretically relevant set of prior adopters, and β is the effect of the intrapopulation diffusion process on the rate of individual adoption. Thus this model combines both individual heterogeneity and the contagious influences of previous adopters on nonadopters and allows to model diffusion within an event history framework.

Since the readiness to enter a union is highly time-dependent and gov-erned to a large extent by women's age and by organizational rules and institutional structures of the educational and employment systems, Nazio and Blossfeld have controlled for the intrinsic propensity of women with a series of time-constant and time-dependent covariates. In particular, they took into consideration women's changing age, their time-dependent en-rollment in the educational system, the connected progressive upgrading of their educational attainment levels, and their changing employment participation. The α-term defined in the formula above is therefore substituted by $\alpha' x(t)$ in the estimated rate equation, incorporating time-constant and time-dependent individual's heterogeneity on women's likelihood to adopt cohabitation.

Because Nazio and Blossfeld assumed knowledge awareness and direct social modeling as the two driving mechanisms of diffusion, knowledge awareness (P_c) was measured at each point in time by the cumulative proportion of prior adopters from previous birth cohorts at each age, and direct social modeling (P_g) was measured as the cumulative proportion of prior adopters belonging to the women's own birth cohort at each age (see Figures 6.6.7 and 6.6.8):

$$P_g = \frac{\Sigma_{i=c} \Sigma_{j<t} \, m_{ij}}{N_c} \cdot 100 \qquad P_c = \frac{\Sigma_{i<c} \Sigma_{j<t} \, n_{ij}}{N_p(t)} \cdot 100$$

where c indicates the birth cohort, t is woman's age, m_{ij} is the number of prior adopters within the woman's own birth cohort at age t, N_c is the total number of women in the woman's own birth cohort, n_{ij} is the number of prior adopters among older birth cohorts at age t, and $N_p(t)$ is the number of women belonging to older birth cohorts at age t. In order to allow for the nonlinearity in the relationships, Nazio and Blossfeld used a third degree polynomial and replaced the A-term of the diffusion formula above by the following combination of these two factors:

$$r_n(t) = \exp(\alpha' x(t)) \cdot$$
$$\exp(\beta_1 P_g + \beta_2 P_g^2 + \beta_3 P_g^3) \exp(\gamma_1 P_c + \gamma_2 P_c^2 + \gamma_3 P_c^3)$$

This individual-level diffusion model does not require the assumption that diffusion occurs only through interpersonal contacts. Thus it is not only direct conversation and immediate personal contacts to near peers that count but also the perception of the practice proper for people at the same age (structural equivalence; see Burt 1987). There is accordingly no assumption of a complete mixing of social members that would imply that there is a complete, pairwise interaction between prior and potential adopters. Rather, a distinction between individuals is made on the basis of their age and birth cohorts in defining the diffusion covariates in the model. Nazio and Blossfeld's model also does not make the assumption that there is a constant and permanent ceiling on the number of potential adopters in the social system. The number of potential adopters is indeed changing over time, because there is a continuous inflow of new birth cohorts of women entering into the risk set. In addition, there is no implicit assumption that the innovative behavior does not change its meaning over the diffusion process. Instead, Nazio and Blossfeld assumed that the meaning and character of cohabitation is subject to change and that knowledge awareness and direct social modeling might change their effects over time.

The application of event history methods to the data of the Fertility and Family Surveys in Italy, West Germany, and East Germany yielded interesting differences with regard to the diffusion of cohabitation. In many countries, the growing tendency among young adults to opt for informal cohabitation instead of marriage might seemed to be a rational reply to the new challenges of a deteriorating young adults labor market. Cohabitation permit postponement of long-term commitments without incurring the penalties of either heterosexual isolation or promiscuity. It also offers the pooling of resources and the economies of scale that living together provides.

Nazio and Blossfeld's empirical analysis shows that young people can choose between various alternatives: they might stay longer in the parental home (mainly in Italy), live in a single household (often the case in West Germany), marry, or cohabit. The degree to which cohabitation is perceived as being more advantageous than its alternatives is strongly determined by the cultural, structural, and political setting.

Nazio and Blossfeld's analysis shows that cohabitation is indeed not an attractive choice in Italy. First, young Italians have great difficulties to secure public housing. The rental market, which is squeezed by specific rental laws and distorted by a black housing market, is rather expensive in these countries. Thus the best choice for young people would often be between staying with their parents or buying a house (see Kurz and Blossfeld 2004). But buying a house not only requires a huge financial investment, it is also a long-term binding decision. For this reason, marital decisions would implicitly have very similar consequences for the life course of young Italians. Second, the Mediterranean welfare state provides only a weak protection against the increasing labor market risks of the young generation, and the cohesive Mediterranean family is the relevant locus of social aid: parents are responsible for their children and vice versa. In other words, increasing youth unemployment and uncertainties of employment relationships together with the peculiarities of the Italian housing market and Catholic familialism make an extended stay of young people in the parental home more attractive than cohabitation or living as a single person. As Nazio and Blossfeld's longitudinal analysis shows, cohabitation in Italy is therefore confined to small, highly selective groups of women who have a good reason to break with traditional gender roles and family models (see the results in Table 6.6.6). As a rule, these women are not religious, have left the educational system and work, grew up in an urban context, and, in the case of Italy, live mainly in the North.

In East Germany, the relatively low average age at marriage was the result of a comparatively high level of individual life-course predictability in the socialist society and a consequence of a specific housing allocation policy. In the historical period between the mid-1970s and 1989, there was a strong incentive to adopt cohabitation for young women, even when they were still

Table 6.6.6 Estimation of covariate effects on the diffusion of cohabitation for women (Exponential model with time-constant and time-dependent covariates).

	West Germany	East Germany	Italy
Constant	-29.59**	-23.18**	-11.39**
Log(Age-15)	0.52**	0.68**	-0.25*
Log(39-Age)	3.79**	2.58**	0.45
Out of education	0.19*	-0.10	1.29**
(Ref. education: compulsory)	0	0	0
MOB	-0.20	-0.39**	–
HMB	0.50**	0.34*	–
MMB	0.68**	0.47**	–
ABI	0.44**	-0.29	–
FHS	0.22	0.82**	–
UNI	0.62**	0.14**	–
Education: secondary	–	–	-0.44**
Education: tertiary	–	–	0.08
Being employed	0.09	-0.05	0.32**
Religiosity	-0.20**	-0.23**	-1.10**
(Ref. residence: rural/small city)	0	0	0
Residence: middle-size city	0.13*	0.09	-0.23
Residence: big city	0.01	0.00	0.29*
(Ref. region: North)	–	–	0
Region: Centre	–	–	-0.38**
Region: South and Islands	–	–	-0.48**
Peer group adoption	0.15**	0.16**	1.22**
(Peer group adoption)^2	-0.00**	-0.01**	-0.18**
(Peer group adoption)^3	0.00**	0.00**	0.01**
Pre-cohort adoption	-0.02	-0.03	0.69
(Pre-cohort adoption)^2	0.00	0.00	-0.18
(Pre-cohort adoption)^3	0.00	-0.00	0.01
Events	895	868	214
Log-likelihood	(-10321.4)	(-12461.6)	(-14626.0)
	-10014.8	-12100.8	-14493.6

* statistically significant at 10 %, or ** at 5 % level.

in school. After the breakdown of the socialist society in 1989, a historical period that could only be partially covered with the data, the institutional framework of West Germany was introduced in East Germany, and economic uncertainty and rising unemployment have increased dramatically. It is wellknown that these changes resulted in rapidly declining nuptiality and fertility rates and have increased the rate of cohabitation and extramarital births in East Germany.

In West Germany, the housing market has been accessible for young people for many decades. It has been easy to rent a flat, and the prices

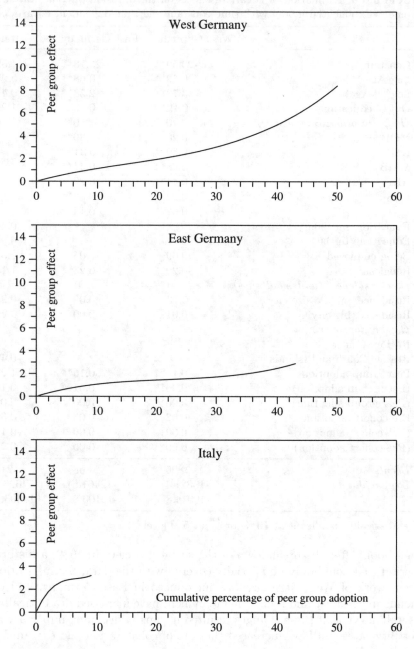

Figure 6.6.9 Effect of peer group adoption in West Germany, East Germany and Italy.

are, with the exception of some few expensive cities, generally affordable. In cross-national comparative terms, the proportion of homeowners is also relatively low in West Germany at 45 % (see Kurz and Blossfeld 2004). If young people don't work, they are normally supported by the conservative welfare state or by their parents. Thus, given increasing unemployment and growing employment uncertainty, cohabitation or living as a single person are attractive options compared to staying with parents in West Germany.

An important result of Nazio and Blossfeld's study is that there is no autonomous cohort trend left on women's rate of entry into cohabitation after controlling for cohort differences in educational participation and attainment levels as well as women's labor force participation. In addition, the diffusion analysis shows that the dissemination of abstract knowledge based on the cohabitation experiences of earlier generations does not seem to have any substantial influence on the diffusion of cohabitation in the population in the studied countries (see Table 6.6.6). Thus the diffusion of cohabitation does not imply a mechanism that links the experiences across generations. Rather, cohabitation seems to be driven mainly by direct social modeling of peers (see the significant estimates in Table 6.6.6). Concrete experiences of the same age group clearly constitute a sort of useful vicarious trial for the potential adopters. In East and West Germany the relationship between peer group adoption and the individual adoption rate is S-shaped and monotonically increasing (see Figure 6.6.9). First, each new cohort seems to start within some specific groups of early innovators with a particular interest in the adoption of cohabitation. Then, with the gradual accumulation of peer-group experience, the diffusion spills over from these specific groups to broader parts of the entire birth cohort population. At the level of about 30 % (in West Germany) to 40 % (in East Germany) of cumulative peer group adoption the effect of direct social modeling then even increases at an accelerating rate. After these points, direct social modeling clearly becomes one of the most important driving forces for the individual adoption rate of cohabitation. Although East and West Germany share the same overall S-shaped diffusion pattern, the diffusion process in East Germany proceeds at a slower pace, and the accelerating phase is triggered at a comparatively later point (see Figure 6.6.9). In the socialist East Germany there was obviously more resistance than in West Germany against the spread of cohabitation to the entire birth cohort population. In Italy, the diffusion of cohabitation to broader groups of the population appears to be blocked (see Figure 6.6.9). Social forerunners who are practising cohabitation in Italy consist of very specific groups of people whose experiences obviously cannot serve as appropriate models for their peers in other groups, so that the mechanism of the strengths-of-weak-ties does not work in the Italian diffusion process.

Chapter 7

Parametric Models of Time-Dependence

In some sociological applications, substantive theory or previous empirical research suggests a specific shape of time-dependence for the transition rate. When this time path can be modeled in terms of a tractable waiting time distribution, the likelihood can be calculated by using its density $f(t)$ and survivor function $G(t)$, as has been shown for the exponential model in section 4.1. An obvious estimation strategy is then to use any computer program or software package (e.g., BMDP, GLIM, GAUSS, LIMDEP, SAS, TDA, Stata) that offers function optimization routines and to maximize the likelihood function with respect to the unknown parameters.[1] This strategy is very flexible because researchers are able to build their own parametric models, but it requires mathematical and programming skills. Our experience, however, shows that applied social scientists normally do not want to be bothered with writing programs and maximizing likelihood functions. Stata therefore offers the opportunity to estimate widely used parametric models with a single command. In Stata, `streg` performs maximum likelihood estimation for parametric event history models.

```
streg varlist, distribution(distname)
```

where `distname` is one of the possible distribution types shown in Box 7.1. The command can be used with single- or multiple-record or single- or multiple-failure data. You must specify the command `stset` before using `streg`. In the case of multiple episodes, as shown in section 4.3, starting and ending times of the successive episodes are coded relative to first entry into the process (e.g., first entry into the labor market). Therefore the starting and ending times of each episode determine the specific location of the successive spells within the distribution of a time-dependent model. We do not demonstrate the estimation of parametric time-dependent models consisting of multiple episodes with Stata because this can be done in exactly the same way as already shown for the exponential model in section 4.3. In the examples in this chapter, we assume that the transition rate only depends on the time spent in an episode and that these durations are independently

---

[1] This strategy has been demonstrated in Blossfeld, Hamerle, and Mayer (1989) using the function optimization subprogram P3R of BMDP and the P3RFUN subroutine written by Petersen (1986a, 1986b, 1988b).

Box 7.1 Stata models with a time-dependent transition rate

Exponential model:	`streg varlist, distribution(exponential)`
Weibull model:	`streg varlist, distribution(weibull)`
Gompertz model:	`streg varlist, distribution(gompertz)`
Log-Normal model:	`streg varlist, distribution(lognormal)`
	`streg varlist, distribution(lnormal)`
Log-Logistic model:	`streg varlist, distribution(loglogistic)`
	`streg varlist, distribution(llogistic)`
Gamma model:	`streg varlist, distribution(gamma)`

and identically distributed. In other words, we study so-called *Semi-Markov models* or *Markov renewal models* (see Tuma and Hannan 1984).

In this chapter we begin with a discussion about the substantive meaning of time-dependence from a causal analytical point of view. Then we survey models with a monotonically decreasing or increasing transition rate, for which the Gompertz (-Makeham) and the Weibull distribution are normally applied. Finally, we demonstrate the log-logistic and the log-normal model that are widely used when the transition rate at first increases and then, after reaching a maximum, decreases. In our examples, these parametric models are estimated as single time-dependent rates[2] as well as models with covariates linked to various parameters of the distributions (see also Blossfeld, Hamerle, and Mayer 1989).

7.1 Interpretation of Time-Dependence

From a causal analytical point of view, it is important to realize that although the models in this chapter are called time-dependent, time itself is no causal factor. Time therefore cannot serve as an explaining variable for the observed pattern of time-dependence. Thus, what does it mean when we say that a transition rate is time-dependent?

The interpretation of time-dependence in parametric transition rate models can be approached from three different angles. First of all, observed time-dependence may be considered *spurious*, that is, it may simply be the consequence of *unobserved heterogeneity*. We discuss this perspective in detail in chapter 10. Second, time-dependence might be seen as the result of a *diffusion process*, reflecting the changing relationship of a set of interdependent individual units in a dynamic system over time (Diekmann 1989). And third, time-dependence can be interpreted as an expression of a causal process taking place in time between a continuously changing quantitative factor and the qualitative outcome variable under study (Tuma and Hannan 1984; Blossfeld, Hamerle, and Mayer 1989).

---

[2]That is, a transition rate model without any covariates.

We first survey the perspective of *diffusion models* on time-dependence. These models are normally based on the idea that some sort of contagion, infection, imitation, or simply social pressure drives the process under study (Rogers 1983; Mahajan and Peterson 1985; Greve, Strang and Tuma 1995, Strang and Tuma 1993; Strang 1991). A diffusion model, for example, has been suggested by Hernes (1972) to explain the bell-shaped transition rate of entry into marriage. In this model he posits two competing structural processes, explaining the time-dependence in the process of entry into marriage. On the one hand, with rising age t there is an increasing proportion $F(t)$ of a cohort that has already entered into first marriage, which in turn enhances the pressure to marry on those who are still unmarried. On the other hand, there is some sort of decreasing social attractiveness and, more importantly, a declining chance $s(t)$ of contact between unmarried peers with increasing time t. In particular, Diekmann (1989) has shown that the differential equation

$$\frac{\mathrm{d}F(t)}{\mathrm{d}t} = s(t)\, F(t)\, (1 - F(t))$$

with $s(t) = m \exp(-c(t - 1))$, corresponds to a bell-shaped transition rate, $r(t) = s(t)\, F(t)$, of entry into marriage (see also Wu 1990).

Although interpretations of time-dependence based on the idea of a diffusion process are illuminating in theoretical terms, they are still only rarely applied in the social sciences (see example 4 in section 6.6). The standard modeling strategy is to use measures of time as proxies for time-varying causal factors, which are difficult to observe directly (see Tuma and Hannan 1984). As discussed earlier, measures of time may serve as proxy variables, for example, for "the amount of marriage-specific investments" in divorce studies, "the stock of job-specific labor force experience" in mobility analyses, "the intensity of information flow" in organizational studies, or "the intensity of ties between a person and a locale" in migration studies. Given the difficulty of measuring such theoretically important concepts over time, time-dependent parametric models become a useful tool for modeling the changes in the transition rates over time.

There is a natural link between the exponential model and some time-dependent parametric models (Tuma and Hannan 1984). It can be shown, for example, that a metric causal variable increasing linearly over duration leads to a Gompertz model when it is included in an exponential model on the basis of the episode-splitting method. Take the application in section 6.5 where we argued that the unobserved variable "job-specific labor force experience," $x_{\mathrm{LFX}}(t)$, starts at 0 at the beginning of each new job and increases linearly over the duration t a person spends in a job. The rate equation with this latent variable $x_{\mathrm{lfx}}(t)$, controlling for a vector of other covariates, x, would therefore be

$$r(t) = \exp\left(x\beta + x_{\text{lfx}}(t)\,\beta_{\text{lfx}}\right)$$

An observable proxy variable for this latent factor is $t \simeq x_{\text{lfx}}$. Applying the method of episode splitting by measuring the proxy variable t intermittently at the beginning of arbitrarily defined subepisodes within each job leads to the following model:

$$r(t) = \exp\left(x\beta + t\,\beta_{\text{lfx}}\right)$$

which can be rewritten

$$r(t) = \exp\left(x\beta\right)\exp\left(t\,\beta_{\text{lfx}}\right)$$

With $b = \exp(x\beta)$ and $c = \beta_{\text{lfx}}$, this is actually a Gompertz model

$$r(t) = b\,\exp\left(c\,t\right)$$

to be explained in more detail in section 7.2. Thus, if we hypothesize a causal mechanism that a linearly increasing stock of "job-specific labor force experience" leads to a monotonic decline in the job-exit rate and include the time path of the duration via episode splitting in an exponential model, this is actually equivalent to *approximating* a Gompertz model.

A Weibull model, conversely, would be approximated if the stock of "job-specific labor force experience" is assumed to change as a *logarithmic function of duration* $(x_{\text{lfx}}(t) = \log(t))$:

$$\begin{aligned}
r(t) &= \exp\left(x\beta + \log(x_{\text{lfx}})\beta_{\text{lfx}(t)}\right)\\
&\simeq \exp\left(x\beta + \log(t)\beta_{\text{lfx}}\right)\\
&= \exp(x\beta)\,t^{\beta_{\text{lfx}}}
\end{aligned}$$

With $a = \exp(x\beta)$ and $b = \beta_{\text{lfx}}$ one obtains a special Weibull model, as can be seen in section 7.3.[3]

To say that the stock of "job-specific labor force experience" affects the job-exit rate *logarithmically* instead of linearly with increasing job duration means that the *same* amount of job duration, t, leads to a *smaller* stock of job-specific experience, $\log(t)$. Of course, the question that arises here is which of these two causal models (Gompertz or Weibull distribution) is the correct one. Because available theory in the social sciences typically provides little or no guidance for choosing one parameterization over another, the problem normally boils down to the question of which model provides a better fit to the data. We discuss some widely used methods for assessing the fit of parametric models in chapter 8.

---

[3]See Blossfeld, Hamerle, and Mayer (1989) for the various forms of the Weibull model.

However, given the issue of unobserved heterogeneity (chapter 10), as well as the difficulties in evaluating which of the models provides the relatively best fit, we recommend that parametric models of time-dependence should only be applied with extreme caution. One should always be aware of the fact that *assumed* causal factors that are (normally) latent or unobserved and measured only on the basis of assumed proxies are being dealt with. Thus any substantive conclusion based on a time-dependent parametric model necessarily rests on a series of untested and/or untestable assumptions: (1) that there is indeed the supposed causal factor, (2) that this factor in fact leads to a specific shape of the transition rate (*via* an assumed causal mechanism), and (3) that the measure of time is a reasonably good proxy for the path of the unobserved factor. In summary, a strong theory is needed for these empirical applications.

In the following examples we do not pretend to have such a strong theory. Our purpose is only a didactical one. We demonstrate from a substantive point of view how different time-dependent parametric models in empirical research can be applied with Stata and how the results of the estimation are to be interpreted.

7.2   Gompertz Models

We begin the discussion of parametric models of time-dependence with the Gompertz distribution. The "Gompertz law," which states that the transition rate decreases monotonically with time, has been successfully applied, for example, in studying the lifetime of organizations (see, e.g., Carroll and Delacroix 1982; Freeman, Carroll, and Hannan 1983; Hannan and Freeman 1989; Lomi 1995; Carroll and Hannan 2000) or the durations in jobs (see, e.g., Sørensen and Tuma 1981; Blossfeld and Mayer 1988). The transition rate is given by the expression

$$r(t) = b \exp(ct) \qquad b \geq 0 \tag{7.1}$$

The corresponding survivor and density functions are

$$f(t) = \exp\left\{-\frac{b}{c}\left(\exp(ct) - 1\right)\right\}\left(b \exp(ct)\right)$$

$$G(t) = \exp\left\{-\frac{b}{c}\left(\exp(ct) - 1\right)\right\}$$

In the case of $c = 0$, it is assumed that these expressions reduce to the density and survivor function for a simple exponential model. Figure 7.2.1 shows graphs of the transition rate function for $b = 1$ and some values of c.

The Gompertz distribution has two parameters to include covariates. Stata uses an exponential link function for the b parameter and a linear link

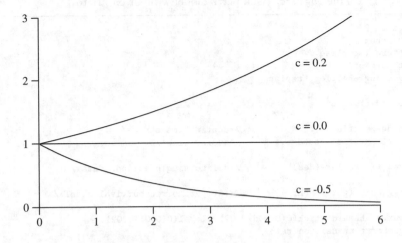

Figure 7.2.1 Gompertz transition rate ($b = 1$).

function for the c parameter. The model formulation for the transition rate from a given origin state to destination state k is

$$
\begin{aligned}
r_k(t) &= b_k \exp(c_k\, t) \\
b_k &= \exp(B^{(k)} \beta^{(k)}) \\
c_k &= C^{(k)} \gamma^{(k)}
\end{aligned}
$$

It is assumed that the first component of each of the covariate (row) vectors $B^{(k)}$ and $C^{(k)}$ is a constant equal to one. The associated coefficient vectors, $\beta^{(k)}$ and $\gamma^{(k)}$, are the model parameters to be estimated. In Stata, the Gompertz model can be requested with the command

```
streg varlist, d(gomp)
```

Linking of the ancillary parameter c can be specified with the option `ancillary(varlist)`.

Models without Covariates (Single Time-Dependent Rate)

In order to demonstrate the estimation and interpretation of the Gompertz model, we first specify a model without covariates:

$$
r(t) = b \exp(ct)\,, \ b = \exp(\beta_0)\,, \ c = \gamma_0
$$

We again analyze the job-exit rate from "being in a job" (origin state $= 0$) to "having left the job" (destination state $= 1$) and regard duration in a

Box 7.2.1 Do-file `ehg1.do` (Gompertz model without covariates)

```
version 9
set scheme sj
capture log close
set more off
log using ehg1.log, replace

use rrdat1, clear

gen des = tfin ~= ti          /*destination state*/
gen tf  = tfin - tstart + 1   /*ending time*/

stset tf, failure(des)        /*define single episode data*/

streg, dist(gomp) nohr        /*fit parametric survival model*/

stcurve, hazard ytick(0(0.005)0.02) ylabel(0(0.01)0.02)
/*gompertz transition rate*/

log close
```

job as a proxy variable for the stock of job-specific skills acquired in each new job. This implies that job-specific experience starts—as the duration itself—with each new job at $t = 0$ and then rises linearly with the time spent in a job. Because training on the job is an investment that is more or less lost when the job is changed, we hypothesize a causal mechanism that with increasing job-specific labor force experience, the transition rate declines monotonically. Given the Gompertz model, this suggests that the estimated parameter for c should be significant and negative (see Figure 7.2.1).

The do-file to estimate this Gompertz model, shown in Box 7.2.1, differs from the do-file for an exponential model in Box 4.1.1 only in that the model selection command has been changed to

```
streg, dist(gomp) nohr
```

The estimation results are shown in Box 7.2.2. _cons refers to parameter b, and `gamma` corresponds to parameter c in 7.1. A comparison of this model with the exponential model in Box 4.1.2, based on a likelihood ratio test, shows that the Gompertz model provides a significant improvement:

$$\text{LR} = 2\left((-898.45) - (-937.97)\right) = 79.04$$

The estimated parameters are $\hat{b} = \exp(\hat{\beta}_0) = \exp(-4.0729) = 0.017$ and $\hat{c} = \hat{\gamma}_0 = -0.0067$. Thus, as hypothesized, the estimated c is negative and significant. We therefore conclude that increasing job-specific labor force

Box 7.2.2 Stata's output using ehg1.do (Box 7.2.1)

```
        failure _d:  des
  analysis time _t:  tf

Iteration 0:   log likelihood = -39205.948
Iteration 1:   log likelihood = -957.17646
Iteration 2:   log likelihood = -904.45409
Iteration 3:   log likelihood =  -898.4633
Iteration 4:   log likelihood = -898.45391
Iteration 5:   log likelihood = -898.45391

Gompertz regression -- log relative-hazard form

No. of subjects =          600    Number of obs   =          600
No. of failures =          458
Time at risk    =        40782
                                  Wald chi2(0)    =         .
Log likelihood  =   -898.45391    Prob > chi2     =

-----------------------------------------------------------------------
   _t |     Coef.   Std. Err.      z    P>|z|    [95% Conf. Interval]
------+----------------------------------------------------------------
 _cons | -4.072898   .0633252   -64.32   0.000   -4.197013   -3.948783
------+----------------------------------------------------------------
 gamma | -.0066923   .0008669    -7.72   0.000   -.0083913   -.0049933
-----------------------------------------------------------------------
```

experience leads to a declining rate of moving out of the job. The estimated rate for this model can be plotted with the command stcurve, hazard (see Box 7.2.1). The resulting plot is shown in Figure 7.2.2. Note that it is also possible to plot the survival function and the cumulative hazard function. To this end you simply need to specify the option survival for the survival function and cumhaz for the cumulative hazard function.

Some illustrations of interpreting the results should be given: If one compares, for example, an employee who has just started a new job ($\hat{r}(0) = 0.017$) with an employee who has already been working for 10 years (120 months) in the same job ($\hat{r}(120) = 0.017 \exp(-0.0067 \cdot 120) = 0.0076$), then the tendency of the second employee to change his or her job has been reduced by about 55 %, due to the accumulation of job-specific skills.[4] Based on the survivor function of the Gompertz model

$$G(t) = \exp\left\{-\frac{b}{c}\left(\exp(ct) - 1\right)\right\}$$

---

[4] Just like a pocket calculator, Stata's display command shows you the result:

```
display exp(_b[_cons])      display exp(_b[_cons])*exp(e(gamma)*120)
```

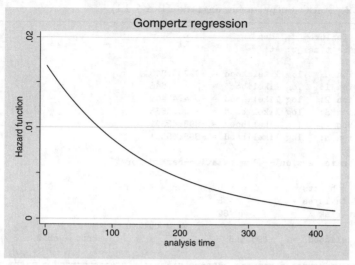

Figure 7.2.2 Gompertz transition rate estimated with do-file `ehg1.do`, (Box 7.2.1). The plot was generated with do-file `ehg1.do`.

it is possible to estimate the median M of the job duration, defined by $G(M) = 0.5$, as

$$G(\hat{M}) = \exp\left\{-\frac{0.017}{-0.0067}\left(\exp(-0.0067\,\hat{M}) - 1\right)\right\} = 0.5$$

The estimated median is about 47.6 months. Thus the Gompertz model estimates a smaller median than the exponential model ($\hat{M} = 61.9$) in section 4.1.2.[5]

Based on the survivor function, one can also compute the probability that an employee is still working in the same job after a period of, say, 10 years:

$$G(120) = \exp\left\{-\frac{0.017}{-0.0067}\left(\exp(-0.0067 \cdot 120) - 1\right)\right\} \approx 0.246$$

or about 25 %. Thus, this estimate is almost the same as for the exponential model in section 4.1.2, where the estimate for this example was 26 %.

However, using this simple model without covariates assumes that there is no important heterogeneity across individuals and job episodes. This assumption is, in fact, not valid, as we have already seen in discussing the exponential and piecewise constant exponential models in chapters 4 and 5. Moreover, ignoring heterogeneity in the present example is particularly

---

[5]In Stata, you can calculate the median with `predict median, median time`.

Box 7.2.3 Do-file `ehg2.do` (Gompertz model with covariates)

```
version 9
capture log close
set more off
log using ehg2.log, replace

use rrdat1, clear

gen des = tfin ~= ti          /*destination state*/
gen tf  = tfin - tstart + 1   /*ending time*/

stset tf, failure(des)        /*define single episode data*/

gen coho2 = tb>=468 & tb<= 504   /*cohort 2*/
gen coho3 = tb>=588 & tb<= 624   /*cohort 3*/
gen lfx   = tstart - te          /*labor force experience*/
gen pnoj  = noj - 1              /*previous number of jobs*/

streg edu coho2 coho3 lfx pnoj pres, dist(gomp) nohr
/*fit parametric survival model*/

log close
```

problematic because a declining duration dependency can be the result of heterogeneity that is not explicitly taken into account.[6] Thus, the conclusion that the transition rate decreases due to the job-specific accumulation of skills could be wrong. It could be the consequence of unobserved heterogeneity. Therefore, in the next step, we estimate a Gompertz model controlling for a set of time-constant covariates.

Models with Covariates Linked to the b Parameter

There are several options to link covariates with the parameters of the Gompertz model. We demonstrate all of them. First of all, time-constant covariates can be linked to the b parameter, so we estimate the following model:

$$r(t) = b \exp(c\,t), \ b = \exp(B\beta) \ , \ c = \gamma_0$$

The do-file for this model, `ehg2.do`, is shown in Box 7.2.3. This do-file is almost identical to the do-file in Box 7.2.1. There is only one difference: A list of time-constant covariates has been added to the instruction.

Results of the model estimation are shown in Box 7.2.4. The value of the log likelihood for this model is -861.9230. Thus, if this Gompertz model is compared with a Gompertz model without covariates (Box 7.2.2), the

---

[6]This is discussed in chapter 10.

Box 7.2.4 Stata's standard output using ehg2.do (Box 7.2.3)

```
          failure _d:  des
   analysis time _t:  tf

Fitting constant-only model:

Iteration 0:   log likelihood =  -937.9681
Iteration 1:   log likelihood = -900.98488
Iteration 2:   log likelihood = -898.46151
Iteration 3:   log likelihood = -898.45391
Iteration 4:   log likelihood = -898.45391


Fitting full model:

Iteration 0:   log likelihood = -898.45391
Iteration 1:   log likelihood = -864.11298
Iteration 2:   log likelihood = -861.92627
Iteration 3:   log likelihood = -861.92295
Iteration 4:   log likelihood = -861.92295


Gompertz regression -- log relative-hazard form

No. of subjects =          600      Number of obs   =          600
No. of failures =          458
Time at risk    =        40782
                                    LR chi2(6)      =        73.06
Log likelihood  =   -861.92295      Prob > chi2     =       0.0000


------------------------------------------------------------------------
    _t |      Coef.   Std. Err.      z    P>|z|     [95% Conf. Interval]
-------+----------------------------------------------------------------
   edu |   .0633836    .024793     2.56   0.011     .0147902    .1119771
 coho2 |   .4129613   .1151944     3.58   0.000     .1871843    .6387383
 coho3 |   .3118589   .1222395     2.55   0.011     .0722738    .5514439
   lfx |  -.0038652   .0009288    -4.16   0.000    -.0056857   -.0020447
  pnoj |   .0627439   .0440582     1.42   0.154    -.0236086    .1490964
  pres |  -.0250146   .0054506    -4.59   0.000    -.0356976   -.0143317
 _cons |  -3.910537   .2813632   -13.90   0.000    -4.461999   -3.359076
-------+----------------------------------------------------------------
 gamma |   -.005876   .0008735    -6.73   0.000    -.0075879    -.004164
------------------------------------------------------------------------
```

likelihood ratio test leads to a χ^2-value of

$$\text{LR} = 2\left((-861.9230) - (-898.45391)\right) = 73.06$$

with six degrees of freedom. The model including covariates obviously provides a better fit.

In addition to this overall goodness-of-fit check, one can use the information provided in the standard errors of the estimation procedure. Assuming a large enough sample, the estimated coefficients divided by their standard errors (provided in column `Std. Err.`) are approximately standard normally distributed. Using this test statistic, one can in particular assess the question of whether the coefficients significantly differ from zero. Box 7.2.4 provides basically the same picture as the estimation results for the simple exponential model (Box 4.1.4). With the exception of `pnoj`, all variables seem to have a statistically significant impact on the transition rate for leaving a job (given the significance level of $\alpha = 0.05$).

Also, the estimate of c, $\hat{c} = \hat{\gamma}_0 = -0.0059$ (the `gamma` coefficient in Box 7.2.4), is still significant and negative. Thus the time-constant factors linked to the b parameter were not able to explain the declining transition rate completely. The c-coefficient is only a little smaller than in Box 7.2.2.

It is interesting to compare the estimates of this Gompertz model with the estimates in Box 6.5.4, where "job-specific labor force experience" in each of the jobs was approximated with the help of the episode-splitting method. The estimates for the models with the maximum subepisode length of 24 and 12 months are almost identical with the Gompertz model in Box 7.2.4. Thus the method of episode splitting provided a quite good approximation of the Gompertz model.

Models with Covariates Linked to the b and c Parameters

In surveying the exponential model with period-specific effects in section 5.4, we have already seen that the effect of time-constant covariates varies over duration. The hypothesis is that the effects of some of the time-constant covariates serving as signals decline with job duration (Arrow 1973; Spence 1973, 1974). This hypothesis has been empirically supported in Box 5.4.2. A similar test, making the parameter c of the Gompertz model dependent on time-constant covariates, can now be conducted with the Gompertz model. The model to be used is

$$r(t) = b \exp(c\,t)\,,\ b = \exp(B\beta)\,,\ c = C\gamma$$

As shown in Box 7.2.5, this model can be estimated by simply adding the option `ancillary` to link a set of covariates with the c parameter of the model. The estimation results are shown in Box 7.2.6.

Looking at the log-likelihood value in Box 7.2.6, which is -857.33, it becomes clear that this model provides only a slight improvement over the model in Box 7.2.4. Thus, if this model is compared with the Gompertz model with covariates linked only to the b parameter (Box 7.2.4), the likelihood ratio test statistic is not significant with

$$\text{LR} = 2\left((-857.33) - (-861.92)\right) = 9.18$$

and six degrees of freedom. However, we briefly want to discuss the results for the c parameter. An inspection of the single estimated coefficients shows

Box 7.2.5 Do-file `ehg3.do` (Gompertz model with covariates)

```
version 9
capture log close
set more off
log using ehg3.log, replace

use rrdat1, clear

gen des = tfin ~= ti            /*destination state*/
gen tf  = tfin - tstart + 1     /*ending time*/

stset tf, failure(des)          /*define single episode data*/

gen coho2 = tb>=468 & tb<= 504  /*cohort 2*/
gen coho3 = tb>=588 & tb<= 624  /*cohort 3*/
gen lfx   = tstart - te         /*labor force experience*/
gen pnoj  = noj - 1             /*previous number of jobs*/

streg edu coho2 coho3 lfx pnoj pres, dist(gomp) nohr ///
ancillary(edu coho2 coho3 lfx pnoj pres) /*fit parametric survival model*/

log close
```

that only the effect of `pnoj` ("number of previously held jobs") is significant. Its effect has a declining relevance over job duration. However, in contradiction to the signal or filter theory, the effects of prestige (`pres`), educational attainment (`edu`), and general labor force experience at the beginning of each job (`lfx`) have no effect on the "shape parameter" c (the gamma coefficients in Box 7.2.6). Thus, the result of this model contradicts the result of the exponential model with period-specific effects in section 5.4. This suggests that caution is required in dealing with highly sophisticated parametric models linking many covariates to various parameters.

Alternatively, a comparison with the results of the exponential model with period-specific effects in Box 5.4.2 also shows that the parameters for the first period from 0 to 24 months are indeed very similar to the coefficients for the b parameter in Box 7.2.6. Thus the b parameter effects of the covariates in the Gompertz model seem to do a good job in describing the effects of the covariates at a starting phase of each new job.

Box 7.2.6 Stata's output using ehg3.do (Box 7.2.5)

```
        failure _d:  des
  analysis time _t:  tf

Fitting constant-only model:

Iteration 0:   log likelihood = -937.9681
Iteration 1:   log likelihood = -889.13039
Iteration 2:   log likelihood = -883.48448
Iteration 3:   log likelihood = -883.46275
Iteration 4:   log likelihood = -883.46274

Fitting full model:

Iteration 0:   log likelihood = -883.46274
Iteration 1:   log likelihood = -858.61766
Iteration 2:   log likelihood = -857.33758
Iteration 3:   log likelihood = -857.33467
Iteration 4:   log likelihood = -857.33467


Gompertz regression -- log relative-hazard form

No. of subjects =          600      Number of obs   =         600
No. of failures =          458
Time at risk    =        40782
                                    LR chi2(6)      =       52.26
Log likelihood  =   -857.33467      Prob > chi2     =      0.0000


------------------------------------------------------------------------
        |    Coef.    Std. Err.      z    P>|z|    [95% Conf. Interval]
--------+---------------------------------------------------------------
_t      |
   edu  |   .091787    .0318233    2.88   0.004    .0294145    .1541596
  coho2 |  .5073593    .1547354    3.28   0.001    .2040835     .810635
  coho3 |  .2069269    .1686586    1.23   0.220   -.123638    .5374918
   lfx  | -.0051039    .0013032   -3.92   0.000   -.007658   -.0025497
  pnoj  |   .151307    .0603776    2.51   0.012    .032969     .269645
  pres  | -.0322516    .0071172   -4.53   0.000   -.0462011   -.0183022
 _cons  | -4.016663    .3663095  -10.97   0.000   -4.734616   -3.298709
--------+---------------------------------------------------------------
gamma   |
   edu  | -.0005215    .0004568   -1.14   0.254   -.0014168    .0003738
  coho2 |  -.001869    .0021518   -0.87   0.385   -.0060864    .0023485
  coho3 |  .0029796    .0028039    1.06   0.288   -.0025161    .0084752
   lfx  |  .0000258    .0000188    1.37   0.170   -.000011    .0000625
  pnoj  | -.0019492    .0009624   -2.03   0.043   -.0038354    -.000063
  pres  |  .0001677    .0001044    1.61   0.108   -.000037    .0003724
 _cons  | -.0053782    .0056633   -0.95   0.342   -.016478    .0057217
------------------------------------------------------------------------
```

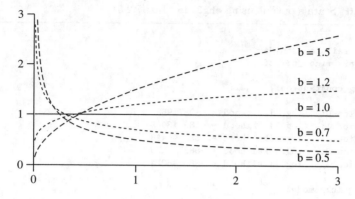

Figure 7.3.1 Weibull transition rates $(a = 1)$.

7.3   Weibull Models

This section describes the Weibull model. In the single transition case, it is derived by assuming a Weibull distribution for the episode durations. Density function, survivor function, and the transition rate are given, respectively, by

$$
\begin{aligned}
f(t) &= b\,a^b\,t^{b-1}\exp\left\{-(at)^b\right\} \qquad a, b > 0 \\
G(t) &= \exp\left\{-(at)^b\right\} \\
r(t) &= b\,a^b\,t^{b-1}
\end{aligned}
$$

Figure 7.3.1 shows graphs of the transition rate for $a = 1$ and different values of b.

     The Weibull model is also flexible and appropriate for a wide variety of situations (e.g., Carroll and Hannan 2000). Like the Gompertz model, the Weibull model can also be used to model a monotonically falling $(0 < b < 1)$ or monotonically increasing rate $(b > 1)$; see Figure 7.3.1. For the special case of $b = 1$, one obtains the exponential model. It is therefore possible to test the hypothesis of a constant risk against the alternative of $b \neq 1$.

     The Weibull model has two parameters, so one has two possibilities to include covariates. Stata uses the following parameterization:[7]

$$
a = \exp(-A\alpha), \quad b = \exp(B\beta)
$$

It is assumed that the first component of each of the covariate (row) vectors A and B is a constant equal to one. The associated coefficient vectors, α and β, are the model parameters to be estimated.

---

[7]This is the so-called accelerated failure time formulation. Note the minus sign in the link function for the a parameter.

Box 7.3.1   Do-file `ehg5.do`   (Weibull model without covariates)

```
version 9
set scheme sj
capture log close
set more off
log using ehg5.log, replace

use rrdat1, clear

gen des = tfin ~= ti          /*destination state*/
gen tf  = tfin - tstart + 1   /*ending time*/

stset tf, failure(des)        /*define single episode data*/

streg, dist(w) time           /*fit parametric survival model*/

stcurve, hazard ytick(0(0.005)0.02) ylabel(0(0.01)0.02)

log close
```

The Stata command to request estimation of a Weibull model is

> `streg, dist(weibull)`

Note that, by default, the model is parameterized as a proportional hazard model. To specify the accelerated failure time version, that we have assumed previously, one has to add the option `time`.

Models without Covariates (Single Time-Dependent Rate)

In order to demonstrate the estimation and interpretation of the Weibull model, we first specify a model without covariates:

$$r(t) = b\,a^{b}\,t^{b-1}, \; a = \exp\left(-\alpha_0\right), \; b = \exp\left(\beta_0\right),$$

Again, we use the job-exit example of movement from "being in a job" (origin state = 0) to "having left the job" (destination state = 1), but now assume that the *logarithm* of the duration in a job is a proxy variable for the change in the stock of job-specific skills acquired in each new job. This means that job-specific experience starts—as the duration itself—in each new job and then rises as a logarithmic function of the time spent in the job. Again, we hypothesize that with increasing job-specific labor force experience the transition rate declines monotonically. Given the Weibull model, this suggests that the estimated parameter b is significant, and its size is between 0 and 1 (see Figure 7.3.1).

The Stata do-file (`ehg5.do`) to estimate this Weibull model, shown in Box 7.3.1, differs from the do-file for the Gompertz model in Box 7.2.1 only

Box 7.3.2 Stata's output using `ehg5.do` (Box 7.3.1)

```
failure _d:  des
analysis time _t:  tf

Fitting constant-only model:

Iteration 0:   log likelihood = -937.9681
Iteration 1:   log likelihood = -928.85373
Iteration 2:   log likelihood = -928.84734
Iteration 3:   log likelihood = -928.84734

Fitting full model:
Iteration 0:   log likelihood = -928.84734

Weibull regression -- accelerated failure-time form

No. of subjects =           600        Number of obs   =        600
No. of failures =           458
Time at risk    =         40782        LR chi2(0)      =       0.00
Log likelihood  =    -928.84734        Prob > chi2     =         .


------------------------------------------------------------------------
    _t |      Coef.   Std. Err.      z    P>|z|     [95% Conf. Interval]
-------+----------------------------------------------------------------
  _cons |   4.461634    .054394   82.02   0.000     4.355023    4.568244
-------+----------------------------------------------------------------
 /ln_p |  -.1477012    .0360025   -4.10   0.000    -.2182648   -.0771377
-------+----------------------------------------------------------------
     p |   .8626888    .0310589                     .8039126    .9257624
   1/p |   1.159167    .0417329                     1.080191    1.243916
------------------------------------------------------------------------
```

in that now the distribution has been changed to `weibull` and we use the option `time` to choose the accelerated failure time parameterization.

The estimation results are shown in Box 7.3.2. The α_0 parameter is called `_cons` in the Stata output, and the β_0 parameter is called `/ln_p`. A comparison with the exponential model in Box 4.1.2 leads to a highly significant likelihood ratio test statistic: 18.24 with one degree of freedom. However, there is little improvement compared to the Gompertz model (see Box 7.2.2). Thus the Gompertz model seems to provide a better fit of the observed data. This highlights an advantage of a linear over a log-linear specification of the accumulation of job-specific labor force experience over duration. For the a term, the estimated parameter is

$$\hat{a} = \exp(-\hat{\alpha}_0) = \exp(-4.4616) = 0.0115$$

For the b term, the estimated parameter is

$$\hat{b} = \exp(\hat{\beta}_0) = \exp(-0.1477) = 0.8627$$

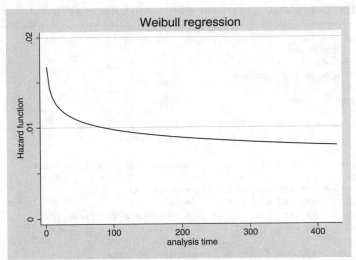

Figure 7.3.2 Weibull transition rate estimated with do-file `ehg5.do` (Box 7.3.1). The plot was generated with do-file `ehg5.do`.

As expected, the estimate of b is significant, positive, and smaller than 1. Thus the Weibull model also predicts a decreasing rate to move out of the job with increasing job-specific labor force experience.

The estimated rate for this model is plotted in Figure 7.3.2. Compared to the Gompertz rate in Figure 7.2.2, the Weibull rate is flat and bears a closer resemblance to the exponential model. This could be why the likelihood ratio test statistic is so small for the Weibull model, as compared to the Gompertz model likelihood ratio test statistic. If we again compare an employee who has just started a new job:

$$\hat{r}(0) = 0.8627 \cdot 0.0115^{0.8627} = 0.018$$

with an employee who has already been working for 10 years (or 120 months), in the same job:

$$\hat{r}(120) = 0.8627 \cdot 0.0115^{0.8627} \cdot 120^{0.8627-1} = 0.0095$$

then the tendency of the second employee to change his or her job has been reduced, through the accumulation of job-specific skills, by about 48 %. Based on the survivor function of the Weibull model, that is

$$G(t) = \exp\left(-(at)^b\right)$$

it is again possible to estimate the median, $\hat{M}$, of the job duration by

$$G(\hat{M}) = \exp\left(-(0.0115\, M)^{0.8627}\right) = 0.5$$

Box 7.3.3 Do-file `ehg6.do` (Weibull model with covariates)

```
version 9
capture log close
set more off
log using ehg6.log, replace

use rrdat1, clear

gen des = tfin ~= ti              /*destination state*/
gen tf  = tfin - tstart + 1       /*ending time*/

stset tf, failure(des)            /*define single episode data*/

gen coho2 = tb>=468 & tb<= 504    /*cohort 2*/
gen coho3 = tb>=588 & tb<= 624    /*cohort 3*/
gen lfx   = tstart - te           /*labor force experience*/
gen pnoj  = noj - 1               /*previous number of jobs*/

streg edu coho2 coho3 lfx pnoj pres, dist(w) time
/*fit parametric survival model*/

log close
```

resulting in $\hat{M} = 56.9$ months. Thus the median estimated with the Weibull model is greater than that estimated with the Gompertz model ($\hat{M} = 47.7$; see section 7.2) and smaller than the estimate resulting from an exponential model ($\hat{M} = 61.9$; see section 4.1.2).

In the next step, we estimate the Weibull model and include our well-known set of time-constant covariates.

Models with Covariates Linked to the a Parameter

The Weibull distribution also offers two parameters to include covariates. In a first step, we link the time-constant covariates only to the a parameter of the Weibull distribution and estimate the following model:

$$r(t) = b\,a^b\,t^{b-1}, \; a = \exp\left(-A\alpha\right), \; b = \exp\left(\beta_0\right)$$

The do-file for this model, `ehg6.do`, is shown in Box 7.3.3. This do-file differs from the do-file for the Gompertz model in Box 7.2.3 only by the model selection, which is now `dist(w)`, and the option `time`, which is used to choose the accelerated failure time parameterization.

The estimation results are presented in Box 7.3.4. As can be seen in that box, the value of the log-likelihood function for this model is -886.71. Thus, if this model is compared with the Weibull model without covariates, one gets a significant likelihood ratio statistic of 84.28 with six degrees

Box 7.3.4 Stata's output using `ehg6.do` (Box 7.3.3)

```
          failure _d:  des
    analysis time _t:  tf

Fitting constant-only model:
Iteration 0:    log likelihood =  -937.9681
Iteration 1:    log likelihood = -928.85373
Iteration 2:    log likelihood = -928.84734
Iteration 3:    log likelihood = -928.84734

Fitting full model:
Iteration 0:    log likelihood = -928.84734
Iteration 1:    log likelihood = -889.15193
Iteration 2:    log likelihood = -886.71221
Iteration 3:    log likelihood = -886.70676
Iteration 4:    log likelihood = -886.70676


Weibull regression -- accelerated failure-time form

No. of subjects =              600      Number of obs   =         600
No. of failures =              458
Time at risk    =            40782
                                        LR chi2(6)      =       84.28
Log likelihood  =       -886.70676      Prob > chi2     =      0.0000


------------------------------------------------------------------------
    _t |      Coef.   Std. Err.       z    P>|z|    [95% Conf. Interval]
-------+----------------------------------------------------------------
   edu |   -.077931    .027014    -2.88   0.004   -.1308776   -.0249845
 coho2 |  -.6062033   .1241684    -4.88   0.000   -.8495689   -.3628377
 coho3 |  -.5776778   .1303482    -4.43   0.000   -.8331555      -.3222
   lfx |   .0036419   .0010393     3.50   0.000    .0016048    .0056789
  pnoj |  -.0637472   .0483515    -1.32   0.187   -.1585144      .03102
  pres |   .0291634    .006026     4.84   0.000    .0173527    .0409741
 _cons |   4.406308   .3060021    14.40   0.000    3.806555    5.006062
-------+----------------------------------------------------------------
 /ln_p |  -.0902791   .0363595    -2.48   0.013   -.1615424   -.0190157
-------+----------------------------------------------------------------
     p |   .9136762   .0332208                     .8508304     .981164
   1/p |    1.09448   .0397948                     1.019198    1.175322
------------------------------------------------------------------------
```

of freedom. So the covariates seem to have an important impact on job duration. This is confirmed by looking at the estimated standard errors. In particular, the estimate of b, $\hat{b} = \exp(-0.0903) = 0.9137$ (see p in Box 7.3.4), is still significant, positive, and less than 1. Again, the included time-constant variables cannot explain the declining transition rate. But note that all coefficients linked to the a parameter (see _t in Box 7.3.4) have to be multiplied by -1 in order to compare these estimates with the estimates of the exponential and Gompertz models.

Box 7.3.5   Do-file `ehg7.do` (Weibull model with covariates)

```
version 9
capture log close
set more off
log using ehg7.log, replace

use rrdat1, clear

gen des = tfin ~= ti              /*destination state*/
gen tf  = tfin - tstart + 1       /*ending time*/

stset tf, failure(des)            /*define single episode data*/

gen coho2 = tb>=468 & tb<= 504    /*cohort 2*/
gen coho3 = tb>=588 & tb<= 624    /*cohort 3*/
gen lfx   = tstart - te           /*labor force experience*/
gen pnoj  = noj - 1               /*previous number of jobs*/

streg edu coho2 coho3 lfx pnoj pres, dist(w) time ///
ancillary(edu coho2 coho3 lfx pnoj pres) /*fit parametric survival model*/

log close
```

Models with Covariates Linked to the a and b Parameters

Finally, we link covariates also to the b parameter of the Weibull distribution. The model specification now becomes

$$r(t) = b\, a^b\, t^{b-1},\; a = \exp\left(-A\alpha\right),\; b = \exp\left(B\beta\right)$$

As shown in Box 7.3.5, this model can be estimated by simply adding the option **ancillary** in order to link covariates to the b parameter. Using the modified do-file (`ehg7.do`), the estimation results are shown in Box 7.3.6.

The log-likelihood value is -883.54 and is only slightly better than that for the model with a single constant in the b parameter (Box 7.3.4). The likelihood ratio test statistic to compare the two models is 5.72 with six degrees of freedom and does not show a significant improvement in model fit. If we look at the estimated coefficients of the b parameter, then only the effect of the cohort dummy variable `coho3` is significant. Its effect has an increasing relevance over the job duration. Again, the result that so few parameters are not significant might also be a consequence of the small number of events in the example data set.

Box 7.3.6 Stata's output using `ehg7.do` (Box 7.3.5)

```
        failure _d:  des
analysis time _t:  tf

Fitting constant-only model:

Iteration 0:   log likelihood = -928.84734
Iteration 1:   log likelihood = -924.09756
Iteration 2:   log likelihood = -924.04382
Iteration 3:   log likelihood = -924.04305
Iteration 4:   log likelihood = -924.04304

Fitting full model:

Iteration 0:   log likelihood = -924.04304
Iteration 1:   log likelihood = -889.85953
Iteration 2:   log likelihood =  -883.8695
Iteration 3:   log likelihood = -883.54403
Iteration 4:   log likelihood = -883.54308
Iteration 5:   log likelihood = -883.54307

Weibull regression -- accelerated failure-time form

No. of subjects =           600      Number of obs   =        600
No. of failures =           458
Time at risk    =         40782
                                     LR chi2(6)      =      81.00
Log likelihood  =   -883.54307       Prob > chi2     =     0.0000


------------------------------------------------------------------------
         |      Coef.   Std. Err.      z    P>|z|     [95% Conf. Interval]
------+-----------------------------------------------------------------
_t       |
     edu |  -.0857577   .0273797    -3.13   0.002    -.1394208   -.0320946
   coho2 |  -.5984699   .1284651    -4.66   0.000    -.8502568    -.346683
   coho3 |  -.5581806   .1297498    -4.30   0.000    -.8124856   -.3038756
     lfx |   .0031906   .0010914     2.92   0.003     .0010516    .0053297
    pnoj |  -.0570866   .0496505    -1.15   0.250    -.1543999    .0402266
    pres |   .0289681   .0061361     4.72   0.000     .0169416    .0409947
   _cons |   4.495128   .3075437    14.62   0.000     3.892354    5.097903
------+-----------------------------------------------------------------
ln_p     |
     edu |  -.0027124   .0184046    -0.15   0.883    -.0387848      .03336
   coho2 |   .0835133   .0854602     0.98   0.328    -.0839856    .2510122
   coho3 |   .2016667   .0914015     2.21   0.027      .022523    .3808103
     lfx |   .0010158   .0007358     1.38   0.167    -.0004264     .002458
    pnoj |  -.0385058   .0358827    -1.07   0.283    -.1088346     .031823
    pres |    .000506   .0040108     0.13   0.900    -.0073549    .0083669
   _cons |  -.1613031   .2129186    -0.76   0.449    -.5786159    .2560097
------------------------------------------------------------------------
```

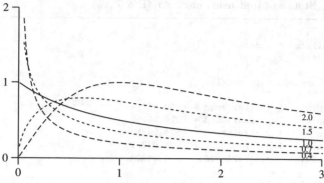

Figure 7.4.1 Log-logistic transition rates ($\lambda = 1$).

7.4 Log-Logistic Models

This section describes the standard log-logistic model.[8] In the single transition case the standard log-logistic model is based on the assumption that the duration of episodes follows a log-logistic distribution. The density, survivor, and rate functions for this distribution are

$$f(t) = \frac{b\, a^b\, t^{b-1}}{[1 + (at)^b]^2} \qquad a, b > 0$$

$$G(t) = \frac{1}{1 + (at)^b}$$

$$r(t) = \frac{b\, a^b\, t^{b-1}}{1 + (at)^b}$$

Figure 7.4.1 shows graphs of the rate function for $a = 1$ and different values of b. The time t_{max} when the rate reaches its maximum, $r_{\max}$, is given by

$$t_{\max} = \frac{1}{a}\,(b-1)^{\frac{1}{b}} \qquad r_{\max} = a\,(b-1)^{1-\frac{1}{b}}$$

Obviously, the log-logistic distribution is even more flexible than the Gompertz and Weibull distributions. As Figure 7.4.1 shows, for $b \leq 1$ one obtains a monotonically declining transition rate, and for $b > 1$ the transition rate at first rises monotonically up to a maximum and then falls monotonically. Thus this model can be used to test a monotonically declining time-dependence against a nonmonotonic pattern. In the literature, the log-logistic model along with the log-normal and the sickle distributions are the

---

[8]A sometimes useful extension of the standard log-logistic model was proposed by Brüderl (1991a; see also Brüderl and Diekmann 1994, 1995). This model can be estimated with TDA as described in Blossfeld and Rohwer (2002, sec. 7.4).

most commonly recommended models if the transition rate is somehow bell-shaped.[9] This is often the case in divorce, marriage, or childbirth studies (see Diekmann 1989; Blossfeld 1995) and research on corporate demography (Brüderl 1991b; Brüderl and Diekmann 1995; Carroll and Hannan 2000).

Stata uses the following parameterization of the distribution parameters:

$$a = \exp(-A\,\alpha) \quad \text{and} \quad b = \exp(-B\beta)$$

It is assumed that the first component of the covariate row vectors A and B are constants equal to one. α and β are the model parameters to be estimated. To estimate a log-logistic model with Stata, type:

```
streg, dist(loglogistic)
```

Models without Covariates (Single Time-Dependent Rate)

Illustrating the application of the log-logistic distribution, we begin with a model without covariates:

$$r(t) = \frac{b\,a^b\,t^{b-1}}{1 + (at)^b}, \ a = \exp(-\alpha_0), \ b = \exp(-\beta_0)$$

Using the job-exit example again, we can examine whether the rate from "being in a job" (origin state $= 0$) to "having left the job" (destination state $= 1$) monotonically declines ($b \leq 1$) or is bell-shaped ($b > 1$) over the duration in a job. As discussed in section 5.2, a bell-shaped transition rate is quite plausible in theoretical terms. It could be the result of an interplay of two contradictory causal forces (increases in job-specific investments and decreases in the need to resolve mismatches) that cannot easily be measured, so that the duration in a job has to serve as a proxy variable for them. Empirical evidence for this thesis has already been provided in Figure 5.2.1.

A Stata do-file to estimate this standard log-logistic model is given in Box 7.4.1. The model selection command is now `streg, dist(logl)`. Estimation results are shown in Box 7.4.2. In Stata's standard output, the parameter α_0 is called _cons, and β_0 is called /ln_gam.

The estimated parameters are $\hat{a} = \exp(-3.8434) = 0.0214$ and $\hat{b} = \exp(0.2918) = 1.34$. As expected on the basis of the results of the piecewise constant exponential model in section 5.2, our estimate of b is greater than 1. Thus we conclude that increasing job-specific labor force experience leads to an increasing and then decreasing rate of job exits. This result demonstrates that the Gompertz and the Weibull models are not able to reflect the increasing rate at the beginning of each job. They can only catch a

---

[9]As demonstrated in the application example 2 of section 6.6, another flexible strategy to model bell-shaped transition rates is to use a combination of two time-dependent variables.

Box 7.4.1 Do-file `ehg8.do` (Log-logistic model without covariates)

```
version 9
set scheme sj
capture log close
set more off
log using ehg8.log, replace

use rrdat1, clear

gen des = tfin ~= ti          /*destination state*/
gen tf  = tfin - tstart + 1   /*ending time*/

stset tf, failure(des)        /*define single episode data*/

streg, dist(logl)             /*fit parametric survival model*/

stcurve, hazard  ytick(0(0.005)0.02) ylabel(0(0.01)0.02)

log close
```

Box 7.4.2 Stata's output using `ehg8.do` (Box 7.4.1)

```
        failure _d:  des
  analysis time _t:  tf

Iteration 0:   log likelihood = -2241.4588  (not concave)
Iteration 1:   log likelihood = -943.12654
Iteration 2:   log likelihood = -884.57982
Iteration 3:   log likelihood =  -884.4348
Iteration 4:   log likelihood = -884.43476

Log-logistic regression -- accelerated failure-time form

No. of subjects =          600     Number of obs   =          600
No. of failures =          458
Time at risk    =        40782
                                   Wald chi2(0)    =          .
Log likelihood  =   -884.43476     Prob > chi2     =          .

-----------------------------------------------------------------------------
     _t |     Coef.   Std. Err.      z    P>|z|     [95% Conf. Interval]
--------+--------------------------------------------------------------------
   _cons |   3.84342   .0548579    70.06   0.000     3.735901    3.95094
--------+--------------------------------------------------------------------
 /ln_gam |-.2917997   .0385254    -7.57   0.000    -.3673081   -.2162913
--------+--------------------------------------------------------------------
   gamma |  .7469181   .0287753                      .6925962    .8055007
-----------------------------------------------------------------------------
```

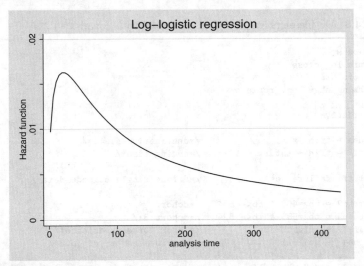

Figure 7.4.2 Log-logistic transition rate estimated with do-file `ehg8.do`, Box 7.4.1. The plot was generated with do-file `ehg8.do`.

monotonic decline or a monotonic increase over time. Because the job-exit rate only increases for some few months at the beginning of each job and then strongly decreases, both fit a model with a decreasing rate to the data. Thus, after "the first job phase," the log-logistic model arrives at the same substantive interpretation as the Gompertz and the Weibull models. However, the log-logistic model offers a more appropriate modeling in the first phase, which is demonstrated in the comparatively high LR test statistic.

The maximum of the log-logistic distribution is reached after a duration of about 21 months:

$$(1/0.0214)(1.34 - 1)^{1/1.34} = 20.89$$

Thus there seems to be an adjustment process leading to a rising rate up to this job duration. However, after this point in time, further increases in job-specific investments will more and more outweigh the force of resolving mismatches, so that the job-exit rate declines with increasing duration. In do-file `ehg8.do` of Box 7.4.1, `stcurve` is used after `streg` to plot the hazard function. The resulting plot is shown in Figure 7.4.2. With the exception of the first part, this plot is very similar to the Gompertz model plot in Figure 7.2.2.

Models with Covariates Linked to the a Parameter

The log-logistic distribution has two parameters to which covariates can be linked. We begin by linking covariates only to the a parameter. Thus we

Box 7.4.3   Do-file `ehg9.do` (Log-logistic model with covariates)

```
version 9
capture log close
set more off
log using ehg9.log, replace

use rrdat1, clear

gen des = tfin ~= ti            /*destination state*/
gen tf  = tfin - tstart + 1     /*ending time*/

stset tf, failure(des)          /*define single episode data*/

gen coho2 = tb>=468 & tb<= 504  /*cohort 2*/
gen coho3 = tb>=588 & tb<= 624  /*cohort 3*/
gen lfx   = tstart - te         /*labor force experience*/
gen pnoj  = noj - 1             /*previous number of jobs*/

streg edu coho2 coho3 lfx pnoj pres, dist(logl)
/*fit parametric survival model*/

log close
```

estimate the following model:

$$r(t) = \frac{b\,a^b\,t^{b-1}}{1 + (at)^b}, \ a = \exp\left(-A\alpha\right), \ b = \exp\left(-\beta_0\right)$$

A do-file to estimate this model is presented in Box 7.4.3. It is very much the same as previously used do-files, except the distribution that had been changed to `loglogistic`.

The estimation results are shown in Box 7.4.4. The value of the likelihood ratio statistic for comparison with a model without covariates is 83.16 with six degrees of freedom. So the model fit has been highly improved by including the covariates. Again, all single coefficients are significant and are quite similar to the parameter estimates for the exponential model.[10] There is only one difference: The effect of `pnoj`, the number of previously held jobs, is now also significant.

Also, the estimated shape parameter, $\hat{b} = \exp(0.3615) = 1.44$, is still significant and greater than 1. However, the included time-constant covariates increased the b value compared to the model without covariates, and the nonmonotonic pattern is therefore steeper and more skewed to the left. We note that a model with covariates also linked to the b parameter would

---

[10]Because of the parameterization of this model in Stata, the signs of the coefficients have to be reversed.

Box 7.4.4 Stata's output using `ehg9.do` (Box 7.4.3)

```
        failure _d:  des
analysis time _t:  tf

Fitting constant-only model:

Iteration 0:   log likelihood = -910.96486
Iteration 1:   log likelihood = -887.72098
Iteration 2:   log likelihood = -884.43728
Iteration 3:   log likelihood = -884.43476
Iteration 4:   log likelihood = -884.43476


Fitting full model:

Iteration 0:   log likelihood = -884.43476
Iteration 1:   log likelihood = -854.71019
Iteration 2:   log likelihood = -842.87048
Iteration 3:   log likelihood =  -842.8523
Iteration 4:   log likelihood =  -842.8523

Log-logistic regression -- accelerated failure-time form

No. of subjects =          600     Number of obs   =          600
No. of failures =          458
Time at risk    =        40782
                                   LR chi2(6)      =        83.16
Log likelihood  =    -842.8523     Prob > chi2     =       0.0000

---------------------------------------------------------------------
     _t |    Coef.   Std. Err.      z    P>|z|     [95% Conf. Interval]
--------+------------------------------------------------------------
    edu | -.0818697   .026856    -3.05   0.002    -.1345066   -.0292328
  coho2 | -.5338245   .1249407   -4.27   0.000    -.7787037   -.2889453
  coho3 | -.4004827   .1318179   -3.04   0.002    -.6588411   -.1421244
    lfx |  .0042518   .0009131    4.66   0.000     .0024622    .0060413
   pnoj | -.0970352   .0476403   -2.04   0.042    -.1904085   -.0036618
   pres |  .0296742   .0056095    5.29   0.000     .0186799    .0406686
  _cons |   3.77846   .2925781   12.91   0.000     3.205017    4.351902
--------+------------------------------------------------------------
/ln_gam | -.3614768   .0385635   -9.37   0.000    -.4370598   -.2858938
--------+------------------------------------------------------------
  gamma |  .6966468   .0268651                     .6459328    .7513424
```

provide basically the same results: Estimates of the α coefficients are almost identical, and the β coefficients are not significant. We therefore do
not present this model here.

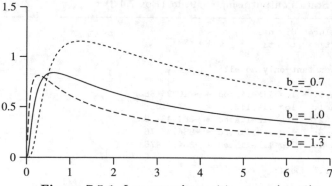

Figure 7.5.1 Log-normal transition rates ($a = 0$).

7.5 Log-Normal Models

Like the log-logistic model, the log-normal model is a widely used model of time-dependence that implies a nonmonotonic relationship between the transition rate and duration: The transition rate initially increases to a maximum and then decreases (see Figure 7.5.1).

This section describes two versions of the log-normal model: a standard log-normal model and a model with an additional shift parameter. The models correspond to the two-parameter and three-parameter log-normal distributions as described, for instance, by Aitchison and Brown (1973). Descriptions of log-normal rate models are given by Lawless (1982, p. 313) and Lancaster (1990, p. 47).

In the single transition case, the standard (two-parameter) log-normal model is derived by assuming that the logarithm of the episode durations follows a normal distribution or, equivalently, that the durations follow a log-normal distribution with density function

$$f(t) = \frac{1}{b\,t}\,\phi\left(\frac{\log(t) - a}{b}\right) \qquad b > 0$$

ϕ and Φ are used, respectively, to denote the standard normal density and distribution functions:

$$\phi(t) = \frac{1}{\sqrt{2\pi}}\exp\left(-\frac{t^2}{2}\right) \quad \text{and} \quad \Phi(t) = \int_0^t \phi(\tau)\,d\tau$$

The survivor function is

$$G(t) = 1 - \Phi\left(\frac{\log(t) - a}{b}\right)$$

and the transition rate can be written as

$$r(t) = \frac{1}{b\,t}\,\frac{\phi(z_t)}{1 - \Phi(z_t)} \quad \text{with} \quad z_t = \frac{\log(t) - a}{b}$$

Box 7.5.1 Do-file `ehg10.do` (Log-normal model without covariates)

```
version 9
set scheme sj
capture log close
set more off
log using ehg10.log, replace

use rrdat1, clear

gen des = tfin ~= ti          /*destination state*/
gen tf  = tfin - tstart + 1   /*ending time*/

stset tf, failure(des)        /*define single episode data*/

streg, dist(ln) time          /*fit parametric survival model*/

stcurve, hazard ytick(0(0.005)0.02) ylabel(0(0.01)0.02)
/*log-normal transition rate*/

log close
```

Figure 7.5.1 shows graphs of the rate function for $a = 0$ and some different values of b. As can be seen, the graphs are very similar for the log-normal and the log-logistic models, provided that $b > 1$ in the latter case.

The standard log-normal distribution has two parameters, so there are two possibilities to include covariates. Stata uses a linear link function for a, but provides in addition the possibility to link covariates to the dispersion parameter, b, via an exponential link function. So one gets the following parameterization of the model:

$$a = A\alpha \quad \text{and} \quad b = \exp(B\beta)$$

It is assumed that the first component of each of the covariate (row) vectors A and B is a constant equal to one. The associated coefficient vectors α and β are the model parameters to be estimated.[11]

Models without Covariates (Single Time-Dependent Rate)

To demonstrate the application of the log-normal distribution, we first estimate a model without covariates:

$$r(t) = \frac{1}{bt}\frac{\phi(z_t)}{1 - \Phi(z_t)}, \; z_t = \frac{\log(t) - a}{b}, \; a = \alpha_0, \; b = \exp(\beta_0)$$

---

[11] In order to link covariates to the b parameter, one can use the option `ancillary(varlist)`.

Box 7.5.2   Stata's output using `ehg10.do` (Box 7.5.1)

```
         failure _d:  des
   analysis time _t:  tf

Iteration 0:    log likelihood = -5130.4981   (not concave)
Iteration 1:    log likelihood = -1186.5402
Iteration 2:    log likelihood = -1094.3427
Iteration 3:    log likelihood = -882.42882
Iteration 4:    log likelihood =  -880.1065
Iteration 5:    log likelihood = -880.08561
Iteration 6:    log likelihood = -880.08561


Log-normal regression -- accelerated failure-time form

No. of subjects =          600          Number of obs   =        600
No. of failures =          458
Time at risk    =        40782
                                         Wald chi2(0)    =          .
Log likelihood  =  -880.08561           Prob > chi2     =          .


------------------------------------------------------------------------
     _t |     Coef.   Std. Err.      z    P>|z|     [95% Conf. Interval]
--------+---------------------------------------------------------------
   _cons |  3.885249   .0548329   70.86   0.000     3.777778    3.992719
--------+---------------------------------------------------------------
 /ln_sig |  .2435508   .0341814    7.13   0.000     .1765564    .3105451
--------+---------------------------------------------------------------
   sigma |  1.275771   .0436076                     1.193102    1.364168
```

Using the job-exit example, we can examine whether the rate from "being in a job" (origin state $= 0$) to "having left the job" (destination state $= 1$) is bell-shaped over the duration in a job. The substantive interpretation is the same as for the log-logistic model in the previous section.

The Stata do-file to estimate this standard log-normal model is shown in Box 7.5.1. Part of the estimation results is shown in Box 7.5.2. The estimated parameters are $\hat{\alpha}_0 = 3.8852$ (`_cons` in the Stata output) and $\hat{\beta}_0 = 0.24355$ (`/ln_sig` in the Stata output). Therefore, $\hat{b} = \exp(0.2436) = 1.28$ (`sigma` in the Stata output). The estimated rate for this model is shown in Figure 7.5.2. The shape of the rate is very similar to the shape of the log-logistic rate in section 7.4 (see Figure 7.4.2). Thus, the interpretation for this model is basically identical to the interpretation of the log-logistic model. In the next step we again include our set of time-constant covariates.

Models with Covariates Linked to the a Parameter

We now link covariates to the a parameter and estimate the following model: $a = A\alpha$ and $b = \exp(\beta_0)$. The Stata do-file for this model is presented in Box

Box 7.5.3 Do-file `ehg11.do` (Log-normal model)

```
version 9
capture log close
set more off
log using ehg11.log, replace

use rrdat1, clear

gen des = tfin ~= ti          /*destination state*/
gen tf  = tfin - tstart + 1   /*ending time*/

stset tf, failure(des)        /*define single episode data*/

gen coho2 = tb>=468 & tb<= 504    /*cohort 2*/
gen coho3 = tb>=588 & tb<= 624    /*cohort 3*/
gen lfx   = tstart - te           /*labor force experience*/
gen pnoj  = noj - 1               /*previous number of jobs*/

streg edu coho2 coho3 lfx pnoj pres, dist(ln)
/*fit parametric survival model*/

log close
```

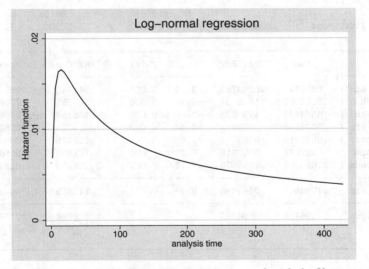

Figure 7.5.2 Log-normal transition rate estimated with do-file `ehg10.do`,
Box 7.5.1. The plot was generated with do-file `ehg10.do`.

7.5.3. The estimation results are shown in Box 7.5.4. The likelihood ratio
test statistics for comparison with a log-normal model without covariates
(Box 7.5.2) is 83.16 with six degrees of freedom, again showing a signifi-

Box 7.5.4 Stata's output using `ehg11.do` (Box 7.5.3)

```
        failure _d:  des
   analysis time _t:  tf

Fitting constant-only model:

Iteration 0:    log likelihood = -917.42548
Iteration 1:    log likelihood = -880.25604
Iteration 2:    log likelihood = -880.08576
Iteration 3:    log likelihood = -880.08561
Iteration 4:    log likelihood = -880.08561

Fitting full model:

Iteration 0:    log likelihood = -880.08561
Iteration 1:    log likelihood = -854.64507
Iteration 2:    log likelihood = -839.93906
Iteration 3:    log likelihood = -839.82987
Iteration 4:    log likelihood = -839.82982

Log-normal regression -- accelerated failure-time form

No. of subjects =        600     Number of obs    =        600
No. of failures =        458
Time at risk    =      40782
                                 LR chi2(6)       =      80.51
Log likelihood  =   -839.82982   Prob > chi2      =     0.0000


---------------------------------------------------------------------
     _t |     Coef.    Std. Err.      z    P>|z|    [95% Conf. Interval]
--------+------------------------------------------------------------
    edu | -.0812716    .0269766   -3.01   0.003   -.1341448   -.0283983
  coho2 | -.5164192    .1246737   -4.14   0.000   -.7607751   -.2720633
  coho3 | -.4514127    .1294633   -3.49   0.000    -.705156   -.1976693
    lfx |  .0038863     .000875    4.44   0.000    .0021713    .0056013
   pnoj | -.0848716    .0463878   -1.83   0.067     -.17579    .0060468
   pres |  .0287017    .0055916    5.13   0.000    .0177423    .0396611
  _cons |  3.856658    .2915528   13.23   0.000    3.285225    4.428091
--------+------------------------------------------------------------
/ln_sig |  .1793801    .0342088    5.24   0.000     .112332    .2464282
--------+------------------------------------------------------------
  sigma |  1.196475     .04093                     1.118884    1.279447
---------------------------------------------------------------------
```

cant improvement of the model fit. In terms of the statistical significance and influence direction of covariates, the result for the log-normal model is basically the same as the result for an exponential model. With regard to the log-logistic model, there is, however, one difference: The effect of the number of previously held jobs (pnoj) is not significant.

The estimated coefficient $\hat{b} = \exp(0.1794) = 1.20$ is still significant and greater than 1. In fact, the included time-constant variables make the non-monotonic pattern even steeper and more skewed to the left than was the case for the log-logistic model.

Again, it would be possible to also link covariates to the b parameter, but this model does not provide different results. We therefore do not present them here.

Conclusion. As shown in this chapter, Stata can be used to estimate a variety of transition rate models with a time-dependent transition rate. It is easy to select different model types and to specify different ways of including covariates. However, we have already remarked that using parametric transition rate models with only limited capabilities to adapt to a given set of data can lead to misleading results, for instance, when using a Weibull model whose transition rate is, in fact, bell-shaped. One provision against this danger is to estimate a variety of different models and see whether the estimation results—for the most interesting covariates—are robust. We come back to this topic at the end of chapter 10.

Chapter 8

Methods to Check Parametric Assumptions

As discussed in the previous chapter, the standard strategy in using parametric models of time-dependence is to consider measures of time as proxies for time-varying causal factors that are difficult to observe directly. However, available theory in the social sciences normally provides little or no guidance for choosing one parametric model over another. For example, as shown in the previous chapter, whether job-specific labor force experience changes linearly (Gompertz model) or log-linearly (Weibull model) over time can hardly be decided on a theoretical basis. Thus it is important to empirically check the adequacy of models upon which inferences are based. One way of doing this was demonstrated in the previous chapter by using likelihood ratio tests as a tool for comparing the improvement in the goodness-of-fit of alternative models. This method is, however, limited to nested models.

In this chapter, we consider two different approaches to checking the suitability of parametric models. First, we survey an informal method for evaluating the fit of parametric models by comparing *transformations of nonparametric estimates of survivor functions* with the predictions from parametric models. And second, we demonstrate how *pseudoresiduals*, also often called *generalized residuals*, can be calculated and used in evaluating distributional assumptions. Although both approaches might give some hints in empirical applications, they still only have the character of *heuristic tools*, as we demonstrate in this chapter.

8.1 Simple Graphical Methods

Several authors have proposed simple graphical methods for identifying systematic departures of parametric models from the data.[1] The basic idea is to produce plots that should be roughly linear, if the assumed family of models is appropriate, because departures from linearity can be readily recognized by the eye. Most of these approaches begin with a nonparametric estimation of a survivor function using the life table method or, preferably, the product limit (Kaplan-Meier) estimator. Then, given a parametric assumption about the distribution of waiting times, one tries to find a suitable transformation of the survivor function so that the result becomes a linear

---

[1]See, among others, Lawless (1982), Wu (1989, 1990), and Wu and Tuma (1990).

function $(y = a + bx)$ that can be plotted for visual inspection. In addition, this approach often provides the first estimates for the parameters of the assumed distribution, which can then be used as starting values for fitting the model via maximum likelihood.[2] We briefly describe this method for four parametric distributions.

Exponential Model. This model was discussed in chapter 4. The survivor function for the basic exponential distribution is

$$G(t) = \exp(-rt)$$

Taking the (always natural) logarithm, we get a straight line

$$\log(G(t)) = -r\,t$$

Thus, if the exponential model holds, a plot of $\log(\hat{G}(t))$ versus t, using the estimated survivor function $\hat{G}(t)$, should provide a roughly linear graph passing through the origin. The negative slope of this line is an estimate of the transition rate r.

Weibull Model. This model was discussed in section 7.3. The survivor function of the Weibull model is

$$G(t) = \exp\left(-(at)^b\right)$$

Taking the logarithm, we get

$$\log(G(t)) = -(at)^b$$

and taking the logarithm again results in the linear function

$$\log\left(\log(-G(t))\right) = b\log(a) + b\log(t)$$

Thus, if the Weibull model holds, a plot of $\log(\log(-\hat{G}(t)))$ versus $\log(t)$ should be approximately linear. The slope of this line is an estimate of b.

Log-logistic Model. This model was discussed in section 7.4. The survivor function for the basic (type I) version of the log-logistic model is

$$G(t) = \frac{1}{1 + (at)^b}$$

This can be transformed in the following way. First, we get

$$1 - G(t) = \frac{(at)^b}{1 + (at)^b}$$

---

[2]Blossfeld, Hamerle, and Mayer (1989) suggested complementing the visual inspection of transformed survivor curves by fitting an ordinary least squares regression line (OLS). However, using OLS can also only be considered a heuristic approach in this case because the data are heteroscedastic and the residuals are highly correlated.

and, dividing by $G(t)$, we get

$$\frac{1 - G(t)}{G(t)} = (at)^b$$

Then, taking logarithms results in the linear function

$$\log\left(\frac{1 - G(t)}{G(t)}\right) = b\log(a) + b\log(t)$$

Therefore, if the log-logistic model holds, a plot of $\log((1 - \hat{G}(t))/\hat{G}(t))$ versus $\log(t)$ should be approximately linear. The slope of this line is an estimate of b.

Log-normal Model. This model was discussed in section 7.5. The survivor function for the basic log-normal model is

$$G(t) = 1 - \Phi\left(\frac{\log(t) - a}{b}\right)$$

with Φ used to denote the standard normal distribution function. Using Φ^{-1} to denote the inverse of this function, one gets the linear function

$$\Phi^{-1}(1 - G(t)) = -\frac{a}{b} + \frac{1}{b}\log(t)$$

Therefore, if the log-normal model holds, a plot of $\Phi^{-1}(1 - \hat{G}(t))$ versus $\log(t)$ should be approximately linear.

Application examples of simple graphical models are not presented here. They can be found in Blossfeld and Rohwer (2002), chapter 8.

8.2   Pseudoresiduals

Additional information for model selection can be gained by using *pseudoresiduals*, also called *generalized residuals*. In OLS regression analysis, the traditional and perhaps best way to evaluate possible violations of the underlying model assumptions is through a direct examination of residuals. Residuals are deviations of the *observed* values of the dependent variable from the values *estimated* under the assumptions of a specific model. In transition rate models the "dependent variable" is the transition rate, which is, however, *not observable*. Thus it is not possible to compute residuals by comparing observed versus predicted transition rates for each unit or episode.

Nonetheless, there is a similar approach that can be used with transition rate models. This approach is based on *pseudoresiduals* (generalized residuals) suggested by Cox and Snell (1968). For applying this method to transition rate models, see, for instance, Blossfeld, Hamerle, and Mayer (1989, p. 82), and Lancaster (1985).

The definition is as follows. Let $\hat{r}(t; x)$ denote the estimated rate, depending on time t and on a vector of covariates, x. The estimation is based on a random sample of individuals $i = 1, \ldots, N$, with duration t_i and covariate vectors x_i. Pseudoresiduals are then defined as cumulative transition rates, evaluated for the given sample observations, that is,

$$\hat{e}_i = \int_0^{t_i} \hat{r}(\tau; x_i)\, d\tau \qquad i = 1, \ldots, N$$

The reasoning behind this definition is that, if the model is appropriate, and if there were no censored observations, the set of residuals should approximately behave like a sample from a standard exponential distribution. If some of the observations are censored, the residuals may be regarded as a censored sample from a standard exponential distribution. In any case, one can calculate a product-limit estimate of the survivor function of the residuals, say $G_{\hat{e}}(e)$, and a plot of $-\log(G_{\hat{e}}(\hat{e}_i))$ versus $\hat{e}_i$ can be used to check whether the residuals actually follow a standard exponential distribution.

Pseudoresiduals are calculated according to

$$\hat{e}_i = \int_{s_i}^{t_i} \hat{r}(\tau; x_i)\, d\tau \qquad i = 1, \ldots, N$$

with s_i and t_i denoting the starting and ending times of the episode, respectively. Also the survivor functions are conditional on starting times, meaning that the program calculates and prints

$$\hat{G}(t_i \mid s_i; x_i) = \exp\left\{ -\int_{s_i}^{t_i} \hat{r}(\tau; x_i)\, d\tau \right\} \qquad i = 1, \ldots, N$$

Therefore, if the starting times are not zero, in particular if the method of episode splitting is applied, the output file will not already contain proper information about residuals.

In order to demonstrate the application of these graphical tests with Stata, we use our standard example data (**rrdat1**). There are three steps.

Step 1. In the first step, you need to **stset** your data. The first part of the do-file **ehh2.do** is similar to **ehd2.do** (Box 4.1.3): **stset tf, failure(des)**. We estimate an exponential model with **streg, dist(e)**. You can then specify a postestimation command **predict cs, csnell** to calculate the generalized Cox-Snell residuals. Stata will generate a new variable, **cs**, containing the Cox-Snell residuals.

You could also include two additional commands, **predict hazard, haz** and **predict survival, sur**, to calculate the predicted hazard and each

Box 8.2.3 Pseudoresiduals for exponential model

```
     +------------------------------------------------------------+
     | id   des   tstart     tf     hazard    survival   residual |
     |------------------------------------------------------------|
  1. | 1    0        555    428   .0161225   .0010074   6.900412  |
     |------------------------------------------------------------|
  2. | 2    1        593     46   .0131337   .5465387    .6041502 |
  3. | 2    1        639     34   .0061498   .8113198    .209093  |
  4. | 2    1        673    220   .0058589   .2755576   1.288959  |
     |------------------------------------------------------------|
  5. | 3    1        688     12   .0153083   .8321857    .1836997 |
  6. | 3    1        700     30   .0156408   .6254874    .4692241 |
  7. | 3    1        730     12   .0138755   .8466178    .1665059 |
  8. | 3    1        742     75   .0141769   .3453265   1.063265  |
  9. | 3    1        817     12   .0118557   .8673888    .1422679 |
     |------------------------------------------------------------|
 10. | 4    1        872     55   .0121056   .5138569    .6658105 |
     +------------------------------------------------------------+
```

observation's predicted survivor probability. A list of the first 10 records of our data is shown in Box 8.2.3. In this file, the estimated rate (column 5) and the pseudoresiduals (column 7) are presented for each episode (column id). For example, for job episode 1, the covariates might have the following values (see Box 2.2.2): `lfx = 0`, `pnoj = 0`, `pres = 34`, `coho2 = 0`, `coho3 = 0`, and `edu = 17`. Thus the estimated rate for this job episode, based on the estimates for the exponential model in Box 4.1.5, is

$$\hat{r}(t \mid x) = \exp\left(-4.4894 + 0.0773 \cdot 17 - 0.0280 \cdot 34\right) = 0.0161$$

This estimate is printed in the column `hazard` in Box 8.2.3. The corresponding pseudoresidual, for the first episode with duration 428 months, is calculated as follows:

$$\hat{e} = -\log\left(\hat{G}(t \mid x)\right) = -\log\left(\exp(-0.0161 \cdot 428)\right) = 6.9004$$

Step 2. If the model fits the data, these residuals should have a standard exponential distribution. One way to check this assumption is to calculate an empirical estimate of the cumulative hazard function. To do this we use the Kaplan-Meier survival estimates. To this end, we first `stset` the data, specifying the Cox-Snell residuals as time variable and keep our censoring variable `des` as before. Then we generate two new variables. First, we specify the `sts generate` command to create a variable `km` with the Kaplan-Meier survival estimates. Second, we generate a new variable `cumhaz` containing the cumulative hazard.

Step 3. Finally, we perform a graphical check of the distribution of the pseudoresiduals. We plot the cumulative hazard against the Cox-Snell residuals.

Box 8.2.4 Do-file ehh2.do

```
version 9
set scheme sj
capture log close
set more off
log using ehh2.log, replace

use rrdat1, clear

gen des = tfin~=ti              /*destination state*/
gen tf  = tfin - tstart + 1     /*ending time*/

gen coho2 = tb>=468 & tb<= 504  /*cohort 2*/
gen coho3 = tb>=588 & tb<= 624  /*cohort 3*/
gen lfx   = tstart - te         /*labor force experience*/
gen pnoj  = noj - 1             /*previous number of jobs*/

stset tf, failure(des)          /*define single episode data*/

streg edu coho2 coho3 lfx pnoj pres, dist(e)   /*Exponential model*/
predict residual, csnell        /*Cox-Snell residuals*/
stset residual, failure(des)    /*define single episode data*/
sts gen km = s                  /*generate Kaplan-Meier survivor function*/
generate cumhaz = -ln(km)       /*generate cumulative hazard*/
line cumhaz residual residual, sort name("exponential, replace") ///
legend(off) t1(Exponential) xtitle("")
drop cumhaz residual km

streg edu coho2 coho3 lfx pnoj pres, dist(weibull) /*Weibull model*/
predict residual, csnell

stset residual, failure(des)
sts gen km = s
generate cumhaz = -ln(km)
line cumhaz residual residual, sort name("weibull, replace") ///
legend(off) t1(Weibull) xtitle("")
drop cumhaz residual km

streg edu coho2 coho3 lfx pnoj pres, dist(llogistic) /*Log-logistic model*/
predict residual, csnell
stset residual, failure(des)
sts gen km = s
generate cumhaz = -ln(km)
line cumhaz residual residual, sort name("llogistic, replace") ///
legend(off) t1(Log-logistic) xtitle("")
drop cumhaz residual km

streg edu coho2 coho3 lfx pnoj pres, dist(lognormal) /*Log-normal model*/
predict residual, csnell

stset residual, failure(des)
sts gen km = s
generate cumhaz = -ln(km)
line cumhaz residual residual, sort name("lognormal, replace") ///
legend(off) t1(Log-Normal) xtitle("")

drop cumhaz residual km

graph combine exponential weibull llogistic lognormal, ///
l1(-ln(Kaplan-Meier)) b1(Cox-Snell residual) saving("Figure 8_1_1")

log close
```

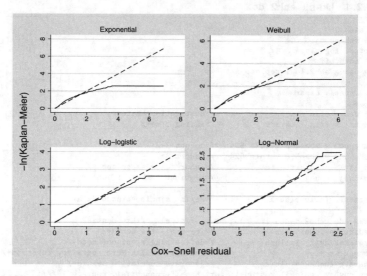

Figure 8.2.1 Graphical check of pseudoresiduals. Plots of logarithm of survivor functions (of residuals) vs. residuals.

If the model fits the data, the plot should be approximately a straight line with a slope of 1 that passes through the origin.

The commands are shown in Box 8.2.4. The same procedure, following the three steps, can be followed for all other transition rate models. Figure 8.2.1 shows the plots for four different models that were discussed in chapters 4 and 7. As can be seen in this figure, the plot for the exponential model has the poorest fit with respect to a straight line with a slope of 1. Also the plot for the Weibull distribution departs strongly from linearity. The log-logistic and the log-normal, on the other hand, provide better fits. But which one fits best? The log-logistic and log-normal models resemble each other closely. Also the estimated shapes of the transition rates are almost identical. These models estimate a nonmonotonic hazard rate. Thus, in substantive terms, it would not matter which one of them we choose. It is important to note, however, that graphical checks of pseudoresiduals should not be understood as goodness-of-fit *tests*. They only provide some hints for model selection; and the final selection should also be based on theoretical considerations.

Chapter 9

Semiparametric Transition Rate Models

Models with a time-dependent transition rate, as surveyed in chapter 7, are based on specific parametric assumptions about the distribution of durations and allow for straightforward maximum likelihood estimations. As demonstrated in detail, time in these models normally serves as a proxy variable for a latent causal factor that is difficult to measure directly. The problem in substantive applications is that theories in the social sciences, at least at their current level of development, rarely offer strong arguments for a specific parametric model. We therefore suggested in chapter 7 to use these models with extreme caution. Estimating a variety of model specifications and comparing the outcomes seems to be an appropriate strategy. However, this leads to another problem: the adequacy of alternative parametric models of time-dependence can only be evaluated with heuristic tools, as demonstrated in chapter 8. Although these goodness-of-fit checks may provide some rough hints as to which classes of models may be preferable, they cannot serve as strict tests to support a specific parametric model. Therefore, an interesting alternative strategy is to specify only a functional form for the influence of covariates, but leave the shape of the transition rate as unspecified as possible. Such models are known as semiparametric models.

The most widely applied semiparametric model is the proportional hazards model proposed by Cox (1972), or the *Cox model*, as stated in the literature. It may be written as

$$r(t) = h(t) \exp\big(A(t)\alpha\big) \tag{9.1}$$

The transition rate, $r(t)$, is the product of an unspecified *baseline rate*, $h(t)$, and a second term specifying the possible influences of a covariate vector $A(t)$ on the transition rate.[1]

Model (9.1) is a special case of so-called *proportional* transition rate models because the effects of covariates can only induce proportional shifts in the transition rate but cannot change its shape. Therefore the Cox model should only be used if this proportionality assumption is justified.

---

[1] The linear combination of a row vector of possible time-dependent covariates, $A(t)$, and a column vector of associated coefficients, α, cannot contain an intercept because this is absorbed in the baseline rate, $h(t)$.

The Cox model has been widely used, although the proportionality assumption restricts the range of possible empirical applications. It is particularly attractive when the researcher (1) has no clear idea about the shape of time-dependence, or (2) has only a weak theory supporting a specific parametric model, or (3) knows the time path of the process, but is not adequately able to model its fluctuations with a tractable waiting time distribution, or (4) is only interested in the magnitude and direction of the effects of observed covariates, controlling for time-dependence.

The Cox model (9.1) can be extended for multiple origin and destination states, and also for multiepisode data. This chapter describes how to estimate such models with Stata. First, we explain the partial likelihood estimation of the model and present an example. Second, we discuss the use of time-dependent covariates based on partial likelihood estimation, in particular, how to use the method of episode splitting with Cox models. Third, we describe some methods for testing the proportionality assumption that is required in Cox models. In particular, we show how to estimate stratified Cox models to cope with the proportionality requirement. Fourth, we describe how to estimate rate and survivor functions for the Cox model. Finally, we give some application examples.

9.1 Partial Likelihood Estimation

The implementation of the Cox model in Stata is based on the following model formulation

$$r_k(t) = h_k(t) \, \exp\left\{ A^{(k)}(t) \, \alpha^{(k)} \right\}$$

$r_k(t)$ is the transition rate at time t for the transition from the given origin state to destination state k. $h_k(t)$ is the unspecified baseline rate for the same transition.[2] $A^{(k)}(t)$ is a (row) vector of covariates, specified for the transition to destination state k, and $\alpha^{(k)}$ is a vector of associated coefficients. The covariates may have time-dependent values; examples are given in section 9.2.

Furthermore, it is possible to explain each transition by a specific set of covariates. One should note, however, that model estimation requires that *all* covariates be defined for all members of a sample of episodes. This is necessary to calculate the risks for all transitions, regardless of the transition that actually happens at the end of an episode. One should also note that it is necessary to include at least one covariate for each transition because Cox models do not contain any intercept terms; all constant effects are included in the baseline rates.

---

[2] The formulation implies that the baseline rates are allowed to vary between different transitions. A special type of Cox model arises if the baseline rates are constrained to be identical for all transitions; see Kalbfleisch and Prentice (1980, p. 170).

Model estimation is based on the method of partial likelihood (Cox 1972, 1975). To explain this method, we first consider the case of a single transition to destination state k. Indices referring to transitions are dropped to simplify notation. With the assumption of no ties (i.e., all ending times in the sample are different), the partial likelihood, L^p, may be written as

$$L^p = \prod_{i \in \mathcal{E}} \frac{\exp(A_i(t_i)\,\alpha)}{\sum_{l \in \mathcal{R}(t_i)} \exp(A_l(t_i)\,\alpha)} \tag{9.2}$$

$\mathcal{E}$ denotes the set of all uncensored episodes with destination state k. $\mathcal{R}(t_i)$ is the risk set at the ending time, say t_i, of the ith episode contained in $\mathcal{E}$. The definition of the risk set is exactly the same as was given for the product-limit estimator: the set of all episodes, exiting with an event or being censored, with starting time less than t_i and ending time equal to or greater than t_i. $A_i(t_i)$ is the (row) vector of covariates for the ith episode (evaluated at t_i), and α is the vector of associated coefficients to be estimated.

Given this notation, the calculation of the partial likelihood is easily understood: One looks at the ending times of episodes ending with an event; then, for each of these points in time, the risk set is created; and finally the expression on the right-hand side of (9.2) is evaluated. This expression may be interpreted as the probability that it is just the ith individual to have an event at this point in time, given the risk set containing all individuals who could have an event. Note that in the calculation of these probabilities time-dependent covariates can be accounted for in a simple way: At each successive point in time, the actual covariate values can be used.

As was shown by Cox and other authors, the partial likelihood defined in (9.2) may be treated as if it were a standard likelihood. Estimates of model coefficients reached by maximizing the partial likelihood have properties similar to those of standard maximum likelihood estimates.

Difficulties only arise if there are tied ending times. Then it is complicated to calculate the partial likelihood exactly. Therefore, several simplifying approximations have been proposed. As computed by BMDP and SAS, the Stata algorithm for the partial likelihood calculation uses an approximation proposed by Breslow (1974).[3] With the `breslow` (Breslow's method), `efron` (Efron's method), `exactm` (exact marginal-likelihood), and `exactp` options (exact partial-likelihood method), you specify the method for handling tied ending times. By default, Stata uses the Breslow method.

Assume there are d_i episodes, with indices contained in a set D_i, all having the same ending time, t_i. The partial likelihood factor for this point

---

[3]We are following the formulation given by Lawless (1982, p. 346). An introduction to Breslow's approximation may also be found in Namboodiri and Suchindran (1987, p. 213).

Box 9.1.1 Do-file `ehi1.do` (Cox model)

```
version 9
capture log close
set more off
log using ehi1.log, replace

use rrdat1, clear

gen des   = tfin ~= ti              /*destination state*/
gen tf    = tfin - tstart + 1       /*ending time*/

gen coho2 = tb>=468 & tb<= 504      /*cohort 2*/
gen coho3 = tb>=588 & tb<= 624      /*cohort 3*/
gen lfx   = tstart - te             /*labor force experience*/
gen pnoj  = noj - 1                 /*previous number of jobs*/

stset tf, failure(des)              /*define single episode data*/

stcox edu coho2 coho3 lfx pnoj pres, nohr
/*fit Cox proportional hazards model*/

log close
```

in time is then approximated by

$$\frac{\exp(S_i(t_i)\,\alpha)}{\left[\sum_{l\in\mathcal{R}(t_i)}\exp(A_l(t_i)\,\alpha)\right]^{d_i}}=\prod_{j\in D_i}\frac{\exp(A_j(t_i)\,\alpha)}{\sum_{l\in\mathcal{R}(t_i)}\exp(A_l(t_i)\,\alpha)}$$

with $S_i(t_i)$ defined as the sum of the covariate vectors for the d_i episodes with events at t_i (evaluated at t_i). As can easily be seen, the use of this approximation is already accounted for in the formulation of the partial likelihood in (9.2), because in this formulation the product goes over all episodes, tied or not, contained in $\mathcal{E}$. As is generally assumed, this approximation is sufficient if there are only "relatively few" ties in a sample of episode data. If there are "too many" ties, it seems preferable to use a discrete time model.

A detailed explanation of how the partial likelihood calculation is done with Stata is given in the Stata manual. An example of a partial likelihood estimation of the Cox model with Stata is shown in Box 9.1.1. The do-file, `ehi1.do`, is almost identical to the do-file for the exponential model in Box 4.1.4. Only the model selection command has been changed to

```
stcox edu coho2 coho3 lfx pnoj pres, nohr
```

Estimation results are shown in Box 9.1.2. The estimated coefficients surprisingly resemble the results obtained for the exponential model in Box

Box 9.1.2 Estimation results using do-file ehi1.do (Box 9.1.1)

```
        failure _d:  des == 1
  analysis time _t:  tf

Iteration 0:   log likelihood = -2584.5701
Iteration 1:   log likelihood = -2548.0198
Iteration 2:   log likelihood = -2546.7823
Iteration 3:   log likelihood = -2546.7756
Iteration 4:   log likelihood = -2546.7756
Refining estimates:
Iteration 0:   log likelihood = -2546.7756


Cox regression -- Breslow method for ties

No. of subjects =          600        Number of obs   =        600
No. of failures =          458
Time at risk    =        40782
                                       LR chi2(6)      =      75.59
Log likelihood  =    -2546.7756        Prob > chi2     =     0.0000

---------------------------------------------------------------------
   _t |    Coef.    Std. Err.     z     P>|z|    [95% Conf. Interval]
------+--------------------------------------------------------------
  edu |  .0668593   .0249149    2.68    0.007    .018027    .1156916
coho2 |  .4113074   .115347     3.57    0.000    .1852314   .6373834
coho3 |  .3052514   .1219834    2.50    0.012    .0661684   .5443344
  lfx | -.003989    .0009324   -4.28    0.000   -.0058166  -.0021615
 pnoj |  .0686267   .0441925    1.55    0.120   -.0179891   .1552426
 pres | -.0261678   .0055004   -4.76    0.000   -.0369484  -.0153871
```

4.1.5. Thus, about the same substantive conclusions must be drawn (at least in terms of direction of influence and statistical significance of effects) with regard to the covariates included. It should be noted that in Box 9.1.2 there is no estimate for the constant anymore. It cannot be identified in the Cox model because all members of a risk set have the same value for each event time, causing it to be canceled from the numerator and denominator of every term in the partial likelihood. Thus the constant becomes part of the baseline hazard rate in the Cox model.

Multiple Origin and Destination States

To extend the Cox model to the case of multiple origin and destination states (see, e.g., Blossfeld and Hamerle 1989b), we follow the general remarks in chapter 4. First, it should be restated that in the context of duration analysis all estimations performed are conditional on given origin states. Therefore, with two or more origin states, the (partial) likelihood may be constructed separately for all of them; each single term may be maximized separately, or the product of all origin-specific terms can be taken and maximized simultaneously.

The case of two or more transitions from a given origin state is also simple (see Kalbfleisch and Prentice 1980, p. 169). One only needs an appropriate definition of the risk set: $\mathcal{R}(t)$ is defined as the set of *all* episodes with the given origin state having a starting time less than t and an ending time equal to, or greater than, t. The partial likelihood may then be written as

$$L^p = \prod_{k \in \mathcal{D}} \prod_{i \in \mathcal{E}_k} \frac{\exp\left(A^{(k)}(t_i)\, \alpha^{(k)}\right)}{\sum_{l \in \mathcal{R}(t_i)} \exp\left(A^{(k)}(t_l)\, \alpha^{(k)}\right)}$$

9.2   Time-Dependent Covariates

Cox models offer an easy way to include time-dependent covariates. The standard method is based on the fact that the partial likelihood calculation gradually goes through all points in time where at least one of the uncensored episodes has an event. Consequently, it is possible to re-evaluate the values of time-dependent covariates at these points in time. This is already provided for in the partial likelihood formula (9.2).

If the time-dependent covariates change their values only at some discrete points in time, the method of episode splitting can be used. The original episodes are split at every point in time where one of the time-dependent covariates changes its value. Each of the original episodes is replaced by a contiguous set of subepisodes (splits) with appropriate values of the covariates. The last of these splits has the same exit status as the original episode; all other splits are regarded as right censored. To use this method with partial likelihood maximization, it is only necessary to be precise in the definition of the risk set. At every point in time, t, the risk set should contain all episodes, or splits, that have a starting time less than t and ending time greater than or equal to t, regardless of their exit status. Consequently, the risk set at every point in time only contains a single split, associated with appropriate values of the time-dependent covariates for each of the original episodes. Clearly, it is necessary for the partial likelihood algorithm to take into account both the different ending and starting times of the episodes (splits).

To illustrate the inclusion of a time-dependent covariate in a Cox model, we again examine whether first marriage has an effect on the job-exit rate (see section 6.4). Thus we must create a time-dependent dummy variable `marr` ("marriage"). Do-file `ehi2.do` (Box 9.2.1) shows how this can be accomplished. First, as described for the exponential model in Box 6.4.4, a variable `marrdate` is created that expresses the marriage date relative to the beginning time of each of the jobs in an occupational career. The variable is

Box 9.2.1 Do-file `ehi2.do` (time-dependent covariates)

```
version 9
capture log close
set more off
log using ehi2.log, replace

use rrdat1, clear

gen des    = tfin ~= ti          /*destination state*/
gen ts     = 0                   /*starting time*/
gen tf     = tfin - tstart + 1   /*ending time*/

gen coho2 = tb>=468 & tb<= 504   /*cohort 2*/
gen coho3 = tb>=588 & tb<= 624   /*cohort 3*/
gen lfx   = tstart - te          /*labor force experience*/
gen pnoj  = noj - 1              /*previous number of jobs*/

gen marrdate = tmar- tstart
gen entrymarr = marrdate>0 & marrdate <tf

gen newid = _n
expand 2 if entrymarr            /*episode splitting*/

by newid, sort: gen postmarr=(_n==2)
by newid, sort: gen t1=tf if _n==_N
by newid, sort: replace t1 = marrdate if _n==1 & _N==2
by newid, sort: replace ts = t1[_n-1] if _n==2
by newid, sort: replace des=0 if _n==1 & _N==2
gen marr=marrdate <= ts & tmar >0

stset t1, failure(des) id(newid)

stcox edu coho2 coho3 lfx pnoj pres marr, nohr
/*fit Cox proportional hazards model*/

log close
```

negative if the individual was still unmarried at the time of the interview; it
is also negative when the marriage took place before the individual entered
into the respective job; it is zero if the marriage took place in the month
when the individual entered into the respective job; and it is positive if the
marriage occured after the individual entered the respective job. Second, a
dummy variable (`entrymarr`) is created that indicates which episodes are
to be split. We then use the command `expand` to split episodes, create some
new variables, `stset` our data and refit the Cox model, this time including
the time-dependent variable `marr`.[4]

---

[4]Note that because partial likelihood estimation is based on the order of events and
censored times, estimation results of the Cox model can differ depending on whether the

Box 9.2.2 Estimation results of do-file `ehi2.do` (Box 9.2.1)

```
        failure _d:  des
  analysis time _t:  t1
               id:  newid

Iteration 0:   log likelihood = -2584.5701
Iteration 1:   log likelihood = -2547.9248
Iteration 2:   log likelihood = -2546.6296
Iteration 3:   log likelihood = -2546.6222
Iteration 4:   log likelihood = -2546.6222
Refining estimates:
Iteration 0:   log likelihood = -2546.6222


Cox regression -- Breslow method for ties

No. of subjects =           600        Number of obs  =        761
No. of failures =           458
Time at risk    =         40782
                                       LR chi2(7)     =      75.90
Log likelihood  =    -2546.6222        Prob > chi2    =     0.0000


-----------------------------------------------------------------------
   _t |     Coef.    Std. Err.      z     P>|z|     [95% Conf. Interval]
------+----------------------------------------------------------------
  edu |   .0664825    .0249497    2.66    0.008     .0175821     .115383
coho2 |   .4055774    .1157551    3.50    0.000     .1787015    .6324532
coho3 |   .2901494    .1249284    2.32    0.020     .0452943    .5350046
  lfx |  -.0041937    .0010035   -4.18    0.000    -.0061606   -.0022268
 pnoj |   .0673956     .044281    1.52    0.128    -.0193935    .1541847
 pres |  -.0262885    .0054992   -4.78    0.000    -.0370667   -.0155102
 marr |   .0660238    .1191552    0.55    0.580     -.167516    .2995636
```

The estimation results of using do-file `ehi2.do` are presented in Box 9.2.2. The time-dependent covariate "marriage" does not seem to be significant, and entry into marriage also does not seem to affect the job-exit rate in the Cox model. This conclusion is in sharp contrast to the one reached for the equivalent exponential in Box 6.4.5, where the variable `marr` ("marriage") was found to be significant. Thus controlling for an unspecified baseline hazard rate in the Cox model seems to strongly affect the coefficient of this time-dependent covariate.[5] However, we already know that the effect

---

greater (`gt`) or *greater/equal* (`ge`) operator is used to define a time-dependent covariate. The decision on a proper definition of time-dependent covariates should be based on substantive considerations, taking into account that, for a causal interpretation, the cause should precede its possible effect.

[5]Our experience with various event history models in social research suggests that changes in the specification of time-dependence may often strongly affect the coefficients of other time-dependent covariates, but they normally have almost no effect on the coefficients of time-constant covariates.

Box 9.2.3 Do-file ehi5.do (Cox model with time-dependent covariates)

```
version 9
capture log close
set more off
log using ehi5.log, replace

use rrdat1, clear

gen des   = tfin ~= ti          /*destination state*/
gen ts    = 0                   /*starting time*/
gen tf    = tfin - tstart + 1   /*ending time*/

gen coho2 = tb>=468 & tb<= 504  /*cohort 2*/
gen coho3 = tb>=588 & tb<= 624  /*cohort 3*/
gen lfx   = tstart - te         /*labor force experience*/
gen pnoj  = noj - 1             /*previous number of jobs*/

gen marrdate = tmar- tstart
gen entrymarr = marrdate>0 & marrdate <tf

gen newid = _n
expand 2 if entrymarr           /*episode splitting*/

by newid, sort: gen postmarr=(_n==2)
by newid, sort: gen t1=tf if _n==_N
by newid, sort: replace t1 = marrdate if _n==1 & _N==2
by newid, sort: replace ts = t1[_n-1] if _n==2
by newid, sort: replace des=0 if _n==1 & _N==2
gen marr=marrdate <= ts & tmar >0

stset t1, failure(des) id(newid)

gen marrmen= sex==1 & marrdate <= ts & tmar >0

stcox edu coho2 coho3 lfx pnoj pres marr marrmen, nohr
/*fit Cox proportional hazards model*/

log close
```

of marriage is different for men and for women, so we should take this into
account in a proper model specification.

We add the time-dependent interaction variable marrmen to capture possible interaction effects of marriage and sex. It is basically the same approach
as already demonstrated in section 6.4 (see do-file ehf3.do in Box 6.4.4).
The do-file now is ehi5.do, shown in Box 9.2.3. The estimated parameters
in Box 9.2.4 are again in accordance with our expectations and basically
in agreement with the results of the exponential model in Box 6.4.6. The
coefficient of marriage on the rate of moving out of the job is still positive for women. This effect is, however, greater than in the exponential

Box 9.2.4 Estimation results with do-file `ehi5.do` (Box 9.2.3)

```
        failure _d:  des
   analysis time _t:  t1
                id:  newid

Iteration 0:   log likelihood = -2584.5701
Iteration 1:   log likelihood = -2530.8076
Iteration 2:   log likelihood = -2528.4647
Iteration 3:   log likelihood = -2528.4461
Iteration 4:   log likelihood = -2528.4461
Refining estimates:
Iteration 0:   log likelihood = -2528.4461


Cox regression -- Breslow method for ties

No. of subjects =          600    Number of obs   =        761
No. of failures =          458
Time at risk    =        40782
                                  LR chi2(8)      =     112.25
Log likelihood  =    -2528.4461   Prob > chi2     =     0.0000

------------------------------------------------------------------
    _t |     Coef.   Std. Err.      z    P>|z|    [95% Conf. Interval]
-------+----------------------------------------------------------
   edu |   .079178   .0240905    3.29   0.001    .0319615    .1263945
 coho2 |  .3767436   .1157905    3.25   0.001    .1497983    .6036888
 coho3 |  .2927654    .124286    2.36   0.018    .0491693    .5363616
   lfx | -.0044539   .0010029   -4.44   0.000   -.0064196   -.0024882
  pnoj |  .1011551   .0449099    2.25   0.024    .0131332    .1891769
  pres | -.0251975   .0053774   -4.69   0.000    -.035737    -.014658
  marr |  .5045789   .1302713    3.87   0.000    .2492518    .7599061
marrmen | -.8608364  .1419966   -6.06   0.000   -1.139145   -.5825282
```

model. In the Cox model marriage *increases* the job-exit rate for women by about 66 %;[6] in the exponential model it is only 31 %. For men the effect of marriage on the job change rate is negative. Marriage *decreases* the rate of moving out of the job by about 30 %;[7] in the exponential model it was 52 %. Thus marriage does indeed make men less mobile. In summary, the exponential as compared to the Cox model underestimated the impact of marriage on women and overestimated it for men.[8] This is the case because the Cox model controls for time-dependence, which is, after the starting phase, negative.

---

[6] $(\exp(0.5046) - 1) \cdot 100\,\% \approx 65.6$.

[7] $(\exp(0.5046 - 0.8608) - 1) \cdot 100\,\% \approx 30\,\%$.

[8] One has to be careful here, because in this example we did not take into account that the covariate effects are not proportional for men and women; see section 9.3.

Box 9.3.1 Do-file `ehi6.do` (graphical proportionality check)

```
version 9
set scheme sj
capture log close
set more off
log using ehi6.log, replace

use rrdat1, clear

gen des    = tfin ~= ti        /*destination state*/
gen tf     = tfin - tstart + 1  /*ending time*/

gen coho2 = tb>=468 & tb<= 504  /*cohort 2*/
gen coho3 = tb>=588 & tb<= 624  /*cohort 3*/
gen lfx    = tstart - te        /*labor force experience*/
gen pnoj   = noj - 1            /*previous number of jobs*/
gen women = sex==2              /*women*/

stset tf, failure(des)

stcox edu coho2 coho3 lfx pnoj pres women, nohr

stphplot, by(women) saving("Figure 9_3_1a",replace)

stcoxkm, by(women) m(i i i i) saving("Figure 9_3_1b",replace)

log close
```

9.3 The Proportionality Assumption

A basic feature of the Cox model is that transition rates for different values
of covariates are proportional. If, for instance, the transition rates, $r(t)$ and
$r'(t)$, corresponding with the values of the ith covariate, A_i and A_i', are
compared, then

$$\frac{r(t)}{r'(t)} = \exp\left\{(A_i - A_i')\,\alpha_i\right\}$$

Models with this feature are called *proportional transition rate models*. This
feature is not specific to the Cox model but is implied in at least some of
the many parametric models shown in chapters 4, 5, 6, and 7. This section
discusses methods of checking whether a sample of episode data satisfies the
proportionality assumption.

Graphical Methods

If there are only a few categorical covariates in a model, it is possible to
perform simple graphical checks to examine the proportionality assumption.

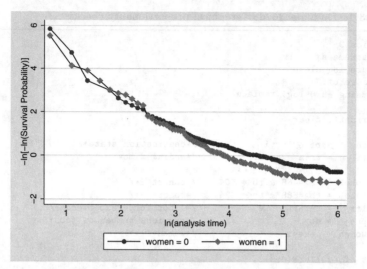

Figure 9.3.1 Graphical check for proportionality of men and women. Plot of $-\log(-\log(\hat{G}(t)))$ against $\log(t)$ (in months).

Let us assume that this is the case and that A and A' are two different vectors of covariate values. The sample can then be split into two groups, and nonparametric, Kaplan-Meier estimates of the survivor function, say $G(t)$ and $G'(t)$, can be calculated for both of these groups. The proportionality assumption implies that

$$\frac{\log\left(G(t)\right)}{\log\left(G'(t)\right)} = \exp\left\{(A - A')\,\alpha\right\}$$

Or, taking (always natural) logarithms once more, this becomes

$$\log\left\{-\log\left(G(t)\right)\right\} = \log\left\{-\log\left(G'(t)\right)\right\} + (A - A')\,\alpha$$

Therefore, a plot of the transformed survivor functions may be used to check whether the proportionality assumption is (nearly) correct.

In Stata, two commands, `stphplot` and `stcoxkm`, provide a graphical check of the proportionality assumption. The command `stphplot` produces plots of $-\log(-\log(\texttt{survival}))$ against $\log(\texttt{analysis time})$. Reasonably parallel lines indicate that the proportional hazards assumption has not been violated. Another graphical method uses the command `stcoxkm` to plot the Kaplan-Meier observed survival curves and compare them with the predicted curves from Cox regression. Similarity between these two curves supports the proportional-hazards assumption. We use our example data `rrdat1` and examine whether the proportional hazards assumption holds for men and women. To give an illustration of diagnostic plots in Stata, we use `stphplot`, followed by `stcoxkm` in Box 9.3.1.

Box 9.3.2 Do-file ehi7.do (test of proportionality)

```
version 9
capture log close
set more off
log using ehi7.log, replace

use rrdat1, clear

gen des   = tfin ~= ti          /*destination state*/
gen tf    = tfin - tstart + 1   /*ending time*/

gen coho2 = tb>=468 & tb<= 504  /*cohort 2*/
gen coho3 = tb>=588 & tb<= 624  /*cohort 3*/
gen lfx   = tstart - te         /*labor force experience*/
gen pnoj  = noj - 1             /*previous number of jobs*/
gen women = sex==2              /*women*/

stset tf, failure(des)

stcox edu coho2 coho3 lfx pnoj pres women, ///
tvc(women) texp(ln(tf)-4.73) nohr

log close
```

The plot generated with the stphplot command is shown in Figure 9.3.1. The figure shows that the lines are not parallel and cross. The difference between observed and predicted values does not seem to be large, however. Thus the question of whether the difference is sufficiently large to violate the proportionality assumption arises. A visual inspection of the plotted curves hardly can answer this question. Thus it is more appropriate to apply a statistical test.

Testing Time-Dependence

This test is based on the idea that if the proportionality assumption is correct, there should be no interaction effect between the covariates and process time. Assuming that the ith component of the covariate vector A is to be tested, a model like the following could be set up and estimated:

$$r(t) = h(t) \exp\left\{A\,\alpha + A_i\left(\log(\texttt{time}) - M\right)\alpha_i'\right\} \qquad (9.3)$$

The constant M is added to facilitate the estimation. It should be the logarithm of the mean (or median) duration of the sample episodes used for the estimation. If the added interaction variable gives a significant coefficient (i.e., if there is a significant interaction effect), the proportionality assumption for this covariate is probably not valid.

As an illustration of this test we again examine whether men and women have proportional transition rates. The used do-file is ehi7.do shown in

Box 9.3.3 Estimation results using do-file `ehi7.do` (Box 9.3.2)

```
            failure _d:  des == 1
    analysis time _t:  tf

Iteration 0:   log likelihood = -2584.5701
Iteration 1:   log likelihood =  -2537.698
Iteration 2:   log likelihood = -2536.2794
Iteration 3:   log likelihood = -2536.2717
Iteration 4:   log likelihood = -2536.2717
Refining estimates:
Iteration 0:   log likelihood = -2536.2717


Cox regression -- Breslow method for ties

No. of subjects =          600        Number of obs   =        600
No. of failures =          458
Time at risk    =        40782
                                       LR chi2(8)      =      96.60
Log likelihood  =    -2536.2717        Prob > chi2     =     0.0000


------------------------------------------------------------------------
      _t |     Coef.   Std. Err.      z    P>|z|    [95% Conf. Interval]
---------+--------------------------------------------------------------
rh       |
     edu | .0803298    .024667     3.26   0.001    .0319834    .1286762
   coho2 | .3936793   .1154586     3.41   0.001    .1673847    .6199739
   coho3 | .2715523   .1221511     2.22   0.026    .0321406     .510964
     lfx |-.0040585   .0009296    -4.37   0.000   -.0058806   -.0022365
    pnoj |  .088772   .0446729     1.99   0.047    .0012147    .1763293
    pres |-.0258837   .0054316    -4.77   0.000   -.0365295   -.0152379
   women | .7110886    .16072      4.42   0.000    .3960831    1.026094
---------+--------------------------------------------------------------
t        |
   women | .2587299   .0987092     2.62   0.009    .0652634    .4521965
------------------------------------------------------------------------

Note: Second equation contains variables that continuously vary with
      respect to time, variables are interacted with current values
      of ln(tf)-4.73.
```

Box 9.3.2. The command includes two new options: `tvc(varlist)` and `texp(exp)`. The first is used to specify variables that vary continuously with respect to time, the latter allows the specification of the function of analysis time that should be multiplied by the time-varying covariates. According to (9.3) we type:

```
stcox edu coho2 coho3 lfx pnoj pres women,
    tvc(women) texp(ln(tf)-4.73) nohr
```

The estimation results of this model specification are shown in Box 9.3.3.

The first part of the equation, rh, reports the results for the time-constant covariates; the second part of the equation, t, reports the results for our time-varying covariate. The time-varying covariate women is obviously significant. In other words, the assumption that men and women have proportional job-exit risks is not justified.

What is the consequence of this result? There are at least two possible reactions: First, the researcher can estimate a stratified Cox model with *group-specific baseline transition rates* for men and women (see following section; or he or she can simply use a *nonproportional* Cox model (i.e., the model just discussed), which includes the interaction effect and automatically corrects the violation of the proportionality assumption.

Stratification

If, for some covariates, the proportionality assumption is not acceptable, it is sometimes sensible to estimate a stratified model. This is possible if the covariates are categorical.[9] The whole sample can then be split into groups (strata), and there is one group for each of the possible combinations of categories. In the simplest case, with only a single dummy variable, there will only be two groups. Let $\mathcal{G}$ denote the set of groups. The model should then be specified so that the baseline rate can be different for each group. There are two possibilities. The first is to define a different model for each group. Then not only the baseline rates but also the covariate effects can vary across all groups.

This approach is, of course, limited to fairly large sets of episode data. When data sets are relatively small, or when there are no significant interaction effects, it may be sensible to build on the assumption that covariate effects are the same in all groups.[10] Based on this assumption, a model for the single transition case can be written as

$$r_g(t) = h_g(t) \exp(A\,\alpha) \qquad g \in \mathcal{G}$$

This model must be estimated for all groups simultaneously. Consequently, the estimation approach given in (9.2) needs a small modification; the partial likelihood must be calculated as being the product of the group-specific likelihoods. This may be written as

$$L^p = \prod_{k \in \mathcal{D}} \prod_{g \in \mathcal{G}} \prod_{i \in \mathcal{E}_{k,g}} \frac{\exp\left(A^{(k)}(t_i)\,\alpha^{(k)}\right)}{\sum_{l \in \mathcal{R}_g(t_i)} \exp\left(A^{(k)}(t_l)\,\alpha^{(k)}\right)} \qquad (9.4)$$

with $\mathcal{G}$ denoting the set of groups of episodes with the given origin state. $\mathcal{E}_{k,g}$ is the set of all uncensored episodes with destination state k *and* belonging

---

[9]Metric covariates could be used by grouping the individual data into appropriate classes.
[10]See Kalbfleisch and Prentice (1980, p. 87), Lawless (1982, p. 365), and Blossfeld, Hamerle, and Mayer (1989).

Box 9.3.6 Do-file `ehi9.do` (stratification)

```
version 9
capture log close
set more off
log using ehi9.log, replace

use rrdat1, clear

gen des   = tfin ~= ti          /*destination state*/
gen tf    = tfin - tstart + 1   /*ending time*/

gen coho2 = tb>=468 & tb<= 504  /*cohort 2*/
gen coho3 = tb>=588 & tb<= 624  /*cohort 3*/
gen lfx   = tstart - te         /*labor force experience*/
gen pnoj  = noj - 1             /*previous number of jobs*/

stset tf, failure(des)

stcox edu coho2 coho3 lfx pnoj pres, nohr strata(sex)

log close
```

to group g. Accordingly, $\mathcal{R}_g(t)$ is the risk set at time t containing all episodes with starting time less than t, ending time equal to or greater than t, and belonging to group g.

To illustrate the estimation of a stratified Cox model with Stata, we use our standard example. The do-file is `ehi9.do` (Box 9.3.6). The sample is stratified according to sex (there are two groups, men and women); this is achieved by using the `strata` option. Estimation results are shown in Box 9.3.7. They are fairly similar to the estimation results shown in Box 9.1.2, where the same model without stratification according to sex was estimated.

9.4   Baseline Rates and Survivor Functions

The partial likelihood method gives estimates of the parameters of a Cox model but no direct estimate of the underlying baseline rate. Clearly, it would be useful to have such estimates, as they could give some information about the type of time-dependence in a set of episode data, and this could give us some insight as to whether a fully parametrical model would be appropriate.

There are different proposals for estimating the baseline rate. One approach is based on a proposal made by Breslow (1974), also discussed in Blossfeld, Hamerle, and Mayer (1989). To explain this method, we begin by assuming a single transition and that all episodes have the starting time zero. Then, in the usual notation, $\mathcal{E}$ denotes the set of, say q, not censored

Box 9.3.7 Estimation results using do-file `ehi9.do` (Box 9.3.6)

```
        failure _d:  des == 1
  analysis time _t:  tf

Iteration 0:   log likelihood = -2259.5669
Iteration 1:   log likelihood =   -2225.69
Iteration 2:   log likelihood = -2224.6371
Iteration 3:   log likelihood = -2224.6321
Iteration 4:   log likelihood = -2224.6321
Refining estimates:
Iteration 0:   log likelihood = -2224.6321


Stratified Cox regr. -- Breslow method for ties

No. of subjects =          600      Number of obs   =        600
No. of failures =          458
Time at risk    =        40782
                                    LR chi2(6)      =      69.87
Log likelihood  =    -2224.6321     Prob > chi2     =     0.0000


------------------------------------------------------------------------
   _t |     Coef.    Std. Err.      z     P>|z|     [95% Conf. Interval]
------+-----------------------------------------------------------------
  edu | .0793089    .0247736     3.20    0.001    .0307535     .1278642
coho2 | .3974667    .1155737     3.44    0.001    .1709465     .6239869
coho3 | .2801267    .1226056     2.28    0.022    .0398241     .5204292
  lfx | -.0040179    .000931    -4.32    0.000   -.0058425    -.0021932
 pnoj | .0888606    .0447533     1.99    0.047    .0011458     .1765754
 pres | -.0257537   .0054493    -4.73    0.000   -.0364341    -.0150734
------------------------------------------------------------------------
                                        Stratified by men women
```

episodes, and the ordered ending times may be given by $\tau_1 < \tau_2 < \ldots < \tau_q$.

Let E_i be the number of events at τ_i and let $\mathcal{R}_i$ be the risk set at τ_i. Furthermore, let $\hat{\alpha}$ be the partial likelihood estimate of the model parameters. Then, defining $\tau_0 = 0$, we can consider

$$\hat{h}_i^b = \frac{E_i}{(\tau_i - \tau_{i-1}) \sum_{l \in \mathcal{R}_i} \exp(A_l \hat{\alpha})} \qquad i = 1, \ldots, q$$

to be an estimate of the baseline rate of the model. It is a constant during each interval $(\tau_{i-1}, \tau_i]$, resulting in a step function with steps at the points in time where at least one event occurs. This step function can now be integrated to provide an estimate of the cumulative baseline rate:

$$\hat{H}^b(t) = \sum_{l=1}^{i} (\tau_l - \tau_{l-1}) \hat{h}_l + (t - \tau_i) \hat{h}_{i+1} \qquad \tau_i < t \leq \tau_{i+1}$$

Box 9.4.1 Do-file `ehi10.do` (baseline rate calculation)

```
version 9
set scheme sj
capture log close
log using ehi10.log, replace

use rrdat1, clear

gen des    = tfin~=ti              /*destination state*/
gen tf     = tfin - tstart + 1     /*ending time*/

gen coho2 = tb>=468 & tb<= 504     /*cohort 2*/
gen coho3 = tb>=588 & tb<= 624     /*cohort 3*/
gen lfx    = tstart - te           /*labor force experience*/
gen pnoj   = noj - 1               /*previous number of jobs*/

stset tf, failure(des)

stcox edu coho2 coho3 lfx pnoj pres, nohr basesurv(s) basehc(h) basec(c)

stcurve, survival /* at mean values of all predictors */

stcurve, cumhaz at1(coho3=1 coho2=0 edu=13 lfx=5 pnoj=1 pres=30) ///
at2(coho2=1 coho3=0 edu=13 lfx=5 pnoj=1 pres=30) ///
at3(coho2=0 coho3=0 edu=13 lfx=5 pnoj=1 pres=30) ///
legend(row(3)) saving("Figure 9_4_1",replace)

stcurve, hazard at1(coho3=1 coho2=0 edu=13 lfx=5 pnoj=1 pres=30) ///
at2(coho2=1 coho3=0 edu=13 lfx=5 pnoj=1 pres=30) ///
at3(coho2=0 coho3=0 edu=13 lfx=5 pnoj=1 pres=30) ///
kernel(gauss) legend(row(3)) saving("Figure 9_4_2",replace)

drop s h c

log close
```

An estimate of the baseline survivor function may then be calculated by

$$\hat{G}^b(t) = \exp\left\{-\hat{H}^b(t)\right\}$$

Finally, due to the assumption of proportional effects, the cumulative transition rate for an arbitrary covariate vector A can be estimated by

$$\hat{H}(t) = \hat{H}^b(t) \exp(A\hat{\alpha}) \tag{9.5}$$

and the corresponding survivor function estimate is

$$\hat{G}(t) = \exp\left\{-\hat{H}^b(t) \exp(A\hat{\alpha})\right\} = \hat{G}^b(t)^{\exp(A\hat{\alpha})} \tag{9.6}$$

We can use these formulas to provide estimates of the cumulative baseline transition rate and the corresponding baseline survivor function. A generalization to the case of multiple origin and destination states can be done analogously: Each transition is treated separately. For instance, with respect to the transition (j, k), the procedure outlined previously is applied to all episodes with the origin state j; all episodes not ending in the destination state k are regarded as censored. The resulting estimates are then pseudo-survivor functions and transition-specific cumulative rates, respectively.

We now illustrate the calculation of baseline rates with Stata (using a somewhat different approach). The do-file is `ehi10.do` (Box 9.4.1), and it is basically identical to do-file `ehi1.do` shown in Box 9.1.1. We simply added three options

```
stcox edu coho2 coho3 lfx pnoj pres, nohr
basesurv(s) basehc(h) basec(c)
```

to the `stcox` command in order to add new variables to the data containing the estimated cumulative baseline hazard (`basechazard`), the estimated baseline hazard contibutions (`basehc`), and the estimated baseline survival function (`basesurv`). It is important to note that the baseline functions correspond to all covariates equal to zero in our Cox model.

In order to request the baseline rate calculation for covariate constellations (i.e., the assignment of different values to the covariates in the model), we will begin by creating variables that, when 0, correspond to the baseline values we desire. For example,

```
gen edu13=edu-13
gen lfx5=lfx-5
gen pnoj1=pnoj-1
gen pres30=pres-30
```

Next, we will refit our model:

```
stcox edu13 coho2 coho3 lfx5 pnoj1 pres30, nohr
basesurv(s) basehc(h) basec(c)
```

There is an easy way to graph estimated survival, cumulative hazard, and hazard functions with Stata. If you type `stcurve, survival`, you will plot the survival function. By default, the curve is evaluated at the mean values of all the predictors, but we can specify other values. For example, we request the plot for three covariate constellations (i.e., the assignment of different values to the covariates in the model). One of these covariate constellations is for birth cohort 1, one for birth cohort 2, and the last one is for birth cohort 3. The other covariates are fixed (`edu=13 lfx=5 pnoj=1 pres=30`; see Box 9.4.1).

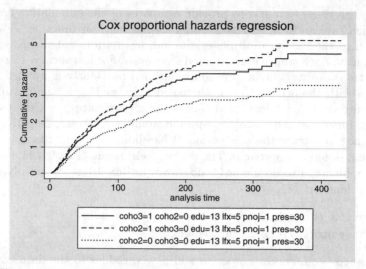

Figure 9.4.1 Cumulative baseline rates for birth cohorts 1, 2, and 3, generated with `ehi10.do`. The plot was generated with do-file `ehi10.do`.

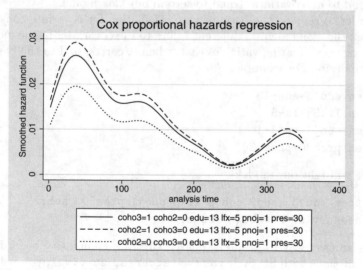

Figure 9.4.2 Smoothed baseline rates for birth cohorts 1, 2, and 3.

Before you can plot the cumulative hazard with Stata, you must add the option `basechazard()` to the `stcox` command. Analogously, to draw a plot of the survival function, you must specify the `basesurv()` option.

Figure 9.4.1 shows a plot of the cumulative baseline rates for the three birth cohorts. Sometimes it would be helpful for interpretation to see a plot of the baseline rate, instead of the cumulative baseline rate. Therefore what we need is the first derivative of the cumulative rate. To calculate this derivative, one can use numerical differentiation. Differentiation of the cumulative rate would, however, result in strong fluctuations. It is therefore useful to first smooth the cumulative rate.

By default, the hazard function is estimated by a kernel smooth of the estimated hazard contributions. Before you can produce such a plot you have to specify `basehc(h)` to the `stcox` command. Do-file `ehi10.do` shown in Box 9.4.1 can be used to plot the estimated hazard functions. Figure 9.4.2 shows the plot of the estimated baseline rate.

9.5   Application Example

Finally, we want to give at least one application example for the Cox model. For this purpose, we use a demographic study of divorce rates (Blossfeld, De Rose, Hoem, and Rohwer 1993). From a methodological point of view, this example is particularly instructive because it compares a piecewise constant exponential model (see chapter 5) with a Cox model. Both models are proportional hazards models. The Cox model leaves the baseline hazard rate completely unspecified, whereas the piecewise constant exponential model tries to approximate the baseline rate with a series of period-specific constants. In other words, with sufficiently small time periods, a piecewise constant exponential model basically becomes a Cox model providing a direct estimation of the baseline hazard rate.

The application example stems from an international collaborative research project, conducted by Alessandra De Rose (Italy) and Jan M. Hoem (Sweden) together with the authors of this book, on the relationship between changes in women's educational attainment and the development of marriage disruption risks in modern societies.

The study focused mainly on two hypotheses. The first is that an increasing educational level raises the risk of marital disruption. This was expected, because women with higher educational attainment normally have higher abilities and are more willing to violate social norms by dissolving unhappy marriages. They are also better able to cope with the consequences, due to being in a better position to deal with any social or religious stigma produced by a divorce. The second hypothesis is that the importance of women's educational attainment on disruption risks is not constant over historical time. In particular, it changes as family systems are transformed. Because the three countries under study (Italy, West Germany, and Sweden) represent quite different stages in the development and differentiation of socially accepted living arrangements and levels of divorce risks, a comparison of the gradient in the effects of women's educational level on divorce risks in these countries should show that the "liberating" impact of a woman's

Table 9.5.1 Estimation results for a Cox model and a piecewise constant exponential model for divorce rates. Results taken from Blossfeld et al. (1993).

Variable	Cox Model			Piecewise Constant		
	Italy	Germany	Sweden	Italy	Germany	Sweden
Period 0– 24				-9.68	-9.58	-7.18
Period 24– 48				-9.37	-7.41	-6.52
Period 48– 72				-9.03	-7.48	-6.30
Period 72– 96				-8.68	-7.31	-6.60
Period 96–120				-8.26	-7.07	-6.37
Period 120–144				-8.42	-7.33	-5.94
Period 144–168				-8.49	-6.65	-6.15
Period 168–				-8.66	-7.42	-5.80
Cohort 1939–43	0.36	-0.52	0.16	0.36	-0.52	0.16
	1.36	*1.54*	*0.69*	*1.36*	*1.55*	*0.71*
Cohort 1944–48	0.37	-0.10	0.49	0.38	-0.09	0.49
	1.38	*0.31*	*2.19*	*1.40*	*0.28*	*2.22*
Cohort 1949–53	0.21	0.29	0.37	0.21	0.33	0.38
	0.69	*0.88*	*1.38*	*0.70*	*0.99*	*1.41*
Cohort 1954–58	0.38	1.01	1.05	0.38	1.07	1.04
	1.08	*2.71*	*2.79*	*1.08*	*2.87*	*2.75*
Age at marriage 20–22	-0.83	-0.30	-0.56	-0.84	-0.30	-0.56
	3.82	*1.22*	*3.55*	*3.82*	*1.21*	*3.55*
Age at marriage 23–25	-0.71	-0.65	-0.74	-0.71	-0.64	-0.74
	3.11	*1.81*	*3.58*	*3.10*	*1.79*	*3.58*
Age at marriage 26–28	-1.21	-0.67	-0.65	-1.21	-0.66	-0.65
	3.44	*1.18*	*2.10*	*3.44*	*1.17*	*2.10*
Age at marriage 28–	-1.04	-1.49	-1.27	-1.03	-1.46	-1.27
	2.39	*1.43*	*2.11*	*2.38*	*1.40*	*2.11*
Second child	-1.04	-0.40	-0.75	-1.04	-0.42	-0.76
	5.32	*1.74*	*4.52*	*5.35*	*1.81*	*4.63*
Third child	-1.31	-0.66	-0.72	-1.31	-0.65	-0.74
	4.02	*1.64*	*2.96*	*4.02*	*1.63*	*3.06*
Education middle level	0.77	0.42	0.30	0.77	0.42	0.30
	4.24	*1.70*	*1.98*	*4.24*	*1.73*	*1.98*
Education high level	1.74	1.22	0.53	1.74	1.24	0.54
	5.79	*2.66*	*2.77*	*5.78*	*2.70*	*2.78*
Pregnant at marriage	0.76	0.87	0.38	0.76	0.88	0.38
	4.12	*4.11*	*2.78*	*4.13*	*4.13*	*2.77*
Log likelihood	-1325.3	-614.4	-1698.2	-1495.8	-759.0	-1849.5
χ^2	117.8	58.4	71.9	118.4	60.3	73.1
df	13	13	13	20	20	20

Note: Coefficients divided by their estimated standard errors are shown in *italic*.

higher educational attainment declines strongly as the family system becomes less "traditional" and as divorce customs get more permissive for all women. Specifically, it was expected that the effect of women's education on divorce is stronger in Italy than in West Germany, and stronger in West Germany than in Sweden.

Using event history data from Italy, West Germany, and Sweden, the authors specified women's divorce rate as a function of time-constant and time-dependent covariates with the help of two models: an exponential model with marriage-duration specific piecewise constant baseline rates, and a proportional hazards model that did not specify the baseline hazard rate at all.

Observation started with the time of first birth within the first marriage and ended with the event of the first date of de facto separation or, for right-censored cases, with the date of the interview, with a marriage duration of 15 years, with the date of birth of the fourth child, or with some other very specific life events (such as the death of the husband, the birth of twins, etc.), whichever occurred first. The reason we did not go beyond a marriage duration of 15 years and did not include women with more than three children was a methodological one: These marriages took place under more specific conditions with very specific divorce risks.

Although the transition rate analysis focused on the effect of women's educational attainment, the authors included a series of covariables to avoid compositional effects and to clearly bring out the direct (or partial) effect of educational level on the disruption risk. Most effect patterns for the controls were as expected and do not get any further attention here.

In the piecewise constant model shown in Table 9.5.1, a set of eight different periods for marriage duration was applied. It is easy to see that, over the whole duration of marriage, the divorce rate is continuously lower in Italy than in Germany, and continuously lower in Germany than in Sweden. Thus there are persistent differences in divorce risks across duration in each country. In all three countries, the divorce rate slightly increases with marriage duration, up to a duration of about 10 years. Then, in Sweden and Germany, the divorce rates become more or less stable, while in Italy we observe some kind of trend reversal: Long-term marriages become increasingly stable. The amount of this marriage duration effect, which may be due to selective attrition through divorce, and the amount that may be due to actual changes in propensity to divorce with duration, cannot be effectively discussed here. Neither can we give an answer to the question of whether the reasons for divorce change with duration. Controlling for marriage duration patterns in the piecewise constant model and in the Cox model at least shows that the piecewise constant model provides almost identical estimates for the observed variables (cohort membership, age at marriage, children, educational level, and pregnancy at marriage) for all three countries. Thus the results are relatively robust against the model specification. The eight period dummies in the piecewise constant model seem to yield a reasonably good approximation of the baseline hazard rate. This model, of course, has an additional advantage over the Cox model, in that it offers direct estimates of the baseline rate.

After having controlled for important covariables on the rate of divorce, it is possible to evaluate the hypothesis described earlier. Women's educational attainment was included in the form of three levels (reference category: "low educational level"). Table 9.5.1 shows that an increasing level of educational attainment does indeed have a positive effect on the rate of divorce in all three countries. In addition, there is in fact the expected order of these effects between the three countries. Compared to women with a lower secondary qualification, the inclination to divorce of women with an upper secondary qualification is in Italy about 470%, in West Germany about 239%, and in Sweden about 70%. This result means that in all three countries women's educational attainment can in fact be considered at least part of the explanation for high divorce rates. This is especially true in Italy, where all significant cohort effects on the divorce rate could be explained by women's increasing educational attainment. In this perspective, the initially accelerating divorce rates from the mid-1960s to the mid-1980s and the following leveling off and stabilization of these rates in countries that have already reached relatively high levels of divorce rates can be understood as a manifestation of a first increasing and then decreasing lack of equilibrium among elements in the macrostructure of society (educational expansion and structure of the family system), as well as in the respective roles and expectations of the microstructure in intimate relationships.

Chapter 10

Problems of Model Specification

Previously, we stressed that time-dependence can be interpreted from various angles. In chapter 7, we discussed time-dependence from a substantive perspective, where it was derived from a theoretically supposed underlying diffusion process, or as an expression of a theoretically important latent causal factor operating in time. In this chapter, we approach time-dependence from a methodological point of view and consider it to be a consequence of unobserved heterogeneity. We will see that such a switch in perspective means that scientists can investigate the same data using different assumptions and logically reach valid but perhaps contradictory substantive conclusions (Manski 1993). Thus, distinguishing between competing (substantive and methodological) interpretations of the same data can be considered one of the most challenging problems in causal analysis. Therefore, it is not surprising that the estimation of event history models in the presence of omitted variables has become a prime focus of much technical work in recent years.

In section 10.1 we discuss the issue of unobserved heterogeneity in general terms and provide some illustrative examples. Some researchers have proposed using so-called mixture models to account for unobserved heterogeneity. These approaches are demonstrated in section 10.2. In particular, we show how to estimate transition rate models, in which it is assumed that the unobserved heterogeneity follows a gamma distribution. However, our discussion is mainly critical of the usefulness of these approaches, because there is, in general, no way to make reliable assumptions about what has *not* been observed. Section 10.3 summarizes the discussion and stresses the fact that unobserved heterogeneity is just *one* aspect of a broad variety of model specification problems.

10.1 Unobserved Heterogeneity

Using transition rate models, we try to find empirical evidence about how the transition rates, describing the movements of individuals (or other units of analysis) in a given state space, depend on a set of covariates. Unfortunately, we are not always able to include all important factors. One reason is the limitation of available data; we would like to include some important variables, but we simply do not have the information. Furthermore, we often do not know what is important. So what are the consequences of this situation? Basically, there are two aspects to be taken into consideration.

The first one is well known from traditional regression models. Because our covariates are normally correlated, the parameter estimates depend on the specific set of covariates included in the model. Every change in this set is likely to change the parameter estimates of the variables already included in previous models. Thus, in practice, the only way to proceed is to estimate a series of models with different specifications and then to check whether the estimation results are stable or not. However, this sequential model specification and estimation can also be seen as a resource for theoretical development. This procedure can provide additional insights into what may be called context sensitivity of causal effects in the social world.

Second, changing the set of covariates in a transition rate model will very often also lead to changes in the time-dependent shape of the transition rate. A similar effect occurs in traditional regression models: Depending on the set of covariates, the empirical distribution of the residuals changes. But, as opposed to regression models, where the residuals are normally only used for checking model assumptions, in transition rate models the residuals become the focus of modeling. In fact, if transition rate models are reformulated as regression models, the transition rate becomes a description of the residuals, and any change in the distribution of the residuals becomes a change in the time-dependent shape of the transition rate. Consequently, the empirical insight that a transition rate model provides for the time-dependent shape of the transition rate more or less depends on the set of covariates used to estimate the model.[1] So the question is whether a transition rate model can provide at least some reliable insights into a time-dependent transition rate.

Before discussing this question, some examples to illustrate possible consequences of "unobserved heterogeneity" are in order (see also Blossfeld and Hamerle 1992; Vaupel and Yashin 1985). Let us assume a single transition from only one origin state to only one destination state so that the episodes can be described by a single random variable T for the duration in the origin state. The distribution of T can be represented by a density function $f(t)$, a survivor function $G(t)$, or by a transition rate $r(t) = f(t)/G(t)$.

Now let us assume that the population consists of two groups to be distinguished by a variable x, with $x = 1$ for Group 1 and $x = 2$ for Group 2. Then we can define duration variables T_1 and T_2 separately for these two groups. And, like T, these duration variables can be described separately by density, survivor, and transition rate functions:

$$T_1 \quad \sim \quad f_1(t), \ G_1(t), \ r_1(t) = f_1(t)/G_1(t)$$
$$T_2 \quad \sim \quad f_2(t), \ G_2(t), \ r_2(t) = f_2(t)/G_2(t)$$

The transition behavior in both groups can be quite different. If we are able

---

[1] It also depends on the type of model. As shown in chapter 7, all parametric models are only able to fit a limited range of shapes of a time-dependent transition rate.

to separate both groups, we can gain some insight into these differences by estimating $f_i(t)$, $G_i(t)$, and $r_i(t)$ separately for both groups ($i = 1, 2$). If, however, we do not have information about group membership, we can only estimate the transition behavior in both groups together, that is, we can only estimate $f(t)$, $G(t)$, and $r(t)$.

The important point is that the distribution describing T can be quite different from the distributions describing T_1 and T_2, or put in more substantive terms, the transition behavior in the population as a whole can be quite different from the transition behavior in the two subpopulations (groups). To describe this more formally, one can proceed as follows. First, let π_1 and π_2 denote the proportions of the two groups at the beginning of the process ($\pi_1 + \pi_2 = 1$). Then we find that

$$f(t) = \pi_1 \, f_1(t) + \pi_2 \, f_2(t) \quad \text{and}$$
$$G(t) = \pi_1 \, G_1(t) + \pi_2 \, G_2(t)$$

Using the general formula $r(t) = f(t)/G(t)$, we can now derive the following expression for the transition rate in the population:

$$r(t) = r_1(t)\,\pi_1 \, \frac{G_1(t)}{G(t)} + r_2(t)\,\pi_2 \, \frac{G_2(t)}{G(t)} \tag{10.1}$$

The transition rate $r(t)$ in the population is a weighted average of the transition rates in the two groups, $r_1(t)$ and $r_2(t)$. But the weights change during the process. In fact, the weights are just the proportions of the two groups in the "risk set" at every point in time.[2] Let us give three examples.

Example 1: Suppose a sample of employees is divided into two subpopulations, denoted by $x = 1$ (men) and $x = 2$ (women). The job-exit rates for these two groups are supposed to be constant:[3]

$$r_1(t) = 0.01$$
$$r_2(t) = 0.04$$

and the proportions of the two groups in the population are assumed to be $\pi_1 = 0.5$ and $\pi_2 = 0.5$. The survivor functions are then

$$G_1(t) = \exp(-0.01\,t)$$
$$G_2(t) = \exp(-0.04\,t)$$
$$G(t) = 0.5\,\exp(-0.01\,t) + 0.5\,\exp(-0.04\,t)$$

and, using (10.1), we find the transition rate

$$r(t) = \frac{0.01\,\exp(-0.01\,t) + 0.04\,\exp(-0.04\,t)}{\exp(-0.01\,t) + \exp(-0.04\,t)}$$

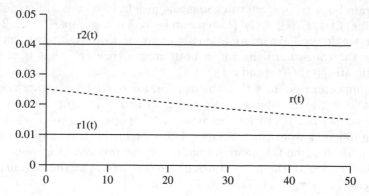

Figure 10.1.1 Mixture of two exponential transition rates.

Figure 10.1.1 illustrates the transition rates. Obviously, the transition rate in the population $r(t)$ declines, although there is a constant transition rate in both subpopulations. The reason is that the proportion of both groups in the risk set continuously changes. For instance, at the beginning of the process there are 50 % men and 50 % women. But women, in this example, leave their jobs faster than men, which is shown by their greater transition rate. Therefore, after (say) 36 months we find

$$
\begin{aligned}
G_1(t) &= \exp(-0.01 \cdot 36) = 0.698 \\
G_2(t) &= \exp(-0.04 \cdot 36) = 0.237 \\
G(t) &= 0.5 \exp(-0.01 \cdot 36) + 0.5 \exp(-0.04 \cdot 36) = 0.468
\end{aligned}
$$

This means that only 30.2 % of the men, but already 76.3 % of the women have left their jobs. So the risk set at $t = 36$ consists of $0.5 \cdot 0.698/0.468 = 74.6 \%$ men and $0.5 \cdot 0.237/0.468 = 25.3 \%$ women.

Example 2: Now assume the same setup as in Example 1, but the transition rate in Group 1 is of the Weibull type, for instance (with $a = 0.01$ and $b = 1.5$):[4]

$$
\begin{aligned}
r_1(t) &= 1.5 \cdot 0.01^{1.5} \cdot t^{0.5} \\
r_2(t) &= 0.04
\end{aligned}
$$

---

[2] The "risk set" at time t is the set of individuals who did not have a transition before t, so it is the number of individuals at $t = 0$ multiplied by the survivor function $G(t)$.

[3] That is, we assume an exponential model for both groups; see chapter 4.

[4] See section 7.3 for a definition of the Weibull model.

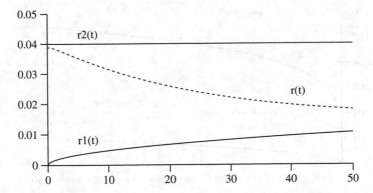

Figure 10.1.2 Mixture of an exponential and a Weibull transition rate.

The survivor functions are then

$$G_1(t) = \exp\left(-(0.01\,t)^{1.5}\right)$$
$$G_2(t) = \exp\left(-0.04\,t\right)$$
$$G(t) = 0.5\exp\left(-(0.01\,t)^{1.5}\right) + 0.5\exp\left(-0.04\,t\right)$$

and, using (10.1), we find the transition rate

$$r(t) = \frac{1.5 \cdot 0.01^{1.5} \cdot t^{0.5}\exp\left(-(0.01\,t)^{1.5}\right) + 0.04\exp\left(-0.04\,t\right)}{\exp\left(-(0.01\,t)^{1.5}\right) + \exp\left(-0.04\,t\right)}$$

Figure 10.1.2 illustrates the transition rates for this example. While the transition rate is increasing in Group 1 and constant in Group 2, the resulting transition rate for the population is *decreasing*.

Example 3: Finally, suppose that both groups follow a Weibull transition rate, for instance,

$$r_1(t) = 1.5 \cdot 0.01^{1.5} \cdot t^{0.5}$$
$$r_2(t) = 1.2 \cdot 0.04^{1.2} \cdot t^{0.2}$$

The survivor functions are then

$$G_1(t) = \exp\left(-(0.01\,t)^{1.5}\right)$$
$$G_2(t) = \exp\left(-(0.04\,t)^{1.2}\right)$$
$$G(t) = 0.5\exp\left(-(0.01\,t)^{1.5}\right) + 0.5\exp\left(-(0.04\,t)^{1.2}\right)$$

and, using (10.1), we find the transition rate $r(t) =$

$$\frac{1.5 \cdot 0.01^{1.5} \cdot t^{0.5}\exp\left(-(0.01\,t)^{1.5}\right) + 1.2 \cdot 0.04^{1.2} \cdot t^{0.2}\exp\left(-(0.04\,t)^{1.2}\right)}{\exp\left(-(0.01\,t)^{1.5}\right) + \exp\left(-(0.04\,t)^{1.2}\right)}$$

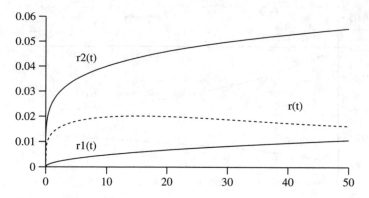

Figure 10.1.3 Mixture of two Weibull transition rates.

Figure 10.1.3 illustrates the transition rates for this example. Both groups
follow an increasing transition rate, but the transition rate for the population $r(t)$ is totally different, as it is bell-shaped (see also Blossfeld and
Hamerle 1989a).

These examples show that the transition rate that is estimated for a
population *can* be the result (a mixture) of quite different transition rates
in the subpopulations. What are the consequences? First, this result means
that one can *explain* an observed transition rate at the population level
as the result of different transition rates in subpopulations. Of course, this
will only be a sensible strategy if we are able to identify important subpopulations. To follow this strategy one obviously needs *observable* criteria
to partition a population into subpopulations. Just to speculate about the
fact that an observed transition rate *might* be the result of quite different transition rates will not further an explanation. Although there might
be unobserved heterogeneity (and we can usually be sure that we were not
able to include all important covariates), just to make more or less arbitrary
distributional assumptions about unobserved heterogeneity will not lead to
better models. On the contrary, the estimation results will be more dependent on assumptions than would be the case otherwise (Lieberson 1985).
Therefore, we would like to stress our view that the most important basis
for any progress in model building is sufficient and appropriate data.

There remains the problem of how to interpret a time-dependent transition rate from a causal view. The question is: Can time be considered as
a proxy for an unmeasured variable producing a time-dependent rate, or is
it simply an expression of unobserved heterogeneity, which does not allow
for any substantive interpretation?[5]

---

[5]There is, however, another aspect to this problem. From a purely descriptive point
of view, a time-dependent transition rate provides some empirically relevant information

10.2 Models with a Mixture Distribution

There have been several proposals to deal with unobserved heterogeneity in transition rate models. The basic idea underlying these proposals is to incorporate an "error term" into the model specification. This is quite familiar from traditional regression models, but specific problems arise if one tries to follow this strategy in the specification of transition rate models. These problems become visible if we begin with the following general specification of a transition rate model:

$$r(t) = f(x, \beta, \epsilon)$$

In this specification, the transition rate, $r(t)$, is a function of a vector of covariates, x, a vector of model parameters, β, to be estimated, and a stochastic variable ϵ to represent an error term. In order to make such a model estimable one needs additional specifications. First, one has to specify the functional relationship $f(.)$. There are many options as already illustrated in previous chapters of this book. But this is not enough. One also needs some assumptions about the distribution of ϵ.

This becomes clearer if we write our transition rate model as a regression model, for instance, in the following way:[6]

$$\log(T) = x\beta + \epsilon$$

---

about the population itself. Some researchers seem to assume that this is *not* the case. The argument runs as follows: Because a time-dependent transition rate could be the result of quite different transition rates in unobserved subpopulations, the transition rate for the population might only be "apparent." We agree with this reasoning insofar as there is always the possibility that the observed transition rate for a population could be the result of quite different transition rates in certain subpopulations. This sometimes produces an opportunity to *explain* the transition rate at the population level by referring to the various transition rates in subpopulations. However, we do not agree with the conclusion that the observed transition rate at the population level is only "apparent." It remains an empirical fact. Otherwise there would be no point in *explaining* the transition rate for the population. The conclusion should be quite different. Instead of using the examples given previously to support speculation about "true" vs. only "apparent" time-dependencies in the transition rate, statements about time-dependent transition rates should be made explicitly dependent on specific populations. Then there can be no contradiction in stating that there are different transition rates for men and women and that there is quite another transition rate for a population consisting of men and women, for example. If, to follow this example, there are constant, but different transition rates for both men and women, the transition rate for the population consisting of men and women will decrease with time. Thus, the statement that there is a decreasing transition rate for the population consisting of men and women will not become false if we learn that this population consists of men and women and that transition rates for men and women are time-constant but different. The statement about the transition rate for the population remains true and provides a more or less valuable *empirical* insight.

[6]Many authors have discussed the formal similarities between regression and transition rate models; see, for instance, Lawless (1982) and Petersen (1990, 1991). See also the discussion of SAS models in Blossfeld, Hamerle, and Mayer (1989).

To simplify the argument, we assume that the logarithm of the duration variable, T, depends on a linear combination of covariates, $x\beta$, and, additively, on an error term, ϵ. Depending on our assumptions about the distribution of ϵ, this becomes a transition rate model. We can, for instance, assume that ϵ is normally distributed, $\epsilon \sim \mathcal{N}(0, \sigma^2)$, a common assumption in regression modeling. Consequently, T (conditional on the covariates) follows a log-normal distribution with density function

$$\frac{1}{t\sigma} \phi \left(\frac{\log(t) - \beta}{\sigma} \right)$$

(ϕ is used to denote the standard normal density function.) In fact, what we get is the log-normal transition rate model, as discussed in section 7.5. However, then there is no longer an error term. What has happened? Our assumption about the error term in the regression model has become an assumption about the distribution of the duration variable T, so in a sense our transition rate model already contains an "error term"; it is, so to speak, the *distribution* of the duration variable T, *conditional* on the covariates. However, this formulation is somewhat misleading because the focus of the model has changed. In traditional regression modeling, the focus is on the *expectation* of the dependent variable, $E(T)$. This focus motivates reference to an "error term," meaning the residuals, in trying to explain the *expectation* of T, given the covariates x. The focus in transition rate models is quite different. It is *not* the expectation of T, but the *distribution* of T (i.e., the transition rate describing how the process in a population proceeds) if time goes on. We are not interested in how the expectation of T depends on covariates, but in how the distribution of T (i.e., the transition rate) depends on the covariates. In statistical terms, there is not much difference in these two modeling approaches, but in terms of substantive theory, there is quite a significant difference. The transition rate has a substantive meaning in event history modeling because it refers to a "propensity" of individuals to change states in a state space. It is, therefore, not just a statistical concept for making assumptions about an error term.

What would a transition rate model containing an *additional* error term look like? We could split, for instance, the error term ϵ into two components: $\epsilon = \epsilon_1 + \epsilon_2$. Written as a regression model, we then get

$$\log(T) = x\beta + \epsilon_1 + \epsilon_2$$

We can then make an assumption about the distribution of ϵ_1 to get a distributional form for T and finally arrive at a transition rate model containing an additional error term, ϵ_2. Of course, to make the model estimable, we also need a distributional assumption about ϵ_2. This is quite possible in purely formal terms, but we will obviously run into a problem. Having made distributional assumptions about ϵ_1 and ϵ_2, we have, in fact, made an assumption about $\epsilon = \epsilon_1 + \epsilon_2$. We have specified a mixture distribution for ϵ and, consequently, for T. Thus, we finally arrive at a mixture model for the duration variable, and we have again lost our error term.

The essential point is that the whole procedure of splitting an error term into components is quite arbitrary. From an empirical point of view, we only have a single set of residuals that is *defined* by a model specification. It would be totally arbitrary to separate these residuals into two parts: one part to be interpreted as a description of the transition rate, the other part to be interpreted as an error term. If strong theoretical and empirical reasons were available to justify a specific distributional assumption about the transition rate, it could make sense to include an additional error term. But, at least in sociological research, this is almost never the case. In fact, we do not know of a single application where the researcher had strong a priori reasons (with respect to the given data) that could be used to justify the selection of a specific type of transition rate model.

Thus it seems that there is no point in specifying and estimating transition rate models based on mixture distributions, at least in the current state of sociological research. However, this result is inconclusive. The fact remains that we almost never have sufficient reasons to decide for one specific transition rate model. Our estimation results will depend on the type of model. We have already discussed this previously, coming to the conclusion that the best strategy is always to estimate a broad variety of different models in order to find robust estimation results. Thus, if one looks at the problem from this perspective, mixture models might be helpful in another way. Although these models have no utility in separating an error term from a "true" transition rate, they broadly enrich the spectrum of models that can be used to look for robust estimation results. Thus, if the previously mentioned strategy is followed, there is some sense in using mixture models. They can be quite helpful in separating robust estimation results (i.e., estimation results that are to a large degree independent of a specific model specification) and "spurious" results, which might be defined by the fact that they heavily depend on a specific type of model.

For these reasons, we give a short technical discussion of mixture models in the following sections. We examine two approaches. One type of approach begins with a fully parametric specification of the distribution of the error term. In particular, the use of a gamma distribution has been proposed (Tuma 1985).[7] This approach is discussed in the following section. Another approach, proposed by Heckman and Singer (1984), is based on a discrete mixture distribution and might be called semiparametric because only very

---

[7] In principle, any other distributional assumption resulting in correspondingly defined mixture models is possible. The gamma distribution is just a particularly convenient choice because the resulting mixture distribution is easily tractable.

weak assumptions are necessary. It is not discussed in this book.[8]

10.2.1 Models with a Gamma Mixture

In this section we follow the usual way of treating the error term in transition rate models. This is based on the assumption that there is a time-invariant unobserved constant specific for each individual. Furthermore, it is assumed that this unobserved constant can be represented as the realization of a random variable, identically distributed for all individuals and independent of observed covariates (Crouchley and Pickles 1987; Davies and Crouchley 1985). This error term is then multiplicatively connected with the transition rate. The idea is to make this random variable capture both individual heterogeneity and deviations from the supposed shape of duration dependence (Galler and Pötter 1990).

To be more specific, it is assumed that the transition rate, $r(t \mid x, v)$, depends on a vector, x, of observed covariates and on a scalar stochastic term, v, which is not observed. Our question is how the variables comprising x influence the transition rate, but this cannot be observed directly. In any observed sample of episodes, the transition rate also depends on the values of v.[9]

The same is true for the associated density and survivor functions. The relation between transition rate, density, and survivor function must therefore be written as

$$r(t \mid x, v) = \frac{f(t \mid x, v)}{G(t \mid x, v)} \tag{10.2}$$

$$G(t \mid x, v) = \exp\left(-\int_0^t r(\tau \mid x, v)\, d\tau\right) \tag{10.3}$$

To find an estimation approach, we make some simplifying assumptions. First, that the transition rate can be expressed as

$$r(t \mid x, v) = r^u(t \mid x)\, v \qquad v \geq 0 \tag{10.4}$$

In fact, we assume that the component $r^u(t \mid x)$ of this expression, called the *underlying* rate, is parametrically given according to one of the standard parametric transition rate models discussed in chapters 4 and 7. The cumulative transition rate may then be written as

$$H(t \mid x, v) = v\, H^u(t \mid x) = v \int_0^t r^u(\tau \mid x)\, d\tau \tag{10.5}$$

---

[8]Trussell and Richards (1985) discussed their experience using this approach.

[9]This stochastic variable v corresponds to the error term ϵ_2, which has been introduced in the regression framework earlier. Because the regression model was formulated in terms of $\log(T)$, the error term now becomes $\exp(\epsilon_2)$, multiplicatively connected with the transition rate.

The second basic assumption is that the stochastic term, v, follows a gamma distribution with expectation $E(v) = 1$. As implied by this assumption, the density function of v can be written as

$$f_v(v) = \frac{\kappa^\kappa v^{\kappa-1}}{\Gamma(\kappa)} \exp(-\kappa v) \qquad \kappa > 0$$

The variance of this distribution is $\text{Var}(v) = 1/\kappa$. The next step is to calculate the resulting mixture distribution for the observed durations. First, for the density and survivor functions, one gets

$$f(t \mid x) = \int_0^\infty f(t \mid x, v) f_v(v) \, dv$$

$$G(t \mid x) = \int_0^\infty G(t \mid x, v) f_v(v) \, dv$$

These mixtures are expectations according to the distribution of v. The calculation is easy because the gamma distribution implies the basic equality

$$\int_0^\infty \exp(-v \, s(t)) f_v(v) \, dv = \left[1 + \frac{1}{\kappa} s(t)\right]^{-\kappa}$$

which holds for any real valued function $s(t)$.[10] Therefore, using (10.3) and (10.5), the unconditional survivor function is

$$G(t \mid x) = \int_0^\infty \exp\left(-v \, H^u(t \mid x)\right) f_v(v) \, dv = \left[1 + \frac{1}{\kappa} H^u(t \mid x)\right]^{-\kappa}$$

$$(10.6)$$

The unconditional density function can be found by differentiating the negative value of the unconditional survivor function, resulting in

$$f(t \mid x) = r^u(t \mid x) \left[1 + \frac{1}{\kappa} H^u(t \mid x)\right]^{-\kappa-1} \tag{10.7}$$

Finally, the unconditional transition rate is

$$r(t \mid x) = \frac{f(t \mid x)}{G(t \mid x)} = r^u(t \mid x) \left[1 + \frac{1}{\kappa} H^u(t \mid x)\right]^{-1} \tag{10.8}$$

Several Destination States. So far we have derived a mixture model for episodes with one origin and one destination state. However, the extension to

---

[10] See, for instance, Lancaster (1990, p. 328).

a situation with several destinations is easy. For the transition to destination state k, the model specification is

$$r_k(t \mid x, v_k) = r_k^u(t \mid x)\, v_k \qquad v_k \geq 0$$

$r_k^u(t \mid x)$ is the underlying rate used for model formulation. The error term v_k is assumed to be specific for each transition and gamma distributed with unit expectation. In the same way, as was shown earlier for the single transition case, one can finally derive expressions for the observed transition rates, which can be used for model estimations.

Maximum Likelihood Estimation. The approach to deriving transition rate models with an additional gamma distributed error term can be summarized as follows. One starts with a parametrically given transition rate, as in (10.4), and assumes that the unobserved heterogeneity is gamma distributed with unit mean and variance $1/\kappa$. Then one derives the observed mixture distribution, described by $f(t \mid x)$, $G(t \mid x)$, and $r(t \mid x)$, given in (10.6), (10.7), and (10.8), respectively. This is for the single transition case, but an extension to the case of several transitions is wholly analogous. It follows that the log likelihood can be set up in the usual way. We only give the formula for the single transition case. With $\mathcal{N}$ and $\mathcal{E}$ denoting the sets of all episodes and of episodes with an event, respectively, the log likelihood can be written as

$$\ell = \sum_{i \in \mathcal{E}} \log(r(t_i)) + \sum_{i \in \mathcal{N}} \log(G(t_i)) =$$

$$\sum_{i \in \mathcal{E}} \log\left(r^u(t_i)\right) - \log\left(1 + \frac{1}{\kappa} H^u(t_i)\right) - \sum_{i \in \mathcal{N}} \kappa \log\left(1 + \frac{1}{\kappa} H^u(t_i)\right)$$

Unfortunately, the usual way of applying the episode-splitting method is no longer possible. Assume an episode $(0, t)$, starting at time zero and ending at time t, and assume that there is a covariate that changes its value at t_x $(0 < t_x < t)$. Then it would be quite possible to include this information into the calculation of the cumulated rate $H^u(t \mid x)$, which is needed for the calculation of the density and survivor functions of the unconditional distribution. However, the episode-splitting method is only applicable in its usual form, if the calculation can be separated into two steps; the first step has the information about the $(0, t_x)$ split, and the second has information about the (t_x, t) split, but obviously the unconditional density and survivor functions cannot be calculated in these two distinct steps. Therefore, we do use split episodes in our examples.

Gamma Mixture Models in Stata. In principle, the approach of adding a gamma distributed error term can be used with any parametric transition rate model. To request estimation of the model with an additional gamma distributed error term, one must only add the option `frailty(gamma)`. The estimation results will show you the estimated parameters, an estimate of the variance of the frailties and a likelihood-ratio test of the null hypothesis that this variance is zero. You may also choose the Inverse-Gaussian distribution by simply typing `frailty(invgauss)`. A generalization of the frailty models is the shared-frailty model. To fit such a model, which assumes that the frailty is group-specific, you use the option `shared(varname)`.

10.2.2   Exponential Models with a Gamma Mixture

To illustrate the estimation of gamma mixture models with Stata, we first use an exponential model. The transition rate, now conditional on v, may be written as

$$r(t \mid v) = a\,v \qquad a,\, v \geq 0$$

The underlying model, already described in chapter 4, is the exponential, implying that $r^u(t) = a$ and $H^u(t) = a\,t$. The observed mixture distribution is described by

$$
\begin{aligned}
G(t) &= (1 + d\,a\,t)^{-\frac{1}{d}} \\
f(t) &= a\,(1 + d\,a\,t)^{-\frac{1}{d}-1} \\
r(t) &= a\,(1 + d\,a\,t)^{-1}
\end{aligned}
$$

d is the variance of the gamma distributed error term. Obviously, if $d > 0$, there will be a negative time-dependence, although the underlying rate is a time-independent constant.

The model has two parameters: a, the constant transition rate of the underlying exponential model, and d, the variance of the mixing gamma distribution. The parameterization is as follows:

$$a = \exp(A\alpha) \quad \text{and} \quad d = \exp(\delta)$$

It is assumed that the first component of the covariate (row) vector, A, is a constant equal to one. The associated coefficient vector, α, together with δ, are the model parameters to be estimated. The estimate of the variance of the mixing gamma distribution is $\exp(\delta)$.

To illustrate the model estimation, we use do-file `ehd2.do` shown in Box 4.1.3 The estimation results for an exponential model without a gamma-distributed error term are shown in Box 4.1.4. In order to estimate a mixture model, type

```
streg edu coho2 coho3 lfx pnoj pres, dist(e) nohr fr(gamma)
```

In Box 10.2.1 estimates of the parameter vector α (see _t) and an estimate of δ (see /ln_the) are shown. Comparing these estimates with the

Box 10.2.1 Estimation results of ehd2.do with a gamma mixture

```
          failure _d:  des
    analysis time _t:  tf

Fitting exponential model:

Fitting constant-only model:
Iteration 0:   log likelihood = -903.19585
Iteration 1:   log likelihood = -902.99555
Iteration 2:   log likelihood = -902.99548

Fitting full model:
Iteration 0:   log likelihood = -912.23868
Iteration 1:   log likelihood = -870.86706
Iteration 2:   log likelihood = -866.14271
Iteration 3:   log likelihood = -866.07659
Iteration 4:   log likelihood =  -866.0763
Iteration 5:   log likelihood =  -866.0763

Exponential regression -- log relative-hazard form
                      Gamma frailty

No. of subjects =          600       Number of obs   =        600
No. of failures =          458
Time at risk    =        40782
                                     LR chi2(6)      =      73.84
Log likelihood  =     -866.0763      Prob > chi2     =     0.0000

------------------------------------------------------------------
     _t |     Coef.   Std. Err.      z    P>|z|   [95% Conf. Interval]
--------+---------------------------------------------------------
    edu |   .0872679   .0310473    2.81   0.005    .0264163    .1481195
  coho2 |   .5706931   .1444685    3.95   0.000     .28754     .8538462
  coho3 |    .416298   .1512207    2.75   0.006    .1199109    .7126851
    lfx |  -.0046331   .0010997   -4.21   0.000   -.0067884   -.0024778
   pnoj |   .0850445    .054537    1.56   0.119   -.0218461    .1919351
   pres |  -.0320635   .0066215   -4.84   0.000   -.0450415   -.0190855
  _cons |  -3.986876   .3430481  -11.62   0.000   -4.659238   -3.314515
--------+---------------------------------------------------------
 /ln_the|  -.8019158   .1836758   -4.37   0.000   -1.161914    -.441918
--------+---------------------------------------------------------
  theta |   .4484689   .0823729                    .3128868    .6428024
------------------------------------------------------------------
Likelihood-ratio test of theta=0: chibar2(01)   =  47.72
                            Prob>=chibar2 = 0.000
```

results of the simple exponential model in Box 4.1.4 shows that there are
no substantial changes in the estimated parameters. However, we get a
quite significant estimate for the variance of the mixing gamma distribution: $\hat{d} = \exp(-0.8019) = 0.448$. This is supported by the likelihood ratio
test statistic to compare the two models, which is 47.7 with one degree

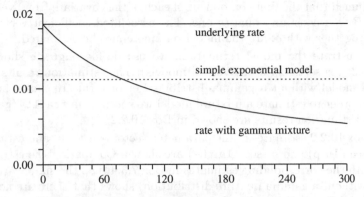

Figure 10.2.1 Transition rates estimated with an exponential model, without (dotted) and with (solid) a gamma mixture distribution. Model specification according to Box 4.1.5, all covariate values set to zero.

of freedom. The result indicates that we have a decreasing transition rate, absorbed by the error term in relation to the assumption of a constant transition rate for the underlying model (see Figure 10.2.1). Of course, this does not prove that all deviations from a constant transition rate are a result of "unobserved heterogeneity." As already discussed at the beginning of this section, the utility of estimating a mixture model lies not in separating an error term from a "true" transition rate, but in providing some means for assessing the robustness of parameter estimates for *observed* covariates.

10.2.3   Weibull Models with a Gamma Mixture

For a second illustration, we use the Weibull model (see section 7.3). The transition rate, now conditional on v, is $r(t \mid v) = r^u(t)\,v$ with $v \geq 0$. The underlying transition rate and the cumulative rate are given by

$$r^u(t) = b\,a^b\,t^{b-1} \quad \text{and} \quad H^u(t) = (a\,t)^b$$

according to the standard Weibull model. The observed mixture distribution is described by

$$
\begin{aligned}
G(t) &= \left(1 + d\,(a\,t)^b\right)^{-\frac{1}{d}} \\
f(t) &= b\,a^b\,t^{b-1}\left(1 + d\,(a\,t)^b\right)^{-\frac{1}{d}-1} \\
r(t) &= b\,a^b\,t^{b-1}\left(1 + d\,(a\,t)^b\right)^{-1}
\end{aligned}
$$

The model has three parameters: a and b are the parameters of the underlying Weibull distribution; d represents the variance of the mixing gamma distribution. The model is parameterized as follows:

$$a = \exp(-A\alpha), \quad b = \exp(B\beta), \quad d = \exp(\delta)$$

It is assumed that the first component of each of the covariate (row) vectors, A and B, is a constant equal to one. The associated coefficient vectors, α and β, together with δ, are the model parameters to be estimated.

To illustrate the model estimation, we use do-file `ehg6.do` shown in Box 7.3.3 (see section 7.3 on Weibull models). The estimation results for a Weibull model without a gamma-distributed error term are shown in Box 7.3.4. In order to estimate a mixture model we specify the `frailty(gamma)` option. Estimation results are shown in Box 10.2.2.

In Box 10.2.2 estimates of the parameter vector α (see `_t`) and estimates of β_0 (see `/ln_p`) and δ (see `/ln_the`) are shown. Comparing the estimates for α with the corresponding estimates in Box 7.3.4 (i.e., the simple Weibull model without a gamma mixture distribution) shows that there are no substantial changes.[11] However, not only we do get a quite significant estimate for the variance of the mixing gamma distribution, $\hat{d} = \exp(\hat{\delta}) = 2.189$. The shape parameter of the underlying Weibull distribution has changed significantly as well. In the simple Weibull model, it was $\hat{b} = 0.914$; now it is $\hat{b} = \exp(0.6693) = 1.953$. In fact, as shown in Figure 10.2.2, the transition rate has changed quite dramatically. Although the Weibull model only allows for monotonic increasing or decreasing transition rates, mixing the Weibull distribution with a gamma distribution allows for bell-shaped transition rates, and because this seems most appropriate for our data, such a rate can finally be estimated. The underlying Weibull transition rate is just an arbitrary part of the mixture distribution, or something like a residual to make the mixing distribution fit the data. This again demonstrates that one should be very careful in interpreting the various parts of a mixture distribution in theoretical terms.

These examples demonstrate that using a mixture model can significantly improve a model's capability to fit a given set of data with one of its possible time-dependent transition rates. As a by-product, this might result in more reliable parameter estimates for the covariates.

As a final example, Figure 10.2.3 shows the transition rates for a log-normal model with and without a mixing gamma distribution.[12] Because we already know that the log-normal distribution is appropriate for our data, we don't expect much improvement from using a mixture distribution. However, as seen in Figure 10.2.3, the final mixing distribution shows that the (population level) transition rate is somewhat steeper than can be expressed with the simple log-normal model.

---

[11] Note, again, that the signs of the estimates of the coefficients in paramter vector α have to be reversed in order to compare these estimates with the other examples in this book.

[12] The model is specified as shown in Box 7.5.3 (do-file `ehg11.do`); see section 7.5 about log-normal models. The gamma mixture model is estimated by using the do-file `ehg11.do` with the additional option `frailty(gamma)`.

Box 10.2.2 Estimation results of `ehg6.do` with a gamma mixture distribution

```
        failure _d:  des
  analysis time _t:  tf

Fitting Weibull model:

Fitting constant-only model:

Iteration 0:   log likelihood = -1010.7268
Iteration 1:   log likelihood = -875.38172
Iteration 2:   log likelihood =  -871.8774
Iteration 3:   log likelihood = -871.85633
Iteration 4:   log likelihood = -871.85632

Fitting full model:

Iteration 0:   log likelihood = -896.80052
Iteration 1:   log likelihood = -838.04895
Iteration 2:   log likelihood = -836.07108
Iteration 3:   log likelihood = -834.66076
Iteration 4:   log likelihood = -834.66053
Iteration 5:   log likelihood = -834.66053

Weibull regression -- accelerated failure-time form
                 Gamma frailty

No. of subjects =          600     Number of obs   =        600
No. of failures =          458
Time at risk    =        40782
                                   LR chi2(6)      =      74.39
Log likelihood  =   -834.66053     Prob > chi2     =     0.0000


------------------------------------------------------------------------
     _t |     Coef.   Std. Err.     z    P>|z|    [95% Conf. Interval]
--------+---------------------------------------------------------------
    edu | -.0719787   .0265541   -2.71   0.007   -.1240239   -.0199335
  coho2 | -.4640506   .1205172   -3.85   0.000    -.70026    -.2278411
  coho3 | -.4014352    .128362   -3.13   0.002    -.65302    -.1498504
    lfx |  .0041267   .0008468    4.87   0.000    .002467    .0057865
   pnoj | -.1143679   .0469785   -2.43   0.015   -.206444    -.0222918
   pres |  .0260338   .0053382    4.88   0.000   .0155711    .0364966
  _cons |  3.492617    .295304   11.83   0.000   2.913832    4.071402
--------+---------------------------------------------------------------
  /ln_p |  .6692704   .0879964    7.61   0.000   .4968007    .8417401
 /ln_the|  .7833431    .171606    4.56   0.000   .4470016    1.119685
--------+---------------------------------------------------------------
      p |  1.952812   .1718404                    1.643455    2.320401
    1/p |   .512082   .0450614                    .4309599    .6084742
  theta |  2.188777   .3756073                    1.563617    3.063888
------------------------------------------------------------------------
Likelihood-ratio test of theta=0: chibar2(01)    = 104.09
                         Prob>=chibar2 = 0.000
```

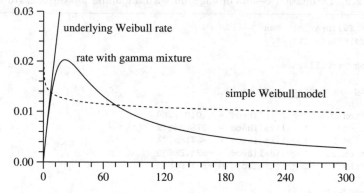

Figure 10.2.2 Transition rates estimated with a Weibull model, without (dotted) and with (solid) a gamma mixture distribution. Model specification according to Box 7.3.4, all covariate values set to zero.

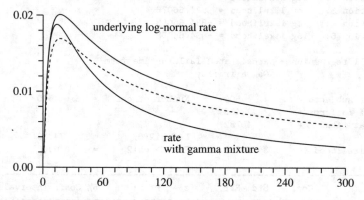

Figure 10.2.3 Transition rates estimated with a log-normal model, without (dotted) and with (solid) a gamma mixture distribution. Model specification according to Box 7.5.3, all covariate values set to zero.

Specification of the Error Term

The main drawback of mixture models is that parameter estimates *can* be highly sensitive to the assumed parametric form of the error term. For example, Heckman and Singer (1982), who based the systematic part of the model on the same assumptions, estimated four different unobserved heterogeneity models: one with a normal, one with a log-normal, and one with a gamma distribution of the error term, as well as a model with a nonparametric specification of the disturbance. They found that the estimates provided by these models were surprisingly different. In other words, the identification problem might only be shifted to another level: Misspecification of the transition rate by neglecting the error term might be replaced by misspecification of the parametric distribution of the error term. Thus a powerful theory would be needed with regard to the distribution of the stochastic error term. However, given the various sources of misspecification that are described later, it is very unlikely that any theory can provide solid guidance to a specific parametric distribution of the error term. In other words, misspecification is likely to occur.

This makes a semiparametric specification of the error term attractive. Heckman and Singer (1982, 1984) proposed to use a discrete distribution with a varying number of mass points to approximate the unknown distribution of the error term. Unfortunately, this solution again only shifts the identification problem to another level. This is because Trussell and Richards (1985) reported a strong dependence of the semiparametric estimator on the choice of the duration dependence in transition rate models. Again, a powerful argument would be needed to justify a specific parametric form of the duration dependence. However, as discussed in section 7.1, this will rarely be the case in empirical applications (see also Heckman and Walker 1987).

A further step in trying to solve the identification problem would be to adopt a nonparametric specification of both the duration dependence and the unobserved heterogeneity term. However, it seems that these models are only identifiable in the case of complete survivor functions for all values of the covariates (Elbers and Ridder 1982). They are also very sensitive to small perturbations in the values of the estimated survivor function (Galler and Pötter 1990). Thus, given the common limitations of event history data in practical research (censored information, measurement error), it seems impossible to estimate both duration dependence and unobserved heterogeneity nonparametrically in one model (Galler and Pötter 1990).[13]

10.3   Discussion

So far we have discussed the topic of "unobserved heterogeneity." We have tried to show that neglecting important covariates is, in fact, a serious source of model misspecification. But we have also tried to show that there are no simple remedies for this problem. In particular, transition rate models with a mixture distribution do not provide an easy solution for the problems generated by unobserved heterogeneity, although they might be quite helpful in a search for robust parameter estimates. This is simply because these models provide a broader range of possible shapes for the transition rate, so

---

[13]A possibly fruitful compromise between a fully nonparametric and a parametric specification of the duration dependence could be a piecewise constant exponential model, as shown in chapter 5. This model could be mixed with a nonparametric specification of the unobserved error term. However, if a larger number of dummy variables is used, the identification of this model, while theoretically possible, would demand a large amount of exact data (see Galler and Pötter 1990).

that they can better fit a given set of data. The most promising strategy to cope with unobserved heterogeneity is to look for more appropriate data.

One should, however, not forget that unobserved heterogeneity is just one source of problems in our search for useful and robust models. In fact, there are many other problems of model specification that are no less important. Therefore it seems sensible to end this book by briefly drawing attention to the most important problems.

(1) The most significant aspect of model specification is to find an appropriate definition of the state space. For example, consider an investigation of women's transition rates between the states "employed," "housewife status," and "unemployed" over the life course. If women in part-time and full-time employment behave differently and/or if covariates have distinct effects that are dependent on the origin and destination states "full-time" and "part-time employment," then a study neglecting the full-time and part-time divide in the state space will produce omitted differences.[14] A further instructive example of misspecification of the state space was given in chapter 4, where we demonstrated that estimating the effect of education on the job-exit rate is problematic because education has a positive effect on upward moves and a negative effect on downward moves. Thus, not taking into account differences in destination states mixes up the contradictory effects of education.

(2) It might not be possible to include all important variables in the model specification. As already stressed earlier, the resulting parameter estimates are more or less dependent on the set of covariates actually used, and leaving out some important covariates is therefore an important source of misspecification.[15] For example, we have shown in some of our examples that the job-exit behavior of men and women is, in some respects, quite different, but in many of our examples we did not take gender differences explicitly into account.[16] Therefore, this might be an important source of misspecification. In serious research, one would include covariates for gender differences and investigate the resulting changes in parameter estimates.

(3) Another important type of misspecification occurs if initial condi-

---

[14]However, to some extent one could also include the differences of full-time and part-time employment by using a dummy variable and some of its interaction effects with other covariates.

[15]We do not speak of "biased" parameter estimates because, outside of descriptively defined estimation problems, the idea of unbiased estimation cannot be given a clear meaning. And without knowing the meaning of unbiased estimates, there is no sense in speculating about "biased" estimation. The problem is that our estimates are more or less dependent on model specification, so the question is how to find an appropriate model that may, in turn, heavily depend on its intended use.

[16]In fact, we did this because our example data set is small, and for didactical purposes, we wanted to use only one basic model throughout the book.

tions at entry into the episode (in single and, much more importantly, in multiepisode models) are not taken into account. Differences at the beginning of the spells are normally the consequence of foregoing selection processes. As discussed previously, most sociological research is based on nonexperimental observations of highly selective processes, which may in themselves be influencing the estimated transition rate. Let us again take the job-exit example. It is very likely that (a) there is self-selection among individual employees depending in part on their preferences for specific jobs, (b) there is selection by employers through their hiring and personnel policies, and (c) there may be selectivity due to forces exogenous to the covariates included in the model (e.g., socioeconomic background, ethnicity, etc.). In short, various sorting processes have already taken place when individuals enter into a new job episode, and they may massively influence the results of estimated transition rates. This is particularly true in models with multiple episodes where one should try to additionally control for the dependencies between successive episodes for each of the individuals (see section 4.3). Although event history models allow for the inclusion of information about process history much better than cross-sectional or panel models, only a few researchers can contend that all relevant variables on the history of the process have been included in their models.

(4) Misspecification can result when important time-dependent covariates are not taken into account, or if time-dependent covariates are modeled as time-constant covariates, measured only once.[17] In chapter 6, we demonstrated that time-dependent covariates are observations of the sample path of parallel processes (at the individual level, the level of small groups, the intermediate level of organizations or households, or at the macrolevel of a society). Omitting these important processes, or including them only as time-constant covariates, is obviously a source of misspecification. Although we have argued that the genuine strength of event history models, at least compared to cross-sectional and panel models, is their ability to include these parallel processes appropriately, it could easily happen that important time-dependent covariates are neglected or must be neglected due to missing data. The effect of the time-dependent covariates may also be highly sensitive with regard to the points in time when they should change their value. This was demonstrated in Example 3 of section 6.6, where the impact of pregnancy on entry into marriage for couples living in consensual unions was analyzed.

(5) Possible misspecification might occur if interaction effects are not taken into account. This is a serious point in many social science applica-

[17] A serious source of misspecification is often a "one time" measurement of explanatory variables (normally at the time of a retrospective interview), which sometimes occurs even after the occurrence of the event being studied (see Sandefur and Tuma 1987).

tions, because often the relationship between the transition rate and any given (time-constant or time-dependent) explanatory variable is not the same across all values of the remaining covariates. When a transition rate model includes more than two covariates, then many interaction terms (also higher order terms) might become necessary. An instructive example for misleading estimation results due to an omitted interaction term was given in chapter 9, where we included marriage as a time-dependent covariate in the job-exit rate model without taking into account that it has opposite effects on the job-exit rate for men and women.

(6) Another problem that might result in misleading estimation results is measurement errors. In transition rate models, this problem concerns not only covariates but also the information about starting and ending times of episodes (see the discussion in Sandefur and Tuma 1987).

(7) Quite another, but no less important, source of misspecification is the model type. As we have discussed in previous chapters, there is a broad range of transition rate models that can be used for practical research. Using different types of models will probably lead to different estimates of the impact of covariates on the transition rate. As discussed in chapter 8, there are some methods of investigating whether a model fits the data, but these methods are quite limited. Based on maximum likelihood estimation, there are, in general, no conclusive statistical criteria that can be used for model selection. Thus, in practice, the most sensible strategy is to estimate and compare a variety of different models and find out to what degree the estimation results are robust (i.e., do not depend on the selected model; see also Galler and Pötter 1992).

(8) Finally, the functional relationship between the various types of covariates just discussed (as well as duration dependence and possible interaction terms) and the transition rate might also be a source of misspecification. Normally, linear or log-linear functions to link model parameters to covariates are used. There are, however, many other possibilities, and estimation results might be dependent on the type of link function used to specify a model.

In summary, specification bias is pervasive in empirical social research. What can be recommended in such a situation—a situation that offers no satisfactory technical solution to settle the problem of model specification? First, it is important to remember that unobserved heterogeneity means that important information is omitted in the model or is not observable. Thus, if we have a clear hypothesis about what it is or could be that is not included in the model, then we can give the following advice: Try to find better data that allow for representation of the important factors in the model. If, however, we have no idea about what is missing from the model, it would certainly be wrong to assume away the problem after diligently attempting to include a large number of variables in the covariate vector as controls. As shown convincingly by Lieberson (1985), this control variable approach will not merely lead to an underestimation or overestimation of the true relationship, but the true relationship in some circumstances will be more closely approximated before controls are applied rather than afterward. A similar situation may occur if a stochastic error term is assumed to capture unobserved heterogeneity. Because, by definition, we do not have information about what is not observed, we are not able to assess assumptions about its distribution.

In particular, we do not believe that all the various sources of misspecification described earlier can be incorporated with just one stochastic error term. For example, including an error term into a job-exit rate model does not bring us closer to a solution of the problem that education has a positive effect on upward moves and a negative effect on downward moves, and that this effect is at least based on the arguments available in the existing literature, without any specific meaning with regard to the job-exit rate as such. Of course, such a conclusion can only be reached on the basis of theoretical considerations. In fact, our short discussion of possible sources of misspecification and the various examples in this book demonstrate that misspecification can at least be greatly reduced when event history model selection is theoretically guided. In our job-exit model, for example, an improvement in the model specification could simply be achieved by estimating it with regard to upward and downward exits, differentiating for men and women, including parallel processes (e.g., family events, events at the level of the firm, changes in the macrostructure), as well as more appropriate information on the history of the process. The choice of a model is therefore not simply a technical decision made at the beginning of an analysis that can then be forgotten. Rather, the results critically depend on a theoretically guided model choice, and any differences among models can only be reconciled by a continuing awareness of the type of model used, and that interpretation may be contingent on the chosen model.

As stated by Manski (1993), identification of causal factors is not an all-or-nothing proposition. Very often, we may only have proxy variables or insufficient data to estimate the value of a parameter, but we may nevertheless be in a position to bound the parameter, to identify its direction of influence or its statistical significance. Sociological theory, at least at its current level of development, rarely predicts a specific value of coefficients. Most of the hypotheses that we have seen in empirical social science applications specify the influence direction of causal variables, or whether they have an effect at all. Thus it seems that the fixation of sociologists on point estimation has inhibited appreciation of the usefulness of statements about bounds (Manski 1993). All in all, we need to develop a greater tolerance for ambiguity. As Manski (1993) expressed it, "Social scientists often seem

driven to draw sharp conclusions, even when these can be generated only
by imposing much stronger assumptions than can be plausibly defended.
Scientific reporting and policy analysis would be improved if we would face
up to the fact that we cannot answer all of the questions that we ask."

References

Aalen, O. O. (1987). Dynamic modelling and causality. *Scand. Actuarial Journal,* *12*, 177–190.

Abbott, A. (1995). Sequence analysis: New methods for old ideas. *Annual Review of Sociology, 21*, 93–113.

Aitchison, J., & Brown, J. A. C. (1973). *The lognormal distribution with special reference to its uses in economics.* Cambridge: Cambridge University Press.

Allison, P. D. (1982). Discrete time methods for the analysis of event histories. In S. Leinhardt (Ed.), *Sociological Methodology* (pp. 61–98). San Francisco: Jossey-Bass.

Allison, P. D. (1984). *Event history analysis: Regression for longitudinal event data.* Beverly Hills, CA: Sage.

Allison, P. D. (1996). Fixed-effect partial likelihood for repeated events. *Sociological Methods & Research, 25*, 207–222.

Allmendinger, J. (1989a). *Career mobility dynamics: A comparative analysis of the United States, Norway, and West Germany.* Studien und Berichte no. 49, Max-Planck-Institut für Bildungsforschung, Berlin.

Allmendinger, J. (1989b). Educational systems and labor market outcomes. *European Sociological Review, 5*, 231–250.

Allmendinger, J. (1994). *Lebensverlauf und Sozialpolitik: Die Ungleichheit von Frau und Mann und ihr öffentlicher Ertrag.* Frankfurt: Campus Verlag.

Andersen, P. K., Borgan, O., Gill, R. D., Keiding, N. (1993). *Statistical models based on counting processes.* New York: Springer-Verlag.

Andreß, H.-J. (1985). *Multivariate Analyse von Verlaufsdaten.* Mannheim: ZUMA.

Andreß, H.-J. (1989). Recurrent unemployment—the West German experience: An exploratory analysis using count data models with panel data. *European Sociological Review, 5*, 275–297.

Andreß, H.-J. (1992). *Einführung in die Verlaufsdatenanalyse.* Köln: Zentrum für historische Sozialforschung.

Arminger, G. (1990). Testing against misspecification in parametric rate models. In K. U. Mayer & N. B. Tuma (Eds.), *Event history analysis in life course research* (pp. 253–268). Madison: University of Wisconsin Press.

Arminger, G., Clogg, C. C. & Sobel, M. E. (Eds.). (1995). *Handbook of statistical modeling for the social and behavioral sciences.* New York: Plenum.

Arminger, G., & Müller, F. (1990). *Lineare Modelle zur Analyse von Paneldaten.* Opladen: Westdeutscher Verlag.

Arrow, K. (1973). Higher education as a filter. *Journal of Public Economics, 2*, 193–216.

Baccaïni, B., & Courgeau, D. (1996). The spatial mobility of two generations of young adults in Norway. *International Journal of Population Geography, 2*, 333–359.

Barron, D. N. (1993). The analysis of count data: Overdispersion and autocorrelation. In P. Marsden (Ed.), *Sociological Methodology* (pp. 179–220). San Francisco: Jossey-Bass.

Becker, G. S. (1975). *Human capital*. New York: Columbia University Press.

Becker, G. S. (1981). *A treatise on the family*. Cambridge: Harvard University Press.

Becker, R. (1993). *Staatsexpansion und Karrierechancen. Berufsverläufe im öffentlichen Dienst und in der Privatwirtschaft*. Frankfurt: Campus.

Becker, R., & Blossfeld, H.-P. (1991). Cohort-specific effects of the expansion of the welfare state on job opportunities: A longitudinal analysis of three birth cohorts in the FRG. *Sociologische Gids, 4*, 261–284.

Bennett, D. S. (1997). Measuring rivalry termination, 1816–1992. *Journal of Conflict Resolution, 41*, 2227–2254.

Bernardi, F. (1999a). Does the husband matter? Married women and employment in Italy. *European Sociological Review, 15*, 285–300.

Bernardi, F. (1999b). *Donne fra famiglia e carriera. Strategie di coppia e vincoli sociali (Women between family and career. The strategy of couples and social constraints)*. Milan: Franco Angeli.

Bernardi, F. (2001). Is it a timing or a probability effect? Four simulations and an application of transition rate models to the analysis of unemployment exit. *Quality and Quantity, 35*, 231–252.

Bernardi, F., Layte, R., Schizzerotto, A., & Jacobs, S. (2000). Who exits unemployment? Institutional features, individual characteristics and chances of getting a job: A comparison of Great Britain and Italy. In D. Gallie & S. Paugam (Eds.), *Welfare regimes and the experience of unemployment*. Oxford University Press.

Bernasco, W. (1994). *Coupled careers. The effects of spouse's resources on success at work*. Amsterdam: Thesis.

Bilsborrow, R. E., & Akin, J. S. (1982). Data availability versus data needs for analyzing the determinants and consequences of internal migration: An evaluation of U.S. survey data. *Review of Public Data Use, 10*, 261–284.

Blau, D. M. (1994). Labor force dynamics of older men. *Econometrica, 62*, 117–156.

Blau, D. M. & Riphahn, R. T. (1999). Labor force transitions of older married couples in Germany. *Labour Economics, 6*, 229–251.

Blau, P. M., & Duncan, O. D. (1967). *The American occupational structure*. New York: Wiley.

Bloom, D. E. (1982). What's happening to the age at first birth in the United States? A study of recent cohorts. *Demography, 19*, 351–370.

Blossfeld, H.-P. (1985). *Bildungsexpansion und Berufschancen*. Frankfurt and New York: Campus.

Blossfeld, H.-P. (1986). Career opportunities in the Federal Republic of Germany: A dynamic approach to the study of life-course, cohort, and period effects. *European Sociological Review, 2*, 208–225.

Blossfeld, H.-P. (1987a). Labor market entry and the sexual segregation of careers in the FRG. *American Journal of Sociology, 93*, 83–118.

Blossfeld, H.-P. (1987b). Zur Repräsentativität der Sfb-3-Lebensverlaufsstudie. Ein Vergleich mit Daten aus der amtlichen Statistik. *Allgemeines Statistisches Archiv, 71*, 126–144.

Blossfeld, H.-P. (1989). *Kohortendifferenzierung und Karriereprozeß. Eine Längsschnittstudie über die Veränderung der Bildungs- und Berufschancen im Lebenslauf*. Frankfurt: Campus.

Blossfeld, H.-P. (1990). Changes in educational careers in the Federal Republic of Germany. *Sociology of Education, 63*, 165–177.

Blossfeld, H.-P. (1992). Is the German dual system a model for a modern vocational training system? *International Journal of Comparative Sociology, 33*, 168–181.

Blossfeld, H.-P. (1994). *Causal modeling in event history analysis*. Paper prepared for the XIII World Congress of Sociology, Bielefeld. University of Bremen: mimeo.

Blossfeld, H.-P. (Ed.) (1995). *The new role of women. Family formation in modern societies*. Boulder: Westview Press.

Blossfeld, H.-P., Buchholz, S., & Hofäcker, D. (2006). *Globalization, uncertainty and late careers in society*. London: Routledge.

Blossfeld, H.-P., & De Rose, A. (1992). Educational expansion and changes in entry into marriage and motherhood: The experience of Italian women. *Genus, 3–4*, 73–91.

Blossfeld, H.-P., De Rose, A., Hoem, J., & Rohwer, G. (1995). *Education, modernization, and the risk of marriage disruption: Differences in the effect of women's educational attainment in Sweden, West-Germany, and Italy*. Stockholm Research Reports in Demography, no. 76, Stockholm. In K. Oppenheim Mason & A.-Magritt Jensen (Eds.), *Gender and family change in industrialized countries* (pp. 200–222). Oxford: Clarendon.

Blossfeld, H.-P., & Drobnič, S. (2001). *Careers of couples in contemporary societies: From male breadwinner to dual-earner families*. Oxford: Oxford University Press.

Blossfeld, H.-P., Drobnič, S., & Rohwer, G. (1998). Les trajectoires professionnelles des couples mariés en Allemagne. Une étude longitudinale de long terme de carrières des époux en Allemagne de l'Ouest. *Revue Française de Sociologie, 39*, 305–351.

Blossfeld, H.-P., Giannelli, G., & Mayer, K. U. (1993). Is there a new service proletariat? The tertiary sector and social inequality in Germany. In G. Esping-Andersen (Ed.), *Changing classes. Stratification and mobility in post-industrial societies* (pp. 109–135). London: Sage.

Blossfeld, H.-P., & Hakim, C. (1997). *Between equalization and marginalization. Part-time working women in Europe and the United States of America*. Oxford: Oxford University Press.

Blossfeld, H.-P., & Hamerle, A. (1989a). Unobserved heterogeneity in hazard rate models: A test and an illustration from a study of career mobility. *Quality and Quantity, 23*, 129–141.

Blossfeld, H.-P., & Hamerle, A. (1989b). Using Cox models to study multiepisode processes. *Sociological Methods and Research, 17*, 432–448.

Blossfeld, H.-P., & Hamerle, A. (1992). Unobserved heterogeneity in event history analysis. *Quality and Quantity, 26*, 157–168.

Blossfeld, H.-P., Hamerle, A., & Mayer, K. U. (1989). *Event history analysis*. Hillsdale, NJ: Lawrence Erlbaum Associates.

Blossfeld, H.-P., & Hofmeister, H. (2006). *Globalization, uncertainty and women's careers: An international comparison*. Cheltenham, UK: Edward Elgar.

Blossfeld, H.-P., & Huinink, J. (1991). Human capital investments or norms of role transition? How women's schooling and career affect the process of family formation. *American Journal of Sociology, 97*, 143–168.

Blossfeld, H.-P., & Jaenichen, U. (1992). Educational expansion and changes in women's entry into marriage and motherhood in the Federal Republic of Germany. *Journal of Marriage and the Family, 54*, 302–315.

Blossfeld, H.-P., Klijzing, E., Mills, M., & Kurz, K. (2005). *Globalization, uncertainty and youth in society*. London: Routledge.

Blossfeld, H.-P., Klijzing, E., Pohl, K., & Rohwer, G. (1999). Why do cohabiting couples marry? An example of a causal event history approach to interdependent systems. *Quality & Quantity, 33*, 229–242.

Blossfeld, H.-P., Manting, D., & Rohwer, G. (1993). Patterns of change in family formation in the Federal Republic of Germany and the Netherlands: Some consequences for solidarity between generations. In H. Becker, & P. L. J. Hermkens (Eds.), *Solidarity between generations. Demographic, economic and social change, and its consequences* (Vol. I, pp. 175–196). Amsterdam: Thesis.

Blossfeld, H.-P., & Mayer, K. U. (1988). Labor market segmentation in the FRG: An empirical study of segmentation theories from a life course perspective. *European Sociological Review, 4*, 123–140.

Blossfeld, H.-P., & Mills, M. (2001). A causal approach to interrelated family events: A cross-national comparison of cohabitation, nonmarital conception, and marriage. *Canadian Journal of Population, 28*, 409–437.

Blossfeld, H.-P., Mills, M., & Bernardi, F. (2006). *Globalization, uncertainty and men's careers: An international comparison*. Cheltenham, UK: Edward Elgar.

Blossfeld, H.-P., & Müller, R. (1997). Sozialstrukturanalyse, Rational Choice Theorie und die Rolle der Zeit. Ein Versuch zur dynamischen Integration zweier Theorieperspektiven. *Soziale Welt*, 382–410.

Blossfeld, H.-P., & Müller, R. (2002/2003). *Assortative partnership selection, division of work in the household, and union separation (I–III)*. Three special issues of the *International Journal of Sociology*: Vol. 31, No. 4; Vol. 33, No. 1; Vol. 33, No. 2. Armonk, NY: Sharpe.

Blossfeld, H.-P., & Nuthmann, R. (1990). Transition from youth to adulthood as a cohort process in the FRG. In H. A. Becker (Ed.), *Life histories and generations* (pp. 183–217). Utrecht: ISOR.

Blossfeld, H.-P., & Prein, G. (1998). *Rational choice theory and large-scale data analysis*. Boulder: Westview Press.

Blossfeld, H.-P., & Rohwer, G. (1997a). Causal inference, time and observation plans in the social sciences. *Quality and Quantity, 31*, 361–384.

Blossfeld, H.-P., & Rohwer, G. (1997b). West Germany. In H.-P. Blossfeld (Ed.), *Between equalization and marginalization. Part-time working women in Europe and the United States of America* (pp. 164–190). Oxford: Oxford University Press.

Blossfeld, H.-P., & Rohwer, G. (2002). Techniques of event history modeling. New approaches to causal analysis. 2nd ed. Mahwah: Lawrence Erlbaum Associates.

Blossfeld, H.-P., & Shavit, Y. (1993). Persisting barriers: Changes in educational opportunities in thirteen countries. In Y. Shavit, & H.-P. Blossfeld (Eds.), *Persistent inequality* (pp. 1–23). Boulder: Westview Press.

Blossfeld, H.-P., & Stockmann, R. (1998/99). *Globalization and changes in vocational training systems in developing and advanced industrialized societies,* Vol. I–III. Armonk, NY: Sharpe (Vol. 28, No. 4; Vol 29, No. 1; and Vol 29, No 2 of *International Journal of Sociology*).

Blossfeld, H.-P., & Timm, A. (1997). Das Bildungssystem als Heiratsmarkt. Eine Längsschnittanalyse der Wahl von Heiratspartnern im Lebenslauf. *Kölner Zeitschrift für Soziologie und Sozialpsychologie, 53*, 440–476.

Blossfeld, H.-P., & Timm, A. (2003). *Who marries whom? Educational systems as marriage markets in modern societies.* Dordrecht: Kluwer Academic.

Blumen, I., Kogan, M., & McCarthy, P. J. (1955). *The industrial mobility of labor as a probability process.* Ithaca, NY: Cornell University Press.

Bollen, K. A. (1989). *Structural equations with latent variables.* New York: Wiley.

Box-Steffensmeier, J. M., & Bradford, S. J. (1997). Time is of the essence: Event history models in political science. *American Journal of Political Science, 41*, 1414–1461.

Box-Steffensmeier, J. M., & Bradford, S. J. (2004). *Event history modeling: A guide for social scientists.* Cambridge, MA: Cambridge University Press.

Breslow, N. (1974). Covariance analysis of censored survival data. *Biometrics, 30*, 89–99.

Brien, M. J., Lillard, L. A., & Waite, L. J. (1999). Interrelated family-building behaviors: Cohabitation, marriage, and nonmarital conception. *Demography, 36*, 535–551.

Brüderl, J. (1991a). *Bell-shaped duration dependence in social processes. A generalized log-logistic rate model.* University of Bern: mimeo.

Brüderl, J. (1991b). *Mobilitätsprozesse in Betrieben. Dynamische Modelle und empirische Befunde.* Fankfurt and New York: Campus.

Brüderl, J., & Diekmann, A. (1994). *The log-logistic rate model. Two generalizations with an application to demographic data.* München/Bern: mimeo.

Brüderl, J., & Diekmann, A. (1995): The log-logistic rate model. *Sociological Methods & Research, 24*, 158–186.

Brüderl, J., Diekmann, A., & Preisendörfer, P. (1991). Patterns of intragenerational mobility: Tournament models, path dependency, and early promotion effects. *Social Science Research, 20*, 197–216.

Brüderl, J., Preisendörfer, P., & Ziegler, R. (1993). Upward mobility in organizations: The effects of hierarchy and opportunity structure. *European Sociological Review, 9*, 173–188.

Brüderl, J., Preisendörfer, P., & Ziegler, R. (1998). *Der Erfolg neugegründeter Betriebe*. Berlin: Duncker & Humblot. 2. Auflage.

Buchmann, M. (1989). *The script of life in modern society*. Chicago: University of Chicago Press.

Burt, R. S. (1987). Social contagion and innovation: Cohesion versus structural equivalence. *American Journal of Sociology, 92*, 1287–1335.

Campbell, D. T., & Stanley, J. C. (1963). *Experimental and quasi-experimental designs for research*. Chicago: Rand McNally.

Campbell, R. T., Mutran, E., & Nash Parker, R. (1987). Longitudinal design and longitudinal analysis: A comparison of three approaches. *Research on Aging, 8*, 480–504.

✓ Carroll, G. R. (1983). Dynamic analysis of discrete dependent variables: A didactic essay. *Quality and Quantity, 17*, 425–460.

Carroll, G. R., & Delacroix, J. (1982). Organizational mortality in the newspaper industries of Argentina and Ireland: An ecological approach. *Administrative Science Quarterly, 27*, 169–198.

Carroll, G. R., & Hannan, M. T. (2000). *The demography of corporations and industries*. Princeton, NJ: Princeton University Press.

Carroll, G. R., & Mayer, K. U. (1986). Job-shift patterns in the FRG: The effects of social class, industrial sector, and organizational size. *American Sociological Review, 51*, 323–341.

Carroll, G. R., & Mosakowski, E. (1987). The career dynamics of self-employment. *Administrative Science Quarterly, 32*, 570–589.

Chamberlain, G. (1984). Panel data. In Z. Griliches & M. D. Intriligator (Eds.), *Handbook of econometrics* (Vol. 2, pp. 1247–1317). Amsterdam: North-Holland.

Chaves, M. (1996). Ordaining women: The diffusion of an organizational innovation. *American Journal of Sociology, 101*, 840–873.

Clogg, C. C., & Arminger, G. (1993). On strategy for methodological analysis. *Sociological Methodology, 23*, 57–74.

Coale, A. (1971). Age patterns of marriage. *Population Studies, 25*, 193–214.

Coleman, J. S. (1964). *Introduction to mathematical sociology*. New York: Free Press.

Coleman, J. S. (1968). The mathematical study of change. In H. M. Blalock & A. Blalock (Eds.), *Methodology in social research* (pp. 428–478). New York: McGraw-Hill.

Coleman, J. S. (1973). Theoretical bases for parameters of stochastic processes. In R. E. A. Mapes (Ed.), Stochastic processes in sociology [monograph]. *The Sociological Review, 19*, 17–28.

Coleman, J. S. (1981). *Longitudinal data analysis*. New York: Basic Books.

Coleman, J. S. (1990). *Foundations of social theory*. Cambridge, MA: Harvard University Press.

Coleman, J. S., & Hao, L. (1989). Linear systems analysis: Macrolevel analysis with microlevel data. *Sociological Methodology, 19*, 395–422.

Collier, D., & Messick, R. E. (1975). Prerequisites versus diffusion: Testing alternative explanations of social security adoption. *American Political Science Review, 69*, 1299–1315.

Conveney, P., & Highfield, R. (1990). *The arrow of time*. London: Allen.

Corijn, M., & Klijzing, E. (2001). *Transitions to adulthood in Europe: From a matter of standard to a matter of choice*. Dordrecht: Kluwer Academic.

Courgeau, D. (1990). Migration, family, and career: A life course approach. In P. B. Baltes, D. L. Featherman, & R. M. Lerner (Eds.), *Life-span development and behavior* (pp. 219–255). Hillsdale, NJ: Lawrence Erlbaum Associates.

σ Courgeau, D. (1995). Event history analysis of household formation and dissolution. In E. Van Imhoff, A. Kuijsten, P. Hooimeijer, & L. van Wissen (Eds.), *Household demography and household modeling* (pp. 185–202). New York: Plenum.

⊕ Courgeau, D., & Baccaïni, B. (1998). Multilevel analysis in the social sciences. In D. Courgeau (Ed.), *Special Issue on New Methodological Approaches in the Social Sciences. Population (English Selection), 10*, 39–70.

Courgeau, D., & Guérin-Pace, F. (1998). Le suivi des itinéraires professionnels des couples par les méthodes de la statistique Textuelle. Lecture des parcours professionnels des couples. In JADT 1998, 4 ème journées internationales d'analyse des données Textuelles, Université de Nice-Sophia Antipolis (pp. 221–232).

ν Courgeau, D., & Lelièvre, E. (1992). *Event history analysis in demography*. Oxford: Clarendon.

Courgeau, D., & Lelièvre, E. (1997). Changing paradigm in demography. *Population (English Selection), 9*, 1–10.

Courgeau, D., Lelièvre, E., & Wolber, O. (1998). Reconstruire des trajectoires de mobilité résidentielle. Eléments d'une analyse biographique des donnés de l'EDP. *Economie et Statistique, 316–317*, pp. 163–173.

Courgeau, D., & Najim, J. (1996). Interval censored event history analysis. *Population (English Selection), 8*, 191–208.

Cox, D. R. (1972). Regression models and life-tables. *Journal of the Royal Statistical Society, 34*, 187–220.

Cox, D. R. (1975). Partial likelihood. *Biometrika, 62*, 269–276.

Cox, D. R., & Oakes, D. (1984). *Analysis of survival data*. London: Chapman and Hall.

Cox, D. R., & Snell, E. J. (1968). A general definition of residuals. *Journal of the Royal Statistical Society, B 30*, 248–275.

Cramm, C., Blossfeld, H.-P., & Drobnič, S. (1998). Die Auswirkungen der Doppelbelastung durch Familie und Beruf auf das Krankheitsrisiko von Frauen. *Zeitschrift für Soziologie, 27*, 341–357.

Crouchley, R., & Pickles, A. R. (1987). An illustrative comparison of conditional and marginal methods for analysing longitudinal data with omitted variables. In R. Crouchley (Ed.), *Longitudinal data analysis* (pp. 177–193). Aldershot: Avebury.

Davies, R. B. (1987). The limitations of cross-sectional analysis. In R. Crouchley (Ed.), *Longitudinal data analysis* (pp. 1–15). Aldershot: Avebury.

Davies, R. B., & Crouchley, R. (1985). Control for omitted variables in the analysis of panel and other longitudinal data. *Geographical Analysis, 17*, 1–15.

Davis, J. A. (1978). Studying categorical data over time. *Social Science Research, 7*, 151–179.

Defo, K. (1998). Fertility response to infant and child mortality in Africa with special reference to Cameroon. In National Research Council (Ed.), *From death to birth* (pp. 254–315). Washington, DC: National Academy Press.

Dex, S. (Ed.). (1991). *Life and work history analyses: Qualitative and quantitative developments*. London: Routledge.

Diamond, I. D., & McDonald, J. W. (1992). Analysis of current-status data. In J. Trussell, R. Hankinson, & J. Tilton (Eds.), *Demographic applications of event-history analysis* (pp. 231–252). Oxford: Clarendon.

Diekmann, A. (1989). Diffusion and survival models for the process of entry into marriage. *Journal of Mathematical Sociology, 14*, 31–44.

Diekmann, A. (1992). The log-logistic distribution as a model for social diffusion processes. *Journal of Scientific & Industrial Research, 51*, 285–290.

Diekmann, A., & Engelhardt, H. (1999). The social inheritence of divorce: Effects of parent's family type in postwar Germany. *American Sociological Review, 64*, 783–793.

Diekmann, A., Jungbauer-Gans, M. Krassnig, H., & Lorenz, S. (1996). Social status and aggression: A field study analyzed by survival analysis. *The Journal of Social Psychology, 136*, 761–768.

Diekmann, A., & Mitter, P. (1983). The "sickle hypothesis". *Journal of Mathematical Sociology, 9*, 85–101.

Diekmann, A., & Mitter, P. (Eds.). (1984). *Stochastic modelling of social processes*. New York: Academic Press.

Diekmann, A., & Preisendörfer, P. (1988). Turnover and employment stability in a large West German company. *European Sociological Review, 4*, 233–248.

Diekmann, A., & Weick, S. (Eds.). (1993). *Der Familienzyklus als sozialer Prozeß*. Berlin: Duncker & Humblot.

Dierckx, P. (1975). An algorithm for smoothing, differentiation and integration of experimental data using spline functions. *Journal of Computational and Applied Mathematics, 1*, 165–184.

DiPrete, T. A. (1993). Industrial restructuring and the mobility response. *American Sociological Review, 58*, 74–96.

DiPrete, T. A., & Whitman, T. S. (1988). Gender and promotion in segmented job ladder systems. *American Sociological Review, 53*, 26–40.

Doeringer, P. B. (1967). Determinants of the structure of industrial type internal labor markets. *Industrial Labor Relations Review, 20*, 205–220.

Doeringer, P. B., & Piore, M. J. (1971). *Internal labor markets and manpower analysis*. Lexington, MA: Heath Lexington.

Doksum, J., & Gasko, M. (1990). On a correspondence between models in binary regression analysis and in survival analysis. *International Statistical Review, 58*, 243–252.

Drobnič, S., & Blossfeld, H.-P. (2004). Career patterns over the life course: Gender, class, and linked lives. *Research in Social Stratification and Mobility, 21*, 139–164.

Drobnič, S., Blossfeld, H.-P., & Rohwer, G. (1998). Dynamics of women's employment patterns over the family life course: A comparison of the United States and Germany. *Journal of Marriage and the Family, 61*, 133–146.

Drobnič, S., & Wittig, I. (1997). Part-time work in the United States. In H.-P. Blossfeld (Ed.), *Between equalization and marginalization*. Oxford: Oxford University Press.

Duncan, O. D. (1966). Methodological issues in the analysis of social mobility. In N. Smelser & S. M. Lipset (Eds.), *Social structure and social mobility* (pp. 51–97). Chicago: Aldine.

Eder, D. (1981). Ability grouping as a self-fulfilling prophecy: A micro-analysis of teacher-student interaction. *Sociology of Education, 54*, 151–162.

Eells, E. (1991). *Probabilistic causality*. Cambridge: Cambridge University Press.

Eerola, M. (1994). *Probabilistic causality in longitudinal studies*. New York: Springer-Verlag.

Elbers, C., & Ridder, G. (1982). True and spurious duration dependence: The identifiability of the proportional hazard model. *Review of Economic Studies, 49*, 403–410.

Elder, G. H. (1975). Age differentiation and the life course. *Annual Review of Sociology, 1*, 165–190.

Elder, G. H. (1978). Family history and the life course. In T. K. Hareven (Ed.), *Transitions: The family and the life course in historical perspective* (pp. 17–64). New York: Academic Press.

Elder, G. H. (1987). War mobilization and the life course: A cohort of World War II veterans. *Sociological Forum, 2*, 449–472.

Engel, U., & Reinecke, J. (1994). *Panelanalyse*. New York: de Gruyter.

Erikson, R., & Goldthorpe, J. H. (1991). *The constant flux*. Oxford: Clarendon.

Erikson, R., & Jonsson, J. (1996). *Can education be equalized? The Swedish case in comparative perspective*. Boulder, CO: Westview Press.

Esping-Andersen, G. (1990). *The three worlds of welfare capitalism*. Cambridge: Polity Press.

Esping-Andersen, G. (Ed.). (1993). *Changing classes*. London: Sage.

Esping-Andersen, G., Leth-Sørensen, S., & Rohwer, G. (1994). Institutions and occupational class mobility: Scaling the skill-barrier in the Danish labor market. *European Sociological Review, 10*, 119–134.

Faulbaum, F., & Bentler, P. M. (1994). Causal modeling: Some trends and perspectives. In I. Borg & P. P. Mohler (Eds.), *Trends and perspectives in empirical social research* (pp. 224–249). Berlin: de Gruyter.

Featherman, D. L., Selbee, K. L., & Mayer, K. U. (1989). Social class and the structuring of the life course in Norway and West Germany. In D. I. Kertzer & W. K. Schaie (Eds.), *Age structuring in comparative perspective* (pp. 55–93). Hillsdale, NJ: Lawrence Erlbaum Associates.

Flinn, C. J., & Heckman, J. J. (1982). Models for the analysis of labor force dynamics. In R. Basmann & G. Rhodes (Eds.), *Advances in econometrics* (pp. 35–95). London: JAI Press.

Fox, J. (1992). Statistical models for nonexperimental data: A comment on Freeman. In J. Popper Shaffer (Ed.), *The role of models in nonexperimental science: Two debates* (pp. 63–66). Washington, DC: American Educational Research Association.

Freedman, R. A. (1991). Statistical analysis and shoe leather. *Sociological Methodology, 21*, 291–313.

Freeman, J., Carroll, G. R., & Hannan, M. T. (1983). The liability of newness: Age dependence in organizational death rates. *American Sociological Review, 48*, 692–710.

Galler, H. P., & Pötter, U. (1990). Unobserved heterogeneity in models of unemployment. In K. U. Mayer & N. B. Tuma (Eds.), *Event history analysis in life course research* (pp. 226–240). Madison: University of Wisconsin Press.

Galler, H. P., & Pötter, U. (1992). Zur Robustheit von Schätzmodellen für Ereignisdaten. In R. Hujer, H. Schneider, & W. Zapf (Eds.), *Herausforderungen an den Wohlfahrtsstaat im strukturellen Wandel* (pp. 379–405). Frankfurt: Campus.

Gardner, W., & Griffin, W. A. (1986). *A structural-causal model for analyzing parallel streams of continuously recorded discrete events*. Unpublished manuscript, University of Washington.

Giere, R. N. (1999). *Science without laws*. Chicago: University of Chicago Press.

Glenn, N. D. (1977). *Cohort analysis*. Beverly Hills, CA: Sage.

Goldthorpe, J. H. (1987). *Social mobility and class structure in modern Britain*. Oxford: Clarendon.

Goldthorpe, J. H. (1991). The use of history in sociology: Reflections on some recent tendencies. *British Journal of Sociology, 42*, 211–230.

Goldthorpe, J. H. (1996). The quantitative analysis of large-scale data-sets and rational action theory: For a sociological alliance. *European Sociological Review, 12*, 109–126.

Goldthorpe, J. H. (2000). *On sociology. Numbers, narratives, and the integration of research and theory*. Oxford: Oxford University Press.

Golsch, K. (2005). *The impact of labour market insecurity on the work and family life of men and women. A comparison of Germany, Great Britain, and Spain*. European University Studies. Frankfurt: Peter Lang.

Goodman, L. A. (1973). Causal analysis of data from panel studies and other kind of surveys. *American Journal of Sociology, 78*, 1135–1191.

Greve, H. R. (1995). Jumping ship: The diffusion of strategy abandonment. *Administrative Science Quarterly, 49*, 444–473.

Greve, H. R., Strang, D., & Tuma, N. B. (1995). Specification and estimation of heterogeneous diffusion models. *Sociological Methodology, 13*, 377–420.

Grundmann, M. (1992). *Familienstruktur und Lebensverlauf. Historische und gesellschaftliche Bedingungen individueller Entwicklungen*. Frankfurt: Campus.

Guo, G. (1993). Event-history analysis of left-truncated data. In P. Marsden (Ed.), *Sociological Methodology* (Vol. 23, pp. 217–242). San Francisco: Jossey-Bass.

Hachen, D. S. (1988). The competing risks model. *Sociological Methods and Research, 17*, 21–54.

Haller, M. (1989). *Klassenstrukturen und Mobilität in fortgeschrittenen Gesellschaften.* Frankfurt: Campus.

Halpin, B., & Chan, T. W. (1998). Class careers as sequences: An optimal matching analysis of work-life histories. *European Sociological Review, 14*, 111–130.

Hamerle, A. (1989). Multiepisode spell regression models for duration data. *Applied Statistics, 38*, 127–138.

Hamerle, A. (1991). On the treatment of interrupted spells and initial conditions in event history analysis. *Sociological Methods & Research, 19*, 388–414.

Hamerle, A., & Tutz, G. (1989). *Diskrete Modelle zur Analyse von Verweildauer und Lebenszeiten.* Frankfurt: Campus.

Handl, J. (1988). *Berufschancen und Heiratsmuster von Frauen.* Frankfurt: Campus.

Handl, J., Mayer, K. U., & Müller, W. (1977). *Klassenlage und Sozialstruktur.* Frankfurt: Campus.

Hannan, M. T., Carroll, G. R., Dobrev, S. D., & Han, J. (1998). Organizational mortality in European and American automobile industries. Part I: Revisiting the effects of age and size. *European Sociological Review, 14*, 279–302.

Hannan, M. T., Carroll, G. R., Dobrev, S. D. Han, J., & Torres, J. C. (1998). Organizational mortality in European and American automobile industries. Part II: Coupled clocks. *European Sociological Review, 14*, 303–313.

Hannan, M. T., & Freeman, J. (1989). *Organizational ecology.* Cambridge, MA: Harvard University Press.

Hannan, M. T., Schömann, K., & Blossfeld, H.-P. (1990). Sex and sector differences in the dynamics of wage growth in the Federal Republic of Germany. *American Sociological Review, 55*, 694–713.

Hannan, M. T., & Tuma, N. B. (1979). Methods for temporal analysis. *Annual Review of Sociology, 5*, 303–328.

Hannan, M. T., & Tuma, N. B. (1990). A reassessment of the effects of income maintenance on marital dissolution in the Seattle-Denver income experiments. *American Journal of Sociology, 95*, 1270–1298.

Heckman, J. J., & Borjas, G. J. (1980). Does unemployment cause future unemployment? *Economica, 47*, 247–283.

Heckman, J. J., & Singer, B. (1982). The identification problem in econometric models for duration data. In W. Hildenbrand (Ed.), *Advances in econometrics* (pp. 39–77). Cambridge: Cambridge University Press.

Heckman, J. J., & Singer, B. (1984). A method of minimizing the impact of distributional assumptions in econometric models for duration data. *Econometrica, 52*, 271–320.

Heckman, J. J., & Walker, J. R. (1987). Using goodness of fit and other criteria to choose among competing duration models: A case study of Hutterite data. In

C. Clogg (Ed.), *Sociological Methodology* (pp. 247–307). San Francisco: Jossey-Bass.

Heckman, J. J., & Willis, R. J. (1977). A beta-logistic model for the analysis of sequential labor force participation by married women. *Journal of Political Economy, 85*, 27–58.

Hedström, P. (1994). Contagious collectivities: On the spatial diffusion of Swedish trade unions, 1890–1940. *American Journal of Sociology, 99*, 1157–1179.

Heinz, W. R. (Ed.), (1991a). *The life course and social change. Status passages and the life course.* Vol. 2. Weinheim: Deutscher Studien Verlag.

Heinz, W. R. (Ed.), (1991b). *Theoretical advances in life course research. Status passages and the life course*, Vol. 1. Weinheim: Deutscher Studien Verlag.

Heinz, W. R. (Ed.), (1992). *Institutions and gate keeping in the life course. Status passages and the life course* (Vol. 3). Weinheim: Deutscher Studien Verlag.

Hernes, G. (1972). The process of entry into first marriage. *American Sociological Review, 37*, 173–182.

Hoem, J. M. (1983). Distortions caused by nonobservation of periods of cohabitation before the latest. *Demography, 20*, 491–506.

Hoem, J. M. (1985). Weighting, misclassification, and other issues in the analysis of survey samples of life histories. In J. J. Heckman & B. Singer (Eds.), *Longitudinal analysis of labor market data* (pp. 249–293). Cambridge: Cambridge University Press.

Hoem, J. M. (1986). The impact of education on modern family-union initiation. *European Journal of Population, 2*, 113–133.

Hoem, J. M. (1989). The issue of weights in panel surveys of individual behavior. In D. Kasprzyk, G. Duncan, G. Kalton, & M. P. Singh (Eds.), *Panel surveys* (pp. 539–565). New York: Wiley.

Hoem, J. M. (1991). To marry, just in case ...: The Swedish widow's pension reform and the peak in marriages December 1989. *Acta Sociologica, 43*, 127–135.

Hoem, J. M., & Rennermalm, B. (1985). Modern family initiation in Sweden: Experience of women born between 1936 and 1960. *European Journal of Population, 1*, 81–111.

Hogan, D. P. (1978). The effects of demographic factors, family background, and early job achievement on age at marriage. *Demography, 15*, 139–160.

Hogan, D. P. (1981). *Transitions and social change: The early lives of American men.* New York: Academic Press.

Holland, P. W. (1986). Statistics and causal inference. *Journal of the American Statistical Association, 81*, 945–960.

Hser, Y.-I., Yamaguchi, K., Chen, J., & Anglin, M. D. (1995). Effects of intervention on relapse to narcotics addiction: An event-history analysis. *Evaluation Review, 19*, 123–140.

Hsiao, C. (1986). *Analysis of panel data.* Cambridge: Cambridge University Press.

Huinink, J. (1987). Soziale Herkunft, Bildung und das Alter bei der Geburt des ersten Kindes. *Zeitschrift für Soziologie, 16*, 367–384.

Huinink, J. (1989). *Mehrebenenanalyse in den Sozialwissenschaften.* Wiesbaden: DUV.

Huinink, J. (1992). Die Analyse interdependenter Lebensverlaufsprozesse. In H.-J. Andreß, H. Huinink, H. Meinken, D. Rumianek, W. Sodeur, & G. Sturm (Eds.), *Theorie, Daten, Methoden. Neue Modelle und Verfahrensweisen in den Sozialwissenschaften* (pp. 343–367). München: Oldenbourg.

Huinink, J. (1993). *Warum noch Familie? Zur Attraktivität von Partnerschaft und Elternschaft in unserer Gesellschaft.* Habilitationsschrift, Freie Universität Berlin.

Huinink, J. (1995). Education, work, and family patterns of men: The case of West Germany. In H.-P. Blossfeld (Ed.), *The new role of women. Family formation in modern societies* (pp. 247–262). Boulder: Westview Press.

Huinink, J., Mayer, K. U., Diewald, M., Solga, H., Sørensen, A., & Trappe, H. (1995): *Kollektiv und Eigensinn. Lebensverläufe in der DDR und danach.* Berlin: Akademie Verlag.

Hunt, M. (1985). *Profiles of social research. The scientific study of human interactions.* New York: Russell Sage Foundation.

Hutchison, D. (1988a). Event history and survival analysis in the social sciences, part I. *Quality and Quantity, 22,* 203–219.

Hutchison, D. (1988b). Event history and survival analysis in the social sciences, part II (Advanced applications and recent developments). *Quality and Quantity, 22,* 255–278.

Jacobs, S. C. (1995). Changing patterns of sex segregated occupations throughout the life-course. *European Sociological Review, 11,* 157–185.

Jöreskog, K. G., & Sörbom, D. (1993). *LISREL 8. Structural equation modeling with the SIMPLIS command language.* Chicago: Scientific Software International.

Kalbfleisch, J. D., & Prentice, R. L. (1980). *The statistical analysis of failure data.* New York: Wiley.

Kaplan, E. L., & Mcicr, P. (1958). Nonparametric estimation from incomplete observations. *Journal of the American Statistical Association, 53,* 457–481.

Kelly, J. R., & McGrath, J. E. (1988). *On time and method.* Newbury Park, CA: Sage.

Kenny, D. A. (1979). *Correlation and causality.* New York: Wiley.

Kiefer, N. M. (1988). Economic duration data and hazard functions. *Journal of Economic Literature, 16,* 646–679.

Klijzing, E. (1992). Wedding in the Netherlands: First-union disruption among men and women born between 1928 and 1965. *European Sociological Review, 8,* 53–70.

Klijzing, E. (1993). A method for the simultaneous estimation of parallel processes in the human life course. *Studia Demograficzne, 3,* 111–124.

Klijzing, E., & Corijn, M. (2001). *Transitions to adulthood in Europe.* London: Routledge.

Kohler, H.-P. (2001). *Fertility and social interaction. An economic perspective.* Oxford: Oxford University Press.

Krain, M. (1997). State-sponsored mass murder: The onset and severity of genocides and politicides. *Journal of Conflict Resolution, 41*, 331–360.

Krempel, L. (1987). *Soziale Interaktionen: Einstellungen, Biographien, Situationen und Beziehungsnetzwerke*. Bochum: Schullwig Verlag.

Kuate Defo, B. (1998). Fertility response to infant and child mortality in Africa with special reference to Cameroon. In National Research Council (Ed.), *From death to birth: Mortality decline and reproductive change* (pp. 254–315). Washington, DC: National Academy Press.

Kurz, K. (2000). Soziale Ungleichheit und Wohneigentum. *Zeitschrift für Soziologie, 29*, 28–44.

Kurz, K., & Blossfeld, H.-P. (2004). *Home ownership and social inequality in comparative perspective*. Studies in Social Inequality. Stanford, CA: Stanford University Press.

Lancaster, T. (1985). Generalized residuals and heterogeneous duration models with applications to the Weibull model. *Journal of Econometrics, 28*, 155–169.

Lancaster, T. (1990). *The econometric analysis of transition data*. Cambridge: Cambridge University Press.

Lauterbach, W. (1994). *Berufsverläufe von Frauen. Erwerbstätigkeit, Unterbrechung und Wiedereintritt*. Frankfurt: Campus.

Lawless, J. F. (1982). *Statistical models and methods for lifetime data*. New York: Wiley.

Lazarsfeld, P. F. (1948). The use of panels in social research. *Proceedings of the American Philosophy of Sociology, 92*, 405–410.

Lazarsfeld, P. F. (1972). Mutual relations over time of two attributes: A review and integration of various approaches. In M. Hammer, K. Salzinger, & S. Sutton (Eds.), *Psychopathology* (pp. 461–80). New York.

Leisering, L., & Leibfried, S. (1998). *Time, life & poverty*. Cambridge: Cambridge University Press.

Leisering, L., & Walker, R. (1998). *The dynamics of modern society. Poverty, policy and welfare*. Southampton: Ashford Press.

Lelièvre, E., Bonvalet, C., & Bry, X. (1998). Event history analysis of groups. The findings of an on-going research project. In D. Courgeau (Ed.), *Special Issue on New Methodological Approaches in the Social Sciences, Population (English Selection), 10*, 11–38.

Lelièvre, E., & Bringe, A. (1998). *Practical guide to event history analysis using SAS, TDA, STATA*. Methodes et Savoirs, Paris: INED.

Leridon, H. (1989). Cohabitation, marriage, separation: An analysis of life histories of French cohorts from 1968 to 1985. *Population Studies, 44*, 127–144.

Li, L., & Choe, M. K. (1997). A mixture model for duration data: Analysis of second births in China. *Demography, 34*, 189–197.

Lieberson, S. (1985). *Making it count. The improvement of social research and theory*. Berkeley: University of California Press.

Lieberson, S. (1991). Small n's and big conclusions: An examination of the reasoning in comparative studies based on a small number of cases. *Social Forces,* *70*, 307–320.

Liefbroer, A. (1991). The choice between a married or unmarried first union by young adults. A competing risks analysis. *European Journal of Population, 7*, 273–298.

Lillard, L. A. (1993). Simultaneous equations for hazards: Marriage duration and fertility timing. *Journal of Econometrics, 56*, 189–217.

Lillard, L. A., Brien, M. J., & Waite, L.J. (1995). Premarital cohabitation and subsequent marital dissolution: A matter of self-selection? *Demography, 32*, 437–457.

Lillard, L. A., & Waite, L. J. (1993). A joint model of marital childbearing and marital disruption. *Demography, 30*, 653–681.

Lomi, A. (1995). The population and community ecology of organizational founding: Italian co-operative banks, 1936–1969. *European Sociological Review, 11*, 75–98.

Mach, B. W., Mayer, K. U., & Pohoski, M. (1994). Job changes in the Federal Republic of Germany and Poland: A longitudinal assessment of the impact of welfare-capitalist and state-socialist labour-market segmentation. *European Sociological Review, 10*, 1–28.

Magnusson, D., & Bergmann, L. R. (Eds.). (1990). *Data quality in longitudinal research.* Cambridge: Cambridge University Press.

Magnusson, D., Bergmann, L. R., & Törestad, B. (Eds.). (1991). *Problems and methods in longitudinal research: Stability and change.* Cambridge: Cambridge University Press.

Mahajan, V., & Peterson, R. A. (1985). *Models of innovation diffusion.* Beverly Hills, CA: Sage.

Manski, C. F. (1993). Identification problems in the social sciences. *Sociological Methodology, 23*, 1–56.

Manting, D. (1994). *Dynamics in marriage and cohabitation. An inter-temporal, life course analysis of first union formation and dissolution.* Amsterdam: Thesis.

Manting, D. (1996). The changing meaning of cohabitation and marriage. *European Sociological Review, 12*, 53–65.

March, J. G., Sproull, L. S., & Tamuz, M. (1991). Learning from samples of one or fewer. *Organization Science, 2*, 1–13.

Marini, M. M. (1978). The transition to adulthood: Sex differences in educational attainment and age at marriage. *American Sociological Review, 43*, 483–507.

Marini, M. M. (1984). Women's educational attainment and the timing of entry into parenthood. *American Sociological Review, 49*, 491–511.

Marini, M. M. (1985). Determinants of the timing of adult role entry. *Social Science Research, 14*, 309–350.

Marini, M. M., & Singer, B. (1988). Causality in the social sciences. In C. C. Clogg (Ed.), *Sociological Methodology* (pp. 347–409). San Francisco: Jossey-Bass.

Mason, K. O. et al. (1973). Some methodological issues in cohort analysis of archival data. *American Sociological Review, 38*, 242–258.

Mason, W. M., & Fienberg, S. E. (Eds.). (1985). *Cohort analysis in social research.* New York: Springer.

Mayer, K. U. (1987). Lebenslaufsforschung. In W. Voges (Ed.), *Methoden der Biographie- und Lebenslaufsforschung* (pp. 51–73). Opladen: Leske & Budrich.

Mayer, K. U. (1988). German survivors of World War II: The impact on the life course of the collective experience of birth cohorts. In M. W. Riley (Ed.), *Social structures and human lives. Social change and the life course* (pp. 229–246). Newbury Park, CA: Sage.

Mayer, K. U. (Ed.) (1990). *Lebensverläufe und sozialer Wandel. Sonderheft 31, Kölner Zeitschrift für Soziologie und Sozialpsychologie.* Opladen: Westdeutscher Verlag.

Mayer, K. U. (1991). Life courses in the welfare state. In W. R. Heinz (Ed.), *Theoretical advances in life course research* (Vol. 1, pp. 171–186). Weinheim: Deutscher Studienverlag.

Mayer, K. U., Allmendinger, J., & Huinink, J. (Eds.). (1991). *Vom Regen in die Traufe: Frauen zwischen Beruf und Familie.* Frankfurt: Campus.

Mayer, U. K., & Baltes, P. B. (1996). *Die Berliner Altersstudie.* Berlin: Academie Verlag.

Mayer, K. U., & Brückner, E. (1989). *Lebensverläufe und Wohlfahrtsentwicklung. Konzeption, Design und Methodik der Erhebung von Lebensverläufen der Geburtsjahrgänge 1929–31, 1939–41, 1949–51. Materialien aus der Bildungsforschung, Nr. 35.* Max-Planck-Institut für Bildungsforschung, Berlin.

Mayer, K. U., & Carroll, G. R. (1987). Jobs and classes: Structural constraints on career mobility. *European Sociological Review, 3*, 14–38.

Mayer, K. U., Featherman, D. L., Selbee, L. K., & Colbjørnsen, T. (1989). Class mobility during the working life: A comparison of Germany and Norway. In M. L. Kohn (Ed.), *Cross-national research in sociology* (pp. 218–239). Newbury Park, CA: Sage.

Mayer, K. U., & Huinink, J. (1990). Age, period, and cohort in the study of the life course: A comparison of classical A-P-C-analysis with event history analysis or farewell to Lexis? In D. Magnusson & L. R. Bergmann (Eds.), *Data quality in longitudinal research* (pp. 211–232). Cambridge: Cambridge University Press.

Mayer, K. U., & Müller, W. (1986). The state and the structure of the life course. In A. B. Sørensen, F. Weinert, & L. R. Sherrod (Eds.), *Human development and the life course* (pp. 217–245). Hillsdale, NJ: Lawrence Erlbaum Associates.

Mayer, K. U., & Schöpflin, U. (1989). The state and the life course. *Annual Review of Sociology, 15*, 187–309.

Mayer, K. U., & Schwarz, K. (1989). The process of leaving the parental home. Some German data. In E. Grebenik, C. Höhn, & R. Mackensen (Eds.), *Later phases of the family cycle. Demographic aspects* (pp. 145–163). Oxford: Clarendon.

Mayer, K. U., & Tuma, N. B. (Eds.). (1990). *Event history analysis in life course research.* Madison: University of Wisconsin Press.

McGinnity, F. (2004). *Welfare for the unemployed in Britain and Germany. Who benefits?* Cheltenham, UK: Edward Elgar.

Medical Research Council. (1992). *Review of longitudinal studies.* London: mimeo.

Menken, J. (1985). Age and fertility: How late can you wait? *Demography, 22,* 469–483.

Meulemann, H. (1990). Schullaufbahnen, Ausbildungskarrieren und die Folgen im Lebensverlauf. Der Beitrag der Lebensverlaufsforschung zur Bildungssoziologie. In K. U. Mayer (Ed.), *Lebensverläufe und sozialer Wandel* (pp. 89–117). Opladen: Westdeutscher Verlag.

Michael, R. T., & Tuma, N. B. (1985). Entry into marriage and parenthood by young men and women: The influence of family background. *Demography, 22,* 515–543.

Mills, M. (2000a). Providing space for time: The impact of temporality on life course research. *Time & Society, 9,* 91–127.

Mills, M. (2000b). *The transformation of partnerships.* Amsterdam: THELA THESIS Population Studies.

Mills, M., & Trovato, F. (2001). The effect of pregnancy in cohabiting unions on marriage in Canada, the Netherlands, and Latvia. *Statistical Journal of the United Nations ECE, 18,* 103–118.

Mincer, J. (1974). *Schooling, experience, and earnings.* New York: National Bureau of Economic Research.

Mincer, J., & Polachek, S. (1974). Family investments in human capital: Earnings of women. *Journal of Political Economy, 82,* 76–108.

Minkoff, D. C. (1997). The sequencing of social movements. *American Sociological Review, 62,* 779–799.

Minkoff, D. (1999). Bending with the wind: Strategic change and adaptation by women's and racial minority organizations. *American Journal of Sociology, 104,* 1666–1703.

Moreau, T., O'Quigley, J., & Mesbah, M. (1985). A global goodness-of-fit statistic for the proportional hazards model. *Applied Statistics, 34,* 212–218.

Mulder, C. H., & Smits, J. (1999). First-time home-ownership of couples. The effect of inter-generational transmission. *European Sociological Review, 15,* 323–337.

Murphy, M. (1991). *The family life cycle.* London: London School of Economics. Unpublished manuscript.

Myers, D. (1997). Racial rioting in the 1960s: An event history analysis of local conditions. *American Sociological Review, 62,* 94–112.

Namboodiri, K., & Suchindran, C. M. (1987). *Life table techniques and their applications.* New York: Academic Press.

Nazio, T., & Blossfeld, H.-P. (2003). The diffusion of cohabitation among young women in West Germany, East Germany and Italy. *European Journal of Population. 19,* 47–82.

Olzak, S. (1992). *The dynamics of ethnic competition and conflict.* Stanford, CA: Stanford University Press.

Olzak, S., & Olivier, J. L. (1998a). Comparative event analysis: Black civil rights protest in South Africa and the United States. In D. Rucht, R. Koopmans, & F. Neidhardt (Eds.), *Acts of dissent* (pp. 253-283). Lanham, MD: Rowman & Littlefield.

Olzak, S., & Olivier, J. L. (1998b). Racial conflict and protest in South Africa and the United States. *European Sociological Review, 14*, 255–278.

Olzak, S., & Shanahan, S. (1996). Deprivation and race riots: An extension of Spilerman's analysis. *Social Forces, 74*, 931–961.

Olzak, S., & Shanahan, S. (1999). The effects of immigrant diversity and ethnic competition on collective conflict in urban America: An assessment of two movements of mass migration, 1869–1924 and 1965–1993. *Journal of American Ethnic History, 18*, 40–64.

Olzak, S., Shanahan, S., & McEneaney, E. H. (1996). Poverty, segregation, and race riots, 1960 to 1993. *American Sociological Review, 61*, 590–613.

Olzak, S., Shanahan, S., & West, E. (1994). School desegregation, interracial exposure, and antibusing activity in contemporary urban America. *American Journal of Sociology, 100*, 196–214.

Olzak, S., & West, E. (1991). Ethnic conflict and the rise and fall of ethnic newspapers. *American Sociological Review, 56*, 458–474.

Oppenheimer, V. K. (1988). A theory of marriage timing. *American Journal of Sociology, 94*, 563–591.

Ostermeier, M., & Blossfeld, H.-P. (1998). Wohneigentum und Ehescheidung. Eine Längsschnittanalyse über den Einfluß gekauften und geerbten Wohneigentums auf den Prozeß der Ehescheidung. *Zeitschrift für Bevölkerungsforschung, 23*, 39–54.

Papastefanou, G. (1987). *Familienbildung und Lebensverlauf. Eine empirische Analyse sozialstruktureller Bedingungen der Familiengründung bei den Kohorten 1929–31, 1939–41 und 1949–51.* Studien und Berichte no. 50. Max-Planck-Institut für Bildungsforschung, Berlin.

Petersen, T. (1986a). Estimating fully parametric hazard rate models with time-dependent covariates. *Sociological Methods and Research, 14*, 219–246.

Petersen, T. (1986b). Fitting parametric survival models with time-dependent covariates. *Applied Statistics, 35*, 281–288.

Petersen, T. (1988a). Analyzing change over time in a continuous dependent variable: Specification and estimation of continuous state space hazard rate models. *Sociological Methodology, 18*, 137–164.

Petersen, T. (1988b). *Incorporating time-dependent covariates in models for analysis of duration data.* CDE working paper.

Petersen, T. (1990). Analyzing event histories. In A. von Eye (Ed.), *Statistical methods in longitudinal research* (Vol. 2, pp. 259–288). New York: Academic Press.

Petersen, T. (1991). The statistical analysis of event histories. *Sociological Methods & Research, 19*, 270–323.

Petersen, T. (1995). Models for interdependent event history data: Specification and estimation. *Sociological Methodology, 20*, 317–375.

Pickles, A. R., & Davies, R. B. (1986). Household factors and discrimination in housing consumption. *Regional Science and Urban Planning, 16*, 493–517.

Pickles, A. R., & Davies, R. B. (1989). Inference from cross-sectional and longitudinal data for dynamic behavioural processes. In J. Hauer et al. (Eds.), *Urban dynamics and spatial choice behaviour* (pp. 81–104). New York: Kluwer Academic.

Piore, M. J. (1968). On-the-job training and adjustment to technological change. *Journal of Human Resources, 3*, 435–445.

Popielarz, P. A., & McPherson, J. M. (1996). On the edge or in between: Niche position, niche overlap, and the duration of voluntary association memberships. *American Journal of Sociology, 101*, 698–720.

Popper Shaffer, J. (Ed.) (1992). *The role of models in nonexperimental science: Two debates.* Washington, DC: American Educational Research Association.

Pötter, U. (1993). Models for interdependent decisions over time. In J. Janssen & C. H. Skiadas (Eds.), *Applied stochastic models and data analysis* (pp. 767–779). World Scientific Publishers.

Pötter, U., & Blossfeld, H.-P. (2001). Causal inference from series of events. *European Sociological Review, 17*, 21–32.

Preisendörfer, P., & Burgess, Y. (1988). Organizational dynamics and career patterns: Effects of organizational expansion and contraction on promotion chances in a large West German company. *European Sociological Review, 4*, 32–45.

Rajulton, G. (1992). *Life history analysis: Guidelines for using the program* LIFEHIST *(PC version).* Discussion paper no. 92-5. Population Studies Centre, London, Ontario: University of Western Ontario.

Ramirez, F. O., Soysal, Y., & Shanahan, S. (1997). The changing logic of political citizenship: Cross-national acquisition of women's suffrage rights, 1890 to 1990. *American Sociological Review, 62*, 735–745.

Rasler, K. (1996). Concessions, repression, and political protest in the Iranian revolution. *American Sociological Review, 61*, 132–152.

Rindfuss, R. R., & Hirschman, C. (1984). The timing of family formation: Structural and societal factors in the Asian context. *Journal of Marriage and the Family, 55*, 205–214.

Rindfuss, R. R., & John, C. S. (1983). Social determinants of age at first birth. *Journal of Marriage and the Family, 45*, 553–565.

Rodgers, W. L. (1982). Estimable functions of age, period, and cohort effects. *American Sociological Review, 47*, 774–787.

Rogers, E. M. (1983). *Diffusion of innovations.* New York: Free Press.

Rohwer, G. (1995). *Kontingente Lebensverläufe. Soziologische und statistische Aspekte ihrer Beschreibung und Erklärung.* Bremen: University of Bremen.

Rosenthal, L. (1991). Unemployment incidence following redundancy: The value of longitudinal approaches. In S. Dex (Ed.), *Life and work history analyses: Qualitative and quantitative developments* (pp. 187–213). London: Routledge.

Sandefur, G. D., & Tuma, N. B. (1987). How data type affects conclusions about individual mobility. *Social Science Research, 16*, 301–328.

Schömann, K., & Becker, R. (1995). Participation in further education over the life course: A longitudinal study of three birth cohorts in the Federal Republic of Germany. *European Sociological Review, 11*, 187–208.

Sewell, W. H., & Hauser, R. M. (1975). *Education, occupation and earnings.* New York: Academic Press.

Shavit, Y., & Blossfeld, H.-P. (Eds.), (1993). *Persistent inequality. Changing educational attainment in thirteen countries.* Boulder, CO: Westview Press.

Shingles, R. D. (1976). Causal inference in cross-lagged panel analysis. *Political Methodology, 3*, 95–133.

Singer, B., & Spilerman, S. (1976a). The representation of social processes by Markov models. *American Journal of Sociology, 82*, 1–54.

Singer, B., & Spilerman, S. (1976b). Some methodological issues in the analysis of longitudinal surveys. *Annals of Economic and Social Measurement, 5*, 447–474.

Singer, J. D., & Willett, J. B. (1991). Modeling the days of our lives: Using survival analysis when designing and analyzing longitudinal studies of duration and the timing of events. *Psychological Bulletin, 110*, 268–290.

Smeenk, W. (1998). *Opportunity and marriage.* Utrecht: Thela Thesis.

Snyder, L. (1991). Modeling dynamic communication processes with event history analysis. *Communication Research, 18*, 464–486.

Sørensen, A. B. (1977). The structure of inequality and the process of attainment. *American Sociological Review, 42*, 965–978.

Sørensen, A. B. (1979). A model and a metric for the analysis of the intragenerational status attainment process. *American Journal of Sociology, 85*, 361–384.

Sørensen, A. B. (1984). Interpreting time dependency in career processes. In A. Diekmann & P. Mitter (Eds.), *Stochastic modelling of social processes* (pp. 89–122). New York: Academic Press.

Sørensen, A. B. (1986). Theory and methodology in social stratification. In U. Himmelstrand (Ed.), *The sociology of structure and action* (pp. 69–95). New York.

Sørensen, A. B., & Blossfeld, H.-P. (1989). Socioeconomic opportunities in Germany in the post-war period. *Research in Social Stratification and Mobility, 8*, 85–106.

Sørensen, A. B., & Sørensen, A. (1985). An event history analysis of the process of entry into first marriage. *Current Perspectives on Aging and Life Cycle, 2*, 53–71.

Sørensen, A. B., & Tuma, N. B. (1981). Labor market structures and job mobility. *Research in Social Stratification and Mobility, 1*, 67–94.

Soule, S. A. (1997). The student divestment movement in the United States and tactical diffusion: The Shantytown protest. *Social Forces, 75*, 855–882.

Soule, S. A., & Van Dyke, N. (1999). Black church arson in the United States, 1989–1996. *Ethnic and Racial Studies, 22*, 724–742.

Soule, S. A., & Zylan, Y. (1997). Runaway train? The diffusion of state-level reform in ADC/AFDC eligibility requirements, 1950–1967. *American Journal of Sociology, 103*, 733–762.

Spence, A. M. (1973). Job market signaling. *Quarterly Journal of Economics, 87*, 355–374.

Spence, A. M. (1974). *Market signaling*. Cambridge, MA: Harvard University Press.

Strang, D. (1991). Adding social structure to diffusion models. *Sociological Methods & Research, 19*, 324–353.

Strang, D., & Meyer, J. W. (1993). Institutional conditions for diffusion. *Theory and Society, 22*, 487–511.

Strang, D., & Tuma, N. B. (1993). Spatial and temporal heterogeneity in diffusion. *American Journal of Sociology, 99*, 614–639.

Sudman, S., & Bradburn, N. M. (1986). *Asking questions*. San Francisco: Jossey-Bass.

Tarone, R. E., & Ware, J. (1977). On distribution-free tests for equality of survival distributions. *Biometrika, 64*, 156–160.

Teachman, J. D. (1983). Analyzing social processes: Life tables and proportional hazards models. *Social Science Research, 12*, 263–301.

Timm, A., Blossfeld, H.-P., & Müller, R. (1998). Der Einfluß des Bildungssystems auf die Heiratsmuster in Westdeutschland und den USA. Eine vergleichende Längsschnittanalyse der Wahl des ersten Ehepartners im Lebenslauf. *Beiträge zur Arbeitsmarkt- und Berufsforschung* (BeitrAB 215), pp. 129–166.

Treiman, D. J. (1977). *Occupational prestige in comparative perspective*. New York: Academic Press.

Trussell, J., & Richards, T. (1985). Correcting for unmeasured heterogeneity in hazard models using the Heckman-Singer procedure. *Sociological Methodology, 15*, 242–276.

Tuma, N. B. (1980). *Invoking RATE*. Mannheim: ZUMA.

Tuma, N. B. (1985). Effects of labor market structure on job-shift patterns. In J. J. Heckman & B. Singer (Eds.), *Longitudinal analysis of labor market data* (pp. 327–363). Cambridge: Cambridge University Press.

Tuma, N. B., & Hannan, M. T. (1984). *Social dynamics. Models and methods*. New York: Academic Press.

Vaupel, J. A., & Yashin, A. I. (1985). The deviant dynamics of death in heterogeneous populations. *Sociological Methodology, 16*, 179–211.

Vermunt, J. K. (1997). *Log-linear models for event histories*. Newbury Park, CA: Sage.

Wagner, M. (1989a). *Räumliche Mobilität im Lebenslauf*. Stuttgart: Enke.

Wagner, M. (1989b). Spatial determinants of social mobility. In J. van Dijk, H. Folmer, & A. M. Herzog (Eds.), *Migration and labor market adjustment* (pp. 241–264). Dordrecht.

Wagner, M. (1990). Education and migration. In K. U. Mayer & N. B. Tuma (Eds.), *Event history analysis in life course research* (pp. 129–145). Madison: University of Wisconsin Press.

Weber, M. (1972). *Wirtschaft und Gesellschaft*. Studienausgabe. Tübingen: Mohr.

Wegener, B. (1985). Gibt es Sozialprestige? *Zeitschrift für Soziologie, 14*, 209–235.

Weymann, A. (1995). Modernization, generational relations and the economy of life-time. *International Journal of Sociology and Social Policy, 16*, 37–57.

Weymann, A., & Heinz, W. R. (1996). *Society and biography*. Weinheim: DSV.

Willett, J. B., & Singer, J. D. (1991). From whether to when: New methods for studying student dropout and teacher attrition. *Review of Educational Research, 61*, 4.

Wu, L. L. (1989). Issues in smoothing empirical hazard rates. *Sociological Methodology, 19*, 127–159.

Wu, L. L. (1990). Simple graphical goodness-of-fit tests for hazard rate models. In K. U. Mayer & N. B. Tuma (Eds.), *Event history analysis in life course research* (pp. 184–199). Madison: University of Wisconsin Press.

Wu, L., & Martinson, B. C. (1993). Family structure and the risk of premarital birth. *American Sociological Review, 58*, 210–232.

Wu, L. L., & Tuma, N. B. (1990). Local hazard models. *Sociological Methodology, 20*, 141–180.

Yamaguchi, K. (1991). *Event history analysis*. Newbury Park, CA: Sage.

Yamaguchi, K. (1994). Some accelerated failure-time regression models derived from diffusion process models: An application to a network diffusion analysis. In P. V. Marsden (Ed.), *Sociological Methodology, 24*, 267–300.

Yamaguchi, K. (1996). Some loglinear fixed-effect latent-trait Markov-chain models: A dynamic analysis of personal efficacy under the influence of divorce / widowhood. *Sociological Methodology, 26*, 39–78.

Yamaguchi, K. (1997). Some cumulative logit models for panel-data analysis: An application to a dynamic analysis of personal efficacy. *Quality and Quantity, 31*, 287–304.

Yamaguchi, K. (1998). Mover-stayer models for analyzing event nonoccurrence and event timing with time-dependent covariates: An application to an analysis of remarriage. *Sociological Methodology, 28*, 327–361.

Yamaguchi, K., & Ferguson, L. (1995). The stopping and spacing of childbirths and their birth-history predictors: Rational-choice theory and event-history analysis. *American Sociological Review, 60*, 272–298.

Yamaguchi, K., & Jin, L. (1999). Event history analysis in human developmental research. In R. K. Sibereisen & A. von Eye (Eds.), *Growing up in times of social change* (pp. 319–339). Berlin: Walter de Gruyter.

Zwick, M. (Ed.). (1998). *Einmal arm, immer arm?* Frankfurt: Campus.

About the Authors

Hans-Peter Blossfeld, Prof., Dr. rer pol., holds the Chair of Sociology I at the Otto Friedrich University in Bamberg, Germany, and is the Director of the Staatsinstitut für Familienforschung an der Universität Bamberg (ifb) (State Institute for Family Research at Bamberg University). He was born in München, Germany (1954), and received his training in sociology, economics, social statistics and computer science at the University of Regensburg (Dipl.-Soz., 1980), the University of Mannheim (Dr. rer. pol., 1984), and the Free University of Berlin (Habilitation, 1987). He worked as research scientist at the University of Mannheim (1980–84) and as senior research scientist at the Max Planck Institute for Human Development and Education in Berlin (1984–89). He was full professor of sociology and political sciences at the European University Institute in Florence (1989–92), professor of sociology (chair of social statistics and sociological research methods) at the University of Bremen (1992–98), and professor of sociology (chair of theory and empirical analysis of social structures and economic systems) at Bielefeld University (1998-2002). In the academic year 1988–89 he was Research Fellow at the Netherlands Institute for the Advanced Study in the Humanities and Social Sciences (NIAS) in Wassenaar, the Netherlands. He has taught and held visiting positions at Harvard University and Cornell University, the Nuffield College, Oxford, and the University of Southampton, the Universities of Haifa and Tel Aviv, the Karl-Franzens University in Graz and the University of Vienna, the Universidad Complutense in Madrid, the Norwegian School of Economics and Business Administration in Bergen, the Universitè de Genéve, the Universities of Utrecht, Nijmegen, and Groningen, the Universities of Trento and Torino, and the State University in St. Petersburg. Blossfeld is the chairman of the European Consortium of Sociological Research and member of the Steering Committee of the European Science Foundation Programme "Quantitative Methods in the Social Sciences." Blossfeld is editor in chief of the European Sociological Review and the Zeitschrift für Familienforschung as well as coeditor of the Zeitschrift für Erziehungswissenschaft. He is on the editorial board of International Sociology and the scientific advisory board of the Kölner Zeitschrift für Soziologie und Sozialpsychologie and the Zeitschrift für Soziologie. Blossfeld has published 18 books and more than 130 articles on social inequality, youth, family, educational sociology, labor market research, demography, social stratification and mobility, the modern methods of quantitative social research and statistical methods for longitudinal data analysis. He has directed several international comparative projects on demography, family, work, and education, among them the Globalife project.

Katrin Golsch is an assistant professor at the Faculty of Economics, Business Administration and Social Sciences, University of Cologne, Germany. Prior

293

to this she was a researcher in the Globalife project and a lecturer in the Department of Sociology, Bielefeld University, Germany. She received her doctorate in sociology in 2004, with a focus on labor market insecurity and its impact on the work and family life of men and women in Germany, Great Britain, and Spain.

Götz Rohwer is professor of methods of social research and statistics at the Ruhr-Universität Bochum. Previously, he was a research fellow at the European University Institute, Florence, and then worked together with Hans-Peter Blossfeld at the University of Bremen. Together with Ulrich Pötter, he is the author of the program TDA (Transition Data Analysis) that is used in Blossfeld and Rohwer (2002).

Index

capture =

277